Management Research

Management Research: Applying the Principles of Business Research Methods supports new researchers on every step of the research journey, from defining a project to communicating its findings, as well as balancing the technical aspects of research with the management of the project itself. Structured around the key stages of a research project, the text reflects the richness and diversity of current business and management research, both in its presentation of methods as well as its choice of examples drawn from different industries and organizations.

This book explains the design, selection, development, and implementation of appropriate research strategies in different management contexts and disciplines, providing practical guidance to the new researcher in carrying out ethical and inclusive research in today's organizational and business environments, whilst also introducing a range of research methods and techniques. Each chapter includes learning outcomes and in-chapter call out boxes with real-life research examples to illustrate concepts and provide basis for discussion, as well as 'next steps' activities to help readers apply the content to their own live research projects. This second edition has been updated throughout to include the following:

- Enhanced pedagogical features such as discussion questions and online quizzes
- New international examples and research-in-practice cases
- Greater emphasis on topics such as diversity and inclusion through the research process, data collection and privacy, digitalisation, and the process of writing up research.

Management Research provides essential reading for undergraduate and postgraduate students undertaking a dissertation, thesis, or research project, as well as professionals currently practising in the field.

Extensive instructor and student resources support the work online, including an instructor's manual, PowerPoint lecture slides, a question bank, and downloadable MS Excel and SPSS data sets.

Susan Rose is Professor Emerita, Henley Business School, University of Reading, UK.

Nigel Spinks is Lecturer in Systems and Processes, Henley Business School, University of Reading, UK.

Ana Isabel Canhoto is Professor of Digital Business, University of Sussex Business School, UK.

Management Research

Applying the Principles of Business Research Methods

SECOND EDITION

Susan Rose, Nigel Spinks and Ana Isabel Canhoto

Routledge
Taylor & Francis Group

LONDON AND NEW YORK

Designed cover image: Eoneren

Second edition published 2024
by Routledge
4 Park Square, Milton Park, Abingdon, Oxon, OX14 4RN

and by Routledge
605 Third Avenue, New York, NY 10158

Routledge is an imprint of the Taylor & Francis Group, an informa business

© 2024 Susan Rose, Nigel Spinks and Ana Isabel Canhoto

The right of Susan Rose, Nigel Spinks and Ana Isabel Canhoto to be identified as authors of this work has been asserted in accordance with sections 77 and 78 of the Copyright, Designs and Patents Act 1988.

First edition published by Routledge 2014

British Library Cataloguing-in-Publication Data
A catalogue record for this book is available from the British Library

Library of Congress Cataloging-in-Publication Data
Names: Rose, Susan (Professor in Marketing management), author. |
    Spinks, Nigel (College teacher), author. | Canhoto, Ana Isabel, author.
Title: Management research : applying the principles of business research
    methods / Susan Rose, Nigel Spinks and Ana Isabel Canhoto.
Description: Second edition. | Abingdon, Oxon ; New York, NY : Routledge,
    2024. | Includes bibliographical references and index. |
Identifiers: LCCN 2023028550 (print) | LCCN 2023028551 (ebook) |
    ISBN 9781032462967 (hardback) | ISBN 9781032462950 (paperback) |
    ISBN 9781003381006 (ebook)
Subjects: LCSH: Management—Research. | Quantitative research.
Classification: LCC HD30.4 .R67 2024 (print) | LCC HD30.4 (ebook) |
    DDC 658.0072—dc23/eng/20230629
LC record available at https://lccn.loc.gov/2023028550
LC ebook record available at https://lccn.loc.gov/2023028551

ISBN: 978-1-032-46296-7 (hbk)
ISBN: 978-1-032-46295-0 (pbk)
ISBN: 978-1-003-38100-6 (ebk)

DOI: 10.4324/9781003381006

Typeset in Berling
by Apex CoVantage, LLC

Access the Support Material: www.routledge.com/9781032462950

Contents

Part II: Design   81

Figures

Tables

Preface

In writing the second edition of our book, our aim has continued to be to produce a textbook that would provide the practical and conceptual resources needed by students undertaking a research project in business and management. Our experience as tutors and supervisors on undergraduate, master's, and doctoral programmes had shown us that such a book was needed. Our students struggled to find a single source that could help them to design and carry out research to answer the questions that interested them whilst meeting the standards required of a rigorous academic assessment. What we felt was required was a book that explained the principles underpinning research in business and management and that guided the reader through their application in practice.

This book is therefore aimed at students undertaking a research project as part of an academic or professional qualification in business and management, or related disciplines, from undergraduate level and above at a business school or similar institution. It is particularly suited to students who plan to carry out their research projects in their own organization or industry. We take an inter-disciplinary approach to support research in different subject areas, different industries, and different sectors. The book is designed to be read while preparing for and carrying out a research project and to act as a reference resource throughout. We have therefore included 'next steps' activities to guide the researcher on that journey. In addition, extensive online resources, including video, are available on the book's companion website to help at key points in the research process.

To achieve our stated aim in the book, we have structured it around the key stages of a research project. We place particular emphasis on how to design research that can help to answer the kinds of research questions that, in our experience, students want to answer. Questions such as, 'What is the impact of new contract arrangements upon employee relations?' 'Why do young people no longer use our brand?' or 'How are new services developed and implemented?' We therefore take a close look at how such questions can be researched, and the types of research design that may be appropriate. In doing so we emphasize the different ways that such questions can be understood and the different ways that they can be investigated. Throughout the book we seek to show how research can be used to generate findings that are both useful and robust and to provide the reader with the knowledge and skills to carry it out. As such, it provides students of business and management with a comprehensive resource.

NEW FEATURES IN THE SECOND EDITION

In this second edition of our book, we have made a number of changes which reflect both the evolution and development of management research but also the very helpful feedback that we have received following the first edition. In particular, the following changes have been made:

- The second edition builds on the achievements of the first whilst at the same time capturing developments and trends that are affecting research today in order to ensure the book remains contemporary. In writing this edition, we have aimed to address changes that have taken place in research thinking and practice and their relevance to management research.
- For this edition we have changed the structure and focus of Part II as it relates to research design. In Chapter 4 we now bring together key considerations in designing research. Chapters 6 and 7 then introduce a range of quantitative, qualitative, and mixed method designs, along with guidance on aligning choice of research design to the research question. The aim of this new structure is to provide greater support to students making the key design decisions at the start of a research project.
- Being mindful of important developments in the recognition of diversity and inclusivity in organizational behaviour, the second edition raises awareness of how researchers can similarly ensure this is reflected in their own practice. Chapter 5 provides guidance for student researchers on this important topic.
- 'Research in Practice' examples have been updated where appropriate to demonstrate the contemporary application of research by students and academics across a wide range of topics and management situations.
- Given the continuous advances in digital technology, the second edition reflects the many ways in which the Internet and technological advances are now being adopted and applied to data collection, analysis, and reporting. At the same time the book engages with the ethical considerations that such advances can create for researchers.
- Each chapter now begins with a statement of learning outcomes that helps the student to recognize the value of each chapter. The five-stage model of research continues to be used to guide the reader through both their research process and the book itself.

Acknowledgements

The authors would like to acknowledge the important contribution made by a number of people to the completion of this book. The original idea for the book came from our experiences of writing course materials for MBA and MSc students and from teaching and supervising them through their research projects. We would like to thank all of our students who have, over the years, provided thought-provoking insights as we worked alongside them in completing their research projects. Several of these projects appear in this book as practical examples of applied research, and we would like to thank the following students for agreeing to our including their work: Rob Garlick, Daniela Castillo, Diana Fandel, Andrew George, Becky Kite, Julia Colin, Melanie Shapiro, Davin MacAnaney, Silvia Lang, Constança Monteiro Casquinho, Abed Kasaji, Laura Wallis, and Debbie McKay. Full reference information can be found in the chapter references.

Additionally we would like to acknowledge the contribution made by our academic colleagues, in particular Moira Clark, Anne Dibley, Kevin Money, Carola Hillenbrand, Chris Brooks, Rebecca Jones, Diana Fandel, Anastasiya Saraeva, Phil Davis, Andrea Tressider, Helen Kara, and Sarah Quinton for their support and where relevant for allowing us to use examples of their own research.

We also acknowledge the role that both of our institutions – Henley Business School and the University of Sussex Business School – have played in the completion of the book and thank them for providing the space and time to do this. Finally we would like to thank the editorial team at Taylor Francis, in particular Sophia Levine, Rupert Spurrier, and Emma Morley, for their constant faith in our ability to deliver this book.

Any remaining errors are, of course, all our own.

Susan Rose, Nigel Spinks, and Ana Isabel Canhoto

PART I

Define

Part I of the book contains three chapters, each of which relates to how you define your research problem. Chapter 1 is an introductory chapter that provides you with an orientation towards research and its purpose. We first define what we understand by business and management research, its distinguishing features, and why it is important to the management of organizations. We introduce the five-stage process model that forms the structure of the book and outline the activities within each stage. We explore the relationship between management practice, theory and research, and discuss different philosophical stances that a researcher may adopt. Chapter 1 also encourages you to take a reflective stance towards your research and your role in it.

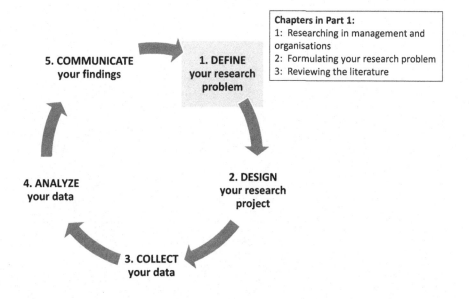

Chapters in Part 1:
1: Researching in management and organisations
2: Formulating your research problem
3: Reviewing the literature

DOI: 10.4324/9781003381006-1

Our approach to research is to view it as providing solutions or insights to problems faced by academics and practitioners. Chapter 2 introduces you to this problem-centred approach and guides you on identifying a research problem and developing suitable research questions. We examine different types of research questions through the lens of three types of research: descriptive/exploratory; explanatory and process. We discuss how they link to the overall aims of a research project and how to formulate them effectively. Before starting a research project, it is good practice to look at what we already know about the topic and how it has been investigated before. Chapter 3 explains the nature and purpose of a literature review in research and how to carry one out.

Researching in business and management

1.1 INTRODUCTION

Management research is an exciting way of learning more about the world of organizations and business. As a management researcher, you will need energy, drive, and a desire to see beyond the expected and the every day. We live in a world where economic, scientific, social, and technological changes are occurring at an ever-increasing pace affecting organizations and the people who work in them. No better example of this than the Covid-19 pandemic that began in 2020 bringing significant changes for us all. It triggered scientific research to understand the virus and create a protective vaccine. At the same time management research was needed to explore and understand the many social and behavioural effects of the pandemic on various stakeholders, including customers and staff. New ways of thinking about all aspects of both our work and home life were required. Much of this relied on research skills by a wide range of individuals from academics through to management practitioners to explore and analyze the changing situation. In Research in Practice 1.1 we give an example of Covid-triggered research undertaken to understand the effects of new hybrid working patterns and the implications for managers.

DOI: 10.4324/9781003381006-2

Research in practice 1.1 Researching hybrid working

One of the key effects of the Covid-19 pandemic in many countries was the change in working patterns that it created. Employees were required to work from home under government policy, with the only exceptions being essential services such as health care and supply of critical goods. As the pandemic eased, a new working pattern emerged referred to as 'hybrid working', which enabled employees to work part of the week at home and part in the office. This new form of flexible working created challenges for organizations and particularly those involved in managing teams, which were no longer fully co-located.

A senior leader from a global banking group studying for his master's degree was interested to learn more about the effects of hybrid working on management practice. The aim was to understand the challenges managers faced and specifically the effects on productivity (level of work output), collaboration (people working well together), and attachment (loyalty to the organization). A cross-sectional quantitative survey study was conducted in February 2022 with a global sample of managers across a range of industries. Participants had managed people with hybrid working patterns over the previous two years. Data were collected using a questionnaire which measured the effects of hybrid working on the three organizational elements. Whilst conducted for a master's level dissertation, the findings and recommendations from the research study were used within the organization to build knowledge and improve management practice and attitudes towards hybrid working patterns.

Source: Garlick (2022)

At this point, particularly if you are new to research, you will probably have more questions than answers about your project. What makes a good research topic? How should I design my research? Where and how will I get my data? How will I analyze my data and report my findings? What skills do I need? This book will help you answer these and many other questions about doing research. It introduces key principles that underpin rigour and relevance in research. It shows you how to apply these principles to your research in order to produce output that has impact and value, whilst making sure you complete your project within the time and resources available.

In this first chapter we begin by defining what we mean by research, identifying its characteristic features, and why we do it. We then introduce a high-level model of the research process which both maps out the sequence of activities that go into a research project and forms the overall structure of the book itself. Next, we explore two important issues: the relationships between management research and practice and between theory and research. These topics prepare the ground for a discussion of different philosophical orientations that characterize present-day management research. Finally, we discuss the importance of reflection and learning from research practice and how this helps you to think through the impact you have had on the research process and to develop your knowledge, expertise, and skills in research.

1.2 DEFINING MANAGEMENT RESEARCH

Management research is usually considered part of the social sciences, which is the field of enquiry concerned with human beings and how they behave and interact either as individuals or as a group. Like many other aspects of management studies, management research is a diverse field. It is used in many different contexts, including commercial and not-for-profit organizations, different industries, and different national and cultural settings. As well as its own, and growing, body of knowledge, it draws on the theories and practices of other disciplines such as economics, sociology, and psychology. But what do we mean by 'research'?

1.2.1 What do we mean by research?

The origins of the word research lie in the French word 'recherche', meaning to look for or seek out (Merriam-Webster, 2023). Table 1.1 presents different definitions of research, drawn from a range of sources both academic and nonacademic. We can see that they emphasize two different but related dimensions. First, that research is a systematic process of investigation and second, that it has the purpose of finding out information or knowledge about a specific problem or issue. Other authors have also emphasized the problem-solving nature of research (e.g. Van de Ven, 2007; Gray, 2018). So we can define **research** as a purposeful, systematic process of investigation in order to find solutions to a problem.

TABLE 1.1 Definitions of research
— 'The systematic gathering and interpretation of information about individuals and organisations. It uses the statistical and analytical methods and techniques of the applied social, behavioural and data sciences to generate insights and support decision-making by corporations, governments, non-profit organisations and the general public'. (Definition of market research, including social and opinion research, ESOMAR, 2023)
— 'research is often about how (process) to solve real problems (content)'. (Gray, 2018: 3)
— 'systematic observation or investigation to find things out. It is the process by which we produce evidence or knowledge about the world'. (McGivern, 2022: 4)
— 'a process that is undertaken in a systematic way with a clear purpose, to find things out'. (Saunders et al., 2019: 5)
— 'the process of finding solutions to a problem after a targeted and systematic study and analysis of materials and sources'. (Bougie and Sekaran, 2020: 1)

1.2.2 Why do a research project?

Management research is used for many different purposes and in many different contexts. It can be done by academics and practitioners or by the two groups in collaboration. As we will see, its aim may be to contribute to the body of management theory or to management practice. At this point, however, it is helpful to stop and consider the situation in which you are working as a researcher and why you are doing your research. This can help you understand the type of research you are likely to have to undertake, identify the stakeholders and their expectations, and understand some of the challenges you may face during the project. We have found it is helpful to consider two key questions:

1. Are you doing the research for an academic qualification? If your research project forms part of an academic qualification programme of study, you are taking the role of student researcher. You may be doing research as a final-year project on an undergraduate or master's programme, for a doctorate, or perhaps as part of a work placement. For a student research project, the outcome will need to meet the assessment criteria of the academic institution in which you are studying as well as meet any commitments that you may have made to other stakeholders in the research. A major benefit of doing research as part of a qualification is the support available. You are likely to be working with an academic supervisor or tutor, who will give guidance and advice during your research project, as well as act as a mentor for your development as a researcher. In addition, you will almost certainly have access to library and other study resources and possibly to specialist software and technical advice. If you are not a student researcher, you are likely to have to develop your contacts and networks to help support you during the process.

2. Are you doing the research in your own organization? If you are, you are taking on the role of **insider researcher**. This presents you with both opportunities and challenges. Opportunities arise because being part of an organization can make it easier to identify a suitable research topic and to gain support and help in getting access to research respondents, data sources, and so on. Challenges arise because of the potential ambiguity of adopting a dual role as both researcher and organizational member. You may face difficulties, for example, because of the need to balance the commitments of a managerial position with the demands for your time as a researcher, or your choice of topic may be constrained by organizational expectations. Being an insider researcher may place particular demands on your ability to deal with a complex and ambiguous situation. If you are not an insider researcher, whilst you may avoid these sorts of problems, you may face greater challenges in gaining access to organizations, respondents, or data. Here your network and personal and professional contacts will be invaluable during the project. If you are a full-time student researcher, your academic institution may be able to help with identifying potential projects or organizations looking for help with research.

Of course these roles are not mutually exclusive. You can be both an insider researcher and a student researcher, for example, a common position for those studying part time

FIGURE 1.1 The five-stage model of research

whilst working in an organization. Whatever your situation, it is important to recognize the implications for how you go about your project and the expectations that are placed on it. We return to these issues in Chapter 8 when we look at planning your research project.

1.2.3 The research process

Successful research is not haphazard and does not happen by chance. Carrying out a research project involves undertaking a series of activities, linked together in a structured and logical process. In Figure 1.1 we provide a high-level model of the research process, separated into five distinctive stages. The model identifies the principal activities involved in carrying out a research project. It provides a working template for planning and monitoring your own project. It also forms the structure for the book, as each of the five stages is covered in a different part of the book. We will now look at each stage in turn in terms of its objectives, key considerations, and the relevant chapters within the book.

Stage 1: Define

In the first stage of your research you will need to identify and define the topic of your investigation. In Chapter 2 we introduce the idea of the research problem and how it provides the focus for you to determine the boundaries of your investigation and set the high-level questions your research will need to answer in order to address your chosen research problem. Having identified the focus of the research, it is important to spend time looking at what is currently known about your topic. Chapter 3 shows how to undertake a critical review of the academic, practitioner, and policy literature that makes up the body of knowledge in your chosen field.

Stage 2: Design

The next stage is design of your research project. Chapter 4 introduces the elements of research design and the key decisions that determine the overall shape of your research and discusses how we can judge the quality of research. Chapter 5 alerts you to ethical considerations that you will need to address when carrying out your research project, including in the context of using new technology and online platforms. This chapter also discusses the importance of diversity and inclusion and your need to be aware of this when you are both designing and conducting your research. In Chapters 6 and 7 we focus on specific research designs using quantitative, qualitative, and mixed methods and how they can be used to answer different research questions. Chapter 8 provides you with guidance on the practical aspects of planning and managing your own research project, along with advice on how to prepare a research proposal at the outset of your project.

Stage 3: Collect

Data collection is one of the key practical tasks in any research project. Depending upon the type of research design you have chosen, you will use different data collection method(s) to collect data from different sources. We begin in Chapter 9 by discussing where and how much data you are going to collect, by introducing the idea of sampling. Chapter 10 looks at one of the most commonly used quantitative data collection methods, the questionnaire. Chapter 11 does the same for an important family of qualitative data collection techniques: in-depth individual and group interviews. In Chapter 12 we turn our attention to data sources where we do not rely on asking participants questions about the phenomenon of interest. These are diaries, observations, social media, documents, big data, and artefacts. In each chapter we discuss how to prepare for and carry out your chosen data collection method.

Stage 4: Analyze

Analysis is the heart of a research project and can often be the most exciting – and demanding – part of doing research. In this part of the book we look at how to prepare your data, carry out your analysis, and draw appropriate, evidence-based conclusions. Chapter 13 is dedicated to quantitative analysis, and in Chapter 14 we cover qualitative data analysis techniques.

Stage 5: Communicate

The audience for your research output may be your academic institution and/or other stakeholders for whom the research has been undertaken. Either way, you must ensure that you communicate your findings clearly, effectively, and in a way that meets the needs of the audience. Communication is the subject of Chapter 15, which looks at how to prepare appropriate written or oral reports of your research findings particularly utilizing technological resources.

1.2.4 Is research a sequential process?

For clarity, the five-stage model has been shown as a sequential process with discrete stages. In practice, research is often much messier, especially early on in a project, where there may be iterations between the definition and design stages as the topic and practical aspects of the research design are clarified. In addition, some research designs are intentionally iterative. Nevertheless, we believe that it is useful to emphasize the high-level sequence of activities that make up the research process in order to make it easier to see the tasks that will need to be carried out to complete your project. We have also shown the process as a circular one to stress the importance of being aware of and, where appropriate, building upon, the results of prior research.

1.3 THE RELATIONSHIP BETWEEN RESEARCH AND PRACTICE

If research is about the application of a process to help solve problems, it is important to understand how management research relates to the practice of management and what this might mean for your own project. As we discuss in the Critical Commentary to this chapter, the relationship between academics and industry practitioners is important in terms of research collaboration but may sometimes be difficult. This is in part due to the fact that there are two broad types of research that differ in terms of their primary focus, their intended audience, and their relationship to management practice. Their key features are summarized in Table 1.2.

TABLE 1.2 Characteristics of pure and applied research

Pure research	Applied research
Primary aim is to add to our theoretical knowledge of the topic area under investigation.	Primary aim is to help to solve a problem or issue of concern to practitioners.
Motivation for research is a particular problem or issue within the domain of theoretical knowledge.	Motivation for research is a particular problem or issue within the domain of management practice.
Research outputs contribute to the body of theoretical knowledge about the topic.	Research outputs are used by managers and policymakers to inform decision-making and action.
Undertaken predominantly for an academic audience.	Undertaken predominantly for a practitioner audience.
Findings disseminated via academic conferences, journals, and books.	Findings disseminated via reports and practitioner publications but often restricted in terms of availability (e.g. for commercial reasons).
Contribution to practice is usually indirect.	Contribution to body of theoretical knowledge is usually secondary and indirect.

1.3.1 Pure research

Pure (or basic) research is often associated with an academic agenda and is aimed primarily at an academic audience. The motivation for the research is a problem, gap, or anomaly identified in the body of theoretical knowledge about a topic. The main aim of the research is to address that problem and thereby extend our knowledge in the field. Findings of the research are likely to be disseminated via academic publishing routes such as conferences, academic journals, and so on. Contribution to practice is likely to be indirect, through a 'trickle down' effect via routes such as higher education, researchers acting as consultants or specialist advisors, or through nonacademic publications. In Research in Practice 1.2 we give an example of pure research, with opportunities to relate findings to practice.

Research in practice 1.2 Using pure research to understand disharmonious co-creation and chatbots

We are all becoming familiar as customers with the use of chatbots powered by artificial intelligence (AI) as part of online service delivery. They are used particularly by consumer facing brands to interact with customers and to encourage active participation by them. However, customer experiences of interacting with chatbots may vary and at times may not lead to a positive outcome. PhD student Daniela Castillo was interested to look at the use of chatbots in the context of co-creation between the customer and the brand. Theoretical positions in existing literature had most often focused on co-creation in the context of harmonious collaboration between two parties. Given that chatbot experience may not always be positive, the researcher set out to investigate customer perceptions of disharmonious co-creation situations and how these influence customer expectations and responsibility attributions during chatbot service failure.

   The researcher used a mixed methods approach. Qualitative research enabled the development of a research framework with hypotheses based on existing theories regarding the relationships between co-creation contexts and the constructs of disconfirmation of expectations and attribution of responsibility. Hypotheses were then tested via two experimental research studies. The outputs of the study were able to challenge the existing views in the literature of co-creation as a harmonious, voluntary collaborative activity and contributed further to the body of knowledge in the co-creation literature.

Source: Castillo (2022)

1.3.2 Applied research

Applied research, on the other hand, is likely to emerge as a direct response to a particular problem faced by practitioners and with the output being aimed directly at a practitioner audience. Note, however, that the research itself may be carried out by academics, practitioners, or by commercial research specialists such as a consultancy or market research agency. In applied research the primary aim is to address the practical problem or issue, and the output is usually intended to be used by practitioners, such as managers or policy-makers, to inform decision-making and action. Dissemination may be by publication (for example, for research commissioned by government or other public bodies) but the findings of applied research may also be very restricted in terms of its circulation, especially if it is commercially sensitive. Applied research varies also in the extent to which it engages with current theory and past research, but by its nature the contribution to the body of theoretical knowledge is likely to be a secondary goal for the research. Nevertheless, applied research can develop awareness of both research methods and theory within the wider management profession. Research in Practice 1.3 shows applied research in action.

Research in practice 1.3 Use of applied research to understand the effects of technology on customer service staff

The Henley Centre for Customer Management conducts research for its corporate members. In autumn 2019, the members were interested in knowing more about how technological changes in the work environment had the potential to affect customer service staff. Whilst digitalisation had been part of the business landscape for some time, changes particularly in relation to artificial intelligence (AI) and the use of robotics were beginning to emerge. A key concern for organizations was how these technological advances were impacting customer service employees and their relationship with customers. Recipients of the research output wanted to use the research in their organizations to understand the changes that are coming in the future and to inform decision-making about customer service provision.

First, the researcher used existing sources of information on the subject from both academic and practitioner literature to explore existing knowledge in the topic. Then, she conducted primary research in the form of qualitative interviews with experts working in the field of AI technology and change. Example organizational cases of the application of these new technologies in the field of customer service were also included to provide rich data. The output of the research was communicated to members via a written report available electronically as well as a live presentation which enabled discussion between the researcher and recipients of the research findings.

Source: Rose (2020)

1.3.3 Implications for your research project

So what is the appropriate type of research for your project? The answer depends, of course, on your situation. If you are doing a doctorate you would be expected to demonstrate the development of your own scholarly and research skills as well as that your work makes a contribution to knowledge. Although this is rather difficult to define, it certainly means that you need to make sure that your research is grounded within the existing body of knowledge in your topic area, so your research is likely to fall within the category of pure research even if your project has a strong practice orientation. For master's level and undergraduate projects, requirements will vary according to the type of project you are doing, but many final projects will offer the opportunity of doing applied research. If you are not bound by the requirements of an academic qualification, you are likely to be able to decide what is most appropriate in view of your reason for undertaking a research project. Whatever your circumstances, however, you should make sure your choice is compatible with the expectations of other stakeholders in your project.

CRITICAL COMMENTARY 1.1

Academic and industry research collaboration

In this chapter we present a generally positive view of the relationship between management research, management theory, and management practice. By implication this suggests that theory and practice work well together. The assumption is that by drawing on both theoretical thinking, rigorous research, and practical input a deeper understanding of business and management will be achieved. It also assumes that academic researchers and industry practitioners can work well together and are of the same mind in terms of the value of pure and applied research. Academics and practitioners are encouraged to collaborate, and much government funding is available today with this as a condition. Such collaborative research partnerships are viewed as important as they encourage knowledge transfer and sharing, which can have benefits economically, socially, and commercially. There are many examples of strong collaborations between universities and industries in the fields of computer science, information systems, pharmaceuticals, or medicine, and the development of the Covid-19 vaccine is an example of such collaboration.

However, academic and industry practitioner research collaborations may not always be harmonious. Being aware of the tensions that may exist is important if such partnerships are to be successful. An investigation into the co-production process in university-industry partnerships by Canhoto et al. (2016) identified that the nature of interactions between the parties and contextual factors, including individual, organizational, and external, determine effectiveness. Key enablers were found to be the level of commitment by each party, similarity of attitudes, and complementarity of skills. Relationship difficulties emerged from differences in end goals (research and publishing versus commercial success), timescales, and ways of working. As with any relationship, levels of trust and effective communication come to the fore in successful academic-industry partnerships.

1.4 THE RELATIONSHIP BETWEEN RESEARCH AND THEORY

In the previous discussion we noted that pure and applied research may differ in terms of how they relate to practice. We now move on to look at what we mean by 'theory' and how it relates to research and to practice.

1.4.1 What is theory?

Christensen and Raynor (2003: 68) define theory as 'a statement predicting what actions will lead to what results and why'. A more technical definition is offered by Gill and Johnson (2010: 43), who define theory as an 'abstract conceptual framework which allows us to explain why specific observed regularities happen'. A theory might explain, for example, why a particular leadership style is more effective than other leadership styles in particular situations or how customers choose between different products when shopping online.

Taking this further, Whetten (1989) argues that a theory should consist of four elements:

1. The concepts that make up the theory. A **concept** is a mental category that groups observations or ideas together on the basis of shared attributes. It can be relatively concrete such as 'age' or 'income', or more tangible, such as 'satisfaction' or 'leadership style'. Concepts form 'the structure of theory' (Corbin and Strauss, 2015: 76).

2. A statement of how the concepts are related, for example, in terms of one causing another.

3. A logical explanation for the relationships between them; this provides the 'theoretical glue' (Whetten, 1989: 491) that holds the theory together.

4. Identification of the contexts, such as the organizational situation, in which the theory applies.

Theory should therefore provide an explanation of a phenomenon in terms of the relevant concepts, how they are related, why they are related, and in what contexts the theory would apply. As we discuss in Chapter 3, such theories are often depicted graphically as a conceptual model that shows the concepts and the relationships between them.

1.4.2 Theory and practice

Theory and practice sometimes seem to belong to separate worlds, and the relevance of theory to everyday management practice is not always obvious. Christensen and Raynor make the point in a light-hearted way:

> Theory often gets a bum rap among managers because it's associated with the word 'theoretical', which connotes 'impractical'. But it shouldn't. . . . Every action that managers take, and every plan they formulate, is based on some theory in the back of their minds that makes them expect the actions they contemplate will have the results they envision. But . . . most managers don't realise they are voracious users of theory.
>
> (Christensen and Raynor, 2003: 68)

Argyris and Schön (1974) make a similar point in their study of theory and professional practice. They argue that any deliberate behaviour is the result of 'theories of action' that human beings hold and which guide those actions. Such theories of action, they suggest, take the form of 'in situation S, if you want to achieve consequence C, do A' (Argyris and Schön, 1974: 4). As humans we therefore find ourselves applying theories every day, whether or not we are aware of doing so.

The inevitability of using some form of theory in our everyday and professional lives means, as Mintzberg (2004: 250) puts it, that 'we use theory whether we realize it or not. So our choice is not between theory and practice as much as between different theories that can inform our practice'. In the view of some writers, theory is even more pervasive. It is a way of 'seeing and thinking about the world' (Alvesson and Deetz, 2000: 37) that shapes how we view reality. Even a simple description is not just a neutral account of what something 'is'. It implicitly involves the concepts, background knowledge, and language available to us as observers. You cannot describe an executive board meeting, for example, without invoking the concepts and language of an executive board, of meetings, and so on (Thorpe and Holt, 2008). Our observations therefore are influenced by the concepts and theories we hold. They are not theory neutral. However, although our theories influence our observations, they do not determine them; instead, our observations can be thought of as 'theory laden' (Sayer, 1992: 83). Being aware of our theories and how they may be influencing what we do and think is one of the reasons for taking a reflexive stance on research, as we discuss in more detail in Section 1.6.

1.4.3 The scope of theory

Theories can vary greatly in their scope. A commonly encountered categorization distinguishes three types of theory in terms of their scale.

Grand theories

Grand theories, sometimes known as meta-theories, are theoretical systems that apply to large-scale social phenomena. Marxist historical materialism and Freudian psychoanalysis are two familiar examples. Grand theory can provide a general orientation towards a problem area and suggest potential explanations for phenomena of interest. It may also be linked to a specific philosophical orientation and thereby incorporate a particular understanding of the nature of research and of the social world. Grand theory may, however, be difficult to test empirically or to use directly in a research project because of its high degree of abstraction, but it may provide an overall orientation for a study.

Middle-range theories

Middle-range theories have a more limited scope than grand theory and provide an explanation of a particular phenomenon, such as leadership or organizational change. As a result they can more readily be used to guide research efforts. Middle-range theories are likely to be important in guiding pure research efforts, but they can also inform applied projects. An example of a middle-range theory is Service Dominant Logic (Vargo and Lusch, 2004, 2017), which challenged existing views of economic exchange that focused on 'tangible resources, embedded value, and transactions' and instead focused on service exchange and the importance of co-creation and relationships. This theory has been used extensively in consumer research and service operations management to challenge traditional goods-centred explanations of markets.

Substantive theories

Substantive theories apply to a specific phenomenon in a specific setting such as leadership in distributed teams or organizational change in entrepreneurial start-ups. Their narrower scope means that they may not be applicable to other contexts, but their closeness to practical problems makes them especially relevant in applied research, where the focus may be a particular situation, and the researcher has less interest in theorizing about other contexts.

For applied research, middle-range or substantive theories will probably be more directly relevant to the immediate needs of the research project. Even if you are carrying out pure research, with a strong theoretical focus, contributing to middle-range or substantive theory in the topic area is likely to be more feasible than aspiring to develop grand theory.

1.4.4 Theory and research

When commencing a research project, you may already be familiar with existing theories in your topic area, and you will encounter further theories as you start to read more about your subject. But how can theory contribute to your research? And how can your research contribute to theory? Figure 1.2 shows two different ways in which theory can be integrated into research.

With a **deductive approach** you start with theory, typically based on existing literature that proposes possible solutions to your research problem. This theory is then tested against data collected in the situation under investigation. The resulting findings provide both a test of the theory and potential solutions to your chosen problem. A deductive

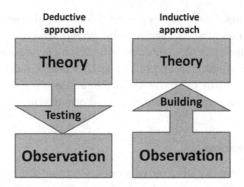

FIGURE 1.2 Deductive and inductive approaches to research

approach might be used, for example, to investigate the factors that influence customers' decisions to shop online. By drawing on existing theory to identify factors seen to influence online shopping behaviour and by collecting suitable data, you could test which factors were influential in the situation you were investigating.

When adopting an **inductive approach**, on the other hand, you begin the collection of data via observations of a specific phenomenon in response to your research problem and then build a theory about what is going on from those observations. For example, an inductive approach might be used to investigate the process by which innovative ideas are developed into a final product in a particular situation. Rather than test an existing theory, you could decide to gather data about what is going on by studying how particular products have been developed from the idea stage in one or more organizations. This would enable you to develop a more detailed understanding of how such product development is done, from which you could build a theory explaining the product innovation process. In an inductive approach, theory is therefore primarily an output; in a deductive approach, it is a key input. The two approaches involve contrasting 'logics of enquiry' (Blaikie and Priest, 2019: 21), using theory and literature in different ways, and making use of different research designs, as we discuss in more detail in Chapter 4.

1.5 RESEARCH AND PHILOSOPHY

Behind any research lie our fundamental assumptions about the world we are researching. This is the domain of philosophy and, in particular, the philosophy of social science. The debates in this area have divided research communities for decades (and even centuries). This is a fascinating area for those who are interested in it but can be mystifying to those who are not. We now introduce you to aspects of this topic that are particularly relevant to management research. Our aim is to assist you in making sense of philosophical issues that you will encounter during your research and to help you develop your own philosophical position in relation to your own project.

1.5.1 Epistemology and ontology

Discussion of research philosophy often proceeds by distinguishing between the **episte-mology** and **ontology** of different philosophical positions. In social sciences, epistemology usually refers to questions of how we know what we claim to know. Since epistemology is concerned with the problem of how we know things, its connection with research as an activity of findings things out is fairly obvious. To illustrate this, we will highlight two contrasting epistemological stances, **objectivism** and **subjectivism**. An objectivist episte-mology assumes the possibility of gathering data through the theory-neutral (objective) and value-free observation of the social world by the application of appropriate methods. A subjectivist epistemology rejects this view and instead assumes that all observation is, at the very least, theory laden, thereby calling into question any claim to produce a value-free, objective account of something. Our epistemological assumptions have sig-nificant implications for how we go about evaluating the research that we and others produce.

Ontology is concerned with our beliefs about the nature of what is out there to know in the social world. At first sight the relevance of ontology to research may not be that clear. But if we think about it in terms of our assumptions about the nature of the world we are investigating, we can see that it does matter. Again we can illustrate this by contrasting two ontological positions, realism and idealism. Ontological **realism** assumes the existence of a mind-independent reality. The tree outside the office window, for example, is there independently of our awareness of it. Ontological **idealism**, on the other hand, challenges that assumption. Idealism, as we use the term here, does not necessarily deny the existence of an object outside our window, but it does suggest that its 'tree-ness' is not something intrinsic to the object but is instead a product, a construction, of cognitive and social processes that make it meaningful for us as humans. If we turn our attention from trees to social phenomena such as organization or culture, we can start to see the importance of ontological questions to research. Is an organization something 'out there' waiting for us to come along and describe and explain it, or is it something that can be understood by investigating the shared meanings of organizational members? How we answer such questions influences how we approach the problem of research in a social setting such as management.

1.5.2 Philosophical orientations

These epistemological and ontological assumptions combine in different ways to contrib-ute to alternative philosophical orientations to business and management research. These alternative orientations have different emphases in terms of the primary goals of research, what constitutes an appropriate research approach, and the preferred research methods. We summarize them in Table 1.3.

Positivism

Positivism, at least as the term is used in the social science, usually refers to a philosophical orientation that looks to apply the methods of the natural sciences to the social sciences.

TABLE 1.3 Philosophical orientations in research

	Philosophical orientation			
	Positivism	Interpretivism	Social constructionism	Realism
Epistemology	Objectivist	Objectivist	Subjectivist	Subjectivist
Ontology	(Direct) Realist	Idealist	Idealist	(Depth) Realist
Emphasis of research	Explanation in terms of universal 'laws'	Understanding lived experience and shared culture	Understanding the process of social construction	Explanation in terms of causal mechanisms
Typical research approach	Deductive	Inductive	Inductive	Abductive/ inductive
Dominant research methods	Quantitative, with qualitative research in a subordinate role	Qualitative	Qualitative	Qualitative/ quantitative

Positivist research aims to establish causal explanations in the form of universal laws by means of controlled observation and measurement and deductive theory testing, in line with its objectivist epistemology. Rigorous and explicit procedures are advocated so as to avoid researcher bias and to ensure that the research is value-free. Positivism is closely associated with quantitative methods and research designs such as experiments. Positivism's ontological position is sometimes described as direct realism because it restricts claims about the world to those that can be observed. Claims about things that cannot be observed or about things about which suitable evidence cannot be gathered (such as some mental processes) are treated with scepticism. This emphasis on the central role of observation is sometimes referred to as empiricism, which term is sometimes used synonymously with positivism. Positivism is often depicted as the dominant research approach in business and management, but it has come in for a great deal of criticism on both philosophical and practical grounds.

One response to the criticisms of positivism has been the emergence of **post-positivism,** sometimes which has been described as a 'less arrogant form of positivism' (Crotty, 1998: 29). Phillips and Burbules sum up the post-positivist position in the following terms:

> [Post-positivists] are united in believing that human knowledge is not based on unchallengeable, rock-solid foundations – it is conjectural. We have grounds, or warrants, for asserting the beliefs, or conjectures, that we hold as scientists, often very good grounds, but these grounds are not indubitable. Our warrants for accepting things can be withdrawn in the light of further investigation.
>
> Phillips and Burbules (2000: 26)

In addition to the quantitative methods typical of positivist research, post-positivist researchers also use qualitative and mixed methods research, particularly those that lend themselves to more structured analysis. Nevertheless, post-positivism retains much of positivism's commitment to the goal of value-free, objective research.

Interpretivism

Interpretivism rejects the positivist assumption that the methods of the natural sciences apply to the social sciences, insisting instead that there are fundamental differences between the objects (such as chemicals and rocks) that natural scientists study and the reasoning human beings that social scientists study. People actively interpret the world around them and do so within a specific sociocultural context. Understanding of the social world therefore requires understanding it from the point of view of the people directly involved in the social process (Burrell and Morgan, 1979). We have therefore classified interpretivist ontology as a form of idealism, in order to stress the importance of meaning and understanding in this approach. Interpretivist researchers are also interested in the lived experience of individuals, in how they understand and make sense of their experiences. The resulting knowledge of particular groups and events in their specific context is often referred to as idiographic, in contrast to positivism's search for nomothetic knowledge in the form of universal laws. Given the very different way in which the nature of the social world is understood, it is not surprising that interpretivism questions the use of the methods of the natural sciences for social research, arguing instead that a different approach is needed. In place of the deductive, quantitative methods that characterize a positivist research, interpretivist research therefore typically adopts an inductive approach, combined with qualitative research methods, such as ethnography and in-depth interviews that allow the researcher to investigate phenomena in context and through the understanding of those involved (Blaikie and Priest, 2019).

In Table 1.3 we show interpretivism as adopting an objectivist epistemology. This is reflected in two commitments that are evident to varying degrees in interpretivist research (Hammersley, 2013). The first is a commitment to the value of detailed and accurate observation via in-depth field research, including audio and even video recording where appropriate. The second is the need for researchers to put aside their presuppositions and own assumptions in favour of understanding the culture being researched on its own terms. This objectivist stance has led some writers to refer to this approach as neo-empiricism, on the basis that interpretivism shares to some degree positivism's empiricist orientation (Johnson et al., 2006), even though it is opposed to other aspects of positivist thought. This objectivist aspect of interpretivism has been challenged by the rise of social constructionism, to the point where today many interpretivist researchers are likely to adopt a more subjectivist epistemological position.

Social constructionism

Social constructionism is a more recent development than either positivism or interpretivism but has been very influential in both the philosophy and method of social science.

As its name suggests, social constructionism emphasizes the 'constructed' nature of social reality. Phenomena like management, organization, and personal identity are not determined by some internal essence that makes them what they are but are instead constructed through our social processes and, in particular, through interaction and language. Researcher interest therefore focuses on investigating the construction process, documenting, for example, how and in what ways things such as 'globalization' or 'competence' get constructed in some ways rather than others. Social constructionist research is generally qualitative and inductive and often with a particular interest in research that investigates language (spoken and written).

As we have seen, social constructionism shares interpretivism's ontological idealism, but it rejects its neo-empiricist leanings in favour of epistemological subjectivism. It thereby draws attention to the constructed nature of the researcher's own account of their own research. Social constructionist researchers have, for example, sought to show the processes through which scientific facts are constructed during the course of laboratory research (such as Latour and Woolgar, 1986). This is a very radical move in many respects: if all accounts, including scientific ones, are socially constructed, what is the basis for preferring one over another? The extreme relativism implied by this question is not accepted by all social constructionists, let alone all researchers, but it draws attention to the problem of how we should decide whether a piece of research should be taken seriously. The problem of deciding on the quality of a piece of research is an important topic which we discuss further in Chapter 4.

Realism

Our final example of a philosophical orientation is **realism**. As we are using the term here, it refers to the relatively recent version of realism that goes under various headings, such as critical realism, subtle realism, and scientific realism. As its name suggests, it is characterized by a form of ontological realism. It replaces the direct realism of positivism, however, with a depth realism that draws a distinction between the events we can observe (the empirical) and the potentially unobservable mechanisms and processes that give rise to them (the real). Explanation, in this view, involves identifying the causal mechanisms that generate the regularities that we observe in the natural and social world. For example, we may observe that gunpowder ignites when it comes into contact with a flame. From a realist point of view, an explanation of this phenomenon would require that we identify the mechanisms, such as gunpowder's chemical composition, that bring this about and the contexts, such as the presence of oxygen, in which it occurs. Identification of such causal mechanisms, along with the contexts in which they are triggered, is a key component of realist research. The research methods for doing this can be qualitative or quantitative, although realists are often critical of the ways in which quantitative methods are used in positivist research. Realism also questions both the deductive and inductive approaches to research in favour of what is sometimes called abduction, a topic we discuss in more detail in Chapter 4.

Realism also departs from positivism in adopting a subjectivist epistemology. In doing so it accepts that we can only know the world through our descriptions of it. Unlike social constructionism, which also espouses a subjectivist epistemological position, realism insists that there is a reality independent of our knowledge of it, and this reality constrains the ways in which we can construct our world and offers the possibility of being able to decide which accounts of reality are more adequate than others. Observation in the realist view is always theory laden, but it is not theory determined.

1.5.3 Axiological assumptions

Axiology deals with questions of value (Saunders et al., 2019). In terms of philosophical positions in research, positivism is traditionally associated with the idea that research should be value-free. The researcher's neutrality is achieved through the application of appropriate research methods and techniques. Other philosophical orientations acknowledge the inevitability of researcher involvement in the research process and thus are more sceptical of the extent to which research can be free of the explicit or implicit values of the researcher. One response to this loss of certainty has been to emphasize the need for researchers to be aware of their own role in and impact upon the research process. This awareness is often referred to as reflexivity, a topic we discuss in more detail later in the chapter.

Values are also at the heart of another debate in business research; namely, on whose behalf and in whose interests is the research being done? We have so far taken it for granted that research that generates knowledge that improves management and organizational practice is a 'good thing'. This is not a view shared by everyone. There is a long tradition in both academic and popular writing that is critical of capitalism in its various manifestations. In business and management research, what are sometimes known as critical management studies have been inspired by various influences, particularly Marxism and feminism, and question what they see as research that operates in the interests of management or other dominant groups. Researchers taking this approach aim to surface issues such as gender imbalance, discrimination, and worker exploitation. We explore these issues further in Chapter 5 when we discuss the ethical aspects of management research and the emergence of participatory research as well as the importance of diversity and inclusivity in research.

1.5.4 Taking it forward

Although we may not be explicitly aware of it, our philosophical orientation shapes the way we frame a research problem and the possible solutions to it. It influences how we go about investigating it in terms of the overall approach and the specific research methods and techniques that we adopt. This is one reason why academic research, especially for dissertations and theses, often includes a discussion of philosophical issues as part of the research report. But where do we start? Our experience is that most new researchers do not begin with strong awareness of, let alone commitment to, a particular philosophical orientation. Instead, this develops over time as they learn more about research methods and as they look at research carried out from different philosophical positions. At this early stage, therefore, do not worry if you do not have a sense of where you stand in relation to the philosophical aspects of research. As you read, talk about, and above all, reflect on your research project, you will develop your own thinking on this complex but fascinating aspect of research.

We conclude this section on a note of caution. It is very easy to get lost in philosophical debate about and lose sight of the research itself. If you find yourself getting into this situation, the advice of Tashakkori and Teddlie is worth noting:

> For most researchers committed to the thorough study of a research problem . . . the underlying world view hardly enters the picture, except in the most abstract sense. . . . [Philosophical] considerations are not as important in the final analysis as the research question that you are attempting to answer.
>
> (Tashakkori and Teddlie, 1998: 21)

1.6 REFLEXIVITY AND THE RESEARCHER

A growing awareness of the impact of the researcher on the research process has led to calls for researchers to pay greater attention to this aspect of their work. This is often talked about in terms of **reflexivity** and involves 'a focus on how does who I am, who I have been, who I think I am, and how I feel affect data collection and analysis' (Pillow, 2003: 176). In this sense, reflexivity goes beyond simply reflecting upon the technical details of our research, to think more deeply about how our underlying assumptions influence what we do and how we do it and how those assumptions are affected in turn by our experiences.

1.6.1 Types of reflexivity

Reflexivity is not constrained by any single aspect of our research but operates on multiple levels simultaneously, as shown by the following examples (Lynch, 2000; Johnson and Duberley, 2003; Haynes, 2012):

- Theoretical reflexivity. How do our existing theories shape our framing of the research problem and our approach to it? How are these theories themselves shaped as the project unfolds?
- Methodological reflexivity. How are our assumptions and preferences about research methods influencing and influenced by the research?
- Philosophical reflexivity. How do our philosophical commitments (epistemological, ontological, and axiological) shape how we go about our research? How are these, in turn, influenced by the research project?
- Standpoint reflexivity. How does our own political, cultural, social, and emotional standpoint influence our approach to the research?

We suggest that reflexivity about our own standpoint in relation to the research is particularly relevant when we are doing research about which we have strong personal feelings or close personal involvement. Such situations can easily arise for the insider researcher doing research in their own organization; reflexivity is therefore important not just with respect to the technical details of the research but also in terms of engagement with stakeholders who may influence or be affected by the research or its findings. Reflexivity should also make us aware of ourselves versus others and raise consideration of diversity and inclusion in our research. It is important, however, not to lose sight of the research. As Alvesson et al. observe:

> A word of caution is in order. Reflexivity does not need to be a heavy, endless source of self-contemplation and doubt but can – and should – be productively used to enhance the quality of any research project. It is the researcher who needs to decide the right level of reflective engagement given the type of the research project s/he is engaged in.
>
> Alvesson et al. (2022: 28)

1.6.2 Being reflexive

What can we do to be more reflexive about our research? Making time and space to think and reflect is the first step, but to develop our skills in reflexivity takes more than that. As part of your research project, we encourage you to keep a research journal or diary (see Chapter 8). This is the ideal place to start writing reflexively. Alongside recording 'factual' information such as the date that an interview took place or the details of a decision that was made, record also your emerging thoughts and feelings about what was happening, why you took a particular decision, how you carried out a particular task, and so on. Use the diary to reflect on the implications of what you are doing, both for the research and yourself. Not only will this help you develop your reflexive skills, it will also provide a valuable record of your actions and thoughts during the research when it comes to writing up your project, especially if you are required or decide to include a reflective component in your final report.

CHAPTER SUMMARY

- Research is a purposeful systematic process of investigation in order to find solutions to problems or issues.
- Pure (or basic) research is focused on adding to the existing body of theoretical knowledge that exists in relation to a particular topic or domain. Its output is primarily aimed at an academic audience. Applied research addresses particular questions or problems faced by practitioners, with the output being aimed at a practitioner audience.

- Theory is an explanation of a phenomenon in terms of relationships between two or more concepts. The role of theory in a research project can vary. With a deductive approach, we begin with theory and test it against data. With an inductive approach we begin by collecting data and then build theory from our observations.
- The philosophy of research helps us to understand the fundamental assumptions about the world that lie behind our approach as a researcher. Four important philosophical orientations are positivism, interpretivism, social constructionism, and realism.
- Reflexivity is important to researchers. It involves the researcher in not only reflecting upon the technical details of a project but also thinking more deeply about how underlying assumptions have influenced what we do and how we do it. Researchers should also reflect upon how these assumptions are themselves affected by the experiences of research.

NEXT STEPS

1.1 Familiarizing yourself with the terms of reference for your project. We recommend that you start your research project by looking at the specification (often called 'terms of reference') of your project. This may be set by your academic institution and/or the organization instigating the project.

1.2 Identifying challenges and issues in your project. Identify any questions or challenges that you have with regard to your intended project. Note these down so that you can review them as you read later chapters.

1.3 Reflecting on your research. Review the types of reflexivity listed in Section 1.6.1. Note down your thoughts with respect to each one to help you develop your awareness of your position with respect to research and your research project.

FURTHER READING

For further reading, please see the companion website.

REFERENCES

Alvesson, M. and Deetz, S. (2000). *Doing Critical Management Research*. London: SAGE Publications.

Alvesson, M., Sandberg, J. and Einola, K. (2022). Reflexive design in qualitative research. In: Flick, U. (ed) *The SAGE Handbook of Qualitative Research Design*. London: SAGE Publications.

Argyris, C. and Schön, D. A. (1974). *Theory in Practice. Increasing Professional Effectiveness.* San Francisco, CA: Jossey-Bass.

Blaikie, N. and Priest, J. (2019). *Designing Social Research.* 3rd ed. Cambridge: Polity Press.

Bougie, R. and Sekaran, U. (2020). *Research Methods for Business.* 8th ed. Hoboken, NJ: John Wiley and Sons.

Burrell, G. and Morgan, G. (1979). *Sociological Paradigms and Organisational Analysis.* Aldershot: Ashgate Publishing Ltd.

Canhoto, A. I., Quinton, S., Jackson, P. and Dibb, S. (2016). The co-production of value in digital, university–industry R&D collaborative projects. *Industrial Marketing Management,* 56(July): 86–96.

Castillo, D. (2022). *When Chatbots Fail: Exploring Customer Responsibility Attributions of Service Failures in Disharmonious Co-creation Contexts.* PhD thesis, Brunel Business School, Brunel University London.

Christensen, C. M. and Raynor, M. E. (2003). Why hard-nosed executives should care about management theory. *Harvard Business Review,* (September): 67–74.

Corbin, J. and Strauss, A. (2015). *Basics of Qualitative Research.* 4th ed. Thousand Oaks, CA: SAGE Publications.

Crotty, M. (1998). *The Foundations of Social Research.* London: SAGE Publications.

ESOMAR (2023). *Guideline for Researchers and Clients Involved in Primary Data Collection [Online].* ESOMAR. Available at: https://esomar.org/uploads/attachments/cktim86vi054wsptru81egz40-guideline-on-primary-data-collection-final.pdf (Accessed 4 April 2023).

Garlick, R. (2022). *Navigating the New World of Hybrid Work: A Study Examining the Biggest Challenges Managers Face.* Master's dissertation, Henley Business School, University of Reading.

Gill, J. and Johnson, P. (2010). *Research Methods for Managers.* 4th ed. London: SAGE Publications.

Gray, D. E. (2018). *Doing Research in the Real World.* 4th ed. London: SAGE Publications.

Hammersley, M. (2013). *What is Qualitative Research?* London: Bloomsbury.

Haynes, K. (2012). Reflexivity in qualitative research. In: Symon, G. and Cassell, C. (eds) *Qualitative Organisational Research.* London: SAGE Publications.

Johnson, P., Buehring, A., Cassell, C. and Symon, G. (2006). Evaluating qualitative management research: Towards a contingent criteriology. *International Journal of Management Reviews,* 8(3): 131–156.

Johnson, P. and Duberley, J. (2003). Reflexivity in management research. *Journal of Management Studies,* 40(5): 1279–1303.

Latour, B. and Woolgar, S. (1986). *Laboratory Life: The Construction of Scientific Facts.* Princeton, NJ: Princeton University Press.

Lynch, M. (2000). Against reflexivity as an academic virtue and source of privileged knowledge. *Theory, Culture & Society,* 17(3): 26–54.

McGivern, Y. (2022). *The Practice of Market Research: From Data to Insight.* 5th ed. Harlow: Pearson Education.

Merriam-Webster (2023). *Merriam Webster Dictionary.* Available at: www.merriam-webster.com/dictionary/research (Accessed 21 April 2023).

Mintzberg, H. (2004). *Managers Not MBAs.* Harlow: Pearson Education.

Phillips, D. and Burbules, N. C. (2000). *Postpositivism and Educational research.* Lanham, MA: Rowman and Littlefield.

Pillow, W. (2003). Confession, catharsis, or cure? Rethinking the uses of reflexivity as methodological power in qualitative research. *International Journal of Qualitative Studies in Education,* 16(2): 175–196.

Rose, S. (2020). *Industrial Revolution 4.0: The Changing Technology Landscape and its Effect upon Customer Service Employees. Report by the Henley Centre for Customer Management.* Henley-on-Thames: Henley Business School, University of Reading.

Saunders, M., Lewis, P. and Thornhill, A. (2019). *Research Methods for Business Students*. 8th ed. Harlow: Pearson Education.

Sayer, A. (1992). *Method in Social Science*. 2nd ed. London: Routledge.

Tashakkori, A. and Teddlie, C. (1998). *Mixed Methodology*. Thousand Oaks, CA: SAGE Publications.

Thorpe, R. and Holt, R. (eds) (2008). *The SAGE Dictionary of Qualitative Management Research*. London: SAGE Publications.

Van de Ven, A. H. (2007). *Engaged Scholarship*. Oxford: Oxford University Press.

Vargo, S. L. and Lusch, R. F. (2004). The four service marketing myths remnants of a goods-based, manufacturing model. *Journal of Service Research*, 6(4): 324–335.

Vargo, S. L. and Lusch, R. F. (2017). Service-dominant logic 2025. *International Journal of Research in Marketing*, 34(1): 46–67.

Whetten, D. A. (1989). What constitutes a theoretical contribution? *Academy of Management Review*, 14(4): 490–495.

CHAPTER 2

Formulating your research problem

LEARNING OUTCOMES

At the end of this chapter you will be able to

- formulate your research project as a problem-solving activity;
- explain different types of research question and state the characteristics of a good research question;
- select and formulate robust research questions that address the research problem for your project.

2.1 INTRODUCTION

Your **research problem** is the specific issue or opportunity that forms the subject of your research. It should give a clear and compelling reason for doing the research and provide the basis for developing the research questions that you need to answer in order to solve the problem. Research questions in turn provide the basis for developing your overall research design. Identifying a suitable problem is therefore a critical stage of your project. It is one of the most challenging aspects of undertaking research, especially for novice researchers, so this chapter takes a step-by-step approach to doing so. We begin by looking at how to take a problem-centred approach to research and how to identify a suitable research problem for your own project. Next we examine different types of research questions and how they relate to the overall aims of your research. We conclude by looking at what makes a good research question.

DOI: 10.4324/9781003381006-3

2.2 A PROBLEM-SOLVING VIEW OF RESEARCH

One way of thinking about research is to see it as a problem-solving activity. Research, according to this view, 'aims to increase our understanding of complex problems or phenomena that exist under conditions of uncertainty found in the world' (Van de Ven, 2007: 72). It applies to both applied and pure research because a research problem may arise from a practical issue or opportunity experienced by practitioners (including the researcher), or it may be the result of anomalies or gaps identified in the theoretical literature. Note that we are using the word 'problem' in a broad sense, so it should not be understood only in negative terms as something harmful or unwelcome; it can equally be an opportunity that merits further investigation, such as the potential offered by a new technology or new form of organization. A research problem may also have an exploratory aspect in response to a situation about which little is known.

2.2.1 The role of the research problem

Your research problem forms the crucial link between the practical or theoretical problem that has motivated your project and the design and conduct of the research itself. It provides the basis for framing clear research questions that will drive how you design your research in order to deliver useful research findings. Those findings ultimately help you to resolve your original practical or theoretical problem. Solving the research problem provides the rationale for undertaking your research and helps you to demonstrate the significance of your results (Creswell and Creswell, 2023). We depict these relationships in Figure 2.1.

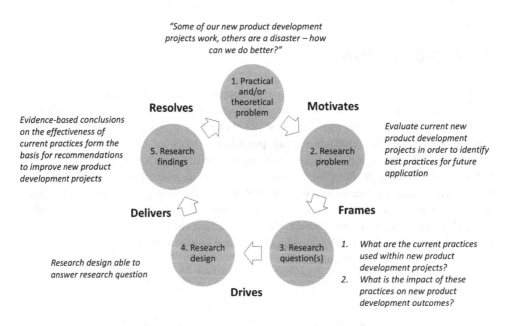

FIGURE 2.1 Linking research problems, questions, design, and findings

Formulating a clear, well-focused research problem is not a simple or quick task. There are likely to be false starts, multiple iterations, and revisions as you read around your potential topic, discuss it with colleagues, supervisors, or others involved in the situation. Given that the process may require input from multiple stakeholders, negotiating access to potential research sites, and even carrying out a preliminary review of the literature in your topic area, it is not surprising that this can take weeks or even months. Be prepared to invest the necessary time and energy into this crucial stage of your research project.

Taking a problem-centred approach draws attention to a more subtle and complex issue in choosing a research subject: problems are a matter of perception and interpretation, and formulating them involves a process known as framing. Van de Ven explains this in the following way:

> All problems, anomalies, or issues motivating a study begin with a perception that something requires attention. Problems are not given by nature, but by how, whom, and why they are perceived. . . . That being the case, any formulation of a problem is a partial representation reflecting the perspectives and interests of the observer.
>
> Van de Ven (2007: 74)

How you frame a problem has a big influence on how you try to solve it. It also affects whether other people share the view that it is a problem. Framing it in a particular way may also blind you to other possible ways of looking at the problem. If you frame a problem in terms of human resources, for example, you will draw attention to some features of the situation and away from others. If someone else sees the same issue in terms of operations management, their perspective may be very different. As well as being aware of how different stakeholders perceive a particular situation, you also need to reflect on your own position and role in the research process. This involves developing a reflexive awareness of yourself as a researcher, as we highlighted in the previous chapter.

2.2.2 Research problems in pure research projects

In pure research, which aims at making an explicit contribution to theory, problem formulation typically involves the identification of some theoretical puzzle that the research is intended to address. In this kind of project, a review of literature (see Chapter 3) plays a central role in refining both your research problem and subsequent research questions. Alvesson and Sandberg (2011: 247) identify 'gap spotting' and 'problematization' as two possible strategies for generating research topics from the literature. Gap spotting, as its name suggests, involves identifying gaps in the literature or opportunities to extend current theories in some way or other. Problematization involves a more fundamental investigation of the assumptions that underlie existing theories. Problematization, according to Alvesson and Sandberg (2011), can lead to more interesting and influential theories. If successful, it may also lead to more radical theoretical innovation in the topic area. However, radical innovation in research is potentially risky and subject to high failure rates (Voss, 2003). If you are new to research, you are probably best advised to take a more incremental and cautious approach, focusing on gaps or anomalies in existing theories that a well-scoped research project could address rather than trying to develop a radically new theory-of-everything.

2.2.3 Research problems in applied research projects

In applied research, your research problem is likely to originate directly from a practical issue or opportunity facing management or other stakeholders. If you are commissioned by a third party to carry out a project, whether on a commercial basis or as part of an academic course of study, the research problem is, to some extent, presented to you. One difficulty, however, is that the problem may not actually be formulated in research terms or even in a way that is researchable. In the context of marketing research, Iacobucci and Churchill (2018) discuss this challenge in terms of the need to move from the 'decision problem' to a 'research problem'. The decision problem relates to the situation faced by the organization and the decisions that management need to take in order to address it. The research problem is essentially a 'translating' of the decision problem into research terms (Iacobucci and Churchill, 2018: 29). Table 2.1 illustrates this distinction. Iacobucci and Churchill (2018: 29) argue that this restatement is made possible by the researcher working closely with those involved to transition from the decision-maker's problem into 'specific operational objectives for the research'.

Problem or symptom?

Understanding the total decision situation can help you to distinguish between surface symptoms and underlying problems. Suppose, for example, that a company's customer service team is making frequent mistakes when processing customer orders. As a result of the mistakes, many customers have complained and stopped using the company's services. In response, the company is offering compensation in an effort to retain them. You will no doubt recognize this as a classic case of treating the symptom rather than the problem. Whilst immediate action to retain customers may be necessary, only by focusing on the root causes of the mistakes in order processing will the problem really be solved.

TABLE 2.1 Examples of the relationship between decision problems and research problems

Management decision problem	Research problem
Selection of offshore distribution channels	Evaluate channel structures and channel members in each of the countries being considered in order to determine their potential
Addressing variable level of performance in new product development	Evaluate new product development practices in order to identify improved practices for future application
Reducing employee turnover	Identify factors influencing employee turnover in order to identify options for policy changes
Building consumer trust in the online brand	Understand drivers of consumer trust in online brands in order to identify improvement opportunities

Similar situations can arise when defining your research problem, particularly in applied research projects. Do not just take the initial statement of the problem for granted. Instead be prepared to do some preliminary investigation to ensure that you understand the situation in sufficient depth to be able to formulate your research problem adequately. Van de Ven (2007: 78) calls this 'grounding the problem'. Careful discussion with stakeholders is a useful starting point for getting a better understanding of what is going on and deeper insights into the problem space. Dialogue with those involved is also essential to ensure a common understanding of the problem and the expected outputs of the research. At this stage, even in applied projects, a preliminary review of literature on the topic area, including existing theories and models, can help you to understand the problem and identify relevant dimensions for subsequent investigation. Remember, however, that you are not expected to solve the problem at this point.

Is your research problem suitable?

Even when your problem is specified in research terms, you will still have to decide whether it is appropriate for you to take on. If you are doing commercial research, the decision will primarily be a business one. If your project is part of an academic course, such as a master's degree, you will need to ensure that it meets the terms of reference set by your institution for your qualification. You should therefore make sure that you fully understand those terms of reference before accepting the task. You will also need to consider whether the proposed research is compatible with your personal goals and can be achieved within the time, word count, and any other resource constraints you are working under. Lastly, regardless of the type of project, you must think through the ethical dimensions of the proposed research, a topic discussed in more detail in Chapter 5.

2.3 CHOOSING A RESEARCH PROBLEM

You may already have a good idea of what research problem you would like to investigate, but equally you may be struggling to come up with a suitable subject. Even where you have a general idea or have even been asked to carry out a particular research project, the problem will still need to be refined and developed. In this section we present some suggestions for choosing your research problem and guidance on how to refine it.

2.3.1 Sources of ideas for your research problem

Many writers have offered suggestions for identifying research topics. What follows is drawn from their suggestions and our own experience and is summarized in Table 2.2.

- A good starting point is to reflect on your own personal experiences and interests. Work or career-related situations can offer a huge source of possible topics, but other areas of personal life such as hobbies, voluntary work, or community activities also provide plenty of scope for projects. A useful approach, in keeping with the

TABLE 2.2 Sources of ideas for your research problem
• Personal experiences and interests • Discussions with practitioners, academics, and colleagues • Academic and practitioner literature, including popular media • Past projects • Projects of opportunity • Seeking a sponsor/client

problem-solving view of research, is to look for anomalies, puzzles, opportunities, or the unexpected in your experiences with organizational and professional life.

• Discussion with practitioners, academics, and other researchers can often generate potential topics. Talking to work colleagues and your broader social and professional network can also throw up interesting ideas. Such discussions can lead to a direct request for help with a problem, a concrete suggestion of a topic, or just more ideas to add to the emerging list of options.

• Read practitioner and academic journals and papers to see what is attracting attention. This is likely to be most fruitful when you have some idea of a general topic area, but practitioner publications can be particularly useful in identifying what is happening in your industry or profession. The general business media can also be a good source of potential topics. There is a risk of picking up on a transient management fad rather than a sound research topic, but this can be checked by further reading and discussion to see whether the topic has real substance.

• Look at past research projects. Past projects can be a useful source of inspiration for ideas, not least because researchers often identify where further research is needed. Looking at previous projects is particularly important if your project has to take a particular form, such as a master's dissertation or doctoral thesis, because it will help you to get a better understanding of the scope, depth, and complexity of what is expected.

• Look out for projects of opportunity. These are projects that just appear out of the blue from time to time. These can arise at work when a particular problem needs investigating, or you may hear about possible projects through your personal contacts. Many academic institutions have close relations with businesses and other organizations and may receive requests for help with issues that they are facing.

• Actively seek a potential client or sponsor organization for which you could conduct a research project. This can also provide you with an opportunity to get in touch with a potential future employer or simply to offer your services to an organization, such as a charity, that you would like to help. Your negotiation skills will be at a premium as you may well be trying to reach agreement on the research problem, access to data and respondents, and the format of any deliverables, such as a research report, all at the same time.

Techniques such as mind mapping or brainstorming can also be helpful, especially if you are trying to move from a general idea to a specific, researchable problem. Whatever sources and techniques you use – and if you are starting from scratch, you will probably

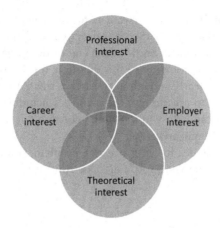

FIGURE 2.2 Looking for potential topics

need to use more than one – keep a record of your thoughts and emerging ideas. You will find it useful to start a research diary at this point, noting down ideas as they come to you so that they are not forgotten (we discuss keeping a research diary in Chapter 8).

A suitable research problem often emerges as a result of bringing together different perspectives. Figure 2.2 shows a simple Venn diagram that can help you to come up with a potential research problem. It brings together four areas of interest.

1. Professional interests. What issues or opportunities have you come across in your professional experiences that are of particular interest to you? Are there any particular skill sets or areas of knowledge that you want to acquire or develop?

2. Career interests. What areas of business and management are interesting for your future career development? Is there a particular topic area in which you want to raise your profile?

3. Employer interests. What issues or opportunities are important for your employing organization (or possible employer)?

4. Theoretical interests. What areas of management or organizational theory do you find particularly interesting?

Record your thoughts on each of these areas and look for any overlaps or interesting juxtapositions. Areas of overlap may suggest topic areas where there is synergy between different aspects of your life. These may be particularly fruitful in terms of the personal benefits they offer. They may also be easier to carry out from a practical point of view if they build on your existing knowledge, skills, and professional and personal network.

2.3.2 Refining your problem

In our experience, if you use the techniques we have discussed, it is not too hard to find a general topic area. The challenge comes in trying to refine a general idea into a clear, focused research problem. One way forward is to ask yourself how your research will contribute to resolving your chosen theoretical or practical problem. In particular, ask yourself what it is that you want to know at the end of the project that you do not now know. If you cannot give a clear answer to this question, it probably means that you have not defined your problem clearly enough in research terms. At this point reading around the topic area and talking to practitioners, academics (including your supervisor, if you have one) and colleagues can help you to refine your thinking and identify researchable problems within a general topic area.

Once you have an initial idea for your research problem, you need to ensure that it is clear and well defined. Van de Ven (2007) discusses this in terms of the problem's focus, level of analysis, and scope.

Problem focus

The focus of the project determines who or what is in the foreground and who or what is in the background of the research. A research study into stress at work, for example, might foreground those individuals experiencing stress, whilst treating the organization or management as the background or context. Alternatively, it might foreground managers involved in managing stressed individuals. It is likely that the audience for whom the research is intended (e.g. the client, the funding body, or the academic institution) will influence the focus of the problem.

Level of analysis

Your level of analysis (individual, group, organizational, or industry) will also shape where the emphasis of the project lies and help you to identify the unit of analysis for your project. The unit of analysis refers to the level of aggregation of the data used during analysis and for reporting your results. Your unit of analysis can be at any level from individual (e.g. a consumer in marketing research), through group (e.g. a project team), or organization (e.g. a firm) to industry or geographical or political region. Being clear on your unit of analysis is important because it will affect how and where you collect your data, how you will carry out your analysis, and how you will report your findings.

Once your level and unit of analysis are chosen, higher levels of aggregation will tend to be treated as context, whilst lower levels become components of the problem domain itself. Suppose, for example, that you were investigating the performance of project teams. The project teams would form your unit of analysis. The organizational and industry levels would be the context in which those project teams operate, whilst the individual project members would be of interest primarily in their role as part of the project team and as potential sources of data on aspects of their team's performance.

Scope

You will also need to decide the scope of your project by setting boundaries to determine what is 'in' and what is 'out'. This is rather like putting up a tent. You have to be very clear about what is inside the tent and what is going to be outside and accept that your tent cannot hold everything. As well as setting boundaries at the outset, you will also need to be very careful about scope creep as the project unfolds. This is a very common problem in dissertations and theses, especially once the literature review is underway. As you learn more about your problem area, you will spot connections with other interesting subjects, and it is very tempting to incorporate these, pushing out the boundaries of your project. Before long, if you are not careful, you will have lost focus and ended up with something unmanageable. Try to keep within your project scope and shift the boundaries only after careful consideration of the implications.

Scope creep can also be a problem when conducting research for a third party, especially if the research context is very dynamic, as it may be in applied projects in an organizational context. Client demands can change and grow as the project proceeds, particularly if the problem was not clearly defined at the outset. In such situations Markham's (2019) advice on handling scope creep in consultancy projects is worth following.

- Assess the implications of the proposed change for the project.
- Discuss these with the client (and your supervisor/tutor if applicable).
- Document the change, noting any changes to deliverables, timings, and resource requirements (and fees for commercial projects).

2.3.3 What makes a good research problem?

A good research problem should be clear, tightly focused, and well scoped. Bougie and Sekaran (2020) suggest that it should also be relevant, feasible, and interesting. Relevance is achieved if the problem relates to a definite need in the domain of either practice (applied research) or theory (pure research) that is recognized by appropriate stakeholders, such as practitioners in a particular work situation or the academic community to which the findings of the research will be addressed. Feasibility addresses two related aspects. Firstly, it must be possible to address the problem through research, and secondly, it must be possible for you to carry out that research within the constraints of ethical conduct, access, time, and other resources. Feasibility is therefore closely connected to the scope of the research. Lastly, the research problem must be interesting to you and to other relevant stakeholders. Sustaining enthusiasm throughout a research project can be a real challenge; make sure that you at least start off interested and enthused by your chosen problem.

When finalizing your research problem, do take time to consider your own motivations and objectives in undertaking it. If you are doing an assessed project as part of an academic course of study, then you may be motivated by the qualification towards which you are working. Beyond the immediate goals of the research project and any qualification, you may have other reasons for undertaking a particular piece of research work. You might want, for example, to learn about a new technology, investigate a new trend in organizational development, or explore an industry sector other than your own. Alternatively, you may want to acquire or develop your skills in a particular type of research. Other benefits can also accrue from careful choice of research problem. You may want to raise your profile in a particular subject area or to use the research to help you make a career change. Whatever the case, a research project can offer great opportunities for personal development, so do not overlook these when choosing your research problem.

2.3.4 Writing down your research problem

As you think about your research problem, capture your thoughts by writing them down. Doing so will help you to develop and clarify your thinking around your topic. Ideas that are written down will also be easier to share and discuss with other people, such as colleagues or your supervisor. They will also be input for a written research proposal (Chapter 8) and even for your final report. In the early stages we have found the following simple structure useful to capture the essence of your research problem.

1. Background (a statement of the theoretical or practical problem, issue, or opportunity motivating the research).
2. *This research will* (the overall aim of the research) *in order to* (how the research will address the problem).

For example:

1. The Company has been successful in attracting online customers but is unable to retain them.
2. *This research will* identify the factors influencing online customer retention *in order to* make recommendations to the Company for improvement.

The structure of the statement is designed to encourage you to think not just about the overall problem but also how your research will contribute to solving it. You will build upon this as you develop your research questions.

2.4 DEVELOPING YOUR RESEARCH QUESTIONS

Research questions are the specific questions that your research needs to answer in order to resolve your research problem. As Maxwell (2013: 73) puts it, they show 'what you specifically want to understand by doing your study'. They form the bridge between your research problem and your research design (Figure 2.1). Clearly formulated, they provide direction for your investigation and selection of a suitable research design. Research questions also help to confirm the boundaries of your study and keep it manageable. They are also important because without clear questions, it is very difficult to have clear answers and therefore to know whether your research has achieved its aims by answering them. Lastly, research questions also help to communicate to the reader what your research is intended to find out.

2.4.1 Research questions and data collection questions

One difficulty that novice researchers often encounter is distinguishing between research questions and those questions that are used in interviews or questionnaires to collect the data needed to answer the research question. The difference is easily illustrated by distinguishing between a research question such as 'what is the average IQ (intelligence quotient) of a group of students?' and the questions included in a test designed to measure the IQ of each individual. In many cases, as in the IQ example, the research question is not actually answerable in a single question because IQ measurement requires more than one question to be asked of participants. Research questions and data collection questions are thus rarely the same. They are likely to be worded differently and to be at very different levels of generality: you are unlikely to ask a respondent your research question directly. When formulating research questions, you should be aware of this distinction.

2.4.2 Categorizing research questions

Different writers have proposed different ways of categorizing research questions. Our start point is to think about the type of research we are undertaking and to ask what is the purpose of our research. The answer will lie broadly in one of three categories of research, each of which leads to the use of a different type of research question and research design. These are the following:

- Descriptive/exploratory research
- Explanatory research
- Process research

Descriptive/exploratory research – 'what' questions

Descriptive research seeks to describe more fully the characteristics of a particular phenomenon, such as the degree of customer satisfaction with a particular service or the experiences of employees working from home. Descriptive research can also include an element of comparison; for example, it might involve comparing the difference in customer satisfaction levels across different retail sites. Alternatively, it may seek to compare over time, for instance, to identify trends in social media use or changing attitudes to environmental issues. It may involve the quantitative measurement of the attributes of a large population, or it may require the in-depth investigation of the experiences of a small number of people involved in a particular situation. We can consider these as 'what' type questions.

When we use 'what' questions, we seek to generate a detailed description of the characteristics and attributes of our phenomenon of interest. Examples might include the following:

- What is the level of satisfaction amongst our customers?
- What is the attitude of employees to the new information system?
- What are the experiences of people participating in a coaching programme?

- What are the characteristics of online shoppers?
- What are consumers saying about our products on social media websites?
- What leadership styles are displayed by project managers in our organization?

'What' questions can also encompass within them such questions as 'who', 'when', 'how much', and 'how many' (Yin, 2018: 10), but all have the same purpose: to provide a description and in-depth understanding of the phenomenon of interest. Descriptive research would not, however, seek to answer 'why' or 'how' such differences had come about. That would require a different type of research question and a different research design as we discuss later in this chapter.

When little is known about the phenomenon and there is a lack of existing knowledge or theory, the researcher will be in exploratory mode aiming to 'probe a topic when the variables, questions, and theory are unknown' (Creswell and Creswell, 2023: 110). The researcher will be seeking to obtain data that will help build an understanding of the phenomenon, such as experiences of working with new technology. Exploratory research may fill gaps in existing knowledge and is often the preliminary stage to the subsequent development of theoretical explanations. Exploratory research is most often associated with qualitative research methods and can be the first stage of a sequential mixed methods design.

Description is 'fundamental to the research enterprise' (de Vaus, 2001: 1) as it forms the basis on which further research can be built. Description may also be required to inform practical action. You might, for example, use research to develop a detailed description of the behavioural or demographic characteristics of your firm's customers in order to focus future marketing efforts. In evaluation, descriptive research methods can be used to gain an understanding of the situation being evaluated, to find out what policy measures are currently in place or to measure programme outcomes. Descriptive studies can also provide a 'call for action' (Yin, 2015: 228) to draw attention to the need for a policy change, although care needs to be taken to avoid the accusation that the research is biased by the policy-making agenda. Descriptive research can also be undertaken as an end in itself. In some cases a topic may be sufficiently novel or interesting for no further justification to be needed. In many cases, however, description is not the end point of the research but provides an impetus and basis for further research into why and how a phenomenon exists. The relationship is not one way. Not only does good description provoke 'why' and 'how' questions, the answers to those questions can in turn help to add to the significance of the descriptive component of your research project.

Explanatory research – 'why' questions

Why is explanation of interest to researchers? Aneshensel (2013) suggests that it is prompted by the findings of descriptive research arousing curiosity about why things are as they are. 'The search for scientific understanding, therefore, tends', she argues, 'to evolve in the direction of explanation' (Aneshensel, 2013: 4). Pure research often involves building or testing theories about why something is happening. Similarly, many applied research problems are related to issues of explanation to find out what is causing something we observe. Behind this often lies the assumption that explanation may help in practical situations: if we can explain something, we may be able to predict it and possibly control (or at least influence) it. In practice, the extent to which such prediction and control are feasible, or even desirable, within complex social systems like an organization is debatable, but given the practical possibilities of knowing why something happens, it is not surprising that the answers to explanatory 'why' questions are of interest to practitioners as well as academics.

'Why'-style questions are therefore concerned with explaining phenomena. De Vaus (2014) suggests three basic forms that such questions can take.

1. Why is something happening? For example, you observe that employee turnover rate is higher than the industry average; your research question may then be aimed at identifying the reasons why.
2. What are the consequences of something? What, for instance, are the consequences of high employee turnover? Your search is therefore for the effects of some phenomenon.
3. What is the effect of something on something else? Here the focus shifts to investigating a relationship between two phenomena. You might, for example, investigate whether employee satisfaction is impacting on employee turnover and, if so, by how much.

Examples of 'why' questions include the following:

- Why do some mergers and acquisitions fail?
- What are the effects of long-term unemployment?
- Why do people get involved in voluntary work?
- What is the effect of performance-related pay on employee motivation?
- What is the impact of online advertising on sales?

The wording is not always as straightforward as in the examples in the previous section. Common variations include expressions such as 'What factors influence/affect/impact . . . ?' or 'What are the determinants of . . . ?' In other situations the explanatory component is implied rather than explicit. For example, evaluating whether or not a particular management initiative works in the way intended means establishing and explaining the linkages between the initiative and the expected outcomes (Patton, 2008). Similarly, investigating 'success factors' for something implies an explanatory component in order to determine the nature of the relationship between the supposed success factors and the outcome of interest. We discuss in Chapter 4 in more depth the nature of 'why' questions and appropriate research designs.

Process research – 'How' questions

Answers to 'how' questions offer a different form of explanation by taking a process view. The focus of research may be on investigating the sequence of events or activities by which entities such as people or organizations change over time. Alternatively, it may take a more micro-level perspective, focusing on how 'things' such as organizing, leading, and strategizing actually get done and how social reality is constituted, reproduced, and maintained through social processes. A process perspective can also contribute to an understanding of causality by identifying the steps through which a cause produces an effect and so complement 'why' type questions. Example 'how' questions could include the following:

- How do high technology start-ups develop over time?
- How do customers select an online insurance provider?
- How is strategy formulated in companies?

Historically, 'how' questions have undoubtedly been neglected in the management literature in favour of other forms of explanation. Nevertheless they have been used in a wide range of applications and have generated a substantial body of research and thinking. They also have significant practical relevance. As Langley and Tsoukas (2010) point out, even well-established answers to 'why' questions may be difficult to put into practice. Knowing, for example, that one particular organizational structure outperforms another in a specific situation does not tell you how you might change your own organization to that new structure. Neither is that knowledge likely to capture the complex sequence of actions and interactions and potential unintended consequences that could arise during such a change. We therefore need process studies not just out of academic curiosity about the world but in order 'to better understand how to act within it' (Langley and Tsoukas, 2010: 10). Process knowledge thereby complements the knowledge gained in response to 'why' questions. Effective management practice, we suggest, requires an understanding of 'how' as well as 'why'.

Mixing research questions

A research project is not, of course, limited to one type of research question. In practice, you will often need answers to 'what' questions before you can go on to address 'why' or 'how' questions. To identify factors influencing employee turnover (a 'why' question), for instance, you might first need to get detailed knowledge of turnover levels by employee group, attitudes to various aspects of conditions in the workplace, and so forth (answers to 'what' questions). Successful use of the resulting 'why' knowledge may depend in turn on understanding 'how' the factors arose in the first place and opportunities for addressing them. The research question types should therefore be seen as complementary rather than mutually exclusive.

'Should' questions

As we noted earlier, practical problems in applied research may not be formulated in research terms. One aspect of this is that solutions to practical problems frequently require explicit or implicit value judgements, often expressed in terms of whether or not we 'should' or 'ought to' take a particular action. Such questions are sometimes referred to as normative questions; they are concerned with what ought to be rather than what is. Whilst they are important questions, they cannot be addressed empirically because there is no correct answer and, as a result, should be avoided as research questions (White, 2009). In this connection, Maxwell (2013: 28) makes the useful distinction between what he calls the 'intellectual' and 'practical' goals of a project. Intellectual goals are concerned with understanding what is going on in a situation in terms of what, why, or how. Practical goals typically involve accomplishing something, such as making a change or achieving some performance objective. Whereas either may be legitimate aims of your project, practical goals cannot typically be translated directly into questions which research can answer. Instead Maxwell recommends that you ask yourself 'what data could I collect, and what conclusions might I draw from these, that would help me accomplish this goal?' (Maxwell, 2013: 76–77). Therefore he suggests framing your research questions so that they provide the information and understanding that will help you to achieve your practical goals or to develop recommendations that will allow you to do so.

To illustrate this approach, suppose that you were asked to investigate whether or not your organization should develop a particular type of product. The practical goal of such a project is to answer the question whether or not the product should be developed. How could research contribute to achieving that goal by providing information and data that would inform decision-making? Possibilities include researching the size of the potential market, customer attitudes to the proposed product, the likely impact of the proposed product on existing product sales, and so on. Discussion with relevant stakeholders could be used to identify what research output would be most helpful to the decision-making process and thereby refine both your problem and your research questions.

Research in practice 2.1 From managerial problem to research question

The research project started with a question asked in a forum on customer management: 'What should we do when people talk negatively about our company on social media.' Further discussion in the forum showed that the motivation for the question was due to a range of different perspectives about what to do. Should companies respond? If so, in what way? What was good practice? What did customers expect?

A review of practitioner literature and conversations with marketing professionals revealed an emphasis on how to deal with crises. The managers in the forum, on the other hand, were more interested in how to handle things on a day-to-day basis and avoid reaching crisis point, rather than in waiting until things got out of control. The academic literature on social media was also limited on how to handle feedback in social media. Much of what was available looked at complaint handling. There was some information on who was using social media and the sorts of things they were saying on social media sites. This would be helpful background and context, but it was not the solution to the problems the forum had raised.

Clearly there was a gap here between the theory and practice of handling social media. Two researchers took up the challenge and kicked off a research project with the goal of helping companies make decisions about how they should handle online customer feedback. Initially they thought that the research questions should focus on identifying best practice within the companies actively engaging with customers in social media. It soon became clear that there was too little knowledge and experience within the companies to make this a viable research approach. Instead, after further discussion, they decided to begin by exploring the problem from a customer perspective. Their unit of analysis was individual customers who were active social media users. The final research question reflected their focus: 'What are social media users' perceptions of best practice in responding to customer feedback online?'

2.4.3 Formulating your research questions

Like your research problem, your research questions need to be carefully formulated, and this can be a time-consuming and challenging task. You will almost certainly have to go through several iterations in order to get them right. Start by reading around your topic, especially the academic or more theoretically oriented practitioner publications, because this will help you to refine the conceptual dimensions of your problem as well as develop your awareness of the questions that have already been answered or are seen as particularly important by other researchers. You will also come across examples of how research questions are formulated in your topic area. At this stage take every opportunity to discuss and share your emerging ideas with colleagues and, if you have one, your supervisor. Robson and McCartan (2016: 64) suggest you 'go public' and 'produce a review paper, do a seminar or other presentation with colleagues whose comments you respect (or fear)'. Opportunities for this may be part of your study process. As well as providing feedback on your research questions, such events can also be an opportunity to generate fresh insights into your problem area, especially from those with different areas of expertise and interest. As always, ensure that you capture these ideas so that you can refer to them later. In Research in Practice 2.1 we show the process of formulating research questions from an initial idea.

How many research questions?

Most research problems, even if tightly scoped, can generate multiple questions that may warrant investigating. This is generally a good thing at the start because it helps you to explore the problem area to the full, but at some point you will need to decide what questions you can feasibly answer within your project. Andrews (2003) suggests writing down all the possible questions that you have identified and then examining how they are related. Is there overlap or duplication between them? Is one question more central than the others? Does one question logically have to be answered before another? Examining your research questions in this way can help you to identify the main question that your research must answer, along with possible subsidiary questions that will need to be answered in order to answer the main question. You should also look out for redundant or overlapping questions that can be eliminated or combined with others. As a result you may have

- a single research question that will address the research problem;
- a principal research question with some subsidiary questions (probably not more than 3–4 unless the project is very large) that, taken together, will allow you to answer the main research question and thereby address the research problem;
- more than one independent main research question, each of which must be answered to address the research problem.

The first two situations can typically be managed by a single researcher. Problems can arise, however, where there are multiple, independent questions to be answered. Lack of time and resources to complete the project is the most obvious difficulty, but multiple questions may indicate that the research problem itself is inadequately focused or that it is simply too large for you to address in a single project. In such situations consider reformulating your research problem or prioritizing particular aspects of the problem. By doing this, the process of developing your research questions can help you to focus your research efforts even more precisely.

Wording your research questions

As you formulate your research questions, you will need to think carefully about how to word them. As well as helping you to clarify what your research is about, clear and unambiguous wording makes it easier to communicate with other stakeholders and to manage their expectations in terms of the research output. Try to keep your questions simple and straightforward. Use a single sentence: if you have to use more, it may indicate that you are actually asking two questions in one. Avoid unnecessary technical language or jargon: when you make use of technical concepts, make sure that you can define them clearly. As a guide, in most research projects the research questions should make sense to an informed reader without elaborate explanation.

One key decision when preparing your questions is how open they should be. This is important because it is an indicator of what research method may be appropriate. Research questions associated with quantitative research designs are often quite specific and narrow, being structured around specific concepts and how they are related (Creswell and Creswell, 2023), for example, 'What is the impact of customer satisfaction on customer loyalty?' Questions of this type are often linked to the testing of existing theory about those relationships. Questions associated with qualitative research, on the other hand, may be worded in more general terms so as to permit a greater degree of exploration of the central issue (Creswell and Creswell, 2023) whilst still putting some boundaries around the study. An example might be, 'How do customers relate to our brand?' Such open questions may indicate a more exploratory approach, be linked to building new theory, or reflect research that seeks to understand a situation from the perspective of those involved. We will discuss the nature of quantitative and qualitative research as well as the relationships between research question and research design in more detail in Chapter 4.

When to formulate your research questions

Formulating the research questions can be a lengthy process, but when should it take place? Our stress on the importance of the research question and its role in the research design suggests that they should be developed first, with everything else flowing logically and in a straight line from there. In practice, it is rarely quite so straightforward. There are also differences between different research approaches. On the one hand, in research designs using a deductive approach, the need to measure concepts quite precisely means that the research questions have to be clear prior to data collection getting underway, although final wording may not be confirmed until after the review of literature. In research designs using an inductive approach, on the other hand, researchers may prefer to start with more open research questions that are refined and developed as the research itself proceeds. Nevertheless, even in inductive research, formulating your research questions should be seen as 'a first and central step' (Flick, 2023: 72), even if your initial questions are likely to 'become more refined and specific as the research progresses and the issues and problems of the area under investigation are identified' (Corbin and Strauss, 2015: 41). Regardless of the research method, our advice is to develop research questions early on, whilst accepting that they may need refining as your project progresses.

2.4.4 Research objectives

Some writers advocate developing specific research objectives from research questions. Whilst this can improve precision and focus, it is not necessary (or even appropriate) in all situations and, in our experience, can cause considerable confusion in distinguishing between the overall aim of the project and the specific, detailed objectives derived from the research questions. Research objectives are likely to be most useful when the research questions themselves can be formulated in very specific terms, for example, in a theory-testing study. In the early stages of a research project, our advice is to stick to research questions, but check what is expected by your own institution if doing an academic project.

CRITICAL COMMENTARY 2.1

The dictatorship of the research question

In this chapter we emphasize the key role played by the research question in providing direction for developing a suitable research design. According to this view, choice of research method is subordinate to choice of research question, a position memorably summed up in the phrase 'the dictatorship of the research question' (Tashakkori and Teddlie, 1998: 20). We believe that this is a useful approach, especially for the novice researcher, because it can help to encourage careful attention to the alignment between research design and the problem being studied. It does, however, simplify what is in reality a more complex process. It downplays, for example, the role of other influences on the choice of method. One of these is the philosophical orientation held either consciously or unconsciously by the researcher, which can influence both the framing of the research problem/questions and the choice of research method. Individual researchers may also have preferences for particular types of research method and, consequently, choose research questions that are appropriate for their preferred method. Those who are more comfortable working with quantitative methods, for example, may formulate research questions in a way that supports the use of a quantitative research design. Other potentially important influences on the choice of research method include the expectations of funding bodies, the preferences of policymakers, and the traditions of the subject discipline regarding what is 'acceptable knowledge' (Bryman, 2007: 17). Of course none of these things renders research questions irrelevant, but they do highlight the complexity of research in practice.

2.4.5 Features of a good research question

Although research questions differ according to the needs of the project, it is possible to offer some guidelines as to what makes a good research question (Andrews, 2003; Van de Ven, 2007; White, 2009; Robson and McCartan, 2016). Your research questions should be the following:

- Address the research problem that you have identified. If you have more than one research question, they should be linked in a coherent way.
- Be clear and unambiguous so that they are understood by the reader. Get feedback from others and use it to help you refine the wording of your research questions.
- Be researchable. As with the overall research problem, your research questions must be answerable by research, and that research must be feasible in the light of practical and ethical considerations. The latter means that the questions must be appropriately scoped so that they are neither too broad nor too narrow.
- Be nontrivial so that they justify the time that will be spent on them. This is linked to the selection and significance of the research problem. If your research questions look insignificant and uninteresting, you may need to revisit your research problem.
- Be questions and not statements. Statements do not give direction to the study nor translate into research designs. Make sure your research questions really are in question format.

Some writers also emphasize that good research questions should also be connected with existing theory. This is obviously the case in pure research, where the relationship between your research problem and existing theory needs to be very clear. In applied research, where the motivation for the research comes from a practical problem, the relationship with theory is likely to be less direct, but knowledge of existing theory is essential to help you develop clear and useful research questions and to locate your research within the existing body of knowledge in your topic area.

Once you have drafted your research questions, review them against the criteria we have identified. It is hard to overestimate the importance of getting this part of your project right, so we will conclude this chapter with a quote from Flick (2023) to underline the point:

> The less clearly you formulate your research question, the greater is the danger that you will find yourself in the end confronted by a mountain of data helplessly trying to analyse them.
>
> Flick (2023: 72)

CHAPTER SUMMARY

- Research can be understood as a problem-solving activity. The research problem provides the context for framing the research questions, which in turn determines the research design able to deliver research findings to resolve the original theoretical or practical problem that motivated the project.
- In pure research the research problem is derived from and grounded in existing theory; in applied research the research problem emerges in response to a practical problem.
- Potential sources of ideas for your research problem include personal experiences and interests; discussions with academics, practitioners, and colleagues; academic, practitioner, and even popular media; past projects of opportunity or through seeking a potential sponsor or client.
- Personal motivations for a particular project can come from professional, theoretical, career, and current or future employer interests.
- Research questions link your research problem to your research design and provide the yardstick against which the success of the project can be judged.
- There are three generic types of research:

  - 'What' questions focus on description or exploration.
  - 'Why' questions focus on explanation for why things are happening.
  - 'How' questions focus on explaining how things change and develop over time.

- Good research questions address the chosen research problem, are clear and unambiguous, researchable, nontrivial, and formulated as questions.

NEXT STEPS

2.1 Identifying a problem. Use one or more of the techniques in the next section to generate a list of potential research problems. Review the potential research problems in terms of their relevance, feasibility, and interest. Select one that looks most promising.

2.2 Research problem statement. Formulate a statement of your research problem in three sentences:

    a. Background (a statement of the theoretical or practical problem, issue, or opportunity motivating the research).

    b. This research will (the overall aim of the research) in order to (how the research will address the problem).

2.3 Personal goals. What are your personal goals (career, professional, skills, knowledge, etc.) in undertaking this project? How will the chosen research problem help you to achieve those goals?

2.4 Research questions. Now start formulating your research questions:

    a. What do you need to know in order to resolve your research problem? Is the knowledge in the form of answers to 'what', 'why', or 'how' questions?

    b. Make a list of possible research questions that, if answered, would provide that knowledge.

    c. Use the evaluation criteria in Section 2.4.5 to refine your research questions.

FURTHER READING

For further reading, please see the companion website.

REFERENCES

Alvesson, M. and Sandberg, J. (2011). Generating research questions through problematization. *Academy of Management Review*, 36(2): 247–271.

Andrews, R. (2003). *Research Questions*. London: Continuum.

Aneshensel, C. (2013). *Theory-Based Data Analysis for the Social Sciences*. 2nd ed. Thousand Oaks, CA: SAGE Publications.

Bougie, R. and Sekaran, U. (2020). *Research Methods for Business*. 8th ed. Hoboken, NJ: John Wiley and Sons.

Bryman, A. (2007). The research question in social research: What is its role? *Social Research*, 10(1): 5–20.

Corbin, J. and Strauss, A. (2015). *Basics of Qualitative Research*. 4th ed. Thousand Oaks, CA: SAGE Publications.

Creswell, J. W. and Creswell, J. D. (2023). *Research Design. Qualitative, Quantitative and Mixed Methods Approaches*. 6th ed. Thousand Oaks, CA: SAGE Publications.

de Vaus, D. (2001). *Research Design in Social Research*. London: SAGE Publications.

de Vaus, D. (2014). *Surveys in Social Research*. 6th ed. Abingdon: Routledge.

Flick, U. (2023). *An Introduction to Qualitative Research*. 7th ed. Los Angeles, CA: SAGE Publications.

Iacobucci, D. and Churchill, G. A., Jr. (2018). *Marketing Research: Methodological Foundations*. 12th ed. Nashville, TN: Earlie Lite Books.

Langley, A. and Tsoukas, H. (2010). Introducing "perspectives on process organization studies". In: Hernes, T. and Maitlis, S. (eds) *Process, Sensemaking and Organizing*. Oxford: Oxford University Press.

Markham, C. (2019). *Mastering Management Consultancy*. London: Legend Business.

Maxwell, J. A. (2013). *Qualitative Research Design. An Interactive Approach*. 3rd ed. Los Angeles, CA: SAGE Publications.

Patton, M. Q. (2008). *Utilisation-Focused Evaluation*. 4th ed. Los Angeles, CA: SAGE Publications.

Robson, C. and McCartan, K. (2016). *Real World Research*. 4th ed. Chichester: John Wiley and Sons.

Tashakkori, A. and Teddlie, C. (1998). *Mixed Methodology*. Thousand Oaks, CA: SAGE Publications.

Van de Ven, A. H. (2007). *Engaged Scholarship*. Oxford: Oxford University Press.

Voss, G. B. (2003). Formulating interesting research questions. *Journal of the Academy of Marketing Science*, 31(3): 356–359.

White, P. (2009). *Developing Research Questions: A Guide for Social Scientists*. New York, NY: Palgrave Macmillan.

Yin, R. K. (2015). *Qualitative Research from Start to Finish*. 2nd ed. New York, NY: Guilford Press.

Yin, R. K. (2018). *Case Study Research and Applications: Design and Methods*. 6th ed. Thousand Oaks, CA: SAGE Publications.

CHAPTER 3

Reviewing the literature

CHAPTER LEARNING OUTCOMES

After reading this chapter you will be able to

- carry out a critical literature review as part of your research project;
- locate, assess, and collate relevant literature;
- analyze and synthesize relevant literature to produce a critical literature review.

3.1 INTRODUCTION

Before starting your research, you need to find out what is already known about your problem. Perhaps your research questions have already been answered and the research is no longer needed. Perhaps there are relevant theories or research methods you could build on in your own study. These are some of the reasons why a critical review of the literature is a key component of many research projects. In the review, you present a critical analysis of literature in your problem area. It is where you examine theories relevant to your research problem and review prior research or other studies that can help you to get a deeper understanding of your topic area. This chapter addresses how to conduct a critical review. We begin by discussing the nature and purpose of a literature review, before looking at the steps involved in carrying one out.

3.2 UNDERTAKING A CRITICAL REVIEW

The seventeenth-century natural philosopher Isaac Newton once wrote that if he had seen further it was by standing on the shoulders of giants (Turnbull, 1959). The idea that knowledge can be cumulative, that we can add to and build on the contributions of those who have gone before, has long been an influential one in science. It is one of the reasons

DOI: 10.4324/9781003381006-4

why academic researchers are expected to review literature in their topic area before actually carrying out their research. According to Boote and Beile:

> 'Good' research is good because it advances our collective understanding. To advance our collective understanding, a researcher or scholar needs to understand what has been done before. . . . A researcher cannot perform significant research without first understanding the literature in the field.
>
> Boote and Beile (2005: 5)

Building on what has gone before does not mean simply accepting existing knowledge: we need to take a critical view of that knowledge. As well as building on what we already know, the literature review is therefore also an opportunity to problematize that knowledge, providing what Alvesson and Sandberg (2020: 1290) describe as 'an "opening up exercise" that enables researchers to imagine how to rethink existing literature in ways that generate new and "better" ways of thinking about specific phenomena'.

3.2.1 Literature and your research

An important objective of your literature review is to ground your own project in previously undertaken research and writing in your topic area. However, this is not the sole purpose, or value, in reviewing literature, and neither is the use of literature restricted to the formal literature review section of your report. Here we explore some of the contributions that literature can make to your research project.

Literature and your research problem

Literature plays an important role when formulating your research problem and research question(s). This is particularly important in academic research where the contribution to theoretical knowledge is emphasized. Early in your project, you can use literature to identify gaps in previous research that your own research might fill. Aside from helping you avoid duplicating existing research, literature can also help confirm the significance of your proposed research. In academic research this may be done by drawing on sources that support the need for the research. In applied research, government statistics, industry surveys, practitioner journals, consultant reports, and even news media can provide useful input for setting the broader scene and significance of your planned fieldwork.

Literature and theory

Literature is the key source of theories, models, and concepts that will be important in investigating your research problem. If you are adopting a deductive theory-testing approach, your literature review will be where you elaborate the theory that your research will test. If you are taking a more inductive approach, the literature review can provide an important source of ideas for developing your study. Once you have completed your research, literature should also be used to help you interpret your findings and assess its broader relevance. In academic research, linking your findings back to existing theory is necessary to show the contribution your research has made. In applied research, it is the opportunity to use your evidence-based findings to inform current thinking on practice and policy.

Literature and practice

The emphasis on academic theory in many guides to doing a literature review can over-shadow the significance of practice and policy literature in your topic area. Such literature is likely to be a major part of any applied project which aims to make recommendations for practice. Identifying what is currently perceived as good practice by practitioners and policymakers and reviewing the evidence of its effectiveness can be an important role for the literature review in applied research projects. A review of practice literature also provides an opportunity to explore links between academic theory and practice. In addition, it can familiarize you with the terminology and language used by practitioners when discussing your chosen topic area, which will be very helpful when carrying out your own research and when writing up.

Literature and research methods

There are three main ways in which literature can help you with the design for your own research. Firstly, other researchers in your subject area may have used research methods that would be useful for your own project. In some cases, this may extend to replicating a previous study in a different context. More likely, you may make use of specific research techniques and tools (such as questions in a questionnaire) that have proved effective in previous studies. Remember that there is no need to reinvent the wheel when it comes to research design, although you must always acknowledge the contribution of others through correct referencing and ensure that, where required, you have permission to use their material. Secondly, you will probably need to draw on literature about research methods in order to develop your own research skills. This might include specialized literature that deals with particular research techniques in greater detail as well as general research methods textbooks such as this one. Thirdly, when writing up the research design component of your report, you will normally be expected to cite relevant literature in support of your choice of research methods and tools.

Literature and academic qualifications

If you are carrying out a research project as part of a course of academic study, a formal literature review is the place where you 'demonstrate a familiarity with the approaches, theories, methods and sources used in your topic area' (Grix, 2004: 38). Your grasp of this aspect of your topic can form a significant part of the final grade awarded, so ensure that you understand the assessment requirements for your particular project to see whether a literature review is expected and, if so, in what format.

3.2.2 Adopting a critical stance in your literature review

Any literature review, whether intended for academic purposes or not, should adopt a critical stance. By 'critical' we do not mean simply drawing attention to flaws or pointing out that a certain writer is 'wrong'. Instead, a critical review involves the exercise of careful judgement and the judicious evaluation of your sources, the theories and ideas they use, the arguments they deploy, and the conclusions they reach. To do so you may have to develop your own skills in analyzing an argument. In Figure 3.1 we show the basic structure of an argument based on the work of Toulmin (1958). It consists of three components: the claim being made, the data or other evidence presented in support of the claim (or on the basis of which the claim has been made), and the warrant. The warrant provides the justification for linking the evidence and the claim.

Separating out the components of an argument in this way allows us to look more critically at what is being claimed and the justification for the claim. In evaluating an argument, consider the following.

- The **claim**. Establish what is being claimed. Is the claim clearly stated and coherent?
- The **evidence**. Is appropriate evidence provided? What type of evidence is presented? Is that evidence credible? What was its source?
- The **warrant**. Is the claim justified on the basis of the evidence? Is the link between the evidence and the claim robust?

Developing your skills in argumentation analysis will stand you in good stead not only in your literature review but also when you come to write up: you should use the same approach to evaluate the strength of your own arguments.

3.2.3 The literature review process

The process of doing a literature review can be broken down into four stages (Figure 3.2):

1. Search for appropriate literature sources.
2. Capture information from individual texts, including evaluating their quality and relevance.

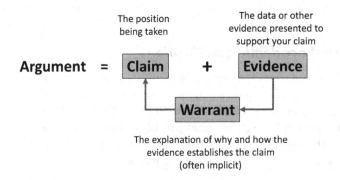

FIGURE 3.1 Structure of an argument (after Toulmin, 1958)

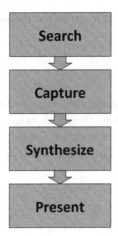

FIGURE 3.2 The literature review process

3. Synthesize the body of literature into a coherent, critical review.

4. Present your review to show how it informs your research project.

The remainder of this chapter is devoted to a discussion of these four stages.

3.3 SEARCH

Searching involves finding relevant literature. The challenge you face in doing so has been described as finding the 'right stuff' whilst avoiding getting too much of the 'wrong stuff' (Petticrew and Roberts, 2006: 83).

3.3.1 What is literature?

We will define **literature** as the body of written material on a particular topic. Written material includes digital and print formats and both academic and nonacademic writing. Wallace and Wray (2021: 122–123) offer a useful categorization of literature types in terms of the kind of knowledge they embody:

1. Theoretical literature, which addresses theories and models relevant to the topic area.

2. Research literature, which presents the results of research into the topic area.

3. Practice literature, which is written by practitioners about their own or other practitioners' experience and practice.

4. Policy literature, which evaluates and proposes changes to current practice.

Depending on your research topic, you may draw on any of the categories in your review. If you are conducting pure research, theoretical and research literature is likely to feature prominently. A critical understanding of such literature will also be important in applied research, but you will probably need to provide a thorough review of applicable practice and policy literature as well.

3.3.2 Literature sources

It is not possible to present a comprehensive review of subject-specific literature sources here as this would have to run to many thousands of items. In any case, identifying relevant material is your role as the reviewer/researcher. Instead, we will look more broadly at what literature sources are available and how and where to find them.

Peer review

Before doing so we need to clarify how quality is controlled in academic writing. Whilst all kinds of literature can have a place within your project, if your research is part of an academic qualification, you will be expected to draw heavily on academic journal articles that have been peer reviewed prior to publication. Peer review (or refereeing) is a quality control process in many academic journals. Articles submitted for publication are sent out for review by other specialists in the field. Often this is double blind so that neither the author nor the reviewer know each other's identity. This process attempts to maintain some objectivity in judging which articles should be published. Submissions may be rejected; others have to be reworked, sometimes extensively, before being accepted for publication. That does not, of course, place a piece of writing above criticism in your review. It may have been overtaken by later work or had its conclusions challenged by authors with alternative views, but in selecting an article from a peer-reviewed journal for your literature review, you can at least be confident that the content has been subject to a level of critical scrutiny.

Not all academic journals are peer reviewed. If you are unsure, you can check by visiting the journal's home page on the Internet, where publishers usually indicate whether or not a journal is peer reviewed. Alternatively, a review of the journal's submission procedures will normally reveal the review process. Many online bibliographic databases also include the option of restricting a search to peer-reviewed articles.

Potential sources

Many different literature sources can contribute to your research project. Table 3.1 reviews some of the main sources, with supporting commentary on how and where you might use them. Most of the sources types listed will not have been through any kind of peer-review procedure, so you will have to undertake much of the analysis of their credibility yourself. You should also be aware that a great deal of 'recycling' goes on. A short article in a newspaper or practitioner journal may just be a summary of something the author (or someone else) has published in more detail elsewhere. Where possible, always go back to the original sources, which will allow you to investigate the arguments in more depth.

TABLE 3.1 Potential literature sources

Source	Comments
Peer-reviewed academic journals	The 'gold standard' for an academic literature review, peer-reviewed journals cover both theory and research. Most articles will include extensive reference lists which help with further searching. Perhaps the biggest drawback is that because of long publishing lead times, new or emerging topics may be less well covered. In some journals special issues dealing with particular topic areas of interest are published more quickly than regular articles.
Non-peer-reviewed academic journals	Articles in these journals may have many of the characteristics of peer-reviewed articles but are likely to vary in quality, so you will have to rely more on your own judgement as to their rigour.
Academic books	Books (or sections of edited books) by academic authors in your topic area can be an important source of ideas, but note that there is generally less quality control than under the journal peer review system. Handbooks and edited collections of journal articles can be useful in getting an overview of a topic area. Academic textbooks can be very helpful in introducing you to a topic area, but you will often still need to consult the original literature on which they were based.
	Obtaining academic books can sometimes be difficult, particularly for highly specialized texts, unless you have access to an academic library or can use a library loan system if a digital version is not available. Prices also vary, although online search can often reveal low-cost options, including second-hand print copies or e-book versions.
Working papers from reputable academic institutions	Some academic institutions publish working papers. These are often works-in-progress, reporting research work that is currently underway; some of which subsequently finds its way into journals. As a result, they can be useful sources of current research and thinking. Accessibility varies and in some cases authors may place restrictions on whether they can be quoted without permission.
Conference papers from leading academic conferences	Conference papers, like working papers, can have the advantage of dealing with on-going and current research topics. There may be some form of review prior to acceptance, but you will still need to make your own judgement regarding quality. Accessibility can be a problem unless the proceedings are published online or you attend the conference yourself.
Theses and dissertations	By their nature, theses tend to be highly specific but can be useful sources, especially for academic research. Getting full-text access can be difficult, although many are now available online. Note that there may be restrictions on using material, including quotations, from a dissertation or thesis without permission.

(Continued)

TABLE 3.1 (Continued)	
Source	*Comments*
Research reports	Research reports can include studies commissioned or carried out by governments, non-governmental organizations (NGOs), profession bodies, consultancies, lobby groups, etc. There is a huge variation in quality, quantity, and accessibility. Some are of a high standard and carried out by leading authorities in the area, whilst others are much less robust, especially in terms of the quality or reporting of empirical research. Copies of research reports for government departments are often available free of charge (as is some NGO literature), whilst commercial consultancy reports can be very expensive. A particular issue with commissioned research can be the problem of bias in either the conduct or reporting of the research. A further problem is that not all reports give details of how the research was carried out (although these are sometimes published separately). You will have to use your own judgement in assessing such sources.
Specialist encyclopae-dias and dictionaries	Specialist encyclopaedias and technical dictionaries can provide useful summaries of particular themes as well as suggestions for further reading. General encyclopaedias (including Wikipedia) can also be helpful, as you get to know your topic, but you should not rely on them as principal sources for your literature review.
Practitioner/consultan-cy literature	Business and management generates an enormous literature from practitioners and consultants. These sources tend to be more practical, less theoretical, and often without a strong empirical content (perhaps based on the authors' experiences of management or consulting). They are also often written in an accessible style. Examples of such sources include the following: • professional/trade journals • white papers by consultancies/companies • nonacademic books aimed at the practising manager/general reader • autobiographies of business leaders Some of this material can be very useful in helping you to identify a topical research question and for identifying current practice and practitioner views in your research area. It may also be the only source for new topics for which little or no academic writing is available. Quality, however, can be very mixed, as can accessibility, although professional body/consultancy websites are often a useful starting point.
News media	Newspapers, news magazines, and other news media can be good ways of identifying topical issues, but their content is, of course, driven by editorial and other concerns rather than by academic criteria. Usually, they report things as they happen and may therefore be unable to offer in-depth, critical, or retrospective analysis. As a result, they are probably best avoided as principal sources for your literature review, but they can help you to pick out potential topic areas. In addition, they can be valuable sources of information for background or commentary on public debates.

Source	Comments
Everything else	Finally, there is everything-else-out-there, and thanks to the Internet, there is an awful lot of it, including blogs, tweets, and other opinion pieces. At this point it will fall almost entirely on your shoulders to judge the quality of material you find. Very often your time would be better spent looking for more academic articles than trawling hopefully through the broader Internet.

3.3.3 Where to search

The Internet is the obvious place to start searching, but do not restrict yourself to your favourite web browser. To help you, Table 3.2 gives some guidance, in rough order of priority, on places to look online for different sources of literature.

The Internet seems such a natural place to search that it is easy to overlook other very useful ways of finding relevant literature. These include the following:

- Course material and academic staff. If your project is part of a course of study, course material and reading lists will often provide a helpful starting point for searching. Your supervisor, if you have one, can also be a useful source of suggestions about where to search or even recommendations for specific sources.
- Library staff. Librarians, particularly in academic or other specialist libraries, can usually suggest places to look for relevant literature. Their expertise is particularly valuable when it comes to developing your literature search skills or when you are trying to locate a hard-to-find book or article.
- Your personal network. An important aspect of doing research is joining the community of academics and practitioners working in your field through conferences, professional organizations, and informal contacts. As you progress your research project, you will build up a network of contacts of people sharing your interests. Your network can become an important way of sharing ideas and accessing sources, especially literature that may not be widely available. This can be further extended through online research forums such as ResearchGate (www. researchgate.net).

3.3.4 How to search

We have addressed what sources you might want to use and where you might look for them, but how do you organize and carry out your search?

Literature review questions

It is hard to search effectively or efficiently without knowing what you are looking for. Wallace and Wray (2021) suggest formulating review questions that your literature review should answer. These can help you focus your reading. For example:

TABLE 3.2 Where to search online

Location	Comments
Bibliographic databases	Bibliographic databases are one of the most important sources available, especially for academic journal articles. They provide a searchable index of journal articles and other material, giving abstracts and citations. Access may also be given to the full text or links to where the full text can be obtained. Most databases are easily accessible online, although commercial ones usually require a subscription for full-text access. Universities and business schools typically include a range of such bibliographic databases as part of their library services so if you are studying at an academic institution, ensure you familiarize yourself with what is available. Other organizations, such as professional institutions, may also offer access to specific collections. Public databases are usually accessible to anyone but may have limited or no full-text sources. A list of commercial and public databases that are particularly relevant for organization and management research can be found at the end of this chapter.
Library databases	Library databases (such as the British Library, www.bl.uk) can be used to search for available books and other material on your topic area. Worldcat (www.worldcat.org/) provides a searchable database covering thousands of libraries around the world and can help you to find the library nearest to you that holds a book for which you are searching. In addition to books and journals (both print and online), university libraries may also hold other publications such as working papers or other sources that may be relevant.
Google Scholar	Google Scholar (http://scholar.google.co.uk/) provides the facility to search for academic and other scholarly articles. It offers some of the capability of bibliographic databases, including the option of downloading citations, although coverage is not as systematic. In some cases links are included to where a full-text version can be found. The 'Cited by' link is useful for forward citation chaining (see next section).
Citation indexes	Citation indexes are a particular form of bibliographic database. They provide an index of the citations between publications, such as journal articles, to allow you to see who has cited a particular article. In literature searching they are very useful to see how an article has been used by other writers and to follow the development of a line of thinking over time (a technique known as citation chaining). Bibliographic databases often include citation links for articles that they reference, as does Google Scholar. You may also be able to access the Web of Science, a subscription citation index, through a university or other library.
ProQuest Dissertations and Theses Global (PQDT)	PQDT provides an index of dissertations and theses from around the world, dating back to 1637, including full text where available.

Location	Comments
Google Books	Google Books (http://books.google.com) offers the ability to search across a large number of books. Some books can be previewed and some are available for download.
Industry, business, and market re-search databases	Industry, business, and market research databases offer access to market reports and to industry and company data. Your university or other organization may have subscriptions to relevant databases. They can be particularly useful for background and context literature.
Other places to search online	
Academic institu-tions' websites	These can be used to locate working papers and specialist research cen-tres (which often have their own working paper/research paper series).
Individual academ-ics' home pages	Academics typically have a webpage on their institution's website or even their own websites. In some cases, you can access copies of their earlier work and work-in-progress or find references to other work they have authored. When you identify a key author in your area, it is well worth checking to see whether they have their own website.
Government/profes-sional associations/ trade bodies/NGO websites	These sites can be very helpful for locating research reports, policy papers, official statistics, etc., although bear in mind the comments made earlier about possible bias. Some professional associations offer extensive access to library resources for their members.
Publishers' websites	Some journal publishers' websites have access to journal contents pages, which can supplement other search strategies for journal articles. This is also normally where individual copies of articles can be purchased if they cannot be accessed in any other way.
Consultancy/com-pany websites	Consultancies and other commercial organizations publish research reports or white papers that can be of interest and which sometimes can be downloaded or read online for free.

- How are the key concepts in your research question defined in the literature?
- What theories/models are being used in relation to your topic?
- How are those theories related to one another (e.g. supporting/contradicting, etc.)?
- What empirical studies have been made of this topic? What were their findings?
- What research methods are used in this topic area? (Answers to this question can also inform your investigation design.)
- What management practices or policies are relevant to the topic area? What evidence is there for their use or effectiveness? (These questions can be particularly important in applied research projects.)

Research in Practice 3.1 provides an example of literature review questions for a specific topic.

Research in practice 3.1 Literature review questions

To illustrate the application of literature review questions, suppose your research question was 'How does job satisfaction influence employee commitment?' Possible questions to answer in your literature review could include the following:

- How is job satisfaction defined in the literature? What are the key dimensions of job satisfaction?
- How is employee commitment defined in the literature? What are the key dimensions of employee commitment?
- What theories are there about the relationship between job satisfaction and employee commitment?
- What does prior research show about the relationship?
- What concepts (variables) were used, and how were they measured?
- In what context (e.g. industry, type of organization)?
- What were the findings?
- What research methods were used (and can I use them for my study)?

Choosing your search terms

For searching bibliographic databases and for general online searching, you will need to identify appropriate search terms or keywords. Initially these can be taken from the concepts included in your research problem, your research questions, and literature review questions. For example, if your research question asks how job satisfaction influences employee commitment, your initial search terms might be 'job satisfaction' and 'employee commitment'. You may find, however, that these terms are too restrictive and that you need either to expand them or to include synonyms in your search. 'Job satisfaction', for instance, may need to be supplemented with 'employee satisfaction'. Alternatively, some of your terms may be too broad, so additional words need to be included in the search to refine the scope. Simply searching on 'satisfaction' without a qualifier, for instance, is likely to produce a lot of irrelevant hits. Adding 'job' or 'employee' should reduce that number. In addition to using additional concept descriptors, particular theories and even the names of key authors in the field can be useful search terms.

As you search, pay attention to the terminology used in your topic area. Look at keywords used by the authors of the articles you are reading. You may find that the terms you are using are not universally recognized. The term 'queue', for example, is common in British English, but 'waiting line' is often preferred in US English. Differences can also exist between academic and practitioner literature. In marketing, for example, academics may refer to customer segmentation, whereas practitioners might describe the same phenomenon as profiling or modelling.

Refining your search

If you find that your search generates a huge number of hits, many of which are totally irrelevant, you have a number of options. Many search engines use Boolean operators such as AND, OR, and NOT. Adding more terms using the AND operator will reduce the number of hits. Using the NOT operator with a search term will exclude references containing that term. Putting inverted commas "" around the search term will return the exact phrase you have entered. If you are still getting a lot of irrelevant hits, you may be able to confine the search to article titles and abstracts; this is usually possible in bibliographic databases, often via an advanced search function. Another option is to use search limiters such as date range, industry, geographic sector, language, or publication type (e.g. peer reviewed), or specific journal titles.

Extending your search

If, on the other hand, your search gets very few hits, you will need to adopt a different strategy. Reducing the number of terms included in your search, making terms more general (e.g. changing from 'employee commitment' to 'commitment'), or replacing the AND operator with OR will generally produce more hits. Removing any search limiters should have a similar effect. You should also review the search terms you are using. Are they appropriate, or are there other terms that are in more common use? Has terminology changed over time? Try searching more than one database and even general web searching. This can be a frustrating point in the search process, but perseverance combined with some creative thinking will usually win through. In our experience, once you have found one or two sources, you can use their reference lists or check using a citation index to see where they have been cited to identify other references.

No literature?

A particular problem arises when you are struggling to identify any relevant academic literature or theory. This can happen when a topic is very narrowly focused or when you are investigating an emergent topic about which there may be very little published material. In such situations you need to think about what other contexts might offer useful insights. In the early days of research on e-commerce, for example, many researchers used literature on direct mail as the reference literature and complemented it with sources looking at the context of the phenomenon, in this case the Internet, in terms of what the web was being used for, how it was being used, and by whom. A bit of imagination and lateral thinking is sometimes needed at this point.

Citation chaining

Once you have found a relevant literature source, **citation chaining** provides a very useful way of expanding your literature search and gaining insights from the discussions around that source. There are two forms of citation chaining. Backward chaining involves looking at the source's reference list and following up on those sources. It allows you to gain insights into the origins of theories in your topic area. Forward chaining involves looking at works that have cited the source you have found. This helps you to identify more recent sources and to explore new thinking and findings about your topic area. Citation indexes and bibliographic databases, including Google Scholar, can support both backward and forward citation chaining from published journal articles, often including direct, click-through access to other sources.

3.3.5 Starting and stopping your search

There is some debate over whether it is better to start by searching for peer-reviewed journals in bibliographic databases or by looking at more general reference literature, such as textbooks or specialist encyclopaedias. In practice it probably depends on your level of background knowledge. If you are reasonably familiar with your topic, you may be able to start searching academic literature straightaway. If, on the other hand, you are new to the topic area, you will probably want to begin with more general, introductory literature to help you formulate appropriate literature review questions, generate relevant search terms, and identify authors, journals, and other literature sources on which you can base a more in-depth search.

Getting started is not always easy, but neither is deciding when to stop. In some projects it can seem that there is no limit to the sources that might be relevant to your study, but clearly you have to conclude your search at some point. Deciding when to do so is a balance between your project timetable and your search progress to date. Whilst it is difficult to suggest universal stopping criteria, we suggest an appropriate stopping point may be approaching when

- you have answered the literature review questions you have set yourself;
- searches of additional bibliographic and library databases fail to find significant new literature;
- examination of literature and reference lists already located does not reveal gaps in your search coverage;
- you have identified a range of perspectives on your topic of interest;
- you have included literature over an appropriate date range, including recent publications (where available);
- theories and models described in nonacademic literature are grounded, where possible, in appropriate academic sources.

Your personal network of subject experts, other researchers, and your supervisor may also be able to help you decide whether you have reached an appropriate stopping point.

3.4 CAPTURE

As you search, you need to capture appropriate information from the sources relevant to your study. This stage involves three key tasks: evaluating your sources, capturing relevant information, and managing the material.

3.4.1 Evaluating your sources

Your searches can generate a very large amount of material, not all of which will be applicable to your topic. When you first locate a source, you should therefore make a preliminary assessment of its relevance to your project. This can be done quickly by scan-reading it, and we find the following sequence useful.

1. Read the abstract or executive summary if there is one.
2. Read the introduction and conclusion.
3. Review the table of contents, main headings, figures, and tables.
4. Review the reference list, if there is one, to check the coverage of other literature.

As you scan, review the source against your literature review questions to help you assess its likely relevance. If it is clearly not applicable, it can be put aside. If you are not sure about its relevance, we suggest that you review it again later when you are more familiar with the topic. Relevant sources should be flagged for further evaluation.

You will need to evaluate sources in terms of two dimensions. The first is the quality of the source itself. If it is an empirical study, you will need to evaluate the quality of the research; if the work is peer reviewed, you may be more confident about its rigour, but you will still need to look at the study's limitations. If it is a work that has been widely cited elsewhere, this may be a positive indication of its quality or suggest that it holds some important place within the body of literature in a topic area. The second dimension is how the source can contribute to your own project. Use your literature review questions to help you make that evaluation. A relevant source is likely to contribute in one or more of four general areas:

1. Problem formulation and context
2. Theories and models
3. Practice and policy
4. Research methods

3.4.2 Capturing relevant information

Two different types of information need to be captured when you find a relevant source: the reference data and content information.

Reference data

Reference data are needed to allow you to reference a literature source accurately within your report. Table 3.3 shows the data required in order to reference some common source types. As you are likely to be reviewing a large amount of material, you should note down the referencing details of each literature source as you go, even if you subsequently decide not to use it. This will help you to keep track of the literature and avoid problems when you come to write up. Online databases usually provide citations in different formats that

TABLE 3.3 Reference data for common source types

Journal article	Book	Chapter of edited book	Report/working paper	Website
Author(s)	Author(s)	Author(s)	Author(s)	Author(s) or originator (e.g. company name)
Year	Year	Year	Year	Year
Title	Title	Title	Title	Title
Journal	Place published	Editor(s)	Series	Publisher
Volume	Publisher	Book title	Publishing institution	Uniform Resource Locator (URL) or Digital Object Identifier (DOI)
Issue		Place published	Place published	Date accessed
Pages		Publisher	Uniform Resource Locator (URL) or Digital Object Identifier (DOI) (if online version)	
		Pages	Date accessed (if online version)	

can be copied and pasted into your records. This process can be made easier and faster by using reference management software. Further details on referencing and reference management software are given later in this chapter.

Content information

Content information includes key points from the source itself and the results of your evaluation of the source. Capture this information systematically as you read. Avoid the temptation just to keep on reading. Unless you record what you are discovering as you work, you will find it very difficult to synthesize and present your review later on. Table 3.4 shows a suggested format for capturing content information in a structured way. Not all sources will need to be recorded to this level of detail, but make sure that you capture the contribution of your main sources. If you come across any pieces of text or data that you think you may wish to quote verbatim in your write-up, note these down, including the number of the page from which they were taken. Remember that the aim at this stage is not just to summarize the source but to evaluate it critically, particularly with respect to its quality and likely relevance for your project.

TABLE 3.4 Capturing reference and content information from a key literature source

Information required	Your notes
Full reference details	Note here the full reference details in the correct format.
Keywords	Record the keywords used for your search and any useful keywords used by the author.
Brief summary of the study	Make a brief summary of the study. Use the abstract/executive summary if there is one.
Type of literature (theoretical, research, practitioner or policy)	Note the type of literature. This can be useful when comparing how your topic is discussed by different sources.
Purpose of the study (e.g. the aims of the study/research questions)	What is the author trying to achieve in the study?
Theories/concepts/models described or reviewed	What are the key theories, concepts, and models discussed in the source? How are they treated (e.g. supported, critiqued)?
Practices/policies described or reviewed	What are the key practices and policies discussed in the source? How are they treated (e.g. supported, critiqued)?
If it is a research study, research methods used	What research methods are used in the study (e.g. quantitative/qualitative, sampling, data collection instrument, data analysis techniques, etc.)?
Study findings	What are the major findings or conclusions of the study? What are its limitations?
Your evaluation	Note your evaluation of the source in terms of its quality and its likely contribution to your project in terms of theories/models, practice/policies, research methods, and background/context. Use your literature review questions to help you decide on the potential relevance of the study.
Any other comments	Record here any other comments or thoughts.

3.4.3 Managing the review material

Data management is a big part of any research project, and the literature review stage is no exception. You will need to decide how to manage the material that your review generates.

Managing your sources

You can easily get overwhelmed by the results of your search efforts. Your first task is managing the sources themselves. If you are downloading material, allocate each document a logical file name. A simple approach is to use citation reference details (i.e. author, date). Ensure that you back up digital data. Online storage can be useful for this, especially if you need access to the material from more than one computer or other device. If you are not downloading a source, make sure you bookmark it and note details of the **Uniform Resource Locator** (URL) or **Digital Object Identifier** (DOI). Printed material needs to be stored securely and archived in a way that allows easy and quick access. You will also need to keep track of your material in a structured way. You can build up a simple database in a spreadsheet to record all reference details and where the source is located. Alternatively, you could consider using specialist reference management software.

Reference management software

A large number of reference management (bibliographic) software packages are available. These typically act as a database in which you record details of individual references and provide an interface with word-processing software (such as Microsoft Word) to allow easy insertion of in-text citations and the automatic creation of a reference list directly from the database. Many also allow you to import reference details directly from online bibliographic databases, Google Scholar, and so on. Some also offer additional functionality, such as annotation of Adobe Acrobat (pdf) documents, or have interfaces with mobile devices. Details vary, depending on the particular software. EndNote (www.endnote.com) and Biblioscape (www.biblioscape.com) are examples of commercial products; versions of Zotero (www.zotero.org) and Mendeley Reference Manager (www.mendeley.com) can be downloaded for free. Microsoft Word also has a referencing facility built in, although this does not offer the database capabilities of full reference management programmes. If you are a student, your institution may offer referencing software and training on how to use it. Reference management software is definitely worth considering if you are going to do a lot of reference work. For smaller projects, a spreadsheet or a table in a word-processing package is usually adequate to manage your references.

Managing your notes

You will also need to manage the notes that you generate during your review. We strongly recommend that you do not just scribble notes on a paper or electronic copy of the document. Instead, record your analysis in a structured format, preferably digital, because this will make it easier to write up. The headings in Table 3.4 can be used to organize your notes. Tabular summaries can also be useful, as we discuss in the next section.

3.5 SYNTHESIZE

As you read your sources you should start to notice connections between them. Some sources may support the views of others; some sources may give alternative perspectives. You may see that there are common ways of researching your topic. You may find that different policies or practices referred to in your literature group together into clear families or categories. When you begin to see such patterns, you are starting to synthesize the literature. You are moving from understanding sources in isolation to understanding the body of literature in your topic area.

3.5.1 From author-centric to concept-centric

A review of literature is not simply a listing of previous research in the manner of

> a laundry list of previous studies, with sentences or paragraphs beginning with the words, 'Smith found . . . ', 'Jones concluded . . . ', 'Anderson stated . . . ', and so on.
>
> Rudestam and Newton quoted in Silverman (2022: 514)

The 'laundry-list' approach is what Webster and Watson (2002: xvi) call author-centric. They contrast this with a concept-centric approach in which the concepts provide the organizing logic for the review, as shown in Table 3.5. Moving from an author-centric to a concept-centric understanding of your reading is a key step in the process of synthesizing your literature.

As you capture content information from your literature, try to group different sources and authors according to the way in which they approach your topic in terms of concepts and theories that they use. Also note whether authors explicitly support or critique a particular approach to your topic. By comparing and contrasting the support for different theories from a range of authors, you can create a more powerful and coherent critical argument than is possible by sequentially reiterating the findings of individual authors. Ordering the literature conceptually also gives you a ready-made framework when it comes to writing up. Each of the main theories or concepts can form a subsection of your review, and you can discuss the arguments for and against each approach as reflected in the literature you have studied.

TABLE 3.5 Author-centric versus concept-centric structure (adapted from Webster and Watson, 2002: Xvii)

Author-centric structure	Concept-centric structure
Author A argues . . . concept/theory x	Concept/theory x . . . [Author A, Author C]
According to Author B . . . concept/theory y	
Author C suggests . . . concept/theory x	Concept/theory y . . . [Author B, Author E]
Author D identifies . . . concept/theory z	Concept/theory z . . . [Author D]
Author E critiques . . . concept/theory y	

Using matrices to synthesize your findings

Tables and matrices provide a useful, practical way of developing such a framework, as shown in Table 3.6. The visual layout of the table allows you to see the different contributions to the theories within the literature you have reviewed. You can build tables such as these in a word-processing or spreadsheet package. The cells in the table can contain short summaries, direct quotations, or symbols, as here. Additional dimensions can be added as required.

Matrices are generally useful ways of organizing, analyzing and displaying textual data, and we look at their use in more detail in the context of qualitative data analysis in Chapter 14. Appropriately organized and edited tables and matrices also provide a useful summary device when presenting your literature review, as we show in Research in Practice 3.2. In this example, the matrix cross-tabulates major theories with relevant dimensions of the topic.

TABLE 3.6 Concept matrix (content based on Mintzberg et al., 2009, after Webster and Watson, 2002: xvii)

Source	Strategy as planning	Strategy as positioning	Etc.
Ansoff (1965)	X		
Henderson (1979)		X	
Porter (1980)		X	
Steiner (1969)	X		
Stewart (1963)	X		
Etc.			X

Note: The sources presented are examples only and are not included in our reference list.

Research in practice 3.2 Using tables to summarize and compare theories of corporate governance

In a critical review of corporate governance, Letza et al. (2004) employ a matrix to summarize and compare four theories (labelled as 'models') of corporate governance in terms of nine dimensions. Their review includes a commentary on the matrix that expands key points of interest. The following table, adapted from Letza et al. (2004: 246), presents a simplified version of the original, showing only five of the nine dimensions to illustrate the principle of using matrices in this way in a literature review.

	The principal-agent model	The myopic-market model	The abuse of executive power model	The stakeholder model
Major contributor	Jensen and Meckling (1976); Manne (1965)	Charkham (1994); Sykes (1994)	Hutton (1995); Kay and Silberston (1995)	Freeman (1984); Blair (1995)
Purpose of corporation	Maximization of shareholder wealth	Maximization of shareholder wealth	Maximization of corporate wealth as a whole	Maximization of stakeholder wealth
Problem of governance	Agency problem	Excessive concern with short-term market value	Abuse of executive power for their own interests	Absence of stakeholders' involvement
Cause	Shareholders do not have enough control	Ineffective market forces	Institutional arrangements leave excessive power to management	Governance failure to represent stakeholders' interests
Proposition	Market efficiency	Importance of long-term relationship	Manager as trustee	Social efficiency of economy

Note: The sources presented are examples only and are not included in our reference list.

Graphical techniques

You may also find graphical techniques useful for exploring the interrelationships in your literature. Literature maps (Creswell and Creswell, 2023) are one way of investigating and displaying the relationships between different concepts and different authors. Figure 3.3 shows an example related to perspectives on feedback in coaching which uses a tree structure.

Concept maps can also be used to help you synthesize the literature you have studied and to develop a theoretical framework for your research (Maxwell, 2013). Concept maps show relationships between concepts. They provide a way of helping you to visualize how the concepts you have identified in your literature fit together. Another option is to use mind maps to help you organize your thinking and to synthesize a body of literature. Note that suitable tables and graphics can also be used in your final write-up to help the reader grasp the essence of your review. Remember, however, that matrices and figures do not alone constitute a synthesis of the literature (Petticrew and Roberts, 2006): you will still need to present a narrative summary of your critical review.

3.5.2 Using CAQDAS to support your literature review

The process of managing and synthesizing multiple literature sources has some strong parallels with analyzing qualitative data, as will be seen in Chapter 14. **CAQDAS** (Computer

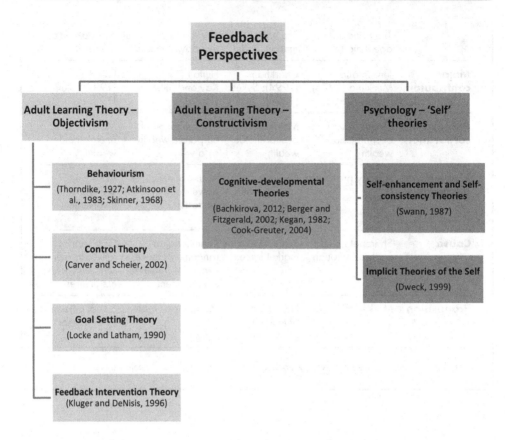

FIGURE 3.3 Example literature map (content based on Maxwell, 2017)

Aided Qualitative Data Analysis Software) are software packages, such as NVivo, MAX-QDA, and Atlas.ti, created to support qualitative data analysis activities. They can also be used to assist with exploring, annotating, note taking, synthesizing, and visualizing literature sources as part of the literature review process. It is arguably most helpful when you have digital copies of the literature being analyzed, but it is also possible to create notes and summaries for print material. Silver (2016) provides a brief overview of using CAQDAS in this context and many of the software providers offer more detailed guidance for their specific programmes. If you are intending to use CAQDAS for qualitative or mixed methods analysis in your own research, you might consider extending its use to include the literature review. See Chapter 14 for more details on CAQDAS in qualitative data analysis.

3.5.3 Developing a conceptual model

A more formal way of synthesizing and presenting literature is through the use of a conceptual model. Such models play a very important part in management and organizational research. They can act as a bridge between theory and the real-world phenomenon you are investigating, making it easier to relate the one to the other.

What is a model?

The term **model** is a common one and is used in many different ways. It can be employed simply as another word for theory. It can refer to a mathematical representation of a theory or of some real-world phenomenon. Queuing models are a good example of this type of model; they can be used to represent or to simulate the behaviour of real waiting lines. Most importantly for current purposes, however, the term is used to refer to a diagrammatic representation of a theory or some real-world phenomenon. This type of model represents visually the features of a theory or of a phenomenon that are relevant to the purpose for which the model has been created. In the case of research, of course, the purpose will be determined by the research questions. Such diagrammatic models are often referred to as conceptual models, a term we will use here. Modelling conventions vary, but typically, **conceptual models** show the key elements/concepts in the theory and how they are related. We give a very simple example in Figure 3.4, which shows the possible relationship between advertising level and sales revenue. The + sign indicates that the relationship is positive: as the advertising level increases, so does sales revenue. The model thereby provides a clear, visual depiction of a possible theory about the impact of advertising on sales.

Types of conceptual model

Conceptual models vary enormously in their form, depending on the theory or phenomenon they are intended to model. Nevertheless, it is possible to identify some generic types of model that you may come across during your reading or use in your own research. We consider three of them here (Figure 3.5).

- **Variance models.** One of the most common types of conceptual model in research depicts cause-and-effect relationships between concepts, for example, the impact of advertising on sales as we discussed in Figure 3.4. In its basic form the causes are shown on the left and connected to the effect by a single-headed arrow. Models like this are sometimes referred to as variance models because they focus on explaining the variability or change in some outcome on the basis of changes in other factors (Mohr, 1982). They are very widely used in explanatory research when answering 'why' type questions, and we discuss them in more detail in Chapter 4.

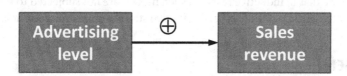

FIGURE 3.4 Conceptual model of the expected relationship between advertising level and sales revenue

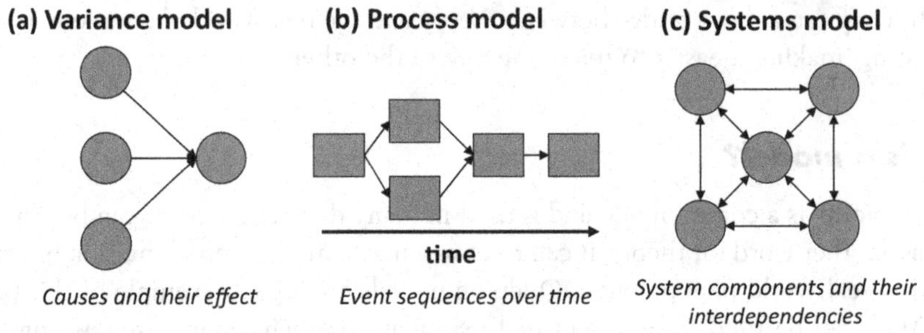

(a) Variance model

(b) Process model

time

(c) Systems model

Causes and their effect   *Event sequences over time*   *System components and their interdependencies*

FIGURE 3.5 Types of conceptual model

- **Process models**. Process models show the sequence of events or activities by which things such as people or organizations change over time, for example, in change programmes, mergers and acquisitions or innovations. Each step in the model represents an event or activity. A well-known example of a simple process model is Lewin's (1952) three-stage Unfreeze-Move-Refreeze model of planned change. We discuss process theories in relation to answering 'how' type questions in Chapter 4.
- **Systems models**. Systems models make up another important, and very diverse, family of conceptual models. They reflect an equally diverse heritage in systems thinking and systems theory. Not intended to represent any particular system model, our simple diagram illustrates the interdependence of system components (via the double-headed arrows) and the emphasis on taking a holistic view that is a feature of much system thinking. Well-known examples of systems thinking in management include Senge's (1990) systems approach to the learning organization and Checkland's soft systems methodology (Checkland and Scholes, 1999).

Using conceptual models in your research

Conceptual models can play different roles in your research, depending on your research problem and the research approach you adopt. In deductive research it is common practice to develop a conceptual model from the theory that is to be tested. The model depicts the concepts and the relationships between them in a very clear way that supports the design of the research and the formulation of suitable hypotheses for testing, as we discuss in Chapter 4. If you are using an inductive approach, it is more likely that a conceptual model will be an output as part of theory building during your analysis, although you might use a preliminary conceptual framework based on the literature to help guide your data collection and analysis. Note that in inductive research such models are not subjected to formal testing as in the deductive approach but serve as tentative starting points for your field research.

3.6 PRESENT

The final stage of the literature review process is to present your findings. General aspects of presenting your research are discussed in Chapter 15, but here we draw attention to some points particularly relevant to presenting your review of the literature.

3.6.1 What the review should cover

Coverage of your review will depend on its purpose, the audience for which it is intended, and the amount of space allowed. A review that forms part of a dissertation or thesis, for example, might be expected to

- demonstrate your critical understanding of the issues which writers and researchers consider important in your topic area;
- provide a critical overview and evaluation of relevant previous work; depending on the topic, this may include the following:

  - key concepts and their definitions
  - relevant theories and models
  - relevant policies and practices
  - a review of research findings from relevant empirical studies

- give a clear demonstration of the link between work you have reviewed and your own research, including identification of any gap(s) that your research will seek to fill.

3.6.2 Integrating your review

One of the decisions you will need to take is how to integrate your review into the overall research report. In academic reports such as journal articles, dissertations or theses, a literature review usually forms a separate chapter or section within the main body of the report, generally just prior to the research design section. Its role and where it is sited in the report are, however, influenced by the research approach that you have taken.

Deductive research

In deductive research approaches, the review is typically positioned immediately before the chapter or section describing the research design. It is where you present your development of the theory to be tested in your research. You should clearly identify the concepts (variables) to be used in the study, the relationships between them, and any hypotheses to be tested. The theory can be summarized in the form of a conceptual model, which may be located at the end of the review or in a separate chapter or section.

Inductive research

In inductive research there is more variability in the role of the literature review, depending on how prior theory is being used in your research. In the context of the qualitative research studies, Creswell and Creswell (2023) suggest three options. The first is to use the literature review in the introduction to 'frame' the research problem. The second option follows the 'traditional' approach of a separate section before the research design. Here the literature review can involve reviewing the theoretical background to the topic and/or identifying broad themes that might be relevant, perhaps including a tentative conceptual framework. The third option, particularly appropriate where the research is very strongly inductive, is to position the literature review later in the report when discussing the findings. Its role here is to compare the findings of your research with existing theory in the topic area. The choice of option, Creswell and Creswell (2023: 30) suggest, should take into account both the nature of the study and the 'audience for the project'.

If you are doing a research project for an academic qualification, check your institution's guidelines on where to position your literature review in the final report. If there are none, the default option is to include your review prior to the research design chapter or section.

Applied research

In applied research reports intended for a nonacademic audience, the position of your literature review can vary even more. In some cases, you may choose to follow traditional academic practice and include it in the main body of the report, before the research design chapter. An alternative, useful if the audience is less interested in the theoretical aspects of your topic, is to include the review as an appendix rather than as part of the main body. In other cases, especially for very large projects, your review may be published or issued separately. Chapter 15 discusses different report formats in more detail.

3.6.3 Structuring your review

In writing up your review, give careful thought to the structure of your argument. Ordering literature by concept will help, but you will still need to develop a clear overall structure and line of argument. Saunders et al. (2019) suggest thinking of your review as a funnel which progressively focuses in on your key themes. Begin by setting the broader scene, introducing the core theories and concepts in your topic area, before narrowing down the discussion to the specific aspects in which you are interested. Here you should discuss in detail the key theories or ideas that relate to your research problem. Finally, you should lead the reader into later sections of your research report.

3.6.4 Writing style

The writing style you adopt will depend on the purpose of your review and the intended audience. It should also conform to the writing style used for your report as a whole. This is discussed in Chapter 15, but the following points are particularly relevant to a literature review.

- *Tense*. When writing a literature review, it is standard practice to use the present rather than the past tense, so 'Jones (2019) argues . . . ', 'Patel (2022) reports that . . . ' rather than 'Jones (2019) argued . . . ' or 'Patel (2022) reported that . . . '.
- *Direct quotations*. Taking direct quotes from key authors is a useful way to emphasize an important point or take advantage of a particularly clear definition or powerful turn of phrase. They should be used sparingly, and very long extracts are generally best avoided. Embed shorter quotes in the body of the text and use separate text blocks only for longer extracts. You should always cite both the source and the number of the page where the quotation appears, so remember to record the page number of any quotations when making notes.

- *Tone*. Although you are doing a critical review, you should avoid setting a tone that is too negative and dismissive of other people's works. It is important to recognize limitations in what has been done, but this can be achieved while still treating others' work with respect.
- *Concept centric*. We have stressed the importance of structuring your review around concepts. An indication that your review is insufficiently concept-centric is when you have a large number of paragraphs that begin with phrases such as 'So and so says . . . ' or 'According to so and so . . . '.

3.6.5 Referencing

As noted earlier in the chapter, knowledge builds on the contributions of earlier scholars, and we acknowledge that debt by referencing their work. Referencing is also important to ground the credibility of your own claims and to allow the reader to refer directly to important or interesting material. You are expected to reference any of the following:

- direct quotations from another source
- paraphrased text based on someone else's work
- data/information/statistics from other sources
- theories/ideas/interpretations from someone else's work
- facts for which the reference provides the evidence.

You do this by means of a referencing system that provides rules for how to cite the work of others in the text of report and rules for how to format a **reference list** that shows all sources cited in your text.

Reference systems vary, and academic institutions, publishers, and other organizations have their own preferences. To illustrate the basic principles, we give an introduction to referencing using two different systems in the companion website: the Harvard system and the Vancouver system. The Harvard system is an author-date system similar to the one used in this book. The Vancouver system is a numbered system which is widely used in medical and other sciences. Ensure that you understand the referencing system you are required to use so that you can collect all of the bibliographic information needed for your final reference list. This, of course, is where a reference management software is invaluable.

You should also check whether you are expected to provide a reference list or a **bibliography**. A reference list contains only those works cited in your text. A bibliography lists all works you have consulted in preparing your report. Unless you have been explicitly asked to provide a bibliography, a reference list is more appropriate for most reports.

Plagiarism

Appropriate referencing is also essential to avoid the accusation of **plagiarism**. You commit plagiarism when you represent someone else's work as your own. 'Work' does not just mean published text but includes ideas, images, or models and so on. It applies to work you have paraphrased as well as direct quotations. The 'someone else' could be a well-known public figure, an anonymous author of a website, or another student. As well as being in breach of ethical standards, plagiarism is a very serious offence in academia and can lead to your dismissal from your programme of study. If you are a student, you should make sure you understand the rules on plagiarism for your institution. You should also take care to ensure that your work does not breach the copyright of another author. Plagiarism is discussed further in Chapter 15 where we discuss writing up your research.

CRITICAL COMMENTARY 3.1

Systematic review

The type of literature review that we have described here requires you to take a structured approach to developing a critical review of the relevant writing in the chosen topic area to support your research project. Reviews produced using this traditional approach, sometimes referred to as **narrative reviews** (Dickson et al., 2017: 10), have been criticized as failing to show how and why sources were selected and what assessment criteria were used to evaluate them and draw conclusions. As a result, according to critics, such reviews 'can be biased by the researcher and often lack rigour' (Tranfield et al., 2003: 207). A further criticism of traditional reviews is that they are not oriented to the needs of policymakers and practitioners in terms of guidance for policy decision-making and implementation.

In light of these criticisms, **systematic review** has been advocated as an alternative to the traditional approach. Originating from the field of medical science and closely associated with the evidence-based management movement, systematic review seeks to provide a systematic, transparent, and reproducible method for locating, appraising, and synthesizing all of the relevant studies in the chosen topic area (Dickson et al., 2017). To achieve this, systematic reviews emphasize the need to prepare a detailed protocol that sets out the research question that the review will answer and the procedures to follow, including the search strategy to be used, the inclusion/exclusion criteria for studies, and the methods for assessing the quality of studies and synthesizing the findings (CRD, 2009). A feature of some systematic reviews is an approach known as **meta-analysis**, which is the use of statistical techniques to synthesize the findings from multiple quantitative studies to provide a single quantitative estimate.

Systematic review is not appropriate in every situation. Petticrew and Roberts (2006) suggest that it is particularly useful as a tool for reviewing existing evidence on whether or not a particular policy or intervention is effective, or where there is a need to get a more accurate picture of previous research to inform future research. Critics have also drawn attention to systematic reviews' perceived positivist leanings in the way that they evaluate studies and the extent to which they are seen to privilege policy-oriented studies over other forms of research (Hammersley, 2001).

Carrying out a systematic review can be a major undertaking: a study of 37 systematic reviews that included meta-analysis found that they took on average 1,139 hours to complete (reported in Petticrew and Roberts, 2006). In practice, therefore, a systematic review is likely to form a study in its own right, rather than be a subordinate component of an empirical research project where a narrative review is more typical. If you are considering undertaking a systematic review and your research forms part of an undergraduate or postgraduate qualification, you should seek further guidance from your tutor/supervisor.

CHAPTER SUMMARY

- A critical review of literature is a component of academic and many other research projects. It provides the opportunity to build on the contribution of others and can help you to formulate your research problem, identify relevant theory, practices, and policy, and develop a suitable research design.
- Literature reviewing involves a systematic process of search, capture, synthesis, and presentation of relevant theoretical, research, practice, and policy literature.
- The literature review requires a critical evaluation of the arguments put forward in your sources and a structured synthesis of the findings from your own review.
- Conceptual models play an important role in research as graphical representations either of theory or of some real-world phenomenon of interest. Variance, process, and systems models are three common types of conceptual model used in research.
- Clear and accurate referencing is essential to acknowledge the contributions of others, to ground your own claims, and to avoid committing plagiarism.

NEXT STEPS

3.1 **Formulating your literature review questions**. Based on your research problem and research questions, formulate questions that your literature review should answer that will help you to (1) develop your understanding of theory and practice in your topic area, (2) design a suitable research approach.

3.2 **Places to look**. Review Table 3.2 and identify databases and other online areas that you can search for sources. Check which of these you can access via your academic institution, professional body, or other organization.

3.3 Preparing to search.

    a. Confirm the reference format you are required to use. If there is no specific requirement, you will have to make your own choice.

    b. Use Table 3.3 and 3.4 to develop your own template for capturing information from the sources you find.

    c. Familiarize yourself with any reference management software you intend to use or decide how you will record reference information.

3.4 Start searching. Make a list of search terms/keywords and the databases and other search locations to use to start searching. Capture your findings using your template created in the previous activity.

3.5 Developing a concept-centric review. As you evaluate and capture individual sources, start looking for patterns and themes in your reading. Use a table and/or graphical technique such as a literature map to develop a concept-centric view of your literature.

3.6 Developing a conceptual model. If you are adopting a deductive research approach, develop a conceptual model and formulate appropriate hypotheses for testing (this activity should be done after deciding on your research design and studying Chapters 4, 6, and 7).

3.7 Make a presentation on your review findings. Find a suitable forum where you can make a presentation on your literature review findings to peers and colleagues. Use the opportunity to refine your overall argument and to get feedback on its structure and coherence.

FURTHER READING

For further reading, please see the companion website.

BIBLIOGRAPHIC DATABASES

The table here shows a selection of bibliographic databases. In addition, most journal publishers have their own databases. The majority of these databases are subscription based; if you are a student, your library services will probably offer access to these and other relevant databases.

TABLE 3.7 Example bibliographic databases

Name	URL	Type
ABI/INFORM Complete (ProQuest)	www.proquest.com/	Bibliographic database
Business Source Complete (EBSCO)	www.ebsco.com/products/research-databases/business-source-complete	Bibliographic database
Directory of Open Access Journals	www.doaj.org/	Database of open-access journals
Emerald Insight	www.emerald.com/insight	Bibliographic database
ERIC (Education Resources Information Center)	https://eric.ed.gov/	Public database of education-related research and information; limited full-text availability
Ingenta Connect	www.ingentaconnect.com/	Bibliographic database
JSTOR	www.jstor.org/	Bibliographic database with full-text journals going back to date of first issue; recent issues less likely to be available
Science Direct	www.sciencedirect.com/	Bibliographic database

REFERENCES

Alvesson, M. and Sandberg, J. (2020). The problematizing review: A counterpoint to Elsbach and Van Knippenberg's argument for integrative reviews. *Journal of Management Studies*, 57(6): 1290–1304.

Boote, D. N. and Beile, P. (2005). Scholars before researchers: On the centrality of the dissertation literature review in research preparation. *Educational Researcher*, 34(6): 3–15.

Checkland, P. and Scholes, J. (1999). *Soft Systems Methodology in Action: A 30-year Retrospective*. Chichester: John Wiley and Sons.

CRD (2009). *Systematic Reviews*. Report, University of York: Centre for Reviews and Dissemination.

Creswell, J. W. and Creswell, J. D. (2023). *Research Design. Qualitative, Quantitative and Mixed Methods Approaches*. 6th ed. Thousand Oaks, CA: SAGE Publications.

Dickson, R., Cherry, M. G. and Boland, A. (2017). Carrying out a systematic review as a master's thesis. In: Boland, A., Cherry, M. G. and Dickson, R. (eds) *Doing a Systematic Review. A Student's Guide*. 2nd ed. London: SAGE Publications.

Grix, J. (2004). *The Foundations of Research*. Basingstoke: Palgrave Macmillan.

Hammersley, M. (2001). On "systematic" reviews of research literatures: A "Narrative" response to Evans & Benefield. *British Educational Research Journal*, 27(5): 543–554.

Letza, S., Sun, X. and Kirkbride, J. (2004). Shareholding versus stakeholding: A critical review of corporate governance. *Corporate Governance: An International Review*, 12: 242–262.

Lewin, K. (1952). *Field Theory in Social Science*. London: Tavistock Publications.

Maxwell, J. A. (2013). *Qualitative Research Design. An Interactive Approach*. 3rd ed. Los Angeles, CA: SAGE Publications.

Maxwell, J. A. (2017). The use of feedback for development in coaching: Finding the coach's stance. In: Bachkirova, T., Spence, G. and Drake, D. (eds) *The SAGE Handbook of Coaching*. London: SAGE Publications.

Mintzberg, H., Ahlstrand, B. and Lampel, J. (2009). *Strategy Safari*. 2nd ed. London: Prentice Hall.

Mohr, L. B. (1982). *Explaining Organisational Behaviour*. San Francisco, CA: Jossey-Bass.

Petticrew, M. and Roberts, H. (2006). *Systematic Reviews in the Social Sciences*. Oxford: Blackwell.

Saunders, M., Lewis, P. and Thornhill, A. (2019). *Research Methods for Business Students*. 8th ed. Harlow: Pearson Education.

Senge, P. M. (1990). *The Fifth Discipline. The Art and Practice of the Learning Organization*. London: Random House.

Silver, C. (2016). The value of CAQDAS for systematising literature reviews. *Revy*, 39(1): 6–8.

Silverman, D. (2022). *Doing Qualitative Research. A Practical Handbook*. 6th ed. London: SAGE Publications.

Toulmin, S. (1958). *The Uses of Argument*. Cambridge: Cambridge University Press.

Tranfield, D., Denyer, D. and Smart, P. (2003). Towards a methodology for developing evidence-informed management knowledge by means of systematic review. *British Journal of Management*, 14(3): 207–222.

Turnbull, H. (ed) (1959). *The Correspondence of Isaac Newton: Volume 1 1661–1675*. Cambridge: Cambridge University Press.

Wallace, M. and Wray, A. (2021). *Critical Reading and Writing for Postgraduates*. 4th ed. London: SAGE Publications.

Webster, J. and Watson, R. T. (2002). Analysing the past to prepare for the future: Writing a literature review. *MIS Quarterly*, 26(2): xiii–xxiii.

PART II

Design

Part II contains five chapters, each of which focuses on helping you at the design stage of your project. In Chapter 4 we begin by laying out key considerations in research design, including how you can integrate theory into your project, categories of research method and their respective data types, the choice of timeframe, and quality criteria. A key consideration for all researchers today is the ethical implications of their work, and we review ethical issues in research in Chapter 5. In Chapters 6 and 7 we introduce you to a range of quantitative, qualitative, and mixed methods designs that you can apply to your own project and explore how the nature of your research questions will influence your choice of research design. Both chapters are supported on the companion website by more detailed guidance on carrying out the research designs introduced in the chapters.

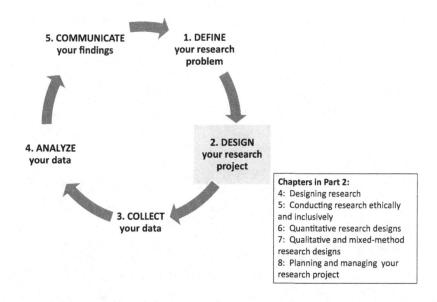

5. COMMUNICATE
your findings

1. DEFINE
your research
problem

2. DESIGN
your research
project

4. ANALYZE
your data

3. COLLECT
your data

Chapters in Part 2:
4: Designing research
5: Conducting research ethically
and inclusively
6: Quantitative research designs
7: Qualitative and mixed-method
research designs
8: Planning and managing your
research project

DOI: 10.4324/9781003381006-5

Chapter 8 moves on to look at how you select an appropriate research design, plan your project, and ultimately manage it. This chapter also introduces you to a crucial part of the planning process – the research proposal. We look at how to write one and provide you with a template for its structure and content.

CHAPTER 4

Designing your research

CHAPTER LEARNING OUTCOMES

After reading this chapter you will be able to

- relate research design to theory;
- select an appropriate research design according to your research questions;
- choose between quantitative, qualitative, and mixed methods;
- recognize the characteristics of primary and secondary data;
- select the time horizon for your research;
- recognize quality in research.

4.1 INTRODUCTION

In Chapter 2 we highlighted the importance of identifying your research problem and developing research questions that your research aims to answer. We introduced three generic types of research questions: 'what', 'why', and 'how' questions. In this chapter we will look at the key dimensions of research design and at the decisions you will need to make. We will look at how different research questions can be investigated using different research designs that employ quantitative, qualitative, or mixed methods. We address each type of research question in turn, examining the implications for how we go about answering them. This chapter provides the background for more specific details about types of research designs that are provided in Chapters 6 and 7.

Your **research design** is the plan that you will adopt for your research in order to answer your research questions. It lays down both the overall structure for your research and the specific methods and techniques that you will use to collect and analyze your data. **Research methods** refer to the general form of your data collection and analysis procedures, in particular whether they are quantitative or qualitative. **Research techniques** are the specific tools and techniques, such as a particular type of statistical analysis or interview procedure.

DOI: 10.4324/9781003381006-6

Designing your research therefore requires decisions at increasing levels of detail to cover each stage of your project. This involves answering a series of questions, as shown in Figure 4.1, where each is linked to chapters in this book where the topics are covered in more depth. At each level your decisions must be aligned so that the overall plan is consistent and coherent. For example, the type of data you collect has major implications for the data analysis techniques you can use. Conversely, the analysis techniques you plan to use will influence your choice of data collection procedure. Mistakes made at one stage can be difficult or even impossible to fix later on. Design is therefore a crucial stage in the overall research process.

Before you can begin a detailed design, you will need to think about your overall research approach. This involves addressing and making decisions about four broad issues that are the topics of this chapter. The first is the relationship between research design and theory, building on the distinction between deductive and inductive approaches that we introduced in Chapter 1. The second is the research questions you have set and a decision about the nature of the data that will enable you to answer them as introduced in Chapter 2. We first introduce you to quantitative, qualitative, or mixed research methods and their data types before we look at how research designs align to research questions. The third decision is the time horizon embedded in the research: do you intend to track events through time or to take a snapshot of what is happening right now? The fourth decision relates to the origin of the data: will you collect new data or make use of data that exists already? The spread of digital technologies such as social media and mobile devices have

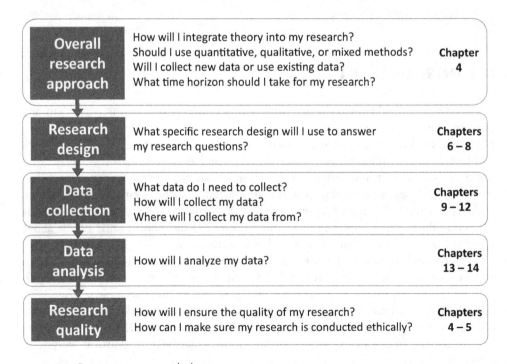

FIGURE 4.1 Decisions in research design

given rise to a wide range of data sources, as well as new technological ways to collect data, and so this can be an important consideration for your research. In addition to addressing these issues, and regardless of what research design you adopt, you will want to have confidence in your findings and for them to be taken seriously by others. We therefore conclude this chapter with an introduction to a very contentious subject: criteria for judging quality in research.

4.2 INTEGRATING THEORY INTO YOUR RESEARCH

Your first decision relates to the relationship between **research** and existing **theory** and what it means for your research design. As we discussed in Chapter 1, a theory explains a phenomenon, often involving relevant concepts, and enables prediction(s) to be made. It is essential that when beginning to design your research that you are clear about your theoretical position and what the purpose of your research is in relation to theory. We start by revisiting the distinction between deductive and inductive approaches introduced in Chapter 1, as these are the theoretical approaches most commonly encountered in business and management research. Later we will also consider a third approach known as abduction.

4.2.1 Deductive research approaches

A deductive (or **hypothetico-deductive**) research approach involves testing theory against observational data, thereby moving from the general (the theory to be tested) to the specific (actual data). In Figure 4.2 we show this proceeding through a series of closely connected sequential steps.

1. The process begins with development of a theory that potentially explains the problem under investigation. The theory must be articulated in a way which allows you to specify the concepts of interest, how they are related, and why. This is often done by developing a conceptual model as described in Chapter 3.

2. Next, specific hypotheses are formulated, derived from the theory. In this context a **hypothesis** can be defined as a testable proposition about the expected association between two or more concepts in the theory. Based on theory, you might, for example, develop the hypothesis that customer satisfaction and customer loyalty are positively related.

3. The concepts identified in the hypotheses are then translated into measurable variables, a process known as **operationalization**. The term **variable** is an important one, particularly in quantitative research, and refers to any characteristic or attribute of something that can take on different values. Such values can be numerical (such as the level of customer satisfaction or customer loyalty) or categorical (such as a respondent's gender or nationality).

4. Suitable data are then collected to measure each variable, for example, by measuring satisfaction and loyalty amongst a randomly chosen sample of customers.

5. The hypotheses are then tested using an appropriate statistical procedure to see whether or not the hypotheses are supported by the data.

6. The results of the hypothesis testing may lead to the rejection of the theory, its modification, or its retention. Either way, the findings are then used to address your original research question.

The deductive approach is closely associated with positivism and the idea of the scientific method and is frequently applied to answer 'why' type research questions. This involves using quantitative research designs such as experiments and survey studies to test theories about the associations between variables in order to determine whether or not a causal relationship exists. This is a very important application of the deductive approach, so we discuss it in more detail in Chapter 6, while the technical details of statistical hypothesis testing are covered in Chapter 13.

Although the deductive approach may appear at first sight to offer a high degree of precision and objectivity, a very important point needs to be made in connection with the truth status of the findings in this type of research. To explain this, we draw on the work of the philosopher of science Karl Popper. Concerned by the ease by which our theories can be 'proved' to be true if we look for evidence that confirms or verifies them, Popper (2002: 48) proposed that the only 'genuine test' of a theory was an attempt to falsify or refute it. The aim of theory testing is therefore the falsification of theories, not their verification. Applying this perspective, we do not prove theories to be true, we fail to reject them. Thus, whilst a theory that has been refuted should be modified or abandoned, those

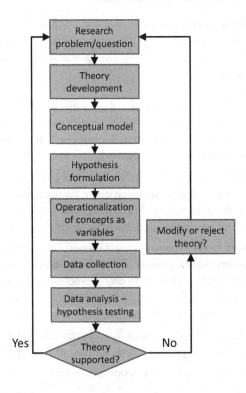

FIGURE 4.2 Stages in the deductive research approach

theories that have survived testing should be seen as provisional rather than 'true' in any simplistic sense. As Blaikie and Priest (2019: 287) warn us, 'theories must be regarded as tentative and open to revision; a cautious and critical approach must be adopted'.

We illustrate the choice to take a deductive approach in Research in Practice 4.1.

Research in practice 4.1 Choosing a deductive approach

Social media as a communication channel is now ubiquitous. It has predominantly been used in the consumer context with organizations and brands using it as a marketing channel to build relationships with individual consumers. For her doctoral research, Diana Fandel was interested to investigate how social media can be used to build business-to-business (B2B) relationships. Three research questions were set:

1. What are the vendor B2B social media communication practices that can influence trust in customer relationships?

2. What is the effect of vendor B2B social media communication practices upon customer loyalty?

3. Is the effect of B2B social media communication practices upon loyalty mediated by trust?

To do this she researched existing theories regarding how social media builds relationships, B2B relationship building, and the twin concepts of trust and loyalty in the B2B context. Her approach then was to build a conceptual model for testing based on these existing theories and prior research. The model was tested within the context of the US Life Sciences industry with data collected from B2B customers such as scientists and laboratory technicians who used social media in the course of their work to connect with a vendor firm. The model was tested using statistical analysis known as PLS – structural equation modelling, and the outputs identified the effects of different practices on customer levels of trust and loyalty.

Adopting a deductive approach allowed the researcher to develop and test a conceptual model of the influencing factors in B2B social media and the effects on building customer relationships. This led to new insights for B2B marketers into this emerging new channel of social media.

Source: Rose et al. (2021)

4.2.2 Inductive research approaches

In contrast to the theory testing of a deductive approach, an **inductive** research approach seeks to build theory on the basis of observations. Theory is therefore the outcome of the research. The process begins with data collection in response to a problem or question (Figure 4.3). Inductive research designs favour open-ended and flexible data collection methods, such as in-depth interviews, rather than the pre-specified measurement

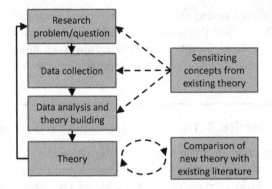

FIGURE 4.3 Stages in the inductive research approach

techniques typical of deductive approaches. Similarly, instead of applying predetermined categories to the data, analysis in inductive research typically proceeds by searching for themes and patterns which form the building blocks of the emerging theory. The resulting theory can then be used to address the original research problem. At this point it is common to compare the findings with existing literature and theory, as we discussed in Chapter 3 and as shown diagrammatically in Figure 4.3.

When you adopt a deductive approach, prior theory determines what data you need to collect. How should you proceed when working inductively? One view is that you should approach the task of data collection without any presuppositions as to what might be important, thereby avoiding imposing your own biases on the data you gather. If, however, we accept that observation is always to some extent theory laden, we have to recognize that 'presuppositionless' observation is not really possible (Blaikie and Priest, 2019: 103). In addition, from a practical point of view, we have to make sure that our data collection efforts generate useful results in whatever time we have available. As a result, many researchers make use of what Blumer (1954: 7) calls **sensitizing concepts**. Sensitizing concepts, which can be developed from the literature review, are not fixed and formally defined in advance as in deductive research. Instead, they are seen as tentative, subject to change, and added to or discarded as the research proceeds. They can guide data collection by suggesting initial lines of enquiry and can help to structure your data analysis, as we discuss further in Chapter 14.

An inductive approach suits pure research projects where the topic area is not well understood and there is little or no prior theory to act as a guide. Flick (2023) suggests that this is increasingly necessary, as rapid social change means that researchers are confronted with new contexts. Inductive approaches are also relevant to applied research projects where the problem under investigation may initially be poorly structured or is completely novel. Moreover, because theory is developed from the data, an inductive approach is attractive to researchers seeking to develop an in-depth understanding of a situation from the perspective of those involved in a situation. This focus on understanding, coupled with the nature of both data collection and analysis, means that qualitative methods are the most common to use when taking an inductive approach, and we introduce a range of suitable qualitative research designs in Chapter 7. There is also growing interest in more inductive quantitative approaches, which we discuss in Chapter 6. Research in Practice 4.2 provides an example of a researcher choosing an inductive qualitative approach.

Research in practice 4.2 Choosing an inductive approach

For his final-year dissertation, MSc student Andrew George wanted to learn more about the virtues of executive coaches. Coaching is still a relatively young profession with emergent practices around ethical behaviour and with new accreditation bodies only recently developing codes of practice. The researcher had a background in ethical practice and specifically an interest in virtue ethics as applied in other traditional, well-established professions such as medicine. He was interested to explore the relevance of virtue ethics in this new profession.

Little theory or research existed about the application of virtue ethics to coaching. Therefore, an inductive approach was adopted that would enable exploration of the subject and the development of a potential explanatory model. An inductive approach enabled exploratory research to be conducted with executive coaches about their practices, their understanding of the moral purpose and virtues required for a 'good' coach, and their view of the development of the coaching profession. Qualitative method using semi-structured 1-2-1 interviews was used to collect data from coaches which was analyzed using thematic analysis. The outputs from the data analysis were used to develop a preliminary conceptual model of the telos of coaching that could be taken forward for further testing.

Source: George (2022)

4.2.3 Abductive research approaches

Abduction (also known as retroduction) offers a third way that involves the interplay of observation and theory during the research process. The term is associated with the philosopher Charles Peirce, who used it to describe a form of reasoning that he called 'inference to the best explanation' (Honderich, 1995: 1). We can illustrate this process with a simple example. Suppose that one morning your car does not start. Faced with this anomaly, you start to theorize why not. If the engine does not turn over, you might decide that a flat battery is a plausible explanation. You could test your new theory by looking for other symptoms of a flat battery, such as the car lights not working. If you found such symptoms you would have more confidence in your theory. If you did not, you might decide that your original theory was wrong and look for an alternative explanation. Your flat battery theory might also prompt you to think more deeply about why the battery was dead in the first place. The process of abduction would thereby lead you on to more theory development as a result of encountering the original anomaly.

Several writers have drawn attention to the possibilities of using abductive reasoning in research, but its application in research practice is not as well documented as either deduction or induction. When considering an abductive approach, there are two requirements to think about beforehand. Firstly, you will need to collect data that is detailed and rich enough to allow you to develop your tentative theory. Secondly, the research process needs to be sufficiently flexible to support the iteration between theory and data. These requirements suggest the use of qualitative or mixed method research designs. Grounded theory is one research design that can employ abduction in its method of constant comparison between data and emerging theory (Reichertz, 2007). Abductive reasoning can also have a role in the cyclical process of action research and in multiple case study designs (see Chapter 7).

4.2.4 Deciding on your research approach

What are the implications of all this for your research? Your approach must have an overall logic to the way in which theory, data collection, and data analysis are combined to answer your research question. It is therefore important at the start of your project to think through the role of theory in relation to your research. This will involve deciding on whether to adopt a deductive, inductive, or abductive approach. Figure 4.4 presents a simple decision tree to help you with that decision.

Your choice of approach will need to be aligned with your choice of research method, the topic we take up next.

4.3 WHAT ARE QUANTITATIVE, QUALITATIVE, OR MIXED METHODS?

Before we look at potential research designs, it is useful to understand research methods and the type of data each employs (Creswell and Creswell, 2023). So far in the book we

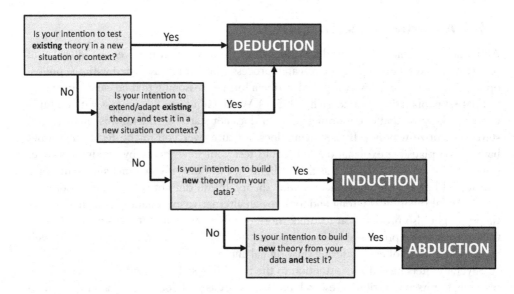

FIGURE 4.4 Research approach decision tree

have referred in passing to quantitative and qualitative methods. As we will see, the distinction between these two types of research methods is complex and controversial but is very widely used both in general textbooks and in more specialized treatments of research methods. It does also provide a helpful framework for classifying research designs discussing important aspects of both designing and carrying out management research. We will start by reviewing some of the perceived differences between the two families of method before considering the possibility of mixing the two methods in one research project.

4.3.1 The quantitative-qualitative distinction

Table 4.1 summarizes some of the ways in which quantitative and qualitative research may be seen as different.

Type of data

Our starting point is to distinguish between the type of data used, with quantitative researchers collecting and analyzing numerical data and qualitative researchers using non-numeric data, primarily words but also images and video. The types of data preferred involve quantitative researchers using statistical analysis procedures, whilst qualitative researchers use techniques such as coding or thematic analysis to interpret their data. The distinction is not so precise in practice. Text (such as advertisements, reports, etc.) can be analyzed quantitatively, whilst qualitative researchers may make explicit or implicit use of some quantification in their analysis. Nevertheless, this difference is widely acknowledged and has significant practical implications for how you design and carry out your research, as well as the skills you will need to develop to do so.

TABLE 4.1 The qualitative-quantitative distinction	
Quantitative research	*Qualitative research*
Collects and analyzes numeric data	Collects and analyzes non-numeric data
Tests theory deductively	Builds theory inductively or abductively
Uses structured, pre-specified, fixed procedures	Uses emergent, flexible procedures
Is variable oriented	Is case oriented
Is concerned with aggregate properties and statistical inference	Is concerned with depth, diversity, and context
Uses researcher's categories (etic approach)	Uses local actors' categories (emic approach)
Works in artificial and/or controlled settings	Works in natural settings
Researcher is at a distance	Researcher is closely involved

Relationship to theory

Quantitative and qualitative research are also often distinguished in terms of their relationship to theory. As we mentioned earlier in the chapter, quantitative research designs are widely used for deductive theory testing, and indeed the hypothetico-deductive approach is so strongly associated with the quantitative methods that the two can appear to be synonymous. Qualitative methods, on the other hand, are more closely associated with inductive or abductive theory building. Use of qualitative methods does not, however, rule out a deductive approach, and quantitative researchers can and do make use of inductive reasoning in their research. Nevertheless the deduction-induction split is widely encountered both in books about research methods and in the actual practice of researchers. It is also connected to other perceived differences between quantitative and qualitative methods.

Specification of procedures

One of these differences is the extent to which the procedures to be followed in the research are specified in advance or are developed as the research unfolds. Quantitative research is commonly characterized as having structured, predetermined, and fixed research designs. A fixed design is consistent with the need to operationalize concepts as measurable variables and to pre-specify appropriate data collection and analysis procedures when taking a deductive approach. Qualitative research does not work under the same strictures, so that research designs can be more flexible, evolving as the research itself unfolds. Cooper et al. (2012: 243) refer to this as a 'developmental' mode of investigation and emphasize its iterative character in support of inductive or abductive theory building. Much quantitative research, on the other hand, operates in what they call 'simultaneous' mode, where all the data are brought together and then analyzed simultaneously.

Variable orientation

Quantitative research is often characterized as having a 'variable orientation'. By operationalizing concepts of interest as measurable variables and specifying the expected association between them, quantitative researchers can apply statistical techniques for analysis, including theory testing. This approach is combined with an interest in the aggregate properties of whatever is being investigated, which often involves a process of statistical inference by which statistical techniques are used to draw conclusions about a larger population on the basis of data drawn from a sample of that population. Qualitative research, on the other hand, tends to adopt a 'case-oriented' or 'case-focused' approach in which the focus is on the 'heterogeneity and particularity of individual cases' (Ragin, 1987: xii). Instead of the aggregate properties of large groups, qualitative researchers usually investigate a small number of cases in depth and in their local context to understand the diversity and complexity of a phenomenon.

Emic or etic approach

Important differences can also be seen in the origin of the conceptual categories used in research. Quantitative research typically adopts an 'outsider' or **etic perspective** in which concepts are specified by the researcher, based, for example, on the theory being tested. Qualitative research, on the other hand, often seeks to take the perspective of those involved in the situation being investigated by adopting what is sometimes called an 'insider' or **emic perspective**. This can involve either staying close to the language and interpretations used by participants in a given situation or actively attempting to understand the lived experience of those involved in a situation. Qualitative research thereby offers a way of 'exploring and understanding the meaning individuals or groups ascribe to a social or human problem' (Creswell and Creswell, 2023: 5). This interest is shared with the philosophy of interpretivism, which has traditionally been associated with qualitative research and contrasts with the positivist orientation that characterizes much quantitative research. As always, however, we need to exercise caution. Some quantitative researchers, for example, in psychology, are interested in 'how people make sense of their experience' (Gomm, 2008: 7), and not all researchers who use qualitative methods seek an interpretivist understanding of phenomena.

Research environment

The final distinctions we will draw relate to the research environment and the role of the researcher. Qualitative research is often seen as preferring to conduct research in natural settings, such as the participants' homes or workplace, whilst quantitative research uses artificial ones, such as a laboratory, in which the researcher can control aspects of the environment. In practice this distinction does not always hold, but it does indicate a difference in emphasis in some research designs. Another difference is how to deal with the influence of the researcher on the research findings. In most quantitative designs, the aim is to minimize researcher impact by striving to be 'independent of and "detached" from, the people and processes that they are studying' (Easterby-Smith et al., 2021: 87). This is sought by careful attention to pre-specified procedures and protocols and the use of standardized data collection techniques. In qualitative research, however, 'issues of instrument trustworthiness ride largely on the skills of the researcher. Essentially, a *person* is observing, interviewing and recording . . . from one field visit to the next' (Miles et al., 2020: 35; italics in the original). Qualitative researchers therefore typically accept that they will have an impact on the research process and stress the need to reflect on the nature of that impact. This is an aspect of reflexivity, a topic we introduced in Chapter 1. Reflexivity should include awareness of how the characteristics, attitudes, and behaviours of the researcher may affect elements of the research design and particularly inclusivity. For example, differences in demographics, culture, values, or belief systems between the researcher and the sample of respondents can have potential effects upon how research is conducted and therefore the outcomes. Note, however, that both quantitative and qualitative methods share a general awareness of researcher effects even if the way in which such effects are understood and addressed varies considerably.

A word of caution

We must be careful not to exaggerate these differences. Particular qualitative and quantitative designs will display these tendencies to different degrees and in different combinations. There is also as much variation between different qualitative or different quantitative designs as there is between quantitative and qualitative research as a whole. Nevertheless, the distinction does provide a framework for discussing important aspects of research design and practice as they relate to choice of method. In addition, the distinctive features of quantitative and qualitative methods suggest different ways in which each may be used in combination to answer particular research questions which we explore further in the next section.

4.3.2 Is it possible to mix methods?

So far our discussion of quantitative and qualitative methods has assumed that the research will involve using one or the other. However, there may be situations in which the aims of the research can best be addressed by utilizing a combination of both types of methods. This is referred to as '**mixed methods**', and the collection of qualitative or quantitative data (utilizing relevant techniques) may be in different sequences over time depending on the reason for using both methods. Decisions about using mixed methods relate to your theoretical position as previously discussed in section 4.2. For example, if the objective is to build and then test theory, then a sequence that involves qualitative method to explore and identify key concepts to build your theory, followed by quantitative method to test theory, may be relevant. Such an example is given in Research in Practice 4.3. There are other types of mixed method designs, and in Chapter 7 we present these with reasons to use each approach. Whilst using a mixed method approach can be beneficial from the perspective of your research aims, it does have some drawbacks for the researcher, such as potential resource implications of time and cost.

Research in practice 4.3 Choosing a mixed method approach

At the start of 2020 the world experienced the Covid-19 pandemic, which resulted in significant disruption to the economy. Specifically, the retail industry in most countries was severely impacted due to governmental quarantine restrictions that required shops and retail outlets to close, with the only exception of essential goods such as food and medicines. Such 'lockdowns' had serious implications for consumers who were unable to purchase via stores and resulted in a significant shift to buying online.

A research team at the Henley Centre for Customer Management recognized that this provided a unique opportunity to research online shopping behaviour in the absence of physical stores. Previously it had not been possible to isolate the effects of physical stores upon buying behaviour online. The team was interested in looking at the purchase of 'high involvement products' (HIP), which are those that are high priced and high risk (e.g. furniture, computers, or cars) and which are usually purchased in store or in combination online and in-store.

Whilst a significant amount of theory and prior research existed regarding the twin subjects of the purchase of HIPs and online shopping, no research had explored their purchase in an online only context. A mixed method approach was therefore used. In the first research phase a qualitative study involved 1-2-1 interviews of consumers forced to buy HIPs online when they would normally have bought in store. This was to elicit exploratory data on this new experience for consumers of being unable to access stores. From this data a conceptual model was developed drawing on the qualitative findings plus existing theories of HIP purchase behaviour and online shopping. In the second phase the model was subjected to hypothesis testing using online survey amongst a wider sample of those shopping for HIPs during retail lockdowns. The findings identified the effect of loss of sensory information when buying HIPs online upon shopper concerns about risk and the consequential effect on future purchase intentions.

Source: Rose et al. (2022)

4.4 LINKING RESEARCH DESIGN TO YOUR RESEARCH QUESTIONS

The second and possibly most important decision is which research design is relevant to your research question. The start point here is to revisit your original research questions. In this section, we consider how different research questions can be investigated, and in Chapters 6 and 7 we discuss them in relation to specific designs using quantitative, qualitative, and mixed methods.

4.4.1 Research designs for answering 'what' questions

As discussed in Chapter 2, answers to 'what' questions are essentially descriptive. To describe means to give a detailed account of something. In research, description involves identifying and describing the characteristics of, and patterns in, a phenomenon of interest. Descriptions can be relatively concrete, such as the age or geographic location of your customer base, or relatively abstract, such as their attitudes or values. They can be qualitative or quantitative, cross-sectional or longitudinal. They can be relatively simple, such as a description of customer satisfaction, or more complex, such as a description of customer satisfaction by customer age and the type of product purchased. Answers to descriptive questions do not attempt to provide explanations of phenomena in terms of 'why' or 'how' they happen, but good description is not just reportage or 'mindless fact gathering' (de Vaus, 2001: 1). Instead it involves drawing conclusions about the phenomenon of interest on the basis of a set of observations in order to reduce a mass of data into something more manageable and useful.

Description and comparison

Description of something in isolation can raise the question 'so what?' because without some frame of reference it can be difficult to make sense of your findings. Knowing, for instance, that the average spend per customer visit to your website is €38.99 may not be very useful on its own. Is 38.99 a big number? Should you be pleased? Concerned? One way of making sense of such data is by making comparisons. For example:

- between groups or subgroups within your own data, for instance, by comparing differences in spend between one customer group and another;
- between the same group at different points in time, for example, by comparing how the level of customer spending has changed over time;
- against a predetermined reference, such as comparison of the average customer spend against organizational sales targets or other relevant (internal or external) benchmarks.

Comparison is not just done in quantitative terms. It can also be qualitative, comparing, for example, different experiences of organizational change or different ways in which customers relate to a company's brand. Comparison has obvious practical application in organizational research, for instance, when evaluating current practices relative to an external benchmark or when seeking a deeper understanding of how groups differ in their perceptions, values, and beliefs. Unexpected or unwelcome findings may prompt further research to find out why or how the situation has arisen and how to close any gap.

Description and classification

An alternative approach to description is to use a classification scheme to divide things into groups or categories according to their similarities and differences. As Bailey (1994: 1) describes the process, 'We arrange a set of entities into groups so that each group is as different as possible from all other groups, but each group is internally as homogenous as possible'. The 'entities' to be categorized might be individuals, organizations, events, or some other phenomenon of interest. The resulting classification scheme should be mutually exclusive and exhaustive so that each entity is in one and only one group. At their best, classification schemes can provide a powerful way of reducing the complexity of your data whilst helping you to identify key distinctions with practical and theoretical relevance.

Classification schemes can be developed using both quantitative and qualitative analysis techniques. Classification can be done along a single dimension such as age or marital status, but more interesting classificatory schemes are likely to be multidimensional. Classification schemes can be built inductively from the data, in which case they are often referred to as **taxonomies**, or they can be developed in advance from existing theory and then applied to the data as a categorizing device, when the expression **typology** is sometimes preferred. You can use a classification scheme to reduce descriptive complexity, but it can be used to help in answering 'why' and 'how' questions, for example, by classifying different patterns of causal factors or types of process.

Classification is applied in demographic data collected about a research sample that may subsequently be used to create 'groups' for analysis. Irrespective of the way a classification system is developed or data is collected, of most importance is that it should be free from bias or prior assumptions based on the researcher's own perspective, background, or grouping. Inappropriate categorization particularly of people can lead to biased findings and at the extreme stereotyping and discrimination. Research in Practice 4.4 illustrates an example of such effects in categorization within the healthcare industry.

Research in practice 4.4 Effects of racial categorization

Categorization of individuals into groups is a way in which a researcher may decide to test the relevance of a theory or to explore new concepts. We may want to know whether our findings differ by some specific characteristic. Grouping people together and then conducting comparative analysis of data at group level is a recognized practice. However, as researchers we should be aware of the basis for such categorization and what assumptions or norms may drive our need for categorization.

Selvarajah et al. (2020) explored the effects of categorization of different racial groups in the context of healthcare. They recognize that categorization can be useful in terms of ensuring fairness in the allocation of health budgets across populations. However, they also point to the way in which power structures can be reinforced via the use of longstanding taxonomies or ways of classifying people. For example, they point to the continued use of categorizations such as BAME (Black, Asian, and minority ethnic), a governmental term in the UK, and BIPOC (Black, Indigenous, and People of Colour) in the US, both of which, they argue, emanate from a colonial need to racially categorize people who were not white.

Whether we are categorizing by race, gender, or age, we should be aware of how such categorization systems are used, but more importantly we should question why there is a need to see differences in people. Is this being driven by a genuine benefit that arises from knowing about how different characteristics affect our theory, or are we following deep-rooted assumptions about differences that should be challenged. Knowing why we are categorizing people into groups is as important as how we do it. As Selvarajah et al. (2020: 3) state: 'We call for data collection and categorizations to be accurate, contextually appropriate and not to reinforce existing power hierarchies'.

Is description enough?

Despite the importance of description, a word of warning is necessary, particularly to those undertaking research for academic assessment: just describing something may not be seen as making sufficient contribution, especially at master's or doctoral level. So while description will almost certainly be a component of any research project, it will not necessarily be the endpoint. In many cases, you will want to go further and build on description as you go on to develop answers to 'why' and 'how' questions. For student research projects, we recommend that you clarify what is expected with your supervisor.

4.4.2 Research designs for answering 'why' questions

Answers to 'why' questions are concerned with explanations for something. What form such an explanation might take, how to produce one, and even whether explanation is feasible are extremely controversial topics in social science. Nevertheless, as we argued in Chapter 2, explanation is an important part of much business and management research, so in this section we take a closer look at different ways of answering 'why' type research questions. We will begin by looking at approaches that seek explanation in terms of cause-and-effect relationships to identify, for example, what factors are causing some observed phenomenon (the effect).

Criteria for inferring causality

Four criteria are commonly suggested for inferring causality:

1. Cause and effect should co-vary. If an independent variable is causally related to a dependent variable, they should co-vary so that as one variable changes, the other systematically changes with it.

2. The cause should precede the effect in time. Establishing the time sequence of cause and effect can help to address the **directionality problem**, which is the problem of deciding, if two variables co-vary, which one is the cause and which is the effect.

3. Alternative potential causes have been ruled out. The researcher must control for the effects of factors other than the presumed cause that might influence the observed outcome.

4. There should be a plausible explanation for the relationship. There should be a theoretical account of why the cause produces the observed effect.

Identifying covariance, establishing the time sequence of cause and effect, and controlling for the effects of **extraneous variables** can give you more confidence that a causal relationship exists, but they do not really explain why it is happening. This is the difference between **causal description** and **causal explanation** (Shadish et al., 2002). The former involves identifying that a causal relationship exists; the latter involves explaining why it exists. Shadish et al. (2002) illustrate this by contrasting the difference between knowing that throwing a light switch causes a light to go on (causal description) and understanding how and why throwing the light switch causes the light to go on (causal explanation). If the light does not work, explanatory knowledge could help us to work out why not and potentially to fix the problem. Both kinds of knowledge are potentially useful. A robust causal description may have practical relevance, even if we cannot provide a full causal explanation; similarly, a potential causal explanation may stimulate further research to establish whether or not there is a causal effect in practice.

The language of explanation

Before going further, it will be useful to introduce some widely used terminology which will help subsequent discussion.

Figure 4.5(a) depicts a simple causal relationship where one variable (X) is shown as causally related to another variable (Y). The arrow in the diagram shows the direction of the causal relationship, which runs from X (the cause) to Y (the effect). The term **dependent** or **outcome variable** refers to the effect in a causal diagram; it is *dependent* on changes in other variables. Conventionally it is labelled as the Y variable. The **independent** or

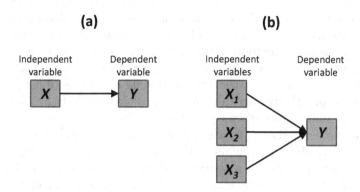

(a)   **(b)**

FIGURE 4.5 Independent and dependent variables

predictor variable is the variable that is identified as the cause of changes in the dependent variable. In experiments it is often called the **treatment variable** because it is the variable that is manipulated by the researcher. It is labelled as the X variable. In some situations there will be more than one independent variable, in which case they are usually labelled $X_1, X_2 \ldots X_n$, as shown in Figure 4.5(b). You will recognize this as a conceptual model of the variance type that we introduced in Chapter 3. Such models are closely associated with positivist and quantitative approaches to causal explanation.

The causal criteria we have identified are closely associated with positivism, but their origins can be traced back to the work of the eighteenth-century philosopher David Hume. Hume argued that causation itself was unobservable and that we could only infer a causal relationship on the basis of observing the 'constant conjunction' of events between a presumed cause and its effect (Maxwell, 2012: 34). This approach, sometimes referred to as the regularity or successionist view of causation, is arguably still the dominant view of causality in business and management research but is not the only way in which causal explanation can be understood. Be aware that other views of causality exist. For example, an approach aligned to the philosophical orientation of realism rejects the regularity view of causation in favour of what is sometimes referred to as generative. Here the emphasis is on causal explanation rather than causal description. Explanation depends on 'identifying causal mechanisms and how they work, and discovering if they have been activated and under what conditions' (Sayer, 2000: 14). Alternatively, explanation may draw on people's reasons or beliefs to explain actions. One way to incorporate people's beliefs, values, and reasons in explanatory research is to treat them as variables in causal models of the type shown in Figure 4.5 in the same way as other (non-reason) variables. Example of reason-based variables of trust and loyalty were included in the deductive research work described in our Research in Practice 4.1 example.

The limits of explanatory research

Regardless of the research designs we employ, we should use the outputs of our explanatory research with due awareness of their potential limitations and be cautious about any causal claims we make. In practice, our ability to make causal inference with absolute certainty will always be limited because in social science we are dealing with complex situations with many interacting and interdependent factors influencing what is happening. These challenges have contributed to a move away from understanding causality in a deterministic way in which X always leads to Y and replacing it with a probabilistic notion of causality in which, instead of certainty, 'we work at the level that a given factor increases (or decreases) the probability of a particular outcome' (de Vaus, 2001: 5). Having a bachelor's degree, for example, increases the probability of a higher salary on leaving university, but it does not make it certain. Even with a probabilistic understanding of causality, however, researchers are often very cautious in the language they use, preferring to use terms such as prediction, correlation, co-variation, and impact, without mentioning the word cause. Although absolute certainty is never possible, we can, with carefully designed and executed research, deepen our understanding of some fundamental questions for business and management: what works, for whom, under what circumstances, and why?

CRITICAL COMMENTARY 4.1

Nonexperimental approaches to causality

As we have seen, causality is a complex and controversial topic in business and management research, and there is a lot of debate over the best way to investigate causal questions. Experimental designs, particularly the randomized controlled trial, are sometimes portrayed as the 'gold standard' for causal research because of their perceived ability to address the requirements for inferring causality that we identified in this chapter. For some writers, nonexperimental research designs are simply not able to demonstrate causality because of the difficulty of achieving high levels of control over extraneous influences. Bleske-Rechek et al. (2015: 49) support this view of the superiority of experimental design in causal research and point to the strong tendency of humans to 'conflate correlation with causation' and that the distinction between the two is 'fundamental'. This is a particularly strong view in social science disciplines such as psychology.

There are, however, many situations in management research where an experiment is not possible or not ethically desirable. An example is in the tourism industry, where much research is based on nonexperimental survey data or panel data. Mazanec (2007) challenges the requirements of experimental causal designs as 'too rigorous' and states, 'A human child acquires causal knowledge without conducting controlled experiments. There must be less restrictive conditions for causal inference' (Mazanec, 2007: 224). He proposes that one way to do this is the application of inferred causation theory and applies this to a model of service quality, tourist satisfaction, loyalty, and repeat visitation. The approach challenges the restrictive nature of experimental data by drawing on a wider range of data sources (such as graph theory, statistics, logic, and artificial intelligence data) that in combination can assess conditional independent relationships and states that 'cross-sectional measurements of variables with no inherent temporal precedence may be sufficient to derive causal conclusions on at least some of the observed relationships' (Mazanec, 2007: 226).

In the complex world of organizations and management, no single research technique, whether quantitative or qualitative, is likely to be able to address all the 'why' questions that we may wish to answer. We have therefore chosen to emphasize the strengths and weaknesses of different approaches in order to support an informed decision on research design when investigating why things are happening.

4.4.3 Research designs for answering 'how' questions

In the previous section we introduced 'why' explanations. This section focuses on a different form of explanation, one that seeks to understand how things come about in terms of process. In business and management we often use the term 'process' quite narrowly to refer to the ways in which organizations go about producing goods and services. Here we will be using the term more broadly to refer to the sequences of events, actions, and activities through which phenomena, such as organizations or innovations, change and develop over time and in context. Viewing a topic through the lens of process involves 'considering phenomena dynamically – in terms of movement, activity, events, change and temporal evolution' (Langley, 2007: 271).

We have already seen one application of process thinking when looking at the sequence of variables linked together to form a causal path. In this section we will explore two other applications where you may find a process approach helpful in answering 'how' questions.

1. The first application is in studying how entities (people, organizations, etc.) change and develop over time, for example, in the context of organizational change, innovation, or mergers and acquisitions.
2. The second application focuses on how 'things' such as organizing, leading, and strategizing actually get done and how social reality is constituted, reproduced, and maintained through social processes, including everyday social interaction.

Although features of process, such as frequency of communication or stakeholder participation, can be included as independent variables in causal models, researchers adopting a process orientation usually investigate process more directly. This typically involves gathering data on how the process unfolds over time by adopting either a prospective or a retrospective longitudinal design. Choice of a specific design, however, depends on the focus of your research, so we will look at options in relation to each of the three applications of process thinking.

Researching change and development processes

Process thinking is commonly used in the context of managing change and development. Models of product and organizational life cycles or stage models of innovation and change are all examples of this approach. Research in this area involves identifying an entity, such as an individual, an organization, or innovative idea that goes through a series of 'events' over time. Unlike cause-and-effect theories that explain outcomes in terms of independent and dependent variables, process theories explain them in terms of sequences of events: do A, then B to get to C (Langley, 1999). Events rather than independent and dependent variables are therefore the building blocks of this kind of process theory. They can include activities such as meetings, administrative reviews, communications, people-related events such as changeover of personnel or roles, changes in the external environment, or outcomes of the process.

The research design can be deductive to test an existing process theory, or inductive or abductive to build process theory. It may use qualitative, quantitative, or mixed methods for collecting and analyzing the data. Despite these differences, we can nevertheless identify common features of this approach.

- Collecting data that will offer insights into process, context, and development over time. Data collection can involve a range of techniques, including interviews, observation, questionnaires, archival, or other documentary data and participant diaries using the logic of triangulation (Pettigrew, 1990).
- Analyzing the data to identify events that are relevant to the process. Event identification can be done deductively, based on event types drawn from prior theory or carried out inductively from the data (Van de Ven, 2007).
- Developing a time-ordered sequence of events.
- Explaining what is causing the event sequences that are observed. This is the domain of process theorizing and can involve looking for common patterns across different cases and explaining how and why process and context interact to produce differences in outcomes across different cases (Pettigrew, 1992).

Research in practice 4.5 A process model of how groups
learn from other groups

Although prior research has indicated that group performance can be enhanced as a result of learning from other groups – so-called vicarious group learning – less attention has been paid to the process by which this happens. Bresman's (2013) study of research and development (R&D) teams sets out to address that gap by investigating how groups change their way of working by using vicarious learning.

The research is a multiple case study examining eight R&D teams across two different sites in a pharmaceutical company recently formed from the merger of two smaller firms. In the absence of sufficient prior theory, the researcher adopted an inductive approach, starting 'with specific observations from which general patterns are identified and theory developed' (Bresman, 2013: 39). Data were collected using a combination of semi-structured and informal interviews, observation, attendance at meetings and other events, along with secondary data such as project reports and process manuals. Analysis was carried out by developing individual case histories, with attention being paid to the sequence of events in each case, before moving on to cross-case analysis. The research identified a four-stage process model of vicarious learning consisting of

1. identification of another group with relevant experience;
2. translation of the knowledge of the other group to assess its value;
3. adoption of the knowledge by the learning group in the form of a change in its routines;
4. continuation in which the learning group decides whether to continue to use the new routine.

The study concludes that the process of vicarious learning by groups is more varied than previously believed and is 'rarely a matter of simply finding and copying best practice routines exactly and in full, but instead is better seen as a set of distinct interlinked activities unfolding over time, each with its own unique demands' (Bresman, 2013: 58).

4.5 TIME HORIZON

The third important decision to take early in your project is the time horizon for your proposed study. Do you want to track events through time or take a single cross-sectional 'snapshot' of the current situation? This decision is driven by your research question and has major implications for your research design. There are three main options, as we explain here.

4.5.1 Cross-sectional studies

Cross-sectional studies (also known as one-shot studies) involve gathering data on your topic at a single, specific point in time. Whilst the term is often linked to quantitative survey research, qualitative studies, such as in-depth interviews, also use cross-sectional designs. Cross-sectional studies can be used to address a range of research questions where the focus is on the current state of the phenomenon of interest, for example, current levels of customer satisfaction or attitudes to a new product. Although in practice you might have to carry out data collection over several days or weeks, due to practical constraint, the nature of cross-sectional studies means that data collection is time-bounded, which brings practical benefits for the researcher. Nevertheless, cross-sectional designs face a major problem when it comes to investigating situations where you need to assign some chronological sequence to events. This can arise, for example, in explanatory research where you want to be sure that a potential cause precedes an effect and not the other way around. Similar problems identifying chronological sequence occur when researching how things change over time. An alternative solution is to carry out a **longitudinal study** to gather data on subjects or events over time.

4.5.2 Prospective studies

A longitudinal research design that follows events as they happen is known as a **prospective study**. Prospective studies do not necessarily involve continuous data gathering.

Instead data may be collected by making repeated observations at specific points in time using cross-sectional techniques, for instance before and after a change management initiative. **Panel studies**, which follow a group of subjects over a time, are classic examples of this type of prospective study. The British Household Panel Survey (ISER, 2022b), for instance, has collected data by questionnaire annually from a representative sample of over 5,000 households in the United Kingdom since 1991. Ethnography (Section 6.3), on the other hand, is an example of a longitudinal qualitative research design where data collection is done during the more continuous presence of a researcher in the research setting.

Longitudinal research provides a way of investigating the effects of time, as well as in some cases allowing you the opportunity to immerse yourself in the research setting. By definition, however, data collection for prospective longitudinal studies will take longer than for cross-sectional ones. There are also other issues that can jeopardize the findings, such as loss of access to the research site or the withdrawal of participants during the study. In addition, some events of importance are not known about in advance, so that a prospective longitudinal study is not feasible. Natural or other disasters fall into this category. In such situations, you may have no option but to study events retrospectively.

4.5.3 Retrospective studies

A **retrospective study** is a form of longitudinal research design that takes place after the events of interest have happened. This raises the challenge of gathering data on past events. Where reliance is placed on the memory of respondents, serious concerns can arise regarding the accuracy of their recall. According to Miller et al. (1997: 189), problems can arise from 'inappropriate rationalisation, oversimplification, faulty post hoc attribution and simple lapses of memory', to which they add the problem of respondents giving answers to present themselves or their organizations in a 'socially desirable' way. In some situations you may be able to use multiple respondents or other sources of data such as company records or other contemporary documents in order to corroborate your findings. Although this can reduce the problems of relying on human recall, there may still be gaps or inconsistencies in retrospective data, so careful attention needs to be paid to data collection.

4.5.4 Implications for your research

During your research design you will need to decide the time horizon for your project. The key driver should be your research question. Can it be answered using a cross-sectional design or is a longitudinal study needed? If the latter, is a prospective or a retrospective design appropriate? Practical considerations will also play a part in the decision. Particularly if you are doing your research for an academic award or for an external client, the time allowed for your project is likely to be fixed, so you will need to make sure that you can complete data collection in the time available. In addition, you should be aware of any problems that may arise during the course of data collection, such as loss of access to the research site.

4.6 PRIMARY AND SECONDARY DATA

The fourth decision area involves whether to collect new data for your project or to use existing data that have been collected for a different purpose. This is the distinction between primary and secondary data.

4.6.1 Primary data

The term **primary data** refers to any data that are collected specifically for the purposes of the research project being undertaken. The data have therefore been collected to answer your own specific research questions, and you are the first user of that data. Primary data can be quantitative or qualitative. In most cases (particularly in a student research project), you are likely to be playing an active role in the actual data collection process. In other situations data collection may be outsourced, for example, to a market research agency. Nevertheless, the term 'primary data' is still applicable.

4.6.2 Secondary data

Secondary data refers to data that were collected, usually by someone else, for purposes other than your own investigation. Examples of secondary data include government statistics, such as census data, or research generated by other research projects such as the British Household Panel Survey that we mentioned earlier. Another important category of secondary data is the data generated by organizational activities, such as customer and employee data and company financial or operating records. Data of this kind are sometimes referred to as administrative or bureaucratic data and are a valuable source for business and management researchers. With the benefit of sophisticated technology now available, both at individual (e.g. customer or citizen) and organizational level, it is possible to capture, store, and analyze ever greater digital data sets that can be used as research data. Referred to as **Big Data,** these extensive data sets can be a source of secondary data, which we explore further in Chapter 12. **Secondary data analysis** (also known as **secondary analysis**) is the reanalysis of these types of data to answer a research question that is distinct from that for which the data were originally collected. The Institute for Social and Economic Research website (ISER, 2022a), for example, lists over 1,000 journal articles that have made use of British Household Panel Survey data. Although much of this sort of data is quantitative, available qualitative data sets, for example, from earlier qualitative research projects, can also be subject to secondary analysis.

4.6.3 Choosing your data type

In choosing what type of data to use, you need to consider the relative advantages and disadvantages that each offers. The main benefit of using primary data is the ability to target data collection precisely to the needs of your research project, thereby ensuring that you have relevant data in the format you want. Additionally, you will be familiar with the data and the quality of the collection process. Against this you have to weigh issues of access, cost, and time that may limit your ability to collect yourself the data that you need. Technology today does enable data collection in a more convenient, cost-efficient, and timely manner. For example, qualitative interviews can be conducted online using virtual meeting software, or quantitative data can be collected using online survey software. You can learn more about these techniques in Chapters 10 to 12.

Using secondary data potentially offsets some of these disadvantages. In particular it may offer access to much larger and better-quality data sets than you would otherwise be able to obtain. Secondary data that have been collected over a period of time can also be used for retrospective analysis. Problems with secondary data can include the size and complexity of the data set, lack of familiarity with the data, and the collection methods used. Moreover, because the data were not specifically gathered for your current project, not all relevant variables may be included, or those that are may be defined differently. Administrative secondary data that have been collected by organizations in the course of their normal activities are also more likely to reflect the collector's interests than yours and may tell you more about the way the organization works than what the data are supposed to represent (Gomm, 2008). Issues of privacy and data protection must also be addressed when using organizational data such as customer records. You are not, however, limited to choosing only one type of data in your project: mixing data types is not unusual and offers further opportunity for **triangulation**, although it can complicate aspects of data collection and analysis. We look at secondary data collection in more detail in Chapter 12.

4.7 QUALITY IN RESEARCH

What does it mean to do good research? One way of answering this question might be to lay down fixed criteria for what constitutes 'good' research. For some writers this means taking the natural sciences as a model, adopting what is sometimes characterized as the 'scientific method', often equated with the hypothetico-deductive approach. As you may imagine, this view is not shared by all researchers. The assumption that the methods of the natural sciences are applicable to the social sciences has long been contested (Guba and Lincoln, 1989), whilst others question whether the standard image of the scientific method is applicable even to the natural sciences, let alone the social sciences (Bhaskar, 1989). Other writers have called into question the possibility of 'objective' science that many accounts of the scientific method emphasize (Johnson and Duberley, 2000) and its association with deduction and, by implication, quantitative research. Behind much of this debate lie competing philosophical worldviews, as we discuss in Chapter 1. However, as Silverman (2022: 432) points out, 'short of reliable methods and valid data conclusions, research descends into a bedlam where the only battles that are won are by those who shout the loudest'.

In the face of such disagreements, Robson and McCartan (2016: 15) propose that researchers should take what they call a 'scientific attitude'. As discussed in Chapter 1, this involves doing research systematically (thinking carefully about what you are doing, how and why), sceptically (subjecting your findings to scrutiny and possible disconfirmation), and ethically (conducting your research so as to ensure the interests of participants are respected). These three criteria would seem a sound guide for research, regardless of your chosen research method or philosophical position. Seale (1999: x) takes a similar stance in advocating 'methodological awareness', emphasizing that you should be 'always open to the possibility that conclusions many need to be revised in the light of new evidence'. Thus the reaction against the assumption of a unified scientific method does not inevitably mean the abandonment of rigour in research or that anything goes.

4.7.1 Quality criteria

Disagreements over status of the 'scientific method' show how difficult it is to establish commonly agreed quality criteria against which we can judge our own research and that of others. Therefore, although we begin by introducing the traditional quality criteria of validity, reliability, and generalizability, you should be aware that these are closely associated with quantitative research and are by no means universally accepted. To complement them we therefore conclude this section by looking at an alternative framework that has been proposed, particularly in the context of qualitative research projects.

Validity

At its most basic, **validity** is about whether your research findings are really about what they claim to be about. Quantitative researchers in particular have developed a complex conceptualization of validity, supported by a range of techniques to assess validity. Some of these focus on the validity of any measures used in the research, such as questions in a questionnaire. Here a key question is whether or not the measures actually measure what they are supposed to measure. For example, does a set of questions in a questionnaire really measure customer satisfaction? Other validity criteria focus more on the validity of the overall research design, in particular the extent to which any causal claims are valid. Table 4.2 summarizes some of the main aspects of validity, particularly as used within quantitative research.

Reliability

Reliability in quantitative research is concerned with the stability and consistency of the measures that researchers use. In the case of a set of questions in a questionnaire, for example, you would want to be confident that they gave the same results if the measure were repeated. As with validity, a number of different dimensions of reliability can be identified, as summarized in Table 4.3.

Generalizability

Generalizability (also known as **external validity**) concerns the extent to which your research findings are applicable to people, time, or settings other than those in which the research was conducted. In quantitative research, this is often done using a process of

TABLE 4.2 Dimensions of validity

Dimension	Definition
Construct validity	The extent to which a measure actually measures the underlying concept it is intended to measure.
Content validity	The extent to which a measure captures all of the dimensions of the concept it is intended to measure.
Convergent validity	The extent to which a measure for one concept is correlated with another measure that measures the same underlying concept. Contrast with discriminant validity.
Criterion validity	The extent to which a measure of a chosen variable predicts the value of another variable known to be related, for example, how well a score on a course entry test predicts performance on that course.
Discriminant validity	The extent to which a measure for one concept is not correlated with another measure that measures a different underlying concept. Contrast with convergent validity.
Ecological validity	The extent to which findings from research in an artificial environment, such as a laboratory, hold in natural settings, such as the home or work-place.
External validity	The extent to which research findings are applicable to people, time, or settings other than those in which the research was conducted. Also known as generalizability.
Face validity	A subjective judgement of the extent to which a measure appears 'on the face of things' to measure what it is supposed to measure.
Internal validity	The extent to which causal inferences about the relationship between two or more variables can be supported by the research design.

statistical inference to make generalizations about the population from which the research sample was drawn. Technically, this is the limit of generalization that is possible statistically (Bell et al., 2022). An alternative approach that does not rely on statistical inference is known as analytic or theoretical generalization. Yin (2015) sees this as a two-stage process in which the researcher proceeds via the development of theory on the basis of research findings to draw out the implications for other settings in which such theory might be relevant. Yin cites the example of a well-known case study of the 1962 Cuban

TABLE 4.3 Dimensions of reliability

Dimension	Definition
Internal consistency reliability	The extent to which items in a multi-item scale are related. Often measured using **Cronbach's alpha**.
Inter-rater (or inter-observer/coder) reliability	The degree of consistency between two or more coders when coding the same set of data. Also known as intercoder reliability.
Test-retest reliability	The extent to which a measure will give the same result if it is repeated.

missile crisis to show how a single study can inform understanding of superpower confrontation in other situations.

4.7.2 Alternative quality criteria

Imposing a one-size-fits-all universal framework raises both theoretical and practical problems. The theoretical problems relate to the appropriateness of using a single set of criteria to judge very different forms of research, sometimes motivated by different philosophical worldviews. The practical problems relate to the difficulty of applying criteria created, for example, for a quantitative survey study to a qualitative ethnography. Not surprisingly, alternative criteria have been proposed, particularly with respect to evaluating qualitative research. Some of these are based on philosophical assumptions that are very different to those claimed to underpin the 'traditional' quality criteria. Here we will illustrate one well-known framework proposed by Lincoln and Guba (1985) in their book *Naturalistic Inquiry*. Lincoln and Guba (1985: 290) argue that researchers need to establish the 'trustworthiness' of any research findings in order to demonstrate that research findings are worth paying attention to. This, they propose, involves addressing four criteria (Table 4.4).

Helpfully, Lincoln and Guba also put forward a range of techniques that can be used to help researchers meet the criteria or confirm that they have been met. These are summarized in Table 4.5.

Lincoln and Guba's framework has been critiqued, not least by the originators, but it provides a helpful alternative perspective to complement validity, reliability, and generalizability as the dominant language and yardstick for quality in research. Further details on the practical aspects these techniques are given in Chapter 14 when we discuss qualitative data analysis.

4.7.3 Implications for your research

Both as part of your research design and as part of your final write-up, you will need to demonstrate the quality of your research. In the first place, regardless of your preferred

TABLE 4.4 Trustworthiness criteria (Lincoln and Guba, 1985)

Criteria	Dimensions
Credibility	Giving confidence in the 'truth' of the findings, in terms of the alignment between the researcher's findings and the lives and experiences of respondents
Dependability	Demonstrating that the findings are consistent and could be repeated
Confirmability	Showing that the findings of the study are shaped by the respondents and not by researcher bias, motivation, or interest
Transferability	Providing sufficient information to allow the reader to assess the findings' relevance to other contexts; analogous to generalizability (external validity) in traditional criteria

TABLE 4.5 Trustworthiness criteria and proposed techniques for meeting them or confirming that they have been met (Lincoln and Guba, 1985)

Trustworthiness criteria	Proposed techniques
Credibility	1. Prolonged engagement with the field and respondents 2. Persistent observation, especially of features that appear to be particularly relevant 3. Triangulation of sources, methods, and investigators to cross-check data 4. Peer debriefing, exposing ideas to a non-involved peer who can help to keep the researcher honest and act as 'devil's advocate' 5. Negative case analysis, looking for negative cases to test emerging theory 6. Member checking (also known as respondent validation), feeding emerging and final findings back to participants for commentary and review
Dependability	Keeping an audit trail and having external audit of the processes used in the research
Confirmability	Keeping an audit trail and having external audit of the data and analysis
Transferability	Sufficient detail, including contextual information, to allow the reader to assess the relevance of the research findings for other situations

research design, you will need to show rigour in its conceptualization and execution. Second, you will need to address appropriate dimensions of research quality as they relate to your own research findings. Further guidance is given in the chapters on data analysis (Chapters 13 and 14).

CHAPTER SUMMARY

- Your research design is your plan for your research in order to answer your research questions; it provides the overall framework for the research and specifies the research methods and techniques to be used to collect and analyze the data.
- Deductive, inductive, and abductive approaches are three ways in which theory can be integrated into research. Deductive research emphasizes theory testing; inductive research is concerned with theory building; abductive research involves the iterative interplay of theory and data. Whatever approach is used, however, findings should always be open to further revision in the light of new evidence.
- There are three generic types of research questions: 'what', 'why', and 'how. Each requires a different approach to research design dependent upon the relationship between the proposed research and theory.
- Quantitative research designs emphasize quantification and measurement in the collection and analysis of data; qualitative research designs emphasize the collection and analysis of data non-numerically. Other distinctive characteristics can also be identified, but the degree to which they are present for a given design varies, and the quantitative-qualitative distinction is a controversial topic.
- Mixed method research designs in which qualitative and quantitative methods are combined in a single study can be characterized in terms of the sequencing and priority given to the different methods.
- Research data options include primary data collected specifically for the purpose of the project and secondary data collected for other purposes and reanalyzed for the current study.
- The time horizon of a research study can be cross-sectional or longitudinal. If the latter, it can involve studying events prospectively, as they unfold, or retrospectively, after they have happened.
- Quality is a contentious subject in research. Traditional criteria of validity, reliability, and generalizability are widely used but have been challenged, particularly for qualitative research, where alternative criteria for establishing trustworthiness have been proposed. Consequently, you will need to think about how you will establish the credibility of your research.

NEXT STEPS

4.1 Theory, research questions, and research design. Select one or more research articles from the literature you have reviewed so far in your topic area. Identify the approach used by the authors to integrate theory into the research design (deductive, inductive, or abductive). Why is this approach adopted? What types of research questions were being asked, and how does the research design help the authors answer their research questions? Identify the type of research method and data used by the authors. Would the approach be suitable for your research project?

4.2 **Time horizon**. Review the research articles that you have identified so far in your topic area. What time horizon is adopted in each study? Why was this time horizon chosen? How does it help the authors answer their research questions? What time horizon would be most suitable for your research project?

4.3 **Choice of data type**. Review the research questions for your project and identify the data you will need in order to answer them. What potential data sources (primary/secondary) are available? What are the strengths and weaknesses of each for your particular project?

4.4 **Research methods**. Review the research articles that you have identified so far in your topic area. What research method (quantitative, qualitative, mixed methods) are adopted in each study? Why was that method chosen? How does it help the authors to answer their research questions? What research method would be most suitable for your research project?

4.5 **Research quality**. Select one or more research articles from the literature you have reviewed so far in your topic area. How do the authors address the quality of their research? What quality criteria do they refer to in their article? How does this help to establish the credibility of their research for the reader?

FURTHER READING

For further reading, please see the companion website.

REFERENCES

Bailey, K. D. (1994). *Typologies and Taxonomies: An Introduction to Classification Techniques*. Thousand Oaks, CA: SAGE Publications.

Bell, E., Bryman, A. and Harley, B. (2022). *Business Research Methods*. 6th ed. Oxford: Oxford University Press.

Bhaskar, R. (1989). *The Possibility of Naturalism*. 2nd ed. Hassocks: Harvester.

Blaikie, N. and Priest, J. (2019). *Designing Social Research*. 3rd ed. Cambridge: Polity Press.

Bleske-Rechek, A., Morrison, K. M. and Heidtke, L. D. (2015). Causal inference from descriptions of experimental and non-experimental research: Public understanding of correlation-versus-causation. *Journal of General Psychology*, 142(1): 48–70.

Blumer, H. (1954). What is wrong with social theory? *American Sociological Review*, 19(1): 3–10.

Bresman, H. (2013). Changing routines: A process model of vicarious group learning in pharmaceutical R&D. *Academy of Management Journal*, 56(1): 35–61.

Cooper, B., Glaesser, J., Gomm, R. and Hammersley, M. (2012). *Challenging the Quantitative-Qualitative Divide*. London: Continuum.

Creswell, J. W. and Creswell, J. D. (2023). *Research Design. Qualitative, Quantitative and Mixed Methods Approaches*. 6th ed. Thousand Oaks, CA: SAGE Publications.

de Vaus, D. (2001). *Research Design in Social Research*. London: SAGE Publications.

Easterby-Smith, M., Jaspersen, L. J., Thorpe, R. and Valizade, D. (2021). *Management and Business Research*. 7th ed. London: SAGE Publications.

Flick, U. (2023). *An Introduction to Qualitative Research*. 7th ed. Los Angeles, CA: SAGE Publications.

George, A. (2022). *A Virtuous Profession? Understanding the Moral Purpose and Character of Coaches*. Master's dissertation, Henley Business School, University of Reading, Reading.

Gomm, R. (2008). *Social Research Methodology: A Critical Introduction*. 2nd ed. Basingstoke: Palgrave Macmillan.

Guba, E. G. and Lincoln, Y. S. (1989). *Fourth Generation Evaluation*. London: SAGE Publications.

Honderich, T. (ed) (1995). *The Oxford Companion to Philosophy*. Oxford: Oxford University Press.

ISER (2022a). *BHPS Publications [Online]*. University of Essex. Available at: www.iser.essex.ac.uk/bhps/publications (Accessed 30 December 2022).

ISER (2022b). *British Household Panel Survey [Online]*. University of Essex. Available at: www.iser.essex.ac.uk/bhps (Accessed 30 December 2022).

Johnson, P. and Duberley, J. (2000). *Understanding Management Research*. London: SAGE Publications.

Langley, A. (1999). Strategies for theorizing from process data. *Academy of Management Review*, 24(4): 691–710.

Langley, A. (2007). Process thinking in strategic organization. *Strategic Organization*, 5(3): 271–282.

Lincoln, Y. S. and Guba, E. G. (1985). *Naturalistic Inquiry*. Newbury Park, CA: SAGE Publications.

Maxwell, J. A. (2012). *A Realist Approach for Qualitative Research*. Thousand Oaks, CA: SAGE Publications.

Mazanec, J. A. (2007). New frontiers in tourist behavior research: Steps toward causal inference from non-experimental data. *Asia Pacific Journal of Tourism Research*, 12(3): 223–235.

Miles, M. B., Huberman, M. A. and Saldaña, J. (2020). *Qualitative Data Analysis*. 4th ed. Thousand Oaks, CA: SAGE Publications.

Miller, C. C., Cardinal, L. B. and Glick, W. H. (1997). Retrospective reports in organisational research: A reexamination of recent evidence. *Academy of Management Journal*, 40(1): 189–204.

Pettigrew, A. M. (1990). Longitudinal field research on change: Theory and practice. *Organization Science*, 1(3): 267–292.

Pettigrew, A. M. (1992). The character and significance of strategy process research. *Strategic Management Journal*, 13(S2): 5–16.

Popper, K. (2002). *Conjectures and Refutations*. London: Routledge.

Ragin, C. C. (1987). *The Comparative Method*. Berkley and Los Angeles, CA: University of California Press.

Reichertz, J. (2007). Abduction: The logic of discovery of grounded theory. In: Bryant, A. and Charmaz, K. (eds) *The SAGE Handbook of Grounded Theory*. London: SAGE Publications.

Robson, C. and McCartan, K. (2016). *Real World Research*. 4th ed. Chichester: John Wiley and Sons.

Rose, S., Clark, M. and Myers, A. (2022). *Sensory Input and Online Purchase of High Involvement Products: A Model of Purchase Intentions in the Absence of Physical Stores*. Henley-on-Thames: Henley Centre for Customer Management, Henley Business School, University of Reading.

Rose, S., Fandel, D., Saraeva, A. and Dibley, A. (2021). Sharing is the name of the game: Exploring the role of social media communication practices on B2B customer relationships in the life sciences industry. *Industrial Marketing Management*, 93: 52–62.

Sayer, A. (2000). *Realism and Social Science*. London: SAGE Publications.

Seale, C. (1999). *The Quality of Qualitative Research*. London: SAGE Publications.

Selvarajah, S., Deivanayagam, T. A., Lasco, G., Scafe, S., White, A., Zembe-Mkabile, W. and Devaku-mar, D. (2020). Categorisation and minoritisation. *BMJ Global Health*, 5(12): 1–3.

Shadish, W. R., Cook, T. D. and Campbell, D. T. (2002). *Experimental and Quasi-Experimental Designs for Generalized Causal Inference*. Belmont, CA: Wadsworth Cengage Learning.

Silverman, D. (2022). *Doing Qualitative Research. A Practical Handbook*. 6th ed. London: SAGE Publications.

Van de Ven, A. H. (2007). *Engaged Scholarship*. Oxford: Oxford University Press.

Yin, R. K. (2015). *Qualitative Research from Start to Finish*. 2nd ed. New York, NY: Guilford Press.

CHAPTER 5

Conducting research ethically and inclusively

CHAPTER LEARNING OUTCOMES

At the end of this chapter you will be able to

- explain the importance of ethical conduct and how to apply the principles of ethical research;
- identify ethical issues that are specific to online research and how to address them;
- ensure that diversity and inclusivity are appropriately addressed in a research project;
- identify ethical concerns within your own research project and be able to secure ethical approval for your project;
- understand the importance of codes of practice and be able to adhere to them;
- recognize the need for research integrity in addressing ethics and inclusivity in research.

5.1 INTRODUCTION

Ethical dilemmas in management have become widely discussed in the academic and practitioner literature, as well as in the wider media (Melé, 2019). Many business organizations and industries have developed rigorous ethical guidelines such as in food technology, pharmaceutical, artificial intelligence, IT, management consultancy, and health care (Perry, 2014; Yardley, 2017; Carroll et al., 2018). Such guidelines are both to ensure that research projects conducted in relation to products or services reach expected ethical and regulatory standards, as well as to provide guidance on expected organizational behaviour. For example, the emergence of products and services utilizing artificial intelligence. There is an increasing questioning of the moral and ethical responsibilities of the organizations involved in terms of the impacts on customers and the wider society. The research and development of new-to-the-world products such as driver-less cars, facial

DOI: 10.4324/9781003381006-7

recognition technology, or automated healthcare diagnoses, all raises questions both about moral decision-making (the appropriateness of developing such products) as well as the ethical responsibility and consequences of those organizations researching and producing them (Liao, 2020). Similarly, as a researcher today you also need to be aware of ethical dimensions of your own research and potential ethical risks.

Ethics concerns what is right or wrong about a particular course of action (Singer, in Remenyi et al., 1998). When carrying out a research project you must ensure that you fully understand the ethical implications of your decisions and how your actions may impact both on those directly involved in the research and on the wider community. In this chapter we introduce the topic of research ethics and highlight the importance of ethical behaviour in management research. We then discuss four key ethical principles in relation to the research process to help you apply these to your own research. This is followed by a discussion of the importance of ensuring any research is inclusive rather than biased by the exclusion of any particular group at any stage of the research design. Special consideration is given to ethical aspects of Internet-based research and the implications of conducting research online. We then look at codes of ethics and regulatory standards, their purpose, and the role they play in gaining ethical approval before commencing your research. Finally, we discuss researcher integrity and provide you with a simple way in which you can be raise your awareness of ethical issues in your own research project.

5.2 ETHICS IN RESEARCH

Research ethics is concerned with the appropriate conduct of research in relation to participants and to others affected by it. Over recent years, the research community has developed an increasingly formalized approach to ethical conduct in both social and business research. Organizations such as ESOMAR, the US Academy of Management, the UK's Market Research Society, for example, provide guidelines regarding ethical conduct (sometimes referred to as a Code of Conduct) both towards those participating in a research project and towards fellow researchers in their community or organization.

As a starting point for understanding your ethical responsibilities as researchers, it is useful to adopt a multi-stakeholder perspective. We can begin by identifying the key stakeholder groups who are impacted by the research process. These include the participants in the research study, the organization or institution on whose behalf the study is being undertaken, the wider society that may be affected by the research and also the researcher. This categorization helps you to understand the range of perspectives that need to be taken into account when conducting your research.

A number of ethical principles can be identified that underpin guidelines for ethical behaviour in research that address these different stakeholder perspectives. In Table 5.1 we summarize them as four key principles and indicate the main **ethical risks** that the researcher needs to consider. We then discuss each in more detail the following sections. These principles provide a useful structure to help you identify the ethical risks you should consider when designing your research project, as well as specific actions that you may need to take while carrying it out. They should be borne in mind throughout your study: before, during, and after your research project.

TABLE 5.1 Key ethical principles in research	
Key principle	Ethical risks to consider
Avoidance of harm or loss of dignity	• Protection from physical or psychological harm • Protection of personal dignity
Transparency and honesty	• Openness regarding the nature of the project • Informed consent • Absence of deception • Full disclosure of researcher affiliations
Right to privacy	• Anonymity • Confidentiality • Data protection

Inclusivity	• Lack of inclusivity in the following:
	  o The research team
	  o The research methods
	  o Sponsorship and/or funding
	  o Research dissemination

5.3 AVOIDANCE OF HARM OR LOSS OF DIGNITY

You have a duty of care as a researcher to ensure that anyone involved in your research remains free from physical and/or psychological harm. This is not limited to the actual respondents taking part but extends to those commissioning the research, recipients of the output of the research, as well as you or others who carry out the research.

Physical harm may result, for example, from some form of direct testing of a service or product, such as skin creams or hair dyes, upon participants. Alternatively, it may arise from insufficient safeguards for the safety of the respondents or the researcher in terms of the research site itself, such as meeting in an unsafe or isolated location. Psychological harm may occur where your research results in distress, anxiety, stress, embarrassment, or loss of self-esteem to others. Such conditions might arise, for example, as a result of insensitive or inappropriate questions during an interview or from a lack of respect for the dignity of others involved in the research. As researchers we therefore need to be aware of cultural differences in the perception of dignity and respect. For example, in some cultures it may be inappropriate for researchers to interview participants of a different gender or to do so without an escort. It is your responsibility as the researcher to consider the nature of your topic and how you intend to investigate it and whether, in so doing, you are likely to cause psychological harm to others.

Potentially harmful outcomes may be difficult for the researcher to recognize, given that they may be highly personal to the individual participant. As the researcher you need to try to step into the participants' shoes and look at the nature of the research, the wording of questions and any activities in which they will be involved, and identify potential harm. Understanding and being sensitive to the background and culture of your respondents is important. Having a research team from diverse and relevant backgrounds can ensure that the data collection method(s) and specific instruments used (e.g. a questionnaire) do not create distress for others. If this is not possible, prior discussions and pretesting of the research method(s) with those familiar with the research context can help you to identify potential sources of harm, as well as ways of avoiding them. When planning your research, you should document the safeguards you are putting in place to ensure the care and safety of those involved in your study, including yourself.

5.4 TRANSPARENCY AND HONESTY

The use of deception to trick respondents into participating in your research or to mislead them about the nature of the study is unethical. As Tai (2012: 219) defines it, deception can be thought of as 'any action designed to mislead others by distorting, falsifying, or misinforming individuals so that they are manipulated to react in a certain manner'. It includes actions such as lying, equivocation (being ambiguous or contradictory), concealment (omitting important information), exaggeration (overstating or extending the truth), and understatement (minimizing the scale of effect or truth) (Tai, 2012). It also includes attempts to deceive people into believing they are taking part in research when in fact the objective of the activity is something else, such as sales promotion or fund-raising, deceptive practices which have become known as sugging and frugging respectively (McGivern, 2022: 43). Research in Practice 5.1 presents a researcher's experiences of a form of deception in an ethnographic study.

Research in practice 5.1 Deception in social research

In discussing the relevance of informed consent and the role of ethical committees, Marzano (2007) reports on his own research conducted in a hospital in Italy in 2000 and 2001. This involved an ethnographic study on 'dying of cancer'. Marzano recounts how he was permitted by a consultant in an oncology unit to join teams of doctors (although he was not one himself) and attend meetings with patients even wearing a white coat to appear to patients as a doctor. Patients were not made aware of his true identity as a researcher, were not told that data was being collected, and no informed consent obtained to their data being collected and used. Marzano reports the growing concern that many in the hospital began to display at his presence as he moved from oncology to palliative care. Ultimately he was required to inform patients of his professional identity but not necessarily the nature of his research. He also writes of his own uncomfortable feelings as patients increasingly demonstrated trust in him, believing him to be a doctor.

In the ethical environment that exists today this form of deception to dying patients would not be deemed ethical given the significant invasion of the patients' privacy and dignity and potential emotional harm. As ethical committees have now become more widespread in Europe, Marzano (2022) makes the point that covert research has now been pushed to the margins due to the impact of ethical committees on restricting the nature of qualitative research involving deception or lack of transparency. What was once acceptable in research may now be seen as ethically questionable.

Any form of deception not only alienates your respondents but also, in the longer term, can have a negative impact upon the reputation of research by seriously undermining the acceptance and participation of the public in such activities. Transparency and openness are therefore important in a research study, and in this section, we introduce you to four key aspects of your research to consider.

5.4.1 Informed consent

One way of achieving transparency and honesty is to ensure that participants are able to make an informed decision as to whether or not they wish to participate in your research. Informed consent is achieved when participants are given enough information about the research to make an informed decision about their involvement and then give their consent on that basis. The principle of informed consent is therefore designed to prevent the use of deception as a means of recruiting people to take part in research.

Informed consent is also intended to prevent coercion and deception and to ensure that participants are involved of their own free will. It is an important ethical principle that people have the right to decide for themselves if they wish to be researched. Our example of the Aboriginal Peoples discussed in Research in Practice 5.4 is an example of a population's right to decide if they are researched and, if so, how this is conducted in an inclusive and culturally relevant way. Participants must therefore be given the right to withdraw from the study if they wish to do so, without facing any repercussions (even though this may be disruptive to your data collection). Informed consent may be particularly important in organizational research where an employee may feel obliged to take part or be told that they have to do so by their line manager. It is therefore important to discuss informed consent with managers when they are commissioning research amongst staff within their own organization.

Establishing informed consent

The process for establishing informed consent typically involves two steps. Firstly, you will need to generate an information sheet providing information about the nature of the research. This should provide sufficient information to the participant in order to decide whether or not they wish to take part. We provide a template based on one in use in one of the authors' own institutions as an example in Research in Practice 5.2.

Research in practice 5.2 Example information sheet for face-to-face interviews

_____ (Title of research project)

This research project investigates _____ (brief topic statement) in order to _____ (broad aims of the research). The research forms part of my _____ qualification at _____ (name of institution).

As part of the research I am interviewing people who _____ (are involved with particular situation/topic, have knowledge/experience of, etc.), and for this reason, I would like to invite you to take part. If you agree, you will be asked to participate in an interview of about _____ (number) minutes.

During the interview I will ask you questions on _____ (brief non-technical outline of subjects to be covered). You can choose not to answer any particular questions, and you are free to withdraw from the study at any time. With your permission, I would like to _____ (record/video the interview/take notes) for later analysis.

The data will be kept securely and destroyed on completion of the project. Your name and identifying information will not be included in the final report. The identity of your organization will not be included in the final report. [Delete if not applicable]

A copy of the completed _____ (project/summary of the project/summary of findings) will be available on request. [Delete if not applicable]

If you have any further questions about the project, please feel free to contact me at the email address provided.

Name of researcher: _____

Email address: _____

Date: _____

Secondly, you should confirm participants' willingness to take part. Such consent should be obtained before you start data collection and is typically required for all research studies involving human participants. The method of evidencing consent depends on the method of data collection, for example:

- For data collection by self-completed questionnaire (for example, online or by post), a disclaimer statement can be included in the introduction to the questionnaire. This should make it clear that by completing and submitting the questionnaire participants will be understood to be giving their consent to take part (see also Chapter 10).
- If the research involves face-to-face contact (such as an interview), evidence of consent is provided by signing a consent form. With the increased use of online interviews where the research may not meet the respondent face-to-face, an e-signature on a consent form or an email giving written consent is often used instead.

In Research in Practice 5.3 we provide you with an example of a consent statement for face-to-face interviews.

Research in practice 5.3 Example informed consent form for face-to-face interviews

_____(Title of research project)

1. I have read and had explained to me by _____ (name of researcher) the information sheet relating to the project and any questions have been answered to my satisfaction.

2. I agree to the arrangements described in the information sheet insofar as they relate to my participation.

3. I understand that my participation is entirely voluntary and that I may withdraw from the project at any time.

4. I agree to the interview being video/audio recorded. [delete if not applicable]

5. I have received a copy of this consent form and of the accompanying information sheet.

6. I am aged 18 or older.

Name of participant: _____

Signed: _____

Date: _____

If interviews are being conducted remotely, for example, over the telephone, evidence of consent can be provided in advance by email or by return of a paper copy of the signed consent statement. If you are administering a closed-ended questionnaire by telephone and no personal data or other identifying information are being collected, a verbal agreement by the participant in response to a suitably worded disclaimer statement by the researcher may be seen as adequate evidence of informed consent (on the grounds that the respondent can break off the phone call at any time). We recommend, however, that you confirm the requirements of your own organization or academic institution before commencing your research.

Evidencing informed consent

Providing evidence of informed consent is a requirement for many organizations and institutions. At first sight, it may seem onerous or likely to impede your ability to get an appropriate number of respondents. In practice, however, the process of gaining informed consent signals to potential participants that you are aware of ethical issues. This can play an important role where a research topic is particularly sensitive and where it is likely that participants may have concerns about the confidentiality of the data being collected. Similarly, informed consent is a mechanism to protect those such as children or the elderly who may be viewed as particularly vulnerable. When interviewing children (under 18 years of age) or those unable to give informed consent, perhaps due to incapacity, you should observe any local protocol or procedure and ensure that you have obtained permission via the informed consent of a parent, guardian, or carer. If your data collection is outsourced to a third party agency, you should ensure that informed consent is obtained by it. Ultimately it is your responsibility as the researcher to ensure all respondents are fully informed and given an informed consent form to sign. In Critical Commentary 5.1 we explore whether potential participants can ever be fully informed and whether an alternative approach should be considered.

If you are conducting your research as part of an academic qualification it is likely that your institution has its own guidelines and templates for use when evidencing informed consent. You should ensure that you understand and comply with the requirements of your institution with respect to informed consent.

CRITICAL COMMENTARY 5.1
Is informed consent truly feasible?

Whilst informed consent is now a recognized and required research practice, some researchers have increasingly questioned the feasibility of informed consent. The concept is based on the assumption that it is possible to provide a potential participant with all necessary information upon which they can make a decision about whether they wish to take part in a research study.

This is being questioned for a number of reasons. First this assumes that it is possible to inform someone fully of all aspects of a research project. Full information disclosure may be difficult due to the complexity or extent of a project. Researchers may differ on what they view as relevant information a participant needs to know. Should information such as the wider objectives, stakeholder involvement, or sources of funding be informed to participants? Second, there may be times when a researcher will not want to divulge the full subject matter of a project as this may distort the participant's perspective on the topic or existing level of information (measurement of which is part of the research objective). Most informed consent forms give a general statement of the nature of the research, and participants may only become fully aware of the topic after they have begun involvement. In such cases is this really informed consent? Potential participants may be told they can withdraw at any time, but will social constraints make a participant feel obliged to continue once having consented (particularly in 1-2-1 interviews)? Using social media for recruitment and/or distribution of surveys may particularly lead to limited levels of informed consent, a method often used by student researchers.

Researcher and author Helen Kara (https://helenkara.com) suggests that informed consent is in fact a myth. She argues that the research environment has now become so complex not just in terms of research topics but in terms of how data is subsequently stored and handled after collection or where research outputs may eventually appear and be distributed. She cites the example of researchers being asked by funders to retain and store data in open access repositories after completion of a project for further use by other researchers. Whilst this is a sensible use of data, Kara points out that consent may never have been given for this to happen. In such a situation according to the informed consent principle, a researcher needs to ask for further consent for this to happen if this was not previously 'informed', and this may be impractical. An alternative approach that Kara proposes is that rather than informing potential participants about the nature of the study, that researchers inform them about the potential risks of involvement, and based on this information participants form decisions about their willingness to be involved.

Source: Kara (2023)

5.4.2 Collecting data covertly

There may be occasions when a researcher wishes to collect data without the awareness of respondents that this is happening. This can occur, for example, in an ethnographic study where the researcher does not wish to be identified to a community or group, or in designs that include covert observation, such as mystery shopping, which is used in the service sector where an organization such as a retailer wishes to undertake observational work of customer/staff interactions in a store, uncontaminated by the known presence of a researcher. Covert observation is sometimes recommended on the grounds that awareness of the researcher can influence the normal behaviour of those being observed, so undermining the validity of your research.

The problem, of course, is that this goes against the principle of informed consent and the right to privacy. Differing views exist amongst researchers of the ethical position of such techniques and their effect upon those being observed. In the case of mystery shopping, for example, Wilson (2001) points out that it can be viewed as involving deception (e.g. service employees being led to believe that the customer is a real customer when they are not) and invasion of the right to privacy (e.g. staff being observed without their knowledge or without consent being given). You should be very cautious and seek further guidance if you are contemplating covert observation as part of your research project.

5.4.3 Researcher affiliation

Often research will be conducted on behalf of a particular organization, industry body, or association. Such organizations may provide funding or other forms of support. Consideration should be given to the degree to which such affiliations or connections are made explicit to participants, and also to those reading the findings, given the effect that such support may have upon the research outcome. Research affiliation, particularly if it involves funding, has the potential to affect the research agenda and how findings are presented. Increasingly now identification of affiliation is a requirement in management research reporting (academic or practitioner). This is consistent with, for example, researchers in the medical field, who must declare any affiliations or financial relationships with organizations involved in a research study, such as with a pharmaceutical or healthcare company. In the design and implementation of your study you should be aware of the effect of affiliation, for example when collecting data from competitors, who may feel they should be informed about all organizations connected to the project at the informed consent stage. You should also be aware of the subjective impact of your own personal affiliations upon your work as a researcher and of any conflicts of interest. For example, when conducting research for your own organization you should be aware of any subjective bias you may have, particularly if requested to conduct the study by someone senior to you in the organization. In such situations, you will need to take special care with respect to the principle of openness and transparency.

Affiliations and conflicts of interest should be clearly stated when presenting findings either in report form or by oral presentation (for example, at an academic conference).

5.4.4 Incentivization

Incentives are sometimes used to encourage participation. They may be in the form of financial incentive, a small gift (such as a pen) or entry into a draw for a prize. Whilst such incentives may encourage participation, they can also create a form of bias. Incentives may encourage participation by those not falling within the chosen target population but who agree to take part for the reward only. Alternatively, they may distort the way in which participants respond, for example, by encouraging particular answers for fear of losing the reward. As a researcher you should give careful consideration to the use of incentives and the effect they will have upon your sample's participation and the quality of the data. You should also be aware of the ethical issues that incentives raise. Participation in research must be free from coercion or undue influence, and The UK's Economic and Social Research Council (ESRC) states as follows:

> Payment should not override the principles of freely given and fully informed consent. Participants should know before they start the research that they can withdraw from the study without losing their payment.
>
> ESRC Consent Guidance (2023)

If you are thinking of offering incentives to potential participants, you should ensure that they are consistent with ethical codes of practice governing your research, and any incentivization methods must be described in your final report and declared in requests for ethical approval. The UK Market Research Society publishes useful guidance on administering incentives (MRS, 2015).

5.5 RIGHT TO PRIVACY

Privacy was originally defined in 1890 by Warren and Brandeis, writing in the Harvard Law Review, as 'the right to be let alone' (Nairn, 2009). Today we may view privacy in broader terms in relation to our personal space, but also in terms of our personal information. As a researcher you should respect the privacy of participants at all times. This means being aware of issues relating to anonymity and confidentiality.

5.5.1 Anonymity

Anonymity protects the personal identity of those taking part in research. This means ensuring that personal information about them as individuals and the data they have provided as part of your study cannot be identified by others. Anonymity may be easily achieved in large-scale survey study where personal contact details (e.g. name, address, email address) are not collected, so it is not possible to link a response to a particular individual, and all results are reported in the aggregate. Maintaining anonymity can be more problematic in qualitative research. At the data collection stage, with relatively small samples, the identity of the participant will be known to the researcher, so anonymous data collection is not really possible. Particular care must be given when reporting findings to ensure that it is not possible to work out the identity of a particular participant by the responses given. Various techniques can be used to protect anonymity, such as using pseudonyms for individuals or for organizations (e.g. by referring to organizations as Company A, TELCO, PHARMACO, and so on) and by replacing specific job titles with generic job descriptions (e.g. senior manager rather than finance director) when completing the final report.

5.5.2 Confidentiality

Confidentiality relates to the protection of the data provided by participants, who will expect that their views, opinions, or information they provide remain confidential and are not communicated to other individuals or organizations. As a researcher you will become privy to a lot of information and be responsible for its confidentiality. The data may be collected in a number or ways, some of which may be directly from the respondents or via online channels such as social media platforms. In Section 5.7 we explore in more details the ethical issues that arise from online research, including the question of confidentiality and privacy even when data is collected from what may be viewed as a public domain such as a social networking platform such as Facebook. Irrespective of the manner in which the data is collected, you will need to think about the security of the data and how you will ensure the confidentiality of the participants. In Section 5.5.3 we explore further the importance of data protection in research and how you should protect the security of both the personal information of participants and their data you collect.

A particular issue in a business research context is that the information revealed may be commercially sensitive and therefore raise concerns regarding disclosure to competitors. Alternatively, there may be instances where release of respondent information could result in someone being denied a service, such as a welfare benefit, a loan, or a product upgrade. More serious ethical dilemmas can arise where the researcher becomes aware of information that should be reported to external authorities regarding illegal activity such as child abuse. In such situations you will need to balance ethical issues regarding confidentiality with your legal and moral position.

5.5.3 Data protection

In order to ensure anonymity and confidentiality you will need to think about the security of your data, whether it is online, held on your computer or other storage device, or in print or hand-written format. In addition to your ethical and legal obligations, this is also good practice to avoid loss or corruption of data disrupting your project. Backing up data storage (as well as your own work) is essential to prevent the distress of losing your work.

In addition to an ethical obligation to respect confidentiality, legal and regulatory controls exist in most countries regarding data protection. For example, in the European Union the General Data Protection Regulation (EU) 2016/679 (GDPR) introduced stringent legal requirements that protected the processing of personal data when people interact with public or private organizations for the provision of services (but not for personal activity). Following the UK exit from the EU, a separate UK GDPR was introduced from 1st January 2021 covering the processing and collection of sensitive personal data which closely aligns to the EU GDPR with some modifications for the UK context. From June 2021 the UK Government and the EU agreed the basis upon which personal data can be shared and safeguards for this until 2025 (ICO, 2023). Given that many UK organizations will continue to operate across the EU, understanding and adhering to EU and UK GDPR is important.

Personal data 'means any information relating to an identified or identifiable natural person (data subject)' (Caride, 2021: 44). This includes personal information such as name, date of birth, or address, as well as other information such as racial origin, religious affiliations, or political views. It also includes data collected from participants during a research study such as surveys, one-to-one interviews, or focus groups. Of particular importance within GDPR is the concept of consent on the part of the individual, that they freely agree to the collection and processing of their personal data. In research terms this requires you as the 'data controller' to ensure that participants give active consent, which can be by electronic or paper-based methods.

Additionally, you are responsible for the storage and handling of the data collected and maintaining its anonymity and confidentiality. This may include consideration of any sharing of original raw data with others with whom the participant did not give consent. You should also be aware of the use of technology, in particular of recording systems. There is now increased use of web conferencing systems such as MS-Teams or Zoom to conduct and record interviews as well as the use of recoding/transcribing systems such as Otter.ai. Consent to the recording and subsequent use and storage of such data so that anonymity and confidentiality is maintained is essential (Sibinga, 2019). You should also confirm that the provider of any technology services that you intend to use is compliant with the relevant GDPR or other legislation.

Regulations also apply to data held by organizations and should be taken into account if your research involves accessing company databases on customers or employees. You will need to work with those responsible in the company for managing the data to identify what is allowed in terms of access to, and use of, such data. Remember that as a researcher it is your responsibility to be familiar with data protection regulations and to adhere to them. Whichever country you are working in, you should also ensure that you are familiar with any local legislation regarding data protection.

You will also need to decide what will be done with the data upon completion of the study. Depending on agreements made when the data were collected, a number of options are available, including:

- secure destruction of data on completion of the project (for an academic qualification this should normally be done only once the award has been confirmed)
- secure storage for later reanalysis (subject to agreement at the time of collection)
- return to the owner of the data and secure destruction of any copies.

Ensure that you understand the rules of your own institution regarding storage, handling, and destruction of data and seek guidance where necessary.

5.6 INCLUSIVITY IN RESEARCH

Equity, diversity, and inclusion (EDI) is now a central focus of both government and commercial organizations. McKinsey (2022) refer to this as 'three closely linked values held by many organizations that are working to be supportive of different groups of individuals, including people of different races, ethnicities, religions, abilities, genders, and sexual orientations'. Inclusivity is particularly focused on ensuring all people, irrespective of background or characteristics, are embraced either in an organization or activity. This is similarly important within research. For research outputs to be meaningful and relevant to organizations and society, research design must be inclusive across all elements of a project. Research that is biased due to lack of inclusivity at the design stage fails to inform adequately and ultimately leads to distortion of knowledge and understanding of the world. As Asmal et al. (2022) state, 'research populations and outcomes should reflect the diverse nature of their population of interest, which is an important basis for acceptance of the accuracy and representativeness of the research output'. Mills and Sachdev (2021) point to the danger of consistent generalizing of findings drawn from narrow samples lacking in diversity. Most often these come from what has been referred to as WEIRD populations: Western, educated, industrialized, rich, and democratic (Henrich et al., 2010). This leads to potential bias and/or inappropriate application of research to other groups.

Asmal et al. (2022) point to four ways in which EDI can be improved in research:

1. The research team should be diverse in both composition and mindset. There should be inclusion of under-represented groups and a recognition of the effect that lack of inclusivity can have on differing perspectives adopted in the design and delivery. As a student researcher you may be working alone so we encourage you to reflect on your awareness of inclusivity as you proceed with your project.

2. The selection of research methods and in particular the manner in which samples are recruited can be barriers to inclusion and should be carefully considered. Student research samples are often obtained via convenience or snowball sampling (see Chapter 9). This may lead to samples that are closely aligned to the characteristics of the researcher and may exclude others. The framing of your research questions should be carefully considered as these may in themselves exclude particular groups by leading to narrow sampling criteria.

3. The sponsorship or funding of research can in itself lead to bias in terms of the topics and areas of interest explored by researchers. Where research is being supported by an external organization or agency, the researcher should be aware of any biases that may exist in the framing of the research topic or objectives being set. Increasingly sources of funding are now being linked to expectations of how EDI is demonstrated in the project.

4. Research dissemination is important if the value of knowledge creation is to be equitable and freely available. Increasingly open access opportunities are making research more widely available, and greater access to public reporting such as at diverse types of conferences is encouraged.

In Research in Practice 5.4 we discuss inclusivity and recognition of different ethical values in Aboriginal Peoples research in Canada.

Research in practice 5.4 Inclusivity and ethical understanding in Aboriginal research

The term Aboriginal refers to the indigenous peoples who were the first inhabitants of a country before colonization. In the context of Canada, the term refers to the First Nation, Inuit and Métis Peoples, as referenced in the Canadian Constitution. Early research conducted into Aboriginal Peoples was most often from a Western perspective. A paper by Castellano (2004) challenges the relevance of such research and in particular the appropriateness of applying Western research approaches and ethics in this context. It is suggested that as a consequence the purpose and activities of such research were often irrelevant to the communities themselves and the outcomes often 'misguided and harmful' (Castellano, 2004: 98). Castellano questions the relevance of Western research philosophies and discusses the differences in 'how Aboriginal perceptions of reality and right behaviour clash with prevailing norms of western research' (Castellano, 2004: 98). In particular that the Western positivist scientific philosophy of research is at odds with Aboriginal philosophies. Positivist thinking is concerned with identifying and measuring observable phenomena, and yet in the Aboriginal culture the 'boundary between material and spiritual realms is easy crossed' suggesting that Western research methods may fail to recognize the important interconnection between the human, natural, and spiritual worlds in the Aboriginal culture.

Catellano proposes a set of principles when researching the aboriginal community that includes inclusivity, that the Aboriginal People must be central to research that 'generates knowledge affecting their culture, identity and well-being' (Castellano, 2004: 98) either as principal researchers or partners in research. The discussion of how researchers have sought to investigate and understand the lives of Aboriginal Peoples demonstrates the need for inclusivity and cultural awareness in research design and practice to ensure that the community under investigation are integrally involved and that research philosophy and practice must recognize and be consistent with the culture and philosophies of the community being researched.

5.7 ETHICS IN ONLINE RESEARCH

The Internet has become an increasingly important medium for researchers from three perspectives. Firstly, it is in itself a phenomenon of interest for research, for example, exploring how consumers use the Internet as a medium for buying, obtaining information, or communicating socially with each other. Secondly, it is a source of data that researchers can use, such as data within blogs, posts, or websites. Thirdly, it is a channel that a researcher can use to collect data, for example, via online surveys or capturing social media exchanges within a community group. In this section we therefore discuss potential ethical issues when carrying out research online.

5.7.1 Public or private data?

Whilst the general ethical principles that we have discussed so far apply, online research does raise some particular issues. A fundamental question is whether data captured from the Internet should be viewed as public or private. The answer to this question has important implications for issues of privacy and confidentiality. On the one hand, individuals may have chosen to place their data in the public domain, such as on Tik Tok or Instagram, open for all to see. On the other, despite the public nature of the platform being used, individuals may nevertheless regard their data as 'private' (Lomborg, 2013: 23). In addition, as Williams et al. (2018: 32) observe, online interactions are 'shaped by ephemerality, anonymity and a reduction in social cues, leading individuals to reveal more about themselves', making people more open to revealing information not intended for other audiences. Consequently, they may have made their personal information more vulnerable (Hong and Thong, 2013). Therefore, although it is possible to argue that online postings made on a public platform are openly available to access, an alternative viewpoint is that the information was not originally provided for research purposes. You should be aware of this ongoing debate as you plan for and conduct any online research.

5.7.2 Use of the Internet as a channel for data collection

As we will see when we look at data collection in Chapters 10–12, the Internet has become a very important, sometimes almost the default, channel for data collection. In quantitative survey research, for example, use of online survey platforms has become the norm. In qualitative research, videotelephony services such as MS Teams and Zoom are now widely used for individual and group interviews. Regardless of the specific channel, it remains the researcher's responsibility to ensure that the ethical principles discussed so far are followed. This includes the securing of informed consent from participants; if video or audio recordings are being made, these also need to be agreed by those taking part. Information on anonymity, confidentiality, and data storage and handling also need to be provided. When using online channels for qualitative research, alongside the formal informed consent procedures, the researcher may have to work to build trust given the reduced contact with participants (Salmons, 2018). This can be achieved for example by enabling participants to find further credentials or information about the researcher(s) online. In addition, as noted earlier, as a researcher, you must also ensure that any online platform or service you are using is compliant with relevant GDPR and other requirements regarding data handling.

5.7.3 Use of social media derived data

In Chapter 12 we discuss the collection of data through social media either via the use of software tools that allow data to be scraped from social media platforms, via direct searching using search engines, or via direct contact with bloggers or influencers. Data collected from social media platforms may be more problematic than direct surveys or interviews from an ethical point of view. There has been much discussion as to whether capturing aggregated data from social media platforms requires consent or can be treated as 'non-personalized information' (Williams et al., 2018: 31). Whilst some online platforms allow or even facilitate researcher collection of public online communications, participants merely agreeing to the terms and conditions of a website does not fully constitute informed consent. In a review of user perspectives on ethics in online research, Williams et al. (2018: 48) suggest that researchers 'should consider users' views and expectations' as well as data protection laws when using social media data.

5.7.4 Taking part in online communities

An alternative online data collection method involves the researcher joining an online community and using the discussions and conversations as sources of data, for example as part of an online netnography study. In this case participants of the community should be made aware that their comments may be used as research data in order to meet the principles of transparency and honesty. To do otherwise would undermine the relationship of trust between the research community and other stakeholders. If you are intending to participate in an online community as a researcher, Harwood and Ward (2013) recommend that you always make your role as a researcher clear. This can be by direct contact with the community members via email, online posting, or an announcement on a bulletin board.

5.7.5 Reporting of online data

When reporting online data, as in the offline environment, you are similarly responsible for adhering to the ethical principle of transparency in the final reporting of data. You should consider carefully whether to report your findings with or without verbatim comments, as this may conflict with the anonymity of an individual and thus with the principle of protecting the personal identity of respondents and avoiding distress or harm. Remember that a section of text in a research report can be copied into an Internet search engine and the originator identified as a result. Hair and Clark (2007) recommend that online researchers report the approach they have adopted with regard to ethical aspects of their work in order that the research practices and protocols used can be appropriately understood and assessed. In addition, as always, you should ensure that you are compliant with any legal, professional, organizational, or institutional guidelines and requirements regarding handling of online data.

5.8 THE ROLE OF CODES OF ETHICS AND GAINING ETHICAL APPROVAL

Ethical guidelines and codes of practice are provided by many research and industry associations or governing bodies. They have emerged alongside a general increased awareness of ethical responsibilities and, specifically within the research community, concerns about the impact of unethical research. Ethics codes of practice provide guidance and procedures with respect to the conduct of research. DeLorme et al. (2001) suggest that they can serve a number of purposes. Firstly, they aim to protect participants from harm or distress, but they also set expectations for participants as to how they will be treated by researchers. Secondly, from a researcher's perspective they are intended to encourage appropriate ethical behaviour by providing guidelines for them, but also guarding them from moral and/or legal problems. Finally, they create awareness of best practice within the research community and thereby encourage those in society to support what researchers do. In Table 5.2 we provide links to different organizations' codes of practice or ethical guidelines. In addition, your own organization or professional body may have its own code of practice, and if you are studying at a university, your academic institution almost certainly will do so. Make sure that you are familiar with any applicable guidelines before starting your research.

5.8.1 Research ethics committees

Many organizations, including most universities in the UK, have **research ethics committees** (RECs) or an equivalent body which is responsible for ensuring that appropriate ethical standards of research conduct are maintained. In a university, for example, this may involve the formulating and maintaining of ethical guidelines and codes of practice, reviewing research applications from an ethical point of view, and providing advice on matters relating to research ethics. There is considerable variation in the roles and responsibilities of RECs within universities, for example, in terms of what types of research are subject to formal review and to what degree of detail, but if you are a student researcher

TABLE 5.2 Research ethics: codes of practice and guidelines	
Organization	*Link to website*
Academy of Management (US)	https://aom.org/about-aom/governance/ethics/code-of-ethics
American Marketing Association (US)	https://myama.my.site.com/s/article/AMA-Code-of-Conduct
The Association of Internet Researchers (AoIR)	http://aoir.org/reports/ethics2.pdf
British Psychological Society (UK)	www.bps.org.uk/guideline/code-ethics-and-conduct
Economic and Social Research Council (ESRC)	www.ukri.org/councils/esrc/guidance-for-applicants/research-ethics-guidance/
ESOMAR Codes and Guidelines)	https://esomar.org/codes-and-guidelines
The Market Research Society (UK)	www.mrs.org.uk/standards/code-of-conduct

you should familiarize yourself early on in your project with any requirements that will be placed on your research.

5.8.2 Gaining ethical approval

Alongside the development of codes of ethics, many organizations, particularly academic institutions, have developed formal requirements for the ethical approval of proposed research projects. This typically involves the researcher submitting a written request for ethical approval. Depending on the nature of the research and the policies in place, this may be very detailed, describing all aspects of the proposed research in full. Alternatively, it may be a brief summary of the proposed research which is then reviewed to see whether further ethical clearance is necessary. The latter might happen, for example, if the proposed project involved working with vulnerable groups, and it was felt that closer scrutiny was required.

It is your responsibility as the researcher to be aware of your institution's and/or organization's procedure for approval and what is required of you. Make sure that you take ethical considerations into account at the planning stage so that you can design a research project that meets the requirements of ethical research. If your research is in an ethically sensitive topic (such as experiments on humans or research with vulnerable groups), you will need to be particularly clear regarding your plans and be prepared for further scrutiny before being allowed to proceed. If you are unsure about any ethical matters relating to your proposed project, you should seek advice from your supervisor or a representative from your institution's REC. Do not begin your research proper until you have secured approval to do so. Note that in some cases you may also have to get approval from more than one body (for example, research in healthcare environments may also require approval of the relevant healthcare authority).

Research in practice 5.5 Ethical Approval in a Mental Health Coaching Research Context

Coaching is a commonly used developmental intervention in organizations today. Coaches are required to recognize when a client may be exhibiting a mental health condition (MHC) and to understand the boundary between coaching and other therapeutic practices and refer clients for further treatment when necessary. A student studying for a MSc in coaching for behavioural change set out to explore what it means to be a coach with an MHC and how this can be managed when coaching. In order to do this, it required researching amongst a sample of coaches who had previously had, or still had, an MHC. Several ethical issues were identified at the design stage which had to be addressed in order to gain ethical approval from the institution's ethics committee.

First the committee would be concerned about the recruitment process and sensitivity to the identification of a MHC. A convenience sampling approach was applied using access to coaches via social media communities. The sampling criteria included the following:

- Can self-certify as having had, or still have, a professional/medically diagnosed mental health condition, but are able to function to a high level day to day, and dealing with coaching clients regularly.

After a prospective participant volunteered, an information email was sent out to them explaining the specific nature of the project and what would be involved and consent forms provided for signature. It was made clear that they could drop out of the research at any time if they wished to.

The protection of the privacy of the participants regarding their MHC was carefully considered and explained in the ethics approval request. No data was collected or stored about the nature of the MHC of a participant or their mental health history. Qualitative 1-2-1 interviews were conducted and so the data collection process involved recording and transcribing the participant's words. All data was stored confidentially and anonymously according to institutional guidelines. After data collection, the researcher emailed to each participant a copy of their transcription in order that they could verify it to be a true reflection of the interview and their willingness for their data to continue to be used. Reporting of data in the final report was anonymized, and all data was destroyed after completion of the project. A final copy of the report was also provided to each participant.

Given the sensitive nature of the research topic, the researcher had to demonstrate to the ethics committee how any distress or anxiety that the interview might cause or trigger would be addressed. A regular series of check-ins were undertaken at the start of the interview, at various points mid-way through the interview and two weeks afterwards. This involved the researcher making sure that the participant felt comfortable and whether they needed any support. If a participant exhibited signs of distress during the interview, the researcher offered to pause or stop, and in cases of extreme distress (which did not arise), they would have also verified if anyone was close-by to sit with them.

If a participant did report difficulties at any stage during or after interview, the research student was required to notify the programme director, and resources were put in place to support the participant. The researcher was also required to be aware of her own mental health and used reflexive practice to maintain herself in a good mental mindset. Addressing these various ethical issues ensured that ethical approval was awarded by the institution's research ethics committee.

Source: Kite (2022)

5.8.3 Following rules or behaving ethically?

Codes of practice, ethics committees, approval processes, and so on have been developed with the purpose of alerting individuals to the ways in which their decision-making or behaviour may contradict ethical criteria or impact on the rights of others. It is relevant to question whether or not this serves to develop ethical behaviour or just blind rule following. Bell and Bryman (2007: 63) point out that the imposition of codes of practice upon individuals 'may encourage instrumental compliance with minimal ethical obligations'. We have to recognize the distinction between merely following ethical procedures (such as completing approval forms or obtaining informed consent forms) and actively recognizing and accepting our responsibility for the rightness of our actions within a particular situation and adjusting our behaviour accordingly.

5.9 RESEARCHER INTEGRITY

Our final key ethical principle relates to the personal behaviour of ourselves as researchers. As researchers we must always act with integrity regarding the way in which we design, implement and report research. You should always conduct research in a way that upholds the previous principles we have discussed, that is to say, act in an honest and respectful way, with an awareness of your responsibility for the care and protection of all stakeholders and/or their data involved in your research.

5.9.1 Misrepresentation of findings

Researchers should take care to ensure that they do not, intentionally or unintentionally, misrepresent the findings. We are responsible for ensuring that the integrity and quality of a research project are not jeopardized by our own actions. The US Academy of Management (AoM, 2023), for example, requires that its members 'do not fabricate data or falsify results in their publications or presentations' [but] 'report their findings fully and do not omit data that are relevant within the context of the research question(s)'. As researchers we should take every care to ensure that our research is rigorous and professional and that we do not mislead the audience regarding the status of our research findings. We should also be mindful of our own influence on the research process. We can develop this awareness through reflexive practice, as discussed further in Chapter 1.

5.9.2 Reciprocity

Research involves one person, or group of people, investigating and exploring the world of another group of people. Often when this occurs, particularly within an organization, a significant difference in the power relationship will exist. Respondents may be less well informed and more vulnerable than the researcher, who may benefit from both their status as an 'expert' researcher and, in some cases, the perceived or actual backing of more powerful stakeholders. This may be a particular concern if the researcher is also a manager in the organization and is conducting the research amongst more junior staff, who may feel obligated to take part or to respond in certain ways. Principles such as informed consent, honesty, and transparency are essential to protect the participant in such cases.

Another response to this situation is to emphasize the need for reciprocity in the relationship between the researcher and participant, in which the research that is done is beneficial to both parties. One version of this is sometimes referred to as **participatory research**. This is not a particular method but instead represents a commitment by the researcher and participants to collaborate with respect to the goals, process, and outcomes of the research project. The degree of collaboration can vary from 'shallow' forms of participation in which the researcher still takes the lead, to 'deeper' modes of participation in which researcher and participants jointly own the agenda and process for the research (Cornwall and Jewkes, 1995). An example of a research design that is well suited to this type of approach is action research, which we introduced in Chapter 7.

5.10 IDENTIFYING THE ETHICAL DIMENSIONS OF YOUR OWN RESEARCH PROJECT

In order to help you to identify key ethical dimensions of your own research project, we provide in Table 5.3 a series of questions that you can ask yourself before, during,

TABLE 5.3 Key ethical questions to ask about your research

What should I consider before the study?	What should I consider during the study?	What should I consider after the study?
• Have I considered diversity and inclusion in my research questions and the selection of my research methods? • Will my sampling strategy ensure inclusivity and prevent any bias or exclusion in my population sample? • Am I aware of any bias from the sponsorship or funding of the research? • Will any physical or psychological harm be caused by my research? • Have I put in place appropriate measures for the safety of participants and anyone else involved in the research? • Have I pretested to check that I understand the impact of my research on respondents? • How will I ensure that coercion is not involved? • Have I prepared information sheets and informed consent forms? • Have I ensured that the research is free of deception?	• Do any of the respondents appear to be upset or distressed? • Am I being considerate of respondent characteristics such as gender, race, disability, or neuro-diversity. • Am I aware of everyone's safety, including my own? • Am I treating everyone with respect and dignity? • Am I ensuring that participants are fully informed of the nature of the research? • Have I collected all the informed consent forms? • Am I disclosing any researcher affiliations to participants? • Am I complying with requirements for anonymity and confidentiality? • Am I storing data securely? • Am I compliant with data protection legislation? • Are my research activities adversely affecting anyone in the wider community? • Am I complying with relevant ethical guidelines?	• Have I retained the informed consent forms for safe keeping, should there be any subsequent query? • Have I declared any affiliations when reporting my research? • Have I maintained the anonymity and confidentiality of the respondents in my final report? • Have I met my obligations regarding data destruction, continued storage, or return? • If relevant, have I ensured the dissemination of my findings to the wider community and inclusive of all relevant groups? • Have I met all my obligations to all stakeholders regarding the project? • Is the final research report free of misleading statements or misrepresentation of the data? • Have I complied with all relevant ethical guidelines?

What should I consider before the study?	What should I consider during the study?	What should I consider after the study?
• Have I put measures in place to ensure the anonymity and confidentiality of all participants? • Have I put in place arrangements for secure data storage? • Am I familiar with relevant data protection legislation? • Do I have permission to collect data from a particular source? • Will there be any impact on the wider community or society by the implementation of my research project? • Have I obtained relevant ethical approval?		

and after your study. We cannot be prescriptive in terms of providing answers to these questions because ultimately these are your decisions to take as the researcher, but these questions should help you by prompting you to think about ethical aspects of your work. As you look through them you may see that there are conflicts in terms of your ethical responsibility towards different stakeholders. For example, maintaining the confidentiality of a respondent regarding the information discussed in an in-depth business-to-business interview may conflict with the expected level of final reporting agreed by you with an organization. These issues should be identified and addressed during the planning stage. As a researcher you have to ensure that you consider all ethical principles and make appropriate decisions, irrespective of how they may affect or constrain your original research intentions. An illustration of the experience of dealing with ethical issues in a sensitive research topic area is given in Research in Practice 5.5.

CHAPTER SUMMARY

- Ethics in research is concerned with the rights and wrongs of how we conduct a research project. Ethical considerations should be made in relation to all stakeholders who are involved in, or affected by, a particular project.
- There are four key ethical principles to consider when planning a research project: avoidance of harm or loss of dignity, transparency and honesty, right to privacy,

and inclusivity. Each should be considered in terms of four key stakeholder groups: the researcher, the participants in the research study, the organization or institution on whose behalf the study is being undertaken, and the wider society or community.

- Inclusivity in research is achieved by consideration of the composition of the research team; the research methods, particularly sampling applied; the sponsorship or funding of the project; and the dissemination of the research outputs.
- The rise of the Internet as a medium for research means that researchers should be alert to how the four ethical principles apply in that context. We must still respect the privacy, anonymity, and confidentiality of respondents and maintain transparency and honesty in the handling and reporting of data.
- Researcher integrity refers to our own personal behaviour as a researcher. It is important that researchers act with integrity in the design, implementation, and reporting of their research.
- Ethical considerations should be identified at the planning stage of a research project and documented during the planning stage.
- Ethical codes of practice and guidelines have been produced by the leading research bodies. Academic institutions and funding bodies will have their own ethical regulation and approval procedures. It is imperative that a research project is compliant with such regulation and that appropriate ethical approval is obtained prior to commencing a research project.

NEXT STEPS

5.1 Preparing the ground. Familiarize yourself with any ethical guidelines or codes of practice that are relevant for your project, for example, those of the academic institution at which you are studying or of the organization or professional body of which you are a member.

5.2 Identifying ethical issues. Before undertaking this activity, look again at Table 5.3, where we provide you with a series of questions to ask yourself about the ethical context before, during, and after your research project. Then consider which of the following four aspects of your research design may raise an ethical issue for you: avoidance of harm or loss of dignity, transparency and honesty, right to privacy, and inclusivity. Think about how you are going to address them.

5.3 Preparing to apply for ethical approval. Confirm the ethical approval process that applies to your project and start preparing the necessary documentation, including information sheets and consent forms.

FURTHER READING

For further reading, please see the companion website.

REFERENCES

AoM (2023). *Code of Ethics [Online]*. Briarcliff Manor, NY: Academy of Management. Available at: https://aom.org/about-aom/governance/ethics/code-of-ethics (Accessed 8 February 2023).

Asmal, L., Lamp, G. and Tan, E. J. (2022). Considerations for improving diversity, equity and inclusivity within research designs and teams. *Psychiatry Research*, 307: 114295.

Bell, E. and Bryman, A. (2007). The ethics of management research: An exploratory content analysis. *British Journal of Management*, 18(1): 63–77.

Caride, C. G. (2021). Respecting the GDPR in online interviewed focus groups. *Journal of Audiovisual Translation*, 4(2): 42–61.

Carroll, A. B., Brown, J. A. and Buchholtz, A. K. (2018). *Business & Society: Ethics, Sustainability and Stakeholder Management*. 10th ed. Boston, MA: Cengage Learning.

Castellano, M. B. (2004). Ethics of aboriginal research. *International Journal of Indigenous Health*, 1(1): 98–114.

Cornwall, A. and Jewkes, R. (1995). What is participatory research? *Social Science & Medicine*, 41(12): 1667–1676.

DeLorme, D. E., Zinkhan, G. M. and French, W. (2001). Ethics and the internet: Issues associated with qualitative Research. *Journal of Business Ethics*, 33(4): 271–286.

ESRC (2023). *Consent Guidance*. Economic and Social Research Council. Available at: www.ukri.org/councils/esrc/guidance-for-applicants/research-ethics-guidance/consent/ (Accessed 20 March 2023).

Hair, N. and Clark, M. (2007). The ethical dilemmas and challenges of ethnographic research in electronic communities. *International Journal of Market Research*, 49(6): 781–800.

Harwood, T. G. and Ward, J. (2013). Market research within 3D virtual worlds: An examination of pertinent issues. *International Journal of Market Research*, 55(2): 247–265.

Henrich, J., Heine, S. J. and Norenzayan, A. (2010). The weirdest people in the world? *Behavioral and Brain Sciences*, 33(2–3): 61–83.

Hong, W. and Thong, J. Y. L. (2013). Internet privacy concerns: An integrated conceptualization and four empirical studies. *MIS Quarterly*, 37(1): 275–298.

ICO (2023). *Guide to Data Protection*. Information Commissioner's Office. Available at: https://ico.org.uk/for-organisations/guide-to-data-protection/ (Accessed 15 February 2023).

Kara, H. (2023). *Why Informed Consent is a Myth [Online Video]*. Available at: https://youtu.be/dEKB-DyMhrHA (Accessed 8 March 2023).

Kite, B. (2022). *Exploring Coaching with a Mental Health Condition*. Dissertation submitted for MSc Coaching and Behavioural Change, Henley Business School, University of Reading, Henley-on-Thames.

Liao, S. M. (ed) (2020). *Ethics of Artificial Intelligence*. New York, NY: Oxford University Press.

Lomborg, S. (2013). Personal internet archives and ethics. *Research Ethics*, 9(1): 20–31.

Marzano, M. (2007). Informed consent, deception, and research freedom in qualitative research. *Qualitative Inquiry*, 13(3): 417–436.

Marzano, M. (2022). Covert research ethics. In: Iphofen, R. and O'Mathuna, D. (eds) *Ethical Issues in Covert, Security and Surveillance Research*. Bingley: Emerald Publishing Limited.

McGivern, Y. (2022). *The Practice of Market Research: From Data to Insight.* 5th ed. Harlow: Pearson Education.

McKinsey (2022). *What is Diversity, Equity, and Inclusion?* McKinsey & Company. Available at: www.mckinsey.com/featured-insights/mckinsey-explainers/what-is-diversity-equity-and-inclusion (Accessed 25 April 2023).

Melé, D. (2019). *Business Ethics in Action: Managing Human Excellence in Organizations.* 2nd ed. London: Bloomsbury Publishing.

Mills, M. J. and Sachdev, A. R. (2021). Descriptives for diversity: Harnessing the potential of Table 1 to advance inclusivity and responsible generalization in psychological research. *Industrial and Organizational Psychology,* 14(4): 505–509.

MRS (2015). *MRS Regulations for Administering Incentives and Free Prize Draws.* London: Market Research Society. Available at: www.mrs.org.uk/pdf/Regulations%2520for%2520Incentives%2520and%2520Prize%2520Draws%2520July%25202015.pdf (Accessed 20 March 2023).

Nairn, A. (2009). Research ethics in the virtual world. *International Journal of Market Research,* 15(2): 276–278.

Perry, F. (ed) (2014). *The Tracks We Leave: Ethics and Management Dilemmas in Healthcare.* 2nd ed. Chicago, IL: Health Administration Press.

Remenyi, D., Williams, B., Money, A. and Swartz, E. (1998). *Doing Research in Business and Management: An Introduction to Process and Method.* London: SAGE Publications.

Salmons, J. (2018). Getting to yes. In: Woodfield, K. (ed) *The Ethics of Online Research.* Bingley: Emerald Publishing.

Sibinga, C. T. S. (2019). Ethical issues in qualitative data collection and management. In: Sibinga, C. T. S. (ed) *Scholarly Ethics and Publishing: Breakthroughs in Research and Practice.* Hershey, PA: IGI Global.

Tai, M. C.-T. (2012). Deception and informed consent in social, behavioral, and educational research (SBER). *Tzu Chi Medical Journal,* 24(4): 218–222.

Williams, M. L., Burnap, P., Sloan, L., Jessop, C. and Lepps, H. (2018). User's views of ethics in social media research: Informed consent, anonymity, and harm. In: Woodfield, K. (ed) *The Ethics of Online Research.* Bingley: Emerald Publishing.

Wilson, A. M. (2001). Mystery shopping: Using deception to measure service performance. *Psychology and Marketing,* 18(7): 721–734.

Yardley, D. (2017). *Practical Consultancy Ethics: Professional Excellence for IT and Management Consultants.* London: Kogan Page.

CHAPTER 6

Quantitative research designs

CHAPTER LEARNING OUTCOMES

After reading this chapter you will be able to

- recognize and evaluate the appropriateness of key quantitative research designs;
- select and justify an appropriate quantitative research design for your own research project.

6.1 INTRODUCTION

In this chapter we introduce a range of quantitative research designs that are used in business and management research. Each design is discussed in terms of its main characteristics and potential applications, along with strengths and weaknesses. Our aim in the chapter is to provide information to help you decide whether a specific quantitative research design may be suitable for your own research project. More details on how to carry out each design are presented in the companion website, along with suggestions for further reading. Data collection and analysis techniques are covered later in the book in Parts III and IV. The majority of designs we discuss here share, to varying degrees, the general characteristics of quantitative research that we introduced in Chapter 4. We begin with experimental designs, before looking at a range of nonexperimental approaches (Figure 6.1). We include a discussion of an increasingly important development in quantitative research: the growth in data-driven approaches. The chapter closes with guidance on the suitability of different research designs to answer different types of research question.

DOI: 10.4324/9781003381006-8

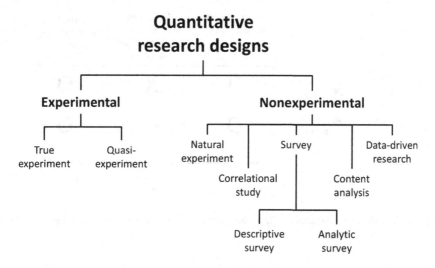

FIGURE 6.1 Quantitative research designs

6.2 EXPERIMENTAL AND QUASI-EXPERIMENTAL DESIGNS

Experiments are the classic quantitative research design for explanatory research. The key feature of an experimental design is that you deliberately vary something in order to find out what happens to something else in order to 'discover the effects of presumed causes' (Shadish et al., 2002: 6). Using the terminology we introduced in Chapter 4, you manipulate one or more independent variables to discover the effect on a dependent variable. Other characteristic features of experimental designs include a deductive approach, the use of **experimental controls** to eliminate extraneous influences, measurement of the effects of the manipulation, and the comparison of the resulting measures.

Figure 6.2 shows these features applied to a 'classic' experimental design that has a single **treatment group**, a **control group** and pre- and posttreatment measures. The levels of the dependent variable are measured for each group both pre- and posttreatment, but only the treatment group receives the treatment. Analysis focuses on the difference in pre- and posttreatment scores for the treatment group, as compared to the difference in pre- and posttreatment scores for the control group. If the change is greater in the treatment group, you would infer that this was due to the treatment, that is, the manipulation of the independent variable caused the change.

The extent to which you can be confident in making this causal claim is a function of the internal validity of the design. Even with the simple example in Figure 6.2, there are several potential threats to internal validity. There may be inaccuracies or inconsistencies

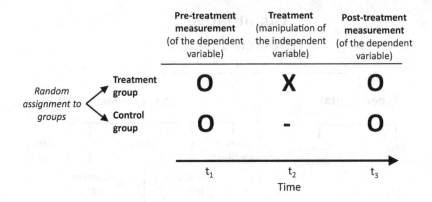

FIGURE 6.2 Classic experimental design with treatment and control groups and pre- and post-test measurement

in the measurement or the way the treatment is administered. If some participants leave during the course of the research or reject treatment, their dropping out may influence the results. Alternatively, particularly if the research is running over a long period, time alone may be introducing changes in participants, giving rise to what are known as **maturation effects**. The researcher may deliberately or unwittingly bias the results through their actions by, for example, behaving differently towards the treatment group, as compared to the control group, thereby leading to what are called **experimenter-expectancy effects**. Additionally, research participants may themselves react to the experience of being in an experiment. Some participants, for example, may be enthusiastic about taking part, and this could influence the outcome, regardless of the actual treatment, creating what are referred to as **subject-expectancy effects**. Experienced experimenters are, of course, well aware of these (and other) issues and seek to address them through careful design and conduct of the experiment.

To achieve high levels of internal validity, you could conduct your experiment in a laboratory or highly controlled environment. However, such experimental conditions may well be different to the normal lives of participants and the naturally occurring conditions of the phenomenon of interest. The term ecological validity is used to describe the degree to which the experiment is representative of the real world. One solution is to conduct your experiment in a natural setting. Such **field experiments** can have higher ecological validity than equivalent **laboratory experiments**, but it may be harder to achieve equally high levels of internal validity because of reduced control over the sort of threats discussed previously.

There are many variations in experimental research designs, but we can usefully distinguish between **true experiments**, which feature random assignment of participants to groups, and so-called **quasi-experiments**, which do not. The logic behind random assignment is that, with a sufficiently large sample size, random selection will ensure that the groups are comparable before treatments are applied, thereby reducing a potential threat to internal validity (Cook and Campbell, 1979). A quasi-experimental design may be the

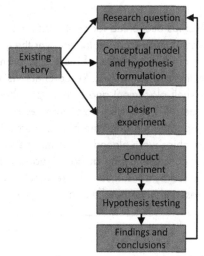

FIGURE 6.3 Steps in an experimental study

only option if random assignment is not possible, in which case careful attention has to be given to sampling procedures.

In Figure 6.3 we show the key steps to be followed when undertaking an experimental study. The variety and complexity of experimental designs precludes an exhaustive discussion, but the basic steps discussed here provide a starting point for approaching more complex experimental designs. We develop these steps in more detail in the chapter supplement on the companion website.

6.2.1 Applications of experimental designs

Experimental designs are primarily used for answering questions about cause and effect. Whilst some organizations, such as pharmaceutical or research and development companies, use experiments as part of their normal business activity, experimental research designs are relatively rare in organization and management research (Podsakoff and Podsakoff, 2019). Despite this, an understanding of the logic of experimental designs is essential to a critical understanding of other ways of doing causal research. Research in Practice 6.1 provides an example of a field experiment.

Research in practice 6.1 The effects of shelf placement on
consumer purchases of potato chips

Sigurdsson et al. (2009) used a field experiment to evaluate the effects of shelf placement on consumers' purchases of potato chips. The experiment involved an alternating treatment design in which the target brand of potato chip was placed on the high, middle, or low shelf in two budget stores. The dependent variable was the proportion of all unit sales of potato chips accounted for by the target brand. The treatment variable was the shelf placement; this was randomized over the course of the experiment to reduce threats to internal validity. Prices of the target brand were kept constant, as were other factors in the marketing mix. Researchers visited each store at least once a day to check on shelf placement and to note possible extraneous variables. In addition, the researchers also collected data on sales prior to the experiment to act as a baseline. The research found that the highest percentage of purchases was recorded when the potato chips were placed on the middle shelf, as compared to the high or low shelf. In their conclusions, the authors suggest that this might be due to lower response effort required by consumers. This research supports the findings from proprietary commercial research into the effects of shelf placement.

6.2.2 Strengths and weaknesses of experimental designs

The key strength of the experimental design is usually seen as its ability to address the causal criteria we identified in Chapter 5. According to Shadish et al. (2002: 6) 'no other scientific method regularly matches the characteristics of causal relationships so well'. Perhaps not surprisingly, the **randomized controlled trial** is often referred to as the 'gold standard' in evidence-based policy-making by both its critics and its advocates. Even when an experiment cannot be used, however, the logic of experimental design can be seen operating in other deductive, quantitative approaches to studying causality, as we will see in the next section.

Against these strengths we have to set some significant limitations that restrict the potential application of experiments within organization and management research:

- In many situations it is simply not feasible to carry out an experiment, for example, when the independent variable(s) cannot be changed by the researcher for practical reasons.
- Experiments involve manipulation of the treatment group, which introduces particular ethical concerns if the subjects are human or animal. Alternatively, it may be deemed unethical to deny treatment to a control group or to use random allocation to different groups. Ethical considerations can mean tight restrictions on what is possible or even rule out an experimental approach altogether.
- Experiments require access to participants willing to take part. Access and recruiting can be difficult, especially if the experiment is demanding in terms of participants' time and effort.
- The time, facilities, and other resources needed may make it impractical to conduct a particular experiment.

Experimental research has also been the subject of more fundamental critiques. These range from questions about the extent to which experimenters in the past have adequately respected the rights of their research subjects to reactions against the perceived privileging of experimental method over other research designs. Experiments, as the archetypal quantitative deductive research design, are closely linked to positivism and subject to similar critiques. Oakley (2000) provides interesting insights into aspects of this broader debate if you are interested in exploring it further.

6.3 NATURAL EXPERIMENTS AND CORRELATIONAL STUDIES

Natural experiments, despite their name, are not really experiments in the true sense because the independent variable is not manipulated. For this reason, they are classified here as nonexperimental. Instead, the researcher looks for naturally occurring comparison between a treatment and a control condition that is as close as possible to those that would have been created in an actual experiment. An example would be a study that compares one factory in which a new quality programme has been introduced (the treatment group) against one in which it has not (the comparison group), in terms of their respective quality levels (the outcome). In **correlational studies** the researcher measures two or more variables as they exist naturally for a set of individual cases (e.g. people) and then tests the relationship between them, for example to investigate the relationship between individual customers' satisfaction levels and their likelihood of making further purchases. Analytic survey studies (see next section) are typical examples of this type of research. (Note that, despite their name, the analysis procedures used in correlational studies are not limited to correlation but can include regression and other statistical techniques as presented in Chapter 13.)

Depending on the chosen design, nonexperimental studies can be cross-sectional or longitudinal. Longitudinal designs may be prospective, following developments over time, or retrospective, researching what has already happened, sometimes in order to set a baseline against which the current situation can be compared. Like experiments, they take a deductive approach, pre-specifying the hypotheses to be tested and emphasizing measurement and comparison. However, since experimental control is not possible, nonexperimental explanatory designs rely on statistical control to deal with extraneous influences. For this reason, as noted in Chapter 4, caution is needed when making causal inferences.

6.3.1 Applications of natural experiments and correlational studies

Nonexperimental designs of this kind are widely used in both pure and applied research. Two applications stand out.

- Theory testing: the theory is often depicted as a conceptual model of the variance type and the hypotheses are expressed in terms of relationships between independent and dependent variables, as discussed in Chapter 4.
- Prediction of the value of a dependent variable from knowledge of the value of one or more independent variables in order, for example, to measure the impact of one variable on another to determine the size of the effect and, in many cases, to compare it relative to other possible factors. In such cases, determining whether any observed relationship is really causal may not be of interest.

From a practical point of view, a nonexperimental design of this sort may be appropriate in situations where an experiment is not an option. Such situations are commonly encountered in practice, so it is not surprising that nonexperimental designs are so widely used. Research in Practice 6.2 presents an example of a correlational design using an analytic survey.

Research in practice 6.2 Do hybrid project management approaches work?

Agile has become a trendy term in business and management in recent years. That is certainly true in the field of project management, particularly since the publishing of the Agile Manifesto in 2001 (https://agilemanifesto.org). Advocates of agile project management argue for its superiority over traditional 'waterfall' approaches, particularly in areas where there is uncertainty over the project goals and methods. In practice, however, many organizations have adopted hybrid approaches that blend elements of agile and waterfall approaches. But do hybrid approaches work?

Gemino et al. (2021) set out to answer that question using a survey study. Recognizing the limited theory available in this emerging topic area, their research sought to measure the impact project management approach, distinguishing between agile, hybrid, and traditional approaches, on project success in terms of budget and time, scope and quality, and stakeholder success. They also included other independent variables relating to the characteristics of the project, the project team, and the organization. These were factors previous research had shown important in project success and the researchers incorporated them to help determine whether or not the degree of project agility added any explanatory power.

Survey participants were asked to answer questions on one or more project. The final sample size was 447 projects. Analysis was performed using multiple regression. The researchers concluded that

> hybrid and agile approaches significantly increase stakeholder success over traditional approaches while achieving the same budget, time, scope, and quality outcomes. Hybrid approaches were found to be similar in effectiveness to fully agile approaches. Results validate decisions by practitioners to combine agile and traditional.
>
> Gemino et al. (2021: 161)

6.3.2 Strengths and weaknesses of nonexperimental explanatory designs

There are many potential attractions to using nonexperimental designs, especially in the form of questionnaire-based correlational studies of the type just described, which also benefit from the advantages of survey designs in general. Above all they avoid many of the practical challenges faced in running an experiment. Nonexperimental designs typically gather their data in naturally occurring settings. As Field and Hole (2003: 10) put it, 'The good thing about this kind of research is it provides us with a very natural view of the question we're researching'. The bad thing is that nonexperimental designs cannot employ the kinds or levels of control enjoyed by experiments. What are the implications of this for investigating causal questions? Recall the criteria for inferring causality that we outlined in Chapter 4. Nonexperimental quantitative designs tend to be strongest on measuring covariance, less strong on assessing whether cause comes before effect (unless they are longitudinal designs) and weakest on ruling out the influence of extraneous variables (Antonakis et al., 2010). These problems lead some writers to deny any causal explanatory role for such designs. Field and Hole (2003: 26), for example, argue that 'correlational research does not allow causal statements to be made', and many researchers avoid using words like 'cause' when reporting their results.

Our own position, as we argued in Chapter 4, is that nonexperimental explanatory research designs do have a role to play in causal research. The identification of strong correlations, for example, can serve to stimulate further research, including experiments, to find whether or not the observed correlation is, in fact, causal. Development of causal theories can be supported by testing the associations implied by causal models (Aneshensel, 2013; Podsakoff and Podsakoff, 2019) although interpreting the results in causal terms remains contentious. A strong theoretical basis can, in turn, support causal analysis using nonexperimental studies, for example by identifying relevant variables, including possible moderators and mediators, that can be included in testing (Rindfleisch et al., 2008). Nevertheless, you should always be cautious when inferring causality on the basis of nonexperimental studies.

6.4 SURVEY STUDIES

The word survey is used in many different ways in research. It is frequently used as a synonym for a **questionnaire** or to refer to a research design that uses a questionnaire. Although questionnaires are widely employed in survey studies, their use is not the determining characteristic of the design. Instead, we can identify four features that typify a **survey study**.

1. It produces quantitative (or quantifiable) data on the variables of interest for the population being studied; the population may be individuals, groups, organizations, or some other entity, such as a project or product.

2. Data are collected using predefined, structured collection procedures. Data are often gathered by questionnaire, but structured observation or secondary data can also be used; some survey studies use more than one source of data.

3. Data are usually collected from only a sample of the population of interest; statistical analysis techniques are then used to generalize the findings to the wider population.

4. The purpose of the survey study may be to describe the phenomenon under investigation (descriptive survey) and/or to test theories relating to the phenomenon (analytic survey).

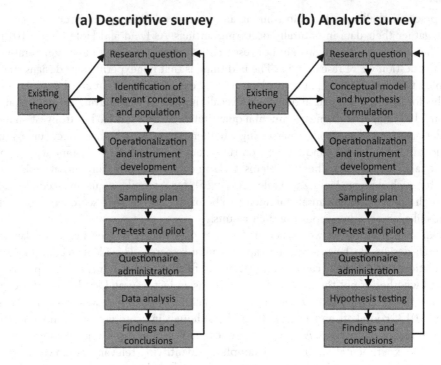

FIGURE 6.4 Steps in questionnaire-based survey studies

More generally, survey studies fall into the category of nonexperimental quantitative research designs.

In Figure 6.4 we show the key steps for using a questionnaire to collect data in descriptive and analytic surveys. Note the development of a conceptual model and hypothesis formulation in analytic surveys. Theory will typically be used in descriptive studies to identify the concepts that need to be measured in the survey. Data collection by questionnaire is reviewed in Chapter 10, and we discuss both of these survey designs in more detail in the companion website chapter supplement.

6.4.1 Applications of survey study design

The survey study is a very versatile research design and is widely used in both pure and applied research for a range of tasks. There are two primary uses of survey study designs.

1. **Descriptive surveys**, which provide a description of a phenomenon in terms of the distribution of relevant variables within a particular population either at a single point in time (cross-sectional) or comparatively over time (longitudinal) by using repeat surveys. An example of a cross-sectional descriptive survey is given in Research in Practice 6.3.

2. **Analytic surveys** (also known as theory-testing or explanatory surveys), which aim to test theories about a phenomenon by examining and testing the associations between

variables. Analytic surveys are a common form of correlational, nonexperimental explanatory research design, as shown in Research in Practice 6.2.

Survey studies can also have an exploratory role (Forza, 2002; Easterby-Smith et al., 2021) in which exploratory statistical techniques such as cluster analysis are used to identify underlying patterns in the data. We discuss such data-driven quantitative research approaches later in this chapter.

Research in practice 6.3 A descriptive survey of executive coaching practices

Bono et al.'s (2009: 386) study sets out 'to describe the current state of executive coaching practices with a special emphasis on comparing the practices of psychologist and non-psychologist coaches'. The research design adopted was a questionnaire-based descriptive survey study. The questionnaire was divided into four sections, looking at coaching practices, coaching outcomes, coaches' backgrounds, and coaching competencies. Section 1, for example, asked questions on such practices as assessment tools, approaches to coaching, and methods of communication. Respondents rated each on a five-point scale indicating frequency of use. Selection of the sample of respondents was done in two stages. In the first stage, screening emails were sent to members of organizations to which coaches are often affiliated to identify executive coaches. In stage two, those identified as executive coaches were invited by email to take part in a web-based survey. This procedure generated 428 usable responses from the 1,260 coaches who were emailed in stage two. Analysis involved summary statistics of responses by subgroup (psychologists and non-psychologists) and inferential statistical tests of intergroup differences. The findings show that differences between psychologists and non-psychologists are generally quite small, and there are as many differences between different types of psychologist as between psychologists and non-psychologists.

6.4.2 Strengths and weaknesses of survey designs

As with any other research design, survey studies have inherent strengths and weaknesses. One of the major advantages is the flexibility in the type and range of variables that can be measured. As Gravetter and Forzano (2012) suggest, some of these variables (such as respondents' attitudes and opinions) may be difficult to investigate in any other way, at least quantitatively. The fact that survey studies are nonexperimental and relatively adaptable in terms of the data collection procedures allows them to be used in situations where other methods cannot be employed. Surveys, particularly sample surveys using self-complete questionnaires, can be very efficient at gathering large amounts of information, whilst statistical analysis supports inference to a larger population from a small sample.

These features make descriptive surveys a useful design for investigating the aggregate properties of groups and subgroups.

Against these benefits must be weighed some potential weaknesses. When the study involves questionnaires, there may be serious problems with response rates and the possibility **of nonresponse bias**, which arises when those who do not respond differ in some systematic way from those who do. Questionnaires rely on self-report and therefore on the accuracy and honesty of respondents. Problems may also arise when a single respondent is asked to report on behalf of a whole organization, for example on an organization's strategy. Lack of knowledge on the part of the respondent, lack of consensus on the issue or the sheer complexity of the topic may lead to unreliable data. Multiple respondents, observation, and/or administrative data can be used to overcome some of these problems, but this may increase the complexity of data collection. Reliance on a single source (e.g. a questionnaire) for both independent and dependent variables can give rise to what is known as **common-method bias**, discussed further in Chapter 10.

To some extent these are practical criticisms of the design, and experienced survey researchers are well aware of the limitations. We discuss some of the ways in which researchers try to address them when we look at quantitative data collection and analysis in Chapters 10 and 13. When used to investigate causal questions, analytic survey studies are subject to similar critiques as other nonexperimental explanatory research designs as we discussed in Chapter 4.

6.5 CONTENT ANALYSIS

Content analysis refers to a family of procedures for the systematic, replicable quantitative analysis of text. In essence it involves the classification of parts of a text through the application of a structured coding scheme from which conclusions can be drawn about the message content. By clearly specifying the coding and other procedures, content analysis is replicable in the sense that other researchers could reproduce the study. Content analysis can be applied to all kinds of written text such as speeches, letters, or articles, whether online or in print. It can also be used to analyze text in the form of pictures, video, film, or other visual media. Content analysis can be carried out quantitatively but also qualitatively (Mayring, 2019). We will focus on quantitative content analysis here and discuss qualitative approaches to message analysis in the following chapter.

Quantitative content analysis shares many of the general characteristics of quantitative research discussed in Chapter 4. Nevertheless, it does have some distinctive features, particularly with respect to the application of a coding scheme to convert textual/visual data to numeric data and the way in which reliability is assessed, which justify treating it as a research design in its own right and not just as a method of analysis. Figure 6.5 outlines the key stages in a content analysis project. We explain these further in the chapter supplement on the companion website.

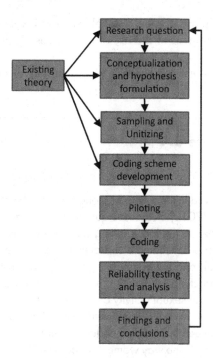

FIGURE 6.5 Key steps in quantitative content analysis

6.5.1 Applications of content analysis

Content analysis provides a structured way of analyzing data that are typically open ended and relatively unstructured. Applications include the following:

- Description. Here the focus is on describing features of the message content. Jain et al. (2010), for example, study how the ways in which celebrities were presented in Indian television commercials varied according to the category of products they were promoting. Descriptive content analysis can be cross-sectional or longitudinal.
- Prediction. Here the main aim is to predict the outcome or effect of the messages being analyzed. A study by Peruta and Shields' (2018), for example, looks at how different content and formats of posts by US universities and colleges on Facebook contribute to different levels of online engagement (such as likes and comments). Researchers interested in, for instance, in the impact of advertisements on consumers can also choose to combine content analysis with other research approaches such as surveys or experiments.

Content analysis has been applied to a wide range of social science topics, including gender and race, media reporting, and political communication; it has obvious applications in the analysis of business communication, particularly marketing. Content analysis is also used to analyze online communication channels, such as Facebook and YouTube; it is of particular interest in the context of the rise of big data, as we discuss in the final section of this chapter.

Research in Practice 6.4 gives an example of a quantitative content analysis study.

Research in practice 6.4 Shaken and stirred: a content analysis of the portrayal of women in James Bond films

How women are portrayed in the media has long been a subject of interest to research-ers. Neuendorf et al.'s (2010) study uses quantitative content analysis to investigate how women are depicted in the long-running and very popular series of James Bond films. Data analysis focused on female characters who met certain criteria (e.g. they speak or are spoken to), and the coding scheme defined a range of variables to be measured for each character, such as race, hair colour, body size, physical attractive-ness, along with aspects of sexual activity and violence by and against the character. Eight coders were used to code 20 films, with tests being carried out to measure the reliability of coding between the different coders. Research findings showed clear links between sex and violence in the way women are portrayed in Bond films. According to the authors, 'the collective body of Bond films . . . stands to serve as an important source of social cognitive outcomes regarding appropriate role behaviour for women – still stereotyped, with persistent allusions to violence and sex (and their linkage), and with unrealistic standards of female beauty' (Neuendorf et al., 2010: 758–759).

6.5.2 Strengths and weaknesses of content analysis

Content analysis is a flexible research approach that can be applied to a wide variety of text sources. Helped by the availability of computer software programmes, content analy-sis can cope with large amounts of data. It can be used to investigate a topic longitudinally through the examination of contemporary texts. Content analysis can also be seen as an unobtrusive research approach in that it can be used to analyze naturally occurring data, as discussed in Chapter 12. As a result, content analysis may be helpful in reducing the problem of social desirability bias amongst respondents when researching sensitive topics (Insch et al., 1997).

Potential weaknesses of the design arise in connection with the process of sampling and coding. Document availability and the sampling process can introduce bias. Developing the coding scheme and coding always involve interpretation, even of manifest content, and thus risk similar biases to those faced by other measurement techniques. Abstraction of content from its context can also create problems. Taking a word or phrase in isolation of other parts of the text, for instance, may result in loss of meaning. In addition, content analysis risks overlooking what is not said in a particular text. In some situations, what is omitted may be as significant as what is included.

There are also broader questions about the extent to which documentary analysis provides access to the world beyond the text. Do job advertisements, for instance, tell us something about real changes in job skill, or do they tell us only about the way in which skill is portrayed in advertising? This is not a criticism of content analysis per se because investigating changes in how subjects are portrayed can be valuable of itself, but it should caution us against any simplistic assumption of a direct correspondence between text and the external world.

6.6 DATA-DRIVEN QUANTITATIVE RESEARCH

The designs we have looked at so far in this chapter are all underpinned by a broadly deductive approach. As we saw in Chapter 4, this is very typical of quantitative research, but the dominance of the hypothetico-deductive approach been criticised for restricting the 'scope and depth of research questions that can be answered with quantitative methods' (Valizade et al., 2022: 2). The last decade, however, has seen growing interest in what has been described as data-driven research, in comparison to the theory-driven research approach typified by deductive methods. Maass et al. provide a working definition:

> Data-driven research is an exploratory approach that analyzes data to extract scientifically interesting insights (e.g., patterns) by applying analytical techniques and modes of reasoning.
>
> Maass et al. (2018: 1253)

One of the consequences of these developments is more focus being given to exploratory quantitative techniques that can support more inductive and abductive research approaches (Valizade et al., 2022; Kitchin, 2014). This has been reinforced by the growth in big data (see Chapter 12) and increased availability of analytic methods and software. In this section, we therefore take a brief look at data-driven quantitative research designs.

Data-driven research can take many different forms but typically follows the steps shown in Figure 6.6. In Research in Practice 6.5, for example, the researchers used a descriptive survey and exploratory analysis techniques. Data-driven research is also often linked to data mining and big data and may, in turn, involve use of machine learning to support the analysis (Kitchin, 2014; Valizade et al., 2022); such approaches lie beyond the scope of this, text but we give further insights into options in the chapter supplement on the companion website.

6.6.1 Applications of data-driven quantitative research

Quantitative data exploration is, of course, nothing new. Indeed, as we will argue in Chapter 13, quantitative data analysis should always include thorough exploration of the data as part of the analysis process. Data-driven research, however, will typically go further using exploratory analytic methods to identify patterns and correlations in the data that offer insights into the phenomenon under study.

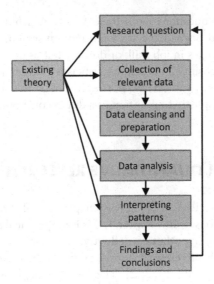

FIGURE 6.6 Typical steps in data-driven quantitative research

A broad range of analysis techniques can be used. We will use cluster analysis as an example. Cluster analysis aims to break down a heterogenous population into a smaller number of homogenous groups (or clusters) (Linoff and Berry, 2011). The resulting clusters will have similar characteristics or properties that differentiate them from the other clusters. A common application of cluster analysis is market segmentation, where different customer segments (clusters) can be identified to support product and service marketing efforts (McGivern, 2022). As Linoff and Berry (2011) point out, cluster analysis is often the starting point for further analysis. For instance, having identified relevant customer segments, investigation could focus on preferred product type, purchasing channels, average spend, etc. Research in Practice 6.5 gives an example of cluster analysis being used to profile shopping mall customers.

Research in practice 6.5 Cluster analysis of shopping mall customers during hard times

A combination of factors, including changing customer buying habits and economic problems, have created challenges for shopping malls in developed countries over recent years. Calvo-Porral and Lévy-Mangin (2019) carried out a customer segmentation analysis of mall customers in the context of economic downturn in order to help mall retailers better understand their customers.

The research was based around a shopping mall in Spain and was built around a survey of mall customers. The final sample size was 511, and the data were subject to a combination of factor and cluster analysis. Calvo-Porral and Lévy-Mangin (2019) identified five clusters:

- Senior hostelry seekers: older customers focusing on leisure and entertainment
- Young enthusiasts: younger customers who are fans of the shopping mall experience
- Deal hunters: lower income shoppers, looking for low price purchases
- Adverse reluctant: customers with low engagement who rarely shop at the mall
- Leisure comfy teens: younger customers who come to browse and enjoy leisure activities and facilities

In their recommendations, the researchers recommend that

mall managers should consider mall customers as five different types, instead of considering them as one single customer. In addition, it is important that retail managers during times of hardship try to maintain the attractiveness of the different aspects of the shopping mall and to remain customer-oriented.

Calvo-Porral and Lévy-Mangin (2019: 246)

6.6.2 Strengths and weaknesses of data-driven quantitative research

As we noted previously, critics have argued that traditional, deductive quantitative research approaches have significant limitations. To some extent, data-driven research designs discussed here seek to address those, or at least to offer alternative ways of investigating a topic quantitatively. In addition, when coupled with the opportunities offered by big data, such designs may provide ways in which researchers can explore new questions and/or better answers to existing questions (George et al., 2016). More practically, exploratory approaches such as cluster analysis can help us to gain additional insights into our data and the phenomena they represent.

Nevertheless, there are several potential limitations. One is the debate that has emerged in connection with the impact of big data on research, famously summed up in an article by Chris Anderson (2008) titled *The End of Theory: The Data Deluge Makes the Scientific Method Obsolete*. Data-driven research as we are using the term here, however, is not intended to be 'theory free'. Rather, both the motivation for the research and the interpretation of the emerging findings can be linked to existing theory (Maass et al., 2018). It is, however, worth noting that the similar research designs may be used in business contexts where the aim is 'to identify new products, markets and opportunities rather than advance knowledge per se' rather than to contribute to our conceptual understanding of a phenomenon (Kitchin, 2014: 3).

There is also concern over some of the analysis approaches that may be used. One is the vulnerability of exploratory data (especially when analyzing big data sets) to **spurious correlations** influencing research findings (Calude and Longo, 2017). Another issue is that some methods, such as cluster analysis, raise concerns over validating findings (Brusco et al., 2017). Researchers need to be aware of such issues when undertaking their analysis. Practical challenges can arise in relation to the skills needed if your project involves accessing and analyzing big data (see also Chapter 12). If you are carrying out your research as part of an academic qualification, it is also helpful to discuss your ideas with your tutor to ensure that the approach is aligned with the assessment brief if you are considering a data-driven research approach.

CRITICAL COMMENTARY 6.1

Critiques of quantitative research

In this chapter we have looked at some of the specific strengths and weaknesses of a range of different quantitative research designs. In this brief commentary we will highlight some of the broader critiques of quantitative methods.

Criticism of quantitative research is often linked to its perceived association with positivism. For researchers working from an interpretivist perspective, for example, quantitative research can be seen as failing to pay sufficient attention to meaning and to understanding of social actors in their particular contexts. A more radical version of this critique is that the data generated by quantitative research 'constructed', for example by the process of respondents making sense of the questions developed by the researcher, rather than reflecting some 'real' underlying state. As Zyphur and Pierides (2017: 3 italics in original) put it, 'by emphasizing formal logics such as statistics and probability, researchers can fail to notice the actual *doing* of research, including the *production* of representations and the *creation and use* of specific tools for testing'.

Some critics also question the dominant role given to variables in quantitative research and the relationships between those variables (Aspers and Corte, 2019). This 'variable orientation' is also often linked to the positivist/regularity view of causation and subject to criticism from those who adopt different views on the nature of causality in social systems (Mingers and Standing, 2017). Concerns are also raised about the emphasis placed on tests for statistical significance in quantitative research. Despite its widespread use, aspects of such testing are controversial, for example, because it downplays practical significance. We explore this point more fully in Chapter 13.

6.7 CHOOSING A QUANTITATIVE RESEARCH DESIGN

We have described a range of different quantitative research designs. In this final section of the chapter we offer guidance on making the choice of which design would be appropriate to answer your research question.

6.7.1 Quantitative designs for answering descriptive and exploratory questions

Some descriptive research questions naturally imply quantification as a component of the answer. Questions such as 'what is the level of . . . ?' 'what is the frequency of . . . ?' 'how many . . . ?' or 'what proportion of . . . ' all suggest quantitative description. At its simplest, such description seeks to identify and describe something in terms of the distribution (e.g. frequencies or average) of one or more variables of interest for a particular population and groups within the population. We can identify four general features that typify a quantitative approach to description:

1. The pre-specification of the concepts of interest (such as age, income, attitude, etc.) so that they can be operationalized as measurable variables for data collection.
2. The use of a standardized data collection instrument, such as a questionnaire, to gather quantitative or quantifiable data on the chosen variables.
3. The selection of a representative sample in a way that will support statistical inferences about the population from which the sample was drawn.
4. The use of statistical techniques to generate a description of the aggregate properties of the population, including any relevant subgroups or classes, based on analysis of the sample data.

Although descriptive research may not involve any formal theory testing, you will notice that these features align closely to the deductive research approach and the general characteristics of quantitative research that we described in Chapter 4. Research design options for answering 'what' questions include questionnaire-based descriptive surveys. Secondary data, such as organizational operating data, are also a useful data source for answering 'what' questions, especially for developing retrospective descriptions. Where the object of interest is text (or other messages), quantitative content analysis can also be used.

Where the question is more exploratory, opportunity exists to use data-driven research approaches. These might be based on a primary data collection method such as a survey (see Research in Practice 6.5) or secondary data, including big data. Appropriate analytical techniques such as cluster analysis can be used to explore and describe patterns in the data.

6.7.2 Quantitative designs for answering explanatory questions

Quantitative research methods are closely associated with the regularity view of causation and use of the hypothetico-deductive approach to test an explanatory theory expressed as a conceptual model of the type shown in Figure 4.5. An experimental design, whether a true or quasi experiment is an obvious starting point when looking at explanatory research designs. As we have said, however, there are many situations in which an experiment cannot be used, for instance, when it is either not practical or not ethical to manipulate the independent treatment variable (such as making someone redundant to observe what happens). In such situations, consider a nonexperimental design of the types we have discussed in Section 6.3 using primary and/or secondary data, including analytic survey design options, as illustrated in Research in Practice 6.2. Content analysis can also be used to research the impact of message content. Particularly where the primary aim of the research is prediction rather than explanation, more exploratory approaches can also be used to look for patterns that may warrant further examination in terms of their causal nature. Regardless of the method used, quantitative explanatory research should be strongly linked to relevant theory if any causal claims are being made.

6.7.3 Quantitative designs for answering process questions

Although investigations of process often use more inductive and qualitative or mixed methods approaches, pure quantitative methods can also be used when answering 'how' questions. Time series analysis can give insights into the development of phenomena over time. Quantitative designs can be employed to measure or test for events that are relevant to a process, for example, using secondary data (Van de Ven, 2007). In Chapter 13 we offer an introduction to time series data and in the further reading section for this chapter on the companion website we suggest sources dealing with some of the more advanced quantitative techniques that fall outside the scope of this book.

CHAPTER SUMMARY

- Experiments involve the manipulation of a treatment variable to observe its effect. True experiments involve random assignment of subjects to groups; quasi-experiments do not. Experimental designs can have very high internal validity for inferring causality but are subject to practical and ethical constraints.
- Natural experiments and correlational studies are examples of nonexperimental explanatory research designs that can be used for testing explanatory theory and for predicting the value of a dependent variable based on the value of one or more independent variables. The extent to which causality can reliably be inferred from nonexperimental designs is controversial.
- Survey studies use pre-specified, structured data collection procedures (such as a questionnaire) to collect quantitative data on variables of interest to the researcher, often from a sample drawn from a larger population. Descriptive surveys generate descriptions of a phenomenon in terms of the distribution of relevant variables. Analytic surveys are used to test theories for explanatory or predictive purposes by investigating relationship between variables.
- Quantitative content analysis provides a way of systematically and quantitatively analyzing text through the application of a structured coding scheme for purposes of description or prediction. Content analysis on its own has limited ability to draw conclusions about the world beyond the text.
- Data-driven quantitative studies offer the opportunity to work more inductively/ abductively to explore phenomena through the identification of patterns in the data, which can inform existing theory and be subject to further investigation.
- Choice of research design should take into account the type of question being asked by the research.

NEXT STEPS

6.1 Quantitative research designs used in your topic area. Review the research articles that you have identified in your literature review that use quantitative research methods.

   a. What specific research designs are used in your topic area?

   b. What types of research question are they used to answer?

   c. What are the strengths and weaknesses of these designs in relation to your topic area?

   d. Evaluate the contribution made by different research designs in your topic area.

6.2 What quantitative research design may be suitable for your own project? Review your research questions and your answers to the Next steps activities in Chapter 4.

   a. What specific quantitative research designs could be used to answer your research question?

   b. What would be the strengths and weaknesses of those designs for your project?

   c. Evaluate the suitability of the research designs you have identified for answering your research questions.

FURTHER READING

For further reading, please see the companion website.

REFERENCES

Anderson, C. (2008). The end of theory: The data deluge makes the scientific method obsolete. *Wired Magazine*, 16(7): 16–07.

Aneshensel, C. (2013). *Theory-Based Data Analysis for the Social Sciences*. 2nd ed. Thousand Oaks, CA: SAGE Publications.

Antonakis, J., Bendahan, S., Jacquart, P. and Lalive, R. (2010). On making causal claims: A review and recommendations. *The Leadership Quarterly*, 21(6): 1086–1120.

Aspers, P. and Corte, U. (2019). What is qualitative in qualitative research. *Qualitative Sociology*, 42(2): 139–160.

Bono, J. E., Purvanova, R. K., Towler, A. J. and Peterson, D. B. (2009). A survey of executive coaching practices. *Personnel Psychology*, 62(2): 361–404.

Brusco, M. J., Singh, R., Cradit, J. D. and Steinley, D. (2017). Cluster analysis in empirical OM research: Survey and recommendations. *International Journal of Operations & Production Management*, 37(3): 300–320.

Calude, C. S. and Longo, G. (2017). The deluge of spurious correlations in big data. *Foundations of Science*, 22(3): 595–612.

Calvo-Porral, C. and Lévy-Mangin, J.-P. (2019). Profiling shopping mall customers during hard times. *Journal of Retailing and Consumer Services*, 48: 238–246.

Cook, T. D. and Campbell, D. T. (1979). *Quasi-Experimentation: Design and Analysis for Field Settings*. Chicago, IL: Rand McNally.

Easterby-Smith, M., Jaspersen, L. J., Thorpe, R. and Valizade, D. (2021). *Management Research*. 7th ed. London: SAGE Publications.

Field, A. and Hole, G. (2003). *How to Design and Report Experiments*. London: SAGE Publications.

Forza, C. (2002). Survey research in operations management: A process-based perspective. *International Journal of Operations & Production Management*, 22(2): 152–194.

Gemino, A., Horner Reich, B. and Serrador, P. M. (2021). Agile, traditional, and hybrid approaches to project success: Is hybrid a poor second choice? *Project Management Journal*, 52(2): 161–175.

George, G., Osinga, E. C., Lavie, D. and Scott, B. A. (2016). Big data and data science methods for management research. *Academy of Management Journal*, 59(5): 1493–1507.

Gravetter, F. J. and Forzano, L.-A. B. (2012). *Research Methods for the Behavioural Sciences: International Edition*. 4th ed. Belmont, CA: Wadsworth Cengage Learning.

Insch, G. S., Moore, J. E. and Murphy, L. D. (1997). Content analysis in leadership research: Examples, procedures, and suggestions for future use. *The Leadership Quarterly*, 8(1): 1–25.

Jain, V., Roy, S., Daswani, A. and Sudha, M. (2010). How celebrities are used in Indian television commercials. *Vikalpa: The Journal for Decision Makers*, 35(4): 45–52.

Kitchin, R. (2014). Big data, new epistemologies and paradigm shifts. *Big Data & Society*, April-June: 1–12.

Linoff, G. S. and Berry, M. J. A. (2011). *Data Mining Techniques: For Marketing, Sales, and Customer Relationship Management*. New York, NY: John Wiley and Sons.

Maass, W., Parsons, J., Purao, S., Storey, V. C. and Woo, C. (2018). Data-driven meets theory-driven research in the era of big data: Opportunities and challenges for information systems research. *Journal of the Association for Information Systems*, 19(12): 1253–1273.

Mayring, P. (2019). Qualitative content analysis: Demarcation, varieties, developments. *Forum: Qualitative Social Research*, 20(3). Available at: https://doi.org/10.17169/fqs-20.3.3343 (Accessed 8 April 2023).

McGivern, Y. (2022). *The Practice of Market Research. From Data to Insight*. 5th ed. Harlow: Pearson Education.

Mingers, J. and Standing, C. (2017). Why things happen – Developing the critical realist view of causal mechanisms. *Information and Organization*, 27(3): 171–189.

Neuendorf, K. A., Gore, T. D., Dalessandro, A., Janstova, P. and Snyder-Suhy, S. (2010). Shaken and stirred: A content analysis of women's portrayals in James Bond films. *Sex Roles*, 62(11–12): 747–761.

Oakley, A. (2000). *Experiments in Knowing. Gender and Method in the Social Sciences*. New York, NY: The New Press.

Peruta, A. and Shields, A. B. (2018). Marketing your university on social media: A content analysis of Facebook post types and formats. *Journal of Marketing for Higher Education*, 28(2): 175–191.

Podsakoff, P. M. and Podsakoff, N. P. (2019). Experimental designs in management and leadership research: Strengths, limitations, and recommendations for improving publishability. *The Leadership Quarterly*, 30(1): 11–33.

Rindfleisch, A., Malter, A. J., Ganesan, S. and Moorman, C. (2008). Cross-sectional versus longitudinal survey research: Concepts, findings, and guidelines. *Journal of Marketing Research (JMR)*, 45(3): 261–279.

Shadish, W. R., Cook, T. D. and Campbell, D. T. (2002). *Experimental and Quasi-Experimental Designs for Generalized Causal Inference*. Belmont, CA: Wadsworth Cengage Learning.

Sigurdsson, V., Saevarsson, H. and Foxall, G. (2009). Brand placement and consumer choice: An in-store experiment. *Journal of Applied Behavior Analysis*, 42(3): 741–745.

Valizade, D., Schulz, F. and Nicoara, C. (2022). Towards a paradigm shift: How can machine learning extend the boundaries of quantitative management scholarship? *British Journal of Management*. https://doi.org/10.1111/1467-8551.12678.

Van de Ven, A. H. (2007). *Engaged Scholarship*. Oxford: Oxford University Press.

Zyphur, M. J. and Pierides, D. C. (2017). Is quantitative research ethical? Tools for ethically practicing, evaluating, and using quantitative research. *Journal of Business Ethics*, 143(1): 1–16.

CHAPTER 7

Qualitative and mixed methods research designs

CHAPTER LEARNING OUTCOMES

After reading this chapter you will be able to

- recognize and evaluate key qualitative and mixed research designs;
- select and justify an appropriate qualitative or mixed research design for your own research project.

7.1 INTRODUCTION

In this chapter we turn our attention to research designs that use primarily qualitative methods, as shown in Figure 7.1. Each design is discussed in terms of its main characteristics and potential applications.

Research that uses only one family of methods (e.g. only quantitative, or only qualitative) is described as mono method. However, as each method has its own limitations, it is sometimes sensible to combine two methods to take advantage of their different features. The combination of quantitative and qualitative methods in a single study is commonly referred to as a mixed method study. In this chapter, we discuss when it is advantageous to mix research methods and how to combine them.

7.2 ETHNOGRAPHY

Ethnography is an in-depth field investigation through which the researcher seeks to describe behaviours within a group setting and from the perspective of group members. Typically this is done by the researcher acting as a participant-observer in the situation under study, sometimes for a long period of time. Ethnographic methods may also be used

DOI: 10.4324/9781003381006-9

FIGURE 7.1 Qualitative research designs

to gain an in-depth understanding of online communities. This is known as netnography. Hammersley and Atkinson (2019) describe what ethnographers do:

- People's actions and interactions are studied in the field, in their natural setting as they go about their daily activities.
- Emphasis is placed on **participant-observation** and informal conversations, although other data collection methods may also be used.
- Field methods are relatively unstructured, developing as the research proceeds.
- Research is focused on a small number of cases, sometimes a single group or setting, to facilitate in-depth study.
- Analysis is inductive, with the focus on 'meaning, sources, functions, and consequences of human actions and institutional practices' (2019: 3), typically in local contexts.

To reflect the developmental nature of ethnographic research, our depiction of the key steps in an ethnographic study in Figure 7.2 has been kept quite general.

7.2.1 Applications of ethnography

A relevant application of ethnographic research in business and management is in the area of organizational ethnography. Within this very broad body of work, it is possible to identify three different categories (Brewer, 2004). One is the study of occupational careers and identities, such as Venkataraman and Joshi's (2020) examination of how workers in the Indian IT industry balanced the organizational and personal dimensions of their identities. The other is study of power in organizations and other social situations, for example Schjøtt Hansen and Hartley's (2021) analysis of a news' personalization algorithm. The final one is the study of routines in professional work and the coping strategies of workers in routine jobs, such as Deken et al.'s (2016) analysis of workers in an automotive company.

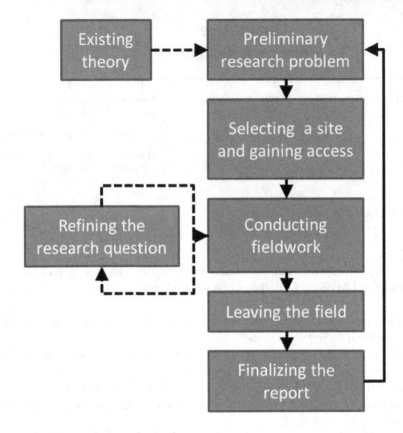

FIGURE 7.2 Steps in an ethnographic study

Ethnography is also used in market research to understand customers and markets in their natural context. An example is Ferreira and Scaraboto's (2016) use of netnography to analyze how consumers use products to shape and reflect their identities.

7.2.2 Strengths and weaknesses of ethnographies

In many respects ethnography is the archetypal qualitative research design embodying many of the general features of qualitative research that we discussed in Chapter 4. In research projects in which taking an emic perspective, working in depth and in context, and studying things in their natural settings are important, ethnography is likely to be a powerful approach. The use of multiple data sources can help offset some of the limitations of individual data collection methods, while prolonged observation overcomes some of the limitations of research designs that involve only brief engagement with the research site and the research participants.

However, gaining and maintaining access to the site may be a challenge. The time required to carry out a prolonged field investigation is another and may preclude an ethnographic research design in some situations. Ethnography also demands a range of skills and attributes from the researcher. Moreover, there may be ethical concerns related to the informed consent of participants: even when the observation is not covert, it may be practically impossible to ensure that everyone is briefed and gives formal consent. The boundary between what is private and what is public may also not be very clear.

Research in Practice 7.1 gives an example of an ethnographic study at a software company.

Research in practice 7.1 An ethnography of algorithm developers

Van den Broek et al. (2021) conducted a two-year ethnography at a software development company, with the goal of understanding 'how the process of machine knowledge production unfolded over time and to unpack the promises, problems, and practices of the actors involved in the process' (van den Broek et al., 2021: 1561). The specific application studied was the development of artificial intelligence algorithms for hiring processes, which, at the time the study was conducted, was an emergent area of application of artificial intelligence. Despite the challenges of ethnographic approach, the authors concluded that the novelty of the application, and the need to develop deep understanding of the process under analysis, required an extended engagement with the organization, as well as the ability to collect multiple types of data.

Data collection included 122 hours of observations, 47 interviews, and analysis of 814 documents. For the observations, the researcher followed different types of machine learning developers and teams, on-site, documenting their work practices and informal practices, as well as participated in various online meetings. 'Whenever possible, the researcher recorded meetings and transcribed the conversations to complement the field notes. Detailed notes made during the day and during meetings were expanded into a 203-page document of written field notes' (van den Broek et al., 2021: 1562). In turn, the interviews with developers and clients allowed the researchers to explore specific aspects of the process. Finally, the internal documents provided insight into the 'companies' statements, vision, and proposed actions' (van den Broek et al., 2021: 1562), as well as an additional opportunity for triangulation.

7.3 GROUNDED THEORY

Grounded theory was originally developed by Glaser and Strauss (1967) as a way of building theory systematically from data, as opposed to the hypothetico-deductive, theory-testing approaches dominant at the time. Key features of grounded theory include the following:

- Data collection is adjusted in response to emerging theory. Additional data may be collected to allow a particular concept to be investigated in more detail.
- Multiple data collection methods may be used, such as in-depth interviews, observation, and document analysis. This allows for the triangulation of sources and enables the gathering of rich data.
- Data analysis may involve different coding approaches, such as open, axial, or selective. Coding is a process in which the researcher derives and develops concepts from the data, which are then given a conceptual label, called a code. The coded concepts form the building blocks of the emerging grounded theory.
- Throughout the coding process, the researcher iterates between data and emerging theory. This is known as constant comparison and involves constantly comparing coded data with other pieces of similarly coded data.
- The cycles of data collection and analysis begin as soon as the first data are collected and continue until no new insights or new dimensions to categories are being identified. This state is called the point of theoretical saturation.

The iterative character of grounded theory is captured in Figure 7.3.

7.3.1 Applications of grounded theory

In terms of our earlier categorization of research questions (section 2.4), grounded theory is particularly suited to investigating process questions. This can include a focus on micro-level actions and interactions in response to a situation or problem, as well as stage models of change and development. One example is Zhang et al.'s (2020) investigation of social media fatigue among WeChat users. Causal research questions can also be addressed using grounded theory. Grounded theory may be particularly helpful when looking at causality through the lens of human agency, for example error prevention in organizations (e.g. Sheikhaboumasoudi et al., 2018).

7.3.2 Strengths and weaknesses of grounded theory

Specific strengths of grounded theory include its potential to capture context and complexity in social action, to investigate emerging topic areas or to shed new light on existing topics. Glaser and Strauss (1967) also argue that the sort of theory produced by grounded theory methods makes sense to people involved in the situation being researched, increasing the potential for grounded theory to be used in applied research for a practitioner audience.

However, divergent accounts of the nature of grounded theory have created difficulties for would-be researchers in wishing to adopt the method. Perhaps as a result of this, some commentators (e.g. Suddaby, 2006) have suggested that researchers' claims to be using grounded theory do not always appear to be borne out by their actual practice. At the same time, as Suddaby (2006) points out, the apparent simplicity of the method can lead new researchers into thinking that grounded theory is 'easy', whereas, in reality, 'the seamless craft of a well-executed grounded theory study . . . is the product of considerable experience, hard work, creativity and, occasionally, a healthy dose of good luck' (Suddaby, 2006: 639).

Research in Practice 7.2 gives an example of a grounded theory study.

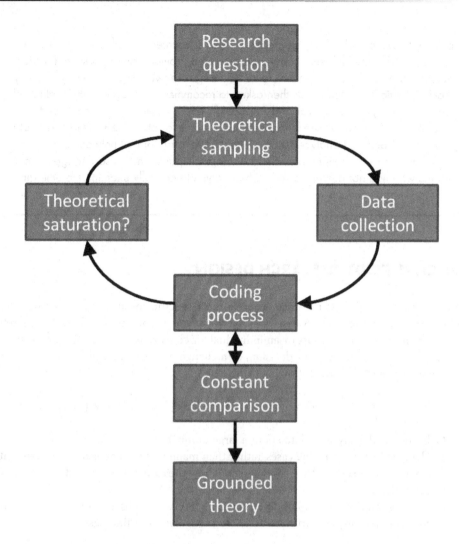

FIGURE 7.3 Steps in a grounded theory research design

Research in practice 7.2 A grounded theory study of bullying among Indian managers

Agarwal and Rai's (2019) investigated workplace bullying, in India, from the victim's perspective. The authors chose grounded theory because it 'moves beyond description to generate or discover a theory that helps to explore the antecedents, outcomes and underlying variables related to the phenomenon under investigation' (Agarwal and Rai, 2019: 592). The authors conducted in-depth interviews with participants who had experienced workplace bullying. The interviewees were also 'asked to draw pictures to express what bullying meant to them, its sources and effects' (Agarwal and Rai, 2019: 593), which enriched the data set and provided an opportunity for triangulation of data. Participants were recruited using a snowballing approach, whereby 'each potential participant was then asked to recommend colleagues who had faced workplace bullying' (Agarwal and Rai, 2019: 592). Sampling was continued until theoretical saturation was reached, which was after a total of 23 interviews. Data were transcribed and analyzed manually, Agarwal and Rai routinely compared their codes with the descriptions provided by the participants; they also engaged a colleague who had not been involved in the analysis to critically examine the emerging categories and concepts.

7.4 CASE STUDY RESEARCH DESIGN

Case study research design investigates one or more specific 'instances of' something that will be the cases in the study. A case in a case study can be something relatively concrete such as an organization, a group, or an individual, or conversely, something more abstract such as an event, a management decision, or a change programme. Common features of case study design include the following (Yin, 2018):

- In-depth study of a small number of cases, often longitudinally (prospectively or retrospectively).
- Collection and analysis of data about a large number of features of each case.
- Studying naturally occurring cases, rather than manipulated ones as in an experiment.
- Examining the cases' context, to understand how the case influences and is influenced by its context.
- Employing multiple sources of data, including interviews, observation, archival documents, and even physical artefacts to allow triangulation of findings.

Case studies are most commonly associated with qualitative data. However, quantitative data can readily be incorporated into a case study where appropriate.

Research case studies differ from the short, descriptive 'vignettes' popular in textbooks and many policy reports. They also differ from the teaching cases widely used in business and management education to stimulate debate in class. Namely, the case study method in research demands a high degree of depth, breadth, and rigour, with careful attention to showing the way in which evidence supports the conclusions reached.

Figure 7.4 illustrates the general steps in case study research to help you formulate your own research design. A multiple case study design is shown, but similar steps apply to single case designs.

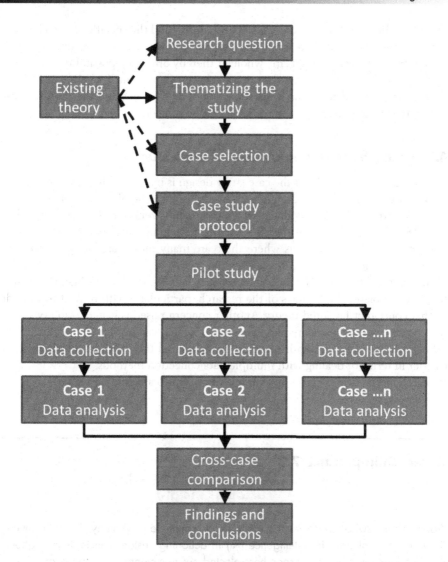

FIGURE 7.4 Steps in a multiple case study research design

7.4.1 Applications of case study design

The ability to investigate instances of the phenomenon being studied in depth, and to employ multiple sources of evidence, makes case study design a useful tool for descriptive studies where the focus is on a specific situation or context and where generalizability is less important. Case study designs can also be employed in applied research, for example, in evaluating the effects of a programme or policy. In explanatory research, case studies offer the possibility of investigating causal mechanisms and the specific contexts in which they are activated. Case study research can also facilitate a holistic perspective on causality because it treats the case as a specific whole. It thereby offers the possibility of investigating causal complexity where there are many relevant factors but few observations. Case study can also be used to research questions about process because the use of multiple data sources supports the retrospective investigation of events.

7.4.2 Strengths and weaknesses of case studies

One of the greatest strengths of the case study design is its adaptability to different types of research question and to different research settings. The use of multiple sources of evidence allows triangulation of findings, which is a major strength of the case study design (Yin, 2018). Case studies also offer the benefit of studying phenomena in detail and in context, particularly in situations where there are many more variables of interest than there are observations.

However, one challenge is a variant of what is known as selection bias, whereby the choice of cases biases the findings of the research, particularly with respect to excluding cases that contradict favoured theory. Another concern raised is generalizability, particularly of single-case studies. Moreover, case study research can be very demanding to carry out due to the need for in-depth access to case sites and the requirement placed on the researcher in terms of dealing with multiple data collection methods.

Research in Practice 7.3 gives an example of multiple case study research.

Research in practice 7.3 Multiple case study research on the role of artificial intelligence in customer insight

Abed Kasaji (2023), a doctoral student, used a multiple case study design to investigate the role of artificial intelligence (AI) in actioning customer insights throughout the customer journey. The researcher selected six non-competing service organizations and collected evidence from multiple informants within each one. A total of 56 in-depth interviews were conducted across a number of relevant departments, which were recorded and transcribed using MS Teams software. In addition, Kasaji reviewed over 40 company documents, including policies, annual reports, and publicly available information.

Within-case analysis was used to describe, understand, and explain what happened in each single, bounded context, while cross-case analysis was used to identify themes that cut across cases. Finally, systematic comparison and synthesis were used to compare and contrast findings across sector-specific and all sectors.

7.5 ACTION RESEARCH

Back in 1946, social psychologist Kurt Lewin (1946) proposed a cyclical, iterative approach to research involving planning what was to be done, taking action, and then, fact finding about the results. Lewin's ideas have since become one of the key influences in what is now known as action research. Over time, action research has taken different directions, but we can nevertheless identify key features of the approach as we are using it here:

- Research is conducted as a collaborative partnership between the researcher and a group (e.g. in an organization) who participate in the process of the action research.
- There is a close relationship between knowledge acquisition and action. Action is taken to improve practice, and the research generates new knowledge about how and why the improvements came about (Coghlan and Brannick, 2010).
- Research proceeds as a cycle of joint planning, action, observation, and reflection, where the reflection phase paves the way for further cycles of planning, acting, observing, and reflecting in a spiral of learning (Figure 7.5).
- The results are shared amongst participants.
- The output is 'actionable knowledge' that is useful to both the practitioner and academic communities.

Participatory action research is one particular type of action research which emphasizes the collaborative and democratic possibilities of this approach. Typically, participatory action research initiatives are designed and led by community members (for example, residents in a particular neighbourhood), though academics and other professional researchers may be involved in the design, execution, and evaluation of the initiative. The underlying assumptions in participatory action research are that those closest to the problem also

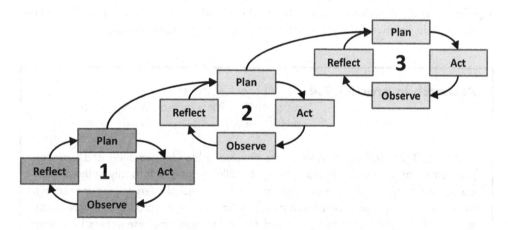

FIGURE 7.5 Action research cycles

know the most about it and that everyone can contribute to the research project. Both qualitative and quantitative methods may be used in action research.

7.5.1 Applications of action research

Action research's action orientation makes it appropriate for investigating causal and process questions where the focus is on producing solutions to problems encountered in practice and understanding what is required to effect change. Within organizations and management, some of the early action research projects investigated issues around autonomous work groups in organizations. Action research has also been used to design and evaluate community and organizational interventions. It is a particularly popular research method among management students who are studying while working and who wish to undertake the research in their own organization.

7.5.2 Strengths and weaknesses of action research

Coghlan (2004: 7) claims that action research 'has the potential to confront the self-perpetuating limitations [such as practical relevance] that befall traditional research approaches'. An action research project can give researchers the opportunity to ameliorate the situation investigated and, in the case of practising managers researching in their own organization, to improve their own professional practice.

Given action research's engagement with problem solving in a particular context, however, questions may be asked about the relevance of any findings beyond the immediate research setting. Action research also raises a number of practical challenges for the would-be action researcher, such as the potential tension between the demands of the practical problem and those of the research project, or the researcher becoming over-involved in the situation or being used as a tool in organizational politics. Some ethical issues may also arise. The principle of informed consent, for instance, may be hard to apply in a rapidly evolving research situation or where the boundaries of the project are ill-defined.

Research in Practice 7.4 gives an example of an action research study.

Research in practice 7.4 Action research study on the adoption of blended learning at a university in Hong Kong

Li et al. (2022) used action research to develop a blended teaching and learning programme at a university in Hong Kong. In collaboration with faculty at the participating university, the researchers developed a first round of interventions concerning installation of a specific type of technology in the classroom. Through interviews with students and instructors, and analysis of server log data, the researchers identified a number of problems and challenges, leading to a redesign of the technology and teaching activities, as well as instructions on how to use the technology for the second round of interventions. Feedback was collected, again, from the participants, this time via interviews, surveys, and server log data. Subsequently, a third combination of technology, instructions, and teaching activities was tried. Additional interviews and surveys were conducted with the participants, alongside analysis of server log data. Based on this action research initiative, the team found that a specific combination of technology solutions, technical instructions, and teaching activities that enabled synchronous delivery as well as asynchronous support, which could effectively facilitate learning for students who were not in the classroom, both those who regularly joined the class remotely and those who faced temporary barriers, such as illness. The authors wrote that using action research had enabled them to 'bridge the gap between research and practice, in which the researchers were involved. The practical problems were identified by one of the authors during teaching, and another author acted as a teaching assistant in the courses. Actions were taken in each round to improve teaching and learning efficiency and student satisfaction' (Li et al., 2022: 223).

7.6 INTERVIEW STUDIES

The word 'interview' is used in different ways in research, including the face-to-face or telephone administration of a quantitative questionnaire, as part of a survey study. Here we will use it to refer to the in-depth interviews used in qualitative research. Such interviews play an important role as a data collection technique in many different qualitative research designs, including case study and ethnography, but often alongside other data collection methods such as observation. There are, however, many qualitative research projects in which interviews are the sole data source (Brinkmann and Kvale, 2018). One such example is interpretative phenomenological analysis, which concerns itself with the study of personal lived experiences and how people make sense of their decisions and choices (Smith et al., 2021). As a result, it is legitimate to talk about an interview study as a research design in business and management.

Interview studies can use a variety of interview formats, including individual and group interviews, open ended or structured, and synchronous or asynchronous. Although there is no generally accepted, standardized format for an interview study, Figure 7.6 gives an outline of the key steps that are involved. You will see that this process has a series of feedback loops. These underline the developmental character of this type of research, which allows emerging findings to be used to shape the project as it unfolds.

7.6.1 Applications of interview study designs

Qualitative interviews, and by extension interview studies, offer the opportunity for participants 'to tell their own stories, in their own words, in depth, and in detail' (Smith et al., 2021: 54). As a result:

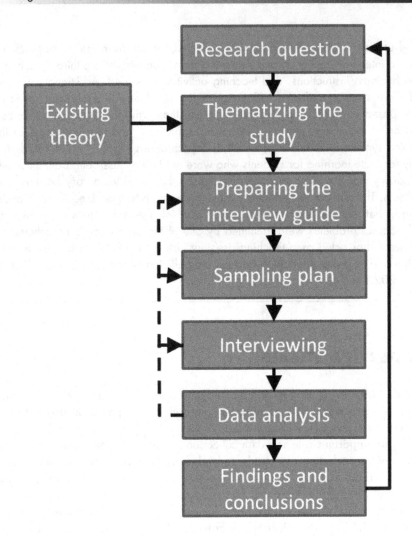

FIGURE 7.6 Steps in an interview study

The qualitative interview is a key venue for exploring the ways in which subjects experience and understand their world. It provides a unique access to the lived world of the subjects, who in their own words describe their activities, experiences and opinions.

Brinkmann and Kvale (2018: 10)

Interviews are also valuable for investigating novel, ill-defined topics where more structured data collection techniques are not feasible or where the ability to follow up emergent issues is likely to be important. Given the widespread use of interviews within different research designs, we explore their use as a data collection method more fully in Chapter 11.

7.6.2 Strengths and weaknesses of interview studies

One of the main strengths of the interview study design is its flexibility: it can be used in many different situations either as a standalone design or as part of a mixed methods study. The familiarity of interviewing in general is undoubtedly an attraction of the method. Interview studies can also be used when other research methods are not possible, for example, due to the nonliteracy of participants. In some situations, an interview study may offer a more efficient way of investigating a topic than other research designs. Convenience alone, however, is not adequate grounds for choosing a particular research design and the key issue is whether or not an interview study is actually adequate to answer the research question.

Questions can be raised regarding the nature of data generated by interviews and therefore by interview studies. Interview data are generated in the interaction in the interviewer and the interviewee, and thus, the data are in that sense constructed. For some commentators this calls into question the possibility that interviews can really offer us access to a reality beyond the interview whether we are wanting to find out about the external world or the meanings and lived experiences of interviewees.

Research in Practice 7.5 gives an example of an interview study.

Research in practice 7.5 Interview study of Pinterest Users' Practices and Views

For her MSc dissertation, White (2013) studied how female users view and use the social media website Pinterest. White chose interviews because her goal was to capture 'the variety of uses and attitudes towards Pinterest, rather than to provide a quantitative portrait of opinions' (White, 2013: 13). The author also deemed interviews to be superior to other qualitative research designs such as ethnographies, because 'although I might be able to glean information from observing women use and navigate their Pinterest home pages, interviews enable the researcher to go beyond pure observation and provide the opportunity to converse with the respondents in order to better understand their attitudes and beliefs' (White, 2013: 13–14). The interview guide was developed from the literature and trialled in a pilot study with three participants. The guide was 'continuously modified during the interview process to accommodate emerging themes and topics' (White, 2013: 16).

The author recruited participants via her personal contacts and posts on social media sites and conducted in-depth, semi-structured interviews face to face and over Skype.

7.7 QUALITATIVE APPROACHES TO LANGUAGE ANALYSIS

Language is central to qualitative research because of the focus upon words, images, and other symbols, rather than numbers. Such inputs can be analyzed for what they can tell us about what is happening in a given situation. For example, you might study a corporate annual report for information about what the company has been doing. In this way, language is treated as a resource through which we can learn about the world. An alternative approach is to see language itself as a topic for analysis. Instead of analyzing the corporate report for what it tells us about the company, we might analyze how the company uses words, images, and other symbols to present itself and to communicate with its shareholders. In this section we will look at three different qualitative research designs that investigate language and language use as a topic rather than a resource. Each uses a different basic research design to achieve its aim.

7.7.1 Qualitative content analysis

Qualitative content analysis (QCA) is a variant of the (quantitative) content analysis approach we introduced in Chapter 6. Like quantitative content analysis, QCA can be used to analyze both verbal and visual text material in either paper or digital format, including online material. It involves classifying language data by following a methodical, sequential procedure in which a coding system and the rules for applying it are developed separately from their application to the bulk of the material to be analyzed (Schreier, 2012). Where QCA differs from quantitative content analysis is in its greater emphasis on developing the coding system from the data rather than from prior theory, along with a recognition that frequency may not always be the best indicator of importance when analyzing the data (Mayring, 2000).

7.7.2 Discourse analysis

In this section we focus on a version of discourse analysis that has been influenced by the work of the French philosopher and historian Michel Foucault regarding how discourse actively constructs meanings:

> Different discourses constitute key entities (be they 'mental illness', 'citizenship' or 'literacy') in different ways, and position people in different ways as social subjects (e.g. as doctors or patients) and it is these social effects of discourse that are focused upon in discourse analysis.
>
> Fairclough (1992: 3–4)

One approach to analyzing discourse that seeks to investigate its social effects is critical discourse analysis (CDA). CDA provides a method for tracing the relationships between language and wider social relations, practices, and structures. To achieve this, CDA brings together both the social and the linguistic aspects of discourse. CDA can be used to understand the discursive component of organizational change, such as how new discourses emerge, how a particular discourse becomes dominant, or how a dominant discourse is enacted in the organization. Doolin (2003), for example, explores how different discourses were employed during a change management programme in a hospital in an attempt to reconstitute clinical care as 'patient flow management' and doctors as 'clinicians-as-managers'. The latter conflicted with a view of the doctor as 'medical professional', and the management role was resisted by clinicians.

7.7.3 Conversation analysis

Although it is sometimes classified as a type of discourse analysis, our third approach to analyzing language is a very distinctive one that focuses on talk in interaction. Known as conversation analysis (CA), it studies how talk is organized sequentially during social interaction. Characteristics of CA include (ten Have, 2007)

- a focus on oral communication involving more than one person;
- fine-grained analysis of the language being used in naturally occurring situations;
- analysis of the context as a means of understanding the sequence of interactions;
- recording of macro-social phenomena relevant to understanding the conversation.

In conversation analysis there is a preference for inductive, data-driven analysis.

The term conversation analysis and the emphasis on naturally occurring talk may suggest that the primary concern of CA is informal conversation, but CA has in practice been applied to a wide range of other settings, including what is referred to as institutional talk or institutional interaction. Applications have included organizational leadership (e.g.Clifton, 2019), improving service helplines (Hepburn et al., 2014) and homeless people street selling the *Big Issue* magazine (Llewellyn and Burrow, 2008). We present an example in Research in Practice 7.6.

Research in practice 7.6 Conversation analysis of group meetings in an organization

Kimura (2021) used conversation analysis (CA) techniques to examine how participants in a university-industry collaborative project, in Japan, influenced each other in meetings, through what they said and how they did so. The meetings between the two academics and four practitioners who were jointly developing a new educational programme were recorded. Subsequently, the researcher coded the various interventions in terms of types, such as whether the speaker was sharing information, expressing an opinion, asking a question, or responding to one. Furthermore, the researcher also noted whether the tone of the speaker was positive, negative, or neutral, as well as interjections such as 'uh-huh' or 'I see'. By including these elements in the analysis, Kimura was able to capture 'how group members' attitudes toward a particular subject have changed in real-time situations at meetings (and) describe what kind of order emerged in the group and caused the attitude change among the group members (Kimura, 2021: 204).

7.8 CHOOSING A QUALITATIVE RESEARCH DESIGN

In this final section, we offer guidance on choosing the qualitative research design that would be appropriate to answer your research question.

7.8.1 Qualitative designs for answering descriptive and exploratory questions

Qualitative approaches to description focus on the in-depth study of a small number of cases in terms of their range and diversity (Jansen, 2010). This focus allows you to develop a rich and detailed description of something, while leaving scope for the unexpected, helped by the flexible and open-ended nature of most qualitative data collection methods.

Another distinctive characteristic of qualitative description is its preference for taking an emic viewpoint emphasizing the experiences and perspectives of those involved in a situation. In this approach, 'the aim [of description] is to grasp in some way what it is like to be the people under investigation and to go through the experiences as they go through them' (Thorpe and Holt, 2008: 7).

One key aspect of description in qualitative research is the development of 'thick' description, a term popularized by the ethnographer Clifford Geertz (1975). Thick description is more than just very detailed description. As Ponterotto (2006: 543) puts it, 'thick description accurately describes observed social actions and assigns purpose and intentionality to these actions, by way of the researcher's understanding and clear description of the context under which the social actions took place'.

The flexible nature of qualitative research means that many of the research designs introduced in this chapter can be used for descriptive purposes. Case study is particularly suited for in-depth description of individual cases and ethnography for studies taking an emic perspective with an emphasis on thick description. Interview studies can be used in a wide range of descriptive research projects, but their flexibility and open-endedness make them particularly useful in exploratory research projects and for investigating the experiences and perspectives of respondents in their own words. Qualitative content analysis can be used for the descriptive analysis of messages, such as advertising, Internet postings, and printed text.

7.8.2 Quantitative designs for answering explanatory questions

The relationship between qualitative research and explanation is not straightforward. Some researchers see the role of qualitative research as primarily one of exploration and discovery, with any causal claims being treated as 'speculative' (Maxwell, 2012: 35). Despite this, many qualitative studies do take an interest in why things are happening and what the consequences are (Hammersley, 2013). Thus, researchers like Miles et al. have stressed the potential for using qualitative methods to answer 'why' questions:

> We consider qualitative analysis to be a very powerful method for assessing causation. . . . Qualitative analysis, with its close-up look, can identify *mechanisms* going beyond sheer association. It is unrelentingly local and deals well with the complex network of events and processes in a situation. It can sort out the *temporal* dimension, showing clearly what preceded what, either through direct observation or *retrospection*.
>
> Miles et al. (2020: 222–225; italics in original)

The language being used here is that of causal explanation rather than causal description and sees qualitative methods providing ways of developing that explanation. Writing from a realist perspective, Maxwell (2012: 38) identifies three specific areas where qualitative methods can help with explanation:

1. Identifying causality in single cases through, for example, investigating the mechanisms and processes involved.
2. Understanding the role of context in causal explanation.
3. Incorporating the meanings, beliefs and values of social actors in causal explanation.

A range of qualitative research designs are candidates for answering 'why' questions. Both grounded theory and case study designs have been used for explanatory research. Ethnography has potential to offer explanatory insights, even if that is not necessarily a primary concern for ethnographers. Interview studies can be used to deepen our understanding of actors' motivations and reasoning. Action research provides a way of investigating why things are happening through direct intervention.

7.8.3 Qualitative designs for answering process-oriented questions

Qualitative methods can be used to understand how things come about in terms of process. That is, the sequences of events, actions, and activities through which phenomena, such as organizations or innovations, change and develop over time and in context. Viewing a topic through the lens of process involves 'considering phenomena dynamically – in terms of movement, activity, events, change and temporal evolution' (Langley, 2007: 271).

Examples of applications where you may find qualitative research designs helpful in answering process or 'how' questions include the following:

1. Studying how entities (people, organizations, etc.) change and develop over time, for example, in the context of organizational change, innovation, or mergers and acquisitions.
2. Understanding how 'things' such as organizing, leading, and strategizing actually get done and how social reality is constituted, reproduced, and maintained through social processes, including everyday social interaction.
3. Deepen our understanding of how phenomena behave dynamically over time.

Although features of process, such as frequency of communication or stakeholder participation, can be included as independent variables in causal models, researchers adopting a process orientation usually investigate process more directly. This typically involves gathering data on how the process unfolds over time by adopting either a prospective or a retrospective longitudinal design. Choice of a specific design, however, depends on the focus of your research.

7.9 MIXED METHOD RESEARCH DESIGNS

Up to now we have made the implicit assumption that choosing a research design will involve choosing either a quantitative or a qualitative method. However, as discussed in Chapter 4, it is very common in business and management research to combine methods from both the quantitative and the qualitative approaches, to compensate for the weakness of each.

7.9.1 Reasons to mix methods

Advocates of mixed methods have identified a number of possible benefits in combining methods. Greene et al. (1989), for example, identify five reasons for doing so.

1. Triangulation. Corroborate the findings of one method with those of the other, to increase confidence in the results.
2. Complementarity. The findings of one type of research can be used to clarify, elaborate upon, or illustrate the findings of the other method.
3. Development. The output of one method is used to support the development of another, for example, interviews used to inform the preparation of a questionnaire.
4. Initiation. The questions or results of different methods are used to offer different perspectives or to uncover contradictions and paradoxes. The desire to gain new perspectives can also lead to the combination of methods, even when the assumption is that they are incompatible philosophically (see Critical Commentary 7.1).
5. Expansion. The scope and range of the study can be increased by adopting different methods as appropriate for different research questions within the study.

Behind these potential benefits is the assumption that both methods should be combined in such a way that the resulting study is stronger than it would have been, had a mono method approach been employed. As Creswell and Creswell put it:

> In a sense more *insight* into a problem must be gained from mixing or integrating the quantitative and qualitative data. This . . . provides a stronger understanding of the problem and the question than either [design] by itself.
> Creswell and Creswell (2023: 227)

7.9.2 Mixed method design options

Morgan (1989) identifies two dimensions of mixed methods designs: priority and sequence. Priority refers to the weighting attached to the different methods. Are they equal or is one predominant over the other? Sequence refers to the ordering of the research methods. Will one follow the other, or will they be done in parallel? This generates a range of options, four of which are illustrated in Figure 7.7.

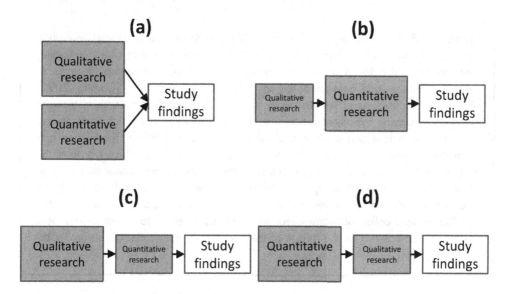

FIGURE 7.7 Example mixed method designs (adapted from Tashakkori and Teddlie, 1998: 44)

In Figure 7.7(a) the researcher is using quantitative and qualitative methods in parallel and with equal weight. The objective may be to achieve methodological triangulation in order to corroborate the findings; alternatively, the approach may be one of 'initiation', whereby the researcher uses different methods to reveal different aspects of a phenomenon. The example in Figure 7.7(b) illustrates how one method may be used to support the development of another, for example, the use of focus groups to help refine a questionnaire as part of a larger survey study. This is a sequential design with the qualitative research coming first but with the quantitative research taking the dominant position with respect to the ultimate findings. An alternative sequential design is given in Figure 7.7(c), where quantitative research is being used to elaborate the findings from a qualitative study. Such research might, for example, involve investigating one dimension of a qualitative study's findings in more breadth by carrying out a survey study, perhaps to establish the prevalence of a particular phenomenon identified by the qualitative research. Figure 7.7(d) uses a qualitative study to elaborate upon or help explain the findings of a quantitative study. We give an example of a mixed method study using this design in Research in Practice 7.7.

Research in practice 7.7 A mixed method study of customer perceptions of chatbot failures

For her doctoral studies, Castillo (2022) set out to investigate customers' assessment of customer service failures caused by chatbots and to understand how their expectations and reactions (for instance, who or what they blamed for the failure) varied with the context. To do that, she conducted three studies. The first one was an interview study which demonstrated how customers perceived three distinct contexts when interacting with chatbots. This initial stage was needed 'due to lack of empirical attention in existing literature, and because of the novelty of the research topic' (Castillo, 2022: 92). From the findings of the first study, Castillo developed a research framework and accompanying hypotheses to test the role of those three distinct contexts on customers' expectations and attribution of responsibility for the failure. The second and third studies were experiments, whereby Castillo manipulated specific elements of the interaction between the customers and the chatbot to test the hypotheses that she had developed. 'The research design is therefore a sequential one, whereby both qualitative and quantitative data collection stages assume equal importance; however, the qualitative data collection stage needs to occur first in order to generate important insight that is required for the design of the quantitative data collection stages' (Castillo, 2022: 91).

7.9.3 Is a mixed method study appropriate?

Despite growing interest in mixed method research and its apparent attractions, it does not follow that mixed method research represents some ideal. Certainly not all research projects would benefit from, let alone require, a mixed method study. Neither is it clear that all the philosophical or technical issues around mixing methods are resolved (see Critical Commentary 7.1). Practical factors intrude as well. The researcher, especially a student researcher, always has finite time and other resources. Spreading those resources too thinly may result in a lower-quality piece of work than if effort had been focused on a single research method. A similar problem comes when reporting research, because of word count or other limits. You will also need to develop the skills to carry out mixed method research, which may be a particular challenge if you are new to research.

If you are considering adopting a mixed method approach, you should think carefully about the logic of doing so. Map out how the different methods are related in terms of sequence and priority. Ask yourself how they combine to answer your research questions. Consider what your mixed method design offers that a mono-method approach would not. Review the practical implications of your research design. Do you have the time, skills, and word count to carry it out successfully? Finally, bear in mind that using more than one method is not a substitute for sound research design and execution.

CRITICAL COMMENTARY 7.1

Mixing methods

Although mixed methods have attracted increased attention over the last few years, there is still some controversy over their role in research. While proponents of mixed methods research argue that combing methods results in the equivalent of '1 + 1 = 3' in terms of findings (Fetters and Freshwater, 2015: 208), this approach is not without challenges.

Cooper et al. (2012) identify the range of perspectives on the benefits and even the possibility of mixing methods. At one end of the debate there are those that argue that quantitative and qualitative research represent incompatible paradigms based on fundamentally different philosophical assumptions (such as positivism versus interpretivism), with supporters of one approach dismissing the other as valueless (or at best subordinate) in terms of producing useful knowledge. In this view there can be no meaningful mixing of methods.

At the other end of the spectrum, there are those that reject any paradigmatic incompatibility between quantitative and qualitative methods. They see the issue of mixing methods more in technical than in philosophical terms, placing emphasis on the characteristics of the methods and their relationship to the research question and, instead, combine them in a single study in order to incorporate the strengths of both approaches.

It is important to be aware of this debate when deciding whether or not to use a mixed method approach.

CHAPTER SUMMARY

- Ethnographic research involves in-depth investigation of a culture-sharing group in which participant-observation and interviews may play a significant role, generating 'thick descriptions' of the phenomenon under investigation.
- Grounded theory research builds theory from data through a systematic, iterative process of constant comparison between emerging theory and data, until theoretical saturation is reached.
- Case study research design involves the study of a relatively small number of naturally occurring cases, in depth and in context, often using multiple sources of evidence.
- Action research requires a collaborative partnership between the researcher and a group of practitioners in a cyclical process of joint planning, action, observation, and reflection that contributes to actionable knowledge.
- Interview studies research focuses on the participants' experiences, points of view, and the meaning that they attach to those experiences, through in-depth probing.
- Qualitative approaches can be used to analyze language in detail. Qualitative content analysis is a data-driven coding system, which stresses the importance of context and interpretation of meaning, and recognizes that frequency is not always the best indicator of importance. Critical discourse analysis recognizes the constitutive properties of discourse and investigates the relationships between discourse

and wider social relations, practices, and structures. Conversation analysis focuses on the detailed analysis of talk-in-interaction to understand how talk is organized sequentially in social interaction.

- Mixed method research combines different methods, to compensate for the weaknesses of each. How the different approaches are combined in a single study can be characterized in terms of sequencing and priority.
- Choice of research design should take into account the type of question being asked by the research.

NEXT STEPS

7.1 Research designs used in your topic area. Review the research articles that you have identified in your literature review.

  a. What specific qualitative or mixed methods research designs are used in your topic area?

  b. What types of research question are they used to answer?

  c. What are the strengths and weaknesses of these designs in relation to your topic area?

  d. Evaluate the contribution made by the different qualitative or mixed methods research designs in your topic area.

7.2 What qualitative or mixed methods research design may be suitable for your own project? Review your research questions and your answers to Next steps in Chapter 4.

  a. What specific qualitative or mixed methods research designs could be used to answer your research question?

  b. What would be the strengths and weaknesses of those designs for your project?

  c. Evaluate the suitability of the qualitative or mixed methods research designs you have identified for answering your research questions.

FURTHER READING

More details how to carry out the designs introduced in this chapter can be found on the companion website, along with suggestions for further reading.

REFERENCES

Agarwal, U. A. and Rai, A. (2019). Exploring bullying among Indian managers: A grounded theory approach. *Journal of Asia Business Studies*, 13(4): 588–611.

Brewer, J. D. (2004). Ethnography. In: Cassell, C. and Symon, G. (eds) *Essential Guide to Qualitative Methods in Organizational Research*. London: SAGE Publications.

Brinkmann, S. and Kvale, S. (2018). *Doing Interviews*. 2nd ed. Los Angeles, CA: SAGE Publications.

Castillo, D. (2022). *When Chatbots Fail: Exploring Customer Responsibility Attributions of Service Failures in Disharmonious Co-creation Contexts*. PhD thesis, Brunel Business School, Brunel University London.

Clifton, J. (2019). Using conversation analysis for organisational research: A case study of leadership-in-action. *Communication Research and Practice*, 5(4): 342–357.

Coghlan, D. (2004). Action research in the academy: Why and whither? Reflections on the changing nature of research. *Irish Journal of Management*, 25(2): 1–10.

Coghlan, D. and Brannick, T. (2010). *Doing Action Research in Your Own Organization*. 3rd ed. London: SAGE Publications.

Cooper, B., Glaesser, J., Gomm, R. and Hammersley, M. (2012). *Challenging the Quantitative-Qualitative Divide*. London: Continuum.

Creswell, J. W. and Creswell, J. D. (2023). *Research Design. Qualitative, Quantitative and Mixed Methods Approaches*. 6th ed. Thousand Oaks, CA: SAGE Publications.

Deken, F., Carlile, P. R., Berends, H. and Lauche, K. (2016). Generating novelty through interdependent routines: A process model of routine work. *Organization Science*, 27(3): 659–677.

Doolin, B. (2003). Narratives of change: Discourse, technology and organization. *Organization* 10(4): 751–770.

Fairclough, N. (1992). *Discourse and Social Change*. Cambridge: Polity Press.

Ferreira, M. C. and Scaraboto, D. (2016). "My plastic dreams": Towards an extended understanding of materiality and the shaping of consumer identities. *Journal of Business Research*, 69(1): 191–207.

Fetters, M. D. and Freshwater, D. (2015). Publishing a methodological mixed methods research article. *Journal of Mixed Methods Research*, 9(3): 203–213.

Geertz, C. (1975). *The Interpretation of Cultures*. London: Hutchinson.

Glaser, B. G. and Strauss, A. (1967). *The Discovery of Grounded Theory. Strategies for Qualitative Research*. Chicago: Aldine.

Greene, J. C., Caracelli, V. J. and Graham, W. F. (1989). Toward a conceptual framework for mixed-method evaluation designs. *Educational Evaluation and Policy Analysis*, 11(3): 255–274.

Hammersley, M. (2013). *What is Qualitative Research?* London: Bloomsbury.

Hammersley, M. and Atkinson, P. (2019). *Ethnography, Principles in Practice*. 4th ed. London: Routledge.

Hepburn, A., Wilkinson, S. and Butler, C. W. (2014). Intervening with conversation analysis in telephone helpline services: Strategies to improve effectiveness. *Research on Language and Social Interaction*, 47(3): 239–254.

Jansen, H. (2010). The logic of qualitative survey research and its position in the field of social research methods. *Forum Qualitative Sozialforschung/Forum: Qualitative Social Research*, 11(2). Available at: www.qualitative-research.net/index.php/fqs/article/view/1450/2946.

Kasaji, A. A. (2023). *The Role of Artificial Intelligence in the Actioning of Customer Insight to Manage Customer Experience Throughout the Customer Journey Within Services Organizations in Jordan*. DBA thesis submission, Henley Business School at the University of Reading.

Kimura, Y. (2021). Attitude change process in group-level collaborative activities: Descriptions of interaction via a conversation analysis approach. *International Journal of Organizational Leadership*, 10(2): 197–213.

Langley, A. (2007). Process thinking in strategic organization. *Strategic Organization*, 5(3): 271–282.

Lewin, K. (1946). Action research and minority problems. *Journal of Social Issues*, 2(4): 34–46.

Li, X., Yang, Y., Chu, S. K. W., Zainuddin, Z. and Zhang, Y. (2022). Applying blended synchronous teaching and learning for flexible learning in higher education: An action research study at a university in Hong Kong. *Asia Pacific Journal of Education*, 42(2): 211–227.

Llewellyn, N. and Burrow, R. (2008). Streetwise sales and the social order of city streets. *The British Journal of Sociology*, 59(3): 561–583.

Maxwell, J. A. (2012). *A Realist Approach for Qualitative Research*. Thousand Oaks, CA: SAGE Publications.

Mayring, P. (2000). Qualitative content analysis. *Forum Qualitative Sozialforschung/Forum: Qualitative Social Research*, 1(2). Available at: www.qualitative-research.net/index.php/fqs/article/view/1089.

Miles, M. B., Huberman, M. A. and Saldaña, J. (2020). *Qualitative Data Analysis*. 4th ed. Thousand Oaks, CA: SAGE Publications.

Morgan, D. L. (1989). Practical strategies for combining qualitative and quantitative methods: Applications to health research. *Qualitative Health Research*, 8(3): 362–376.

Ponterotto, J. G. (2006). Brief note on the origins, evolution, and meaning of the qualitative research concept thick description. *The Qualitative Report*, 11(3): 538–549.

Schjøtt Hansen, A. and Hartley, J. M. (2021). Designing what's news: An ethnography of a personalization algorithm and the data-driven (re)assembling of the news. *Digital Journalism*. https://doi.org/10.1080/21670811.2021.1988861.

Schreier, M. (2012). *Qualitative Content Analysis in Practice*. London: SAGE Publications.

Sheikhaboumasoudi, A., Isfahani, A. N. and Barzoki, A. S. (2018). Designing a model for identifying key factors of error management culture using grounded theory: An empirical study. *International Journal of Learning and Intellectual Capital*, 15(3): 219–241.

Smith, J. A., Flowers, P. A. and Larkin, M. A. (2021). *Interpretative Phenomenological Analysis: Theory, Method and Research*. 2nd ed. London: SAGE Publications.

Suddaby, R. (2006). From the editors: What grounded theory is not. *Academy of Management Journal*, 49(4): 633–642.

Tashakkori, A. and Teddlie, C. (1998). *Mixed Methodology*. Thousand Oaks, CA: SAGE Publications.

ten Have, P. (2007). *Doing Conversation Analysis*. 2nd ed. London: SAGE Publications.

Thorpe, R. and Holt, R. (eds) (2008). *The SAGE Dictionary of Qualitative Management Research*. London: SAGE Publications.

van den Broek, E., Sergeeva, A. and Huysman, M. (2021). When the machine meets the expert: An ethnography for developing AI hiring. *MIS Quarterly*, 45(3): 1557–1580.

Venkataraman, A. and Joshi, C. S. (2020). Who am I? An ethnographic study exploring the construction of organizational and individual self among Indian IT employees. *IIM Kozhikode Society & Management Review*, 9(1): 72–83.

White, E. (2013). *Pinning Pretty: A Qualitative Study of Pinterest Users' Practices and Views*. Master's thesis, Media@LSE, London School of Economics and Political Science, London. Available at: www.lse.ac.uk/media-and-communications/assets/documents/research/msc-dissertations/2013/117-White.pdf.

Yin, R. K. (2018). *Case Study Research and Applications: Design and Methods*. 6th ed. Thousand Oaks, CA: SAGE Publications.

Zhang, Y., Liu, Y., Li, W., Peng, L. and Yuan, C. (2020). A study of the influencing factors of mobile social media fatigue behavior based on the grounded theory. *Information Discovery and Delivery*, 48(2): 91–102.

Planning and managing your research project

8.1 INTRODUCTION

Carrying out a research project is not just an intellectual activity. You will also need to apply practical organizational skills, effective engagement with multiple stakeholders, and manage the commitment of time and other resources. A successful research project involves a series of decisions at both the planning and implementation stages. In this chapter we look at how you reach these decisions. We start with guidance on how to select the most appropriate research design for your project and the factors that you should consider when making your decision. Having selected your research design, you will then need to plan your project in terms of the activities you need to carry out and the time and other resources you will need, so we discuss what to consider at the planning stage. You will also need to think about how to manage your project once it is underway, so we move on to look at the various activities that are involved in doing so effectively. As you work you will need to keep track of your thoughts and reflections on your project and your role in it. To help you do this, we introduce the idea of a research diary or journal kept either paper based or digitally. Finally, we look at how to prepare a research proposal. This is a document written at the start of your project, for review by a supervisor, client, or funding body, that sets out your proposed research and how you will carry it out. We provide you with guidance as to the structure and content of an effective research proposal.

DOI: 10.4324/9781003381006-10

8.2 SELECTING A RESEARCH DESIGN

Before you can begin detailed planning, you will need to finalise what type of research design is appropriate for your research project. Your decision will be influenced by a number of factors, as we show in Figure 8.1. Some of these relate to the nature of the research problem itself, others to practical aspects of the project or to you as the researcher. As you consider each in turn, write down your thoughts as these will help you when it comes to describing and justifying your research design in your final report. These notes will also be useful to you as the basis of your research proposal.

8.2.1 Research question(s)

The starting point for choosing a design should be your research questions. This is because the design must be capable of providing you with appropriate data from which to answer your research questions and so resolve your research problem. To help you to link your choice of research design to your research questions, Table 8.1 maps different research designs onto the three generic research types and the respective research questions

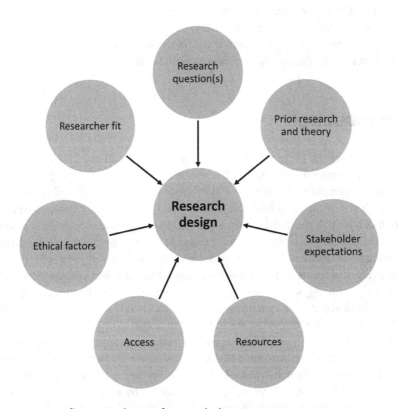

FIGURE 8.1 Factors influencing choice of research design

TABLE 8.1 Mapping your research questions to research designs

Type of research question	Quantitative methods		Qualitative methods	
	Possible research focus	Possible research design(s)	Possible research focus	Possible research design(s)
Descriptive/exploratory research questions *What?*	• Measurement and frequency distribution of key variables of a population or phenomenon • Description of aggregate properties of a population or phenomenon	• Descriptive surveys • Content analysis (for text) • Data-driven quantitative research	• In-depth, thick description of a phenomenon and its context • Lived experience and perspectives of those involved in a particular situation • Understanding of the diversity of a phenomenon	• Interview study • Ethnography • Case study • Qualitative content analysis (for text)
Explanatory research questions *Why?*	• Testing of explanatory theory • Measurement of the impact of one variable on another • Prediction of a dependent variable from the value of one or more independent variables	• Experiments and quasi experiments • Nonexperimental explanatory designs (e.g. natural experiment, analytic survey) • Content analysis (for testing the impact of message content)	• Building explanatory theory • Identification of causal mechanisms, process, and context • Understanding of actors' reasoning, values, and beliefs from their perspective	• Case study • Grounded theory • Action research • Interview study • Ethnography
Process research questions *How?*	• Testing of process theory • Modelling of development of phenomena over time	• Analytic survey (for testing causal models) • Time series analysis	• Building process theory • Identification of process of change and development • Analysis of social construction of phenomena through social processes and language	• Grounded theory • Case study • Ethnography • Conversation analysis • Critical discourse analysis

identified in Chapter 2 and discussed in Chapters 4, 6, and 7. In Table 8.1 we have split out quantitative and qualitative research methods to emphasize that they each offer different insights into the research question(s) under investigation. Mixed method designs may also be appropriate where a single method will not be adequate to address all aspects of your research questions. For further details on each design, you should refer back to the relevant sections in Chapters 6 and 7.

Guidelines such as in Table 8.1 provide a useful starting point for thinking about how to align your research design with your research questions. However, they should not be treated as a prescriptive framework in which the required design is simply 'read off' from the table. Developing a research design requires careful thought and reflection about your research problem, along with a sound understanding of the options available. Your decision process must also take into account the many other factors that can influence the final choice of research design and which we explore next.

8.2.2 Prior research and theory

Your critical review of literature will give you a thorough understanding of the research problem, what is already known, and how it has been researched in the past. It will help you to gain an understanding of the existing world view of your research problem. Prior research can also be a useful source of inspiration and methods for your own project. For example, you may decide to replicate a study found in the literature in a different context (with, of course, appropriate acknowledgement to the original research). Alternatively, you may make use of specific elements of an earlier study, such as measurement scales in a questionnaire, that have been shown to be useful and reliable. At the same time, prior research can also help you to identify whether certain approaches to research are commonly used or widely accepted in a particular field. Your chosen research field may have developed specific research designs that are particularly appropriate to the nature of the problem under investigation, thereby providing you with a useful starting point when selecting your own research design. Your critical analysis of literature will help you to become aware of any biases in prior research which you should aim not to repeat.

8.2.3 Stakeholder expectations

As a researcher, decisions about your research design are rarely taken in isolation. For many research projects, key stakeholders will have to give explicit approval before the project can proceed. A principal stakeholder is the community, organization, or group of individuals in your research population represented by your sample. It is important to ensure that participants are willing to be researched and give consent to be involved. This is particularly important, for example, in internal organizational research. It should not be assumed that all employees will willingly wish to participate in, for example, a staff survey or work audit.

Gaining other forms of approval may be necessary depending on your research situation. As a student researcher you will probably have to submit a research proposal and gain agreement from your supervisor before starting your research project. In such cases you will have to ensure that your proposed research design meets the requirements for your programme of study. Alternatively, approval may be required if you are applying for research funding or if you are conducting research for and on behalf of another body, such as your own organization as an insider researcher. In such situations the expectations of organizational stakeholders will be set by their perceptions of the value to them of the research you are proposing to carry out. Gaining formal approval goes beyond choice of the research design, so we return to this important aspect of research planning at the end of this chapter. Note that as well as setting explicit requirements for your project, stakeholders may also have expectations and preferences regarding what they believe are suitable research methods based on their own experiences, professional background, and so on. It is important to be aware of these when considering your choice of design. In some cases, considerable negotiation may be needed to reach agreement on what is acceptable as an approach. Remember, however, that you must always ensure that your research design is able to answer the research questions you have set.

8.2.4 Resources

Researchers rarely enjoy unlimited availability of resources such as time, money, people, or technology. Lack of resources can significantly constrain the scale and scope of a research project. In some circumstances, resource limitations can actually prevent the desired research approach being carried out. The selection of a research design must therefore take into account practical resource constraints. Do you have sufficient time or travel budget, for example, to conduct a face-to-face interview study with respondents in different countries? Do you have access to technology that can enable online interviews and so reduce cost? Do you have sufficient funds to acquire specialized software for a computer simulation design or data analysis? Whilst resource constraints should not determine the research design, you will have to be aware of their potential impact and find ways of managing them at the design and planning stage. In particular, be aware of any time limits, especially with regard to submission dates for qualification programmes and deadlines for commercial projects.

8.2.5 Access

As researchers we may be able to think of many interesting research problems and ways of investigating them but the ultimate feasibility of many research projects is constrained by the availability of, and access to, appropriate sources of data. This may be access to a sufficient number of suitable participants who will agree to be interviewed or to take part in a survey for primary research, or it may be access to relevant documents or databases for secondary analysis. For example, exclusion of particular individuals in a survey due to access difficulties can impact your research output and the validity of your findings. Access to data is therefore an important consideration when choosing your research design because different research designs place different demands on data collection. Accessibility may not be an easy issue to assess at the start of a project and problems are often recognized or experienced only part way through a project (sometimes with disastrous consequences).

It is therefore important to develop a good strategy for gaining and maintaining access early in your project, a topic we return to in Chapter 9 when we discuss sampling for data collection in more detail.

8.2.6 Ethical factors

It is essential that your research design takes account of appropriate ethical standards and practices as discussed in Chapter 5. Ethical issues must be considered right from the start of the project, as these can affect your design decisions, especially when the research involves respondents from potentially vulnerable groups or involves some form of researcher intervention such as in an experiment. Remember the importance of inclusivity as discussed in Chapter 5. Ensure that at the planning stage your research design is not biased in any way by excluding a particular group. Diversity in the research team is particularly important or if you are working alone make sure to consult widely with others relevant to your research population.

In addition, as we highlighted in Chapter 5, most research projects require that formal ethical approval is obtained before you begin data collection. Ensure that you think through the ethical implications of your proposed research design at an early stage, allow enough time to obtain ethical approval and consider alternative design options should approval be denied.

8.2.7 Researcher fit

Your own philosophical orientation, interests, preferences, experiences, and skills will all influence your choice of research design, just as they will influence your choice of research topic. You may instinctively be more comfortable with some research methods and techniques than others. Alternatively, you may wish to gain new research skills or to build on particular skills you have already developed. The role of personal preference in design choice is a contentious subject because, as Buchanan and Bryman (2007: 495) note, 'novice researchers are typically instructed not to allow personal preference and bias to intrude on "technical" decisions concerning research methods'. Research students often worry about whether their personal view of research philosophy ('am I Positivist or Interpretivist?') has to align to their proposed research design, which is often more attuned to their skills and competencies to handle the project. Feeling guilty about selection of a research design is not helpful. The influence of personal preferences on the choice of research design should nevertheless be the subject of reflection by the researcher, as we have discussed in Chapter 1. In addition, a research project can be a great opportunity to build your skills and competencies in research and in a new topic area by moving beyond your comfort zone. Ultimately, however, you will still have to be able to complete the project successfully, so give careful thought to the feasibility of a project in terms of your current levels of knowledge and personal circumstances.

8.3 PLANNING YOUR RESEARCH PROJECT

Having chosen your overall research design, you should turn your attention to planning how you will carry out the project itself. Whether you are researching in an academic or organizational setting, effective planning will be an important factor in achieving a successful outcome. Planning a research project does not have to be enormously complex. With the exception of large-scale research projects with multiple researchers, you will usually need to use only some basic techniques of project management with which you may already be familiar. You should aim to produce a project plan that identifies the following elements:

- project activities and deliverables
- project time schedule
- project risks

If there is a larger research team involved, a resource schedule showing who is carrying out the various tasks is also useful. The resulting plan can then feed into your research proposal and be used as your guide during your project. Table 8.2 outlines the steps in generating a plan for a simple project.

8.3.1 Project activities

The precise activities that you will need to carry out depend on the details of the project. We can, however, identify some typical activities based on our five-stage research model and the generic elements of research design. We summarize these activities for a typical student research project in Table 8.3, to help you start your planning. You should adjust the content to match the format of your particular project.

Note that we have included interim outputs in the form of draft work, on which you may have the opportunity to get feedback from your supervisor if you have one.

8.3.2 Developing a time schedule

One of the biggest challenges in planning a research project is working out how long you will need for the various activities. This is partly because doing research can be highly dependent upon the availability of others, for example, interview respondents, whose availability may be unknown at the start of the project. In addition, it can be hard to gauge how long certain activities will take you without prior experience (for example, doing data analysis for the first time). Unfortunately it is very difficult to give firm guidance here because it depends so much on the nature of the project, the willingness of others to participate, scheduling arrangements, and your own circumstances and experience as a researcher (especially if you are researching for your studies while working full time). We

TABLE 8.2 Developing a plan for your research project

Step	Task
1	Identify the key activities and outputs in the project.
2	Estimate how long each activity will take and what resources you will need. This can be difficult for novice researchers, so always consult your tutor or supervisor if you are unsure.
3	Work out the relationships and dependencies between the different activities. For example, do some activities (such as data collection) have to be carried out before others (such as data analysis), or can some be worked on in parallel?
4	Identify any schedule constraints such as deadlines, public holidays, resource availability, turnaround times for feedback and so on.
5	Develop a schedule for time and (where needed) for resources.
6	Identify and develop a plan for managing risks in the project.

TABLE 8.3 Typical activities in a student research project

Stage	Typical activities	Typical outputs
Research design and planning	• Choose research design • Develop research project plan	• Research proposal • Ethical approval submission
Literature review	• Search, capture, synthesize, and present critical review of relevant literature	• Draft of literature review section for final report
Data collection	• Finalize sampling plan • Develop, pretest, and pilot data collection instruments (e.g. questionnaire or interview guide) • Carry out data collection plan	• Sampling plan • Data collection instruments • Raw data • Draft of research design section for final report
Data analysis	• Prepare data for analysis • Analyze data • Draw conclusions	• Draft of analysis and findings section for final report
Writing up	• Draft final report • Review of draft with supervisor • Final editing • Printing and binding (if required) • Submit report plus any informed consent evidence required	• Final draft • Final report

therefore provide the following tips which may help you avoid drawing up an over-optimistic time schedule.

- Allow sufficient time for your literature review. Students often underestimate the time this will take. Becoming familiar with the search process, locating and reading articles, and capturing the right information will take a significant amount of time.
- Be realistic about how long it will take you to arrange access to respondents and for them to be available to participate. This is particularly important when organizing appointments for face-to-face interviews. The more senior the person or the busier their lifestyle, the more difficult it will be to schedule appointments. Do not expect your research participants to be available to see you at short notice, so start planning this part of your research early if you are doing an interview study.
- Always factor in turnaround times for any forms of response to correspondence or contact from you (including return of questionnaires, review of drafts by a supervisor, requests for access, and so on), whether it is electronic or not.
- Allow time for pretesting and piloting any data collection instrument (such as a questionnaire) that you plan to use.
- Do not underestimate the time it takes to carry out data analysis, particularly if you are doing it for the first time. Consider how long it may take you to obtain and then learn to use any new software.
- Allow sufficient time for writing up. We recommend that you write your research report as your project progresses. This should reduce the time it takes you to complete the final report, but you will still need time to collate, review, and edit the final version.
- Finally, allow enough time for printing, binding, and physical submission if you have to produce a hard copy of your report.

Once you have identified the activities and their dependencies and estimated how long each will take, you can draw up the time schedule for your project. This can be done as a table but is probably most easily communicated to others using a Gantt chart, as shown in Figure 8.2, for a research project for a part-time student.

8.3.3 Assessing risk

A **research risk** is any uncertain event or condition that, if it occurs, has an effect upon the project. Therefore identifying risks is an important step when planning your research. In Chapter 5 we learnt about ethical risks. Here we are primarily concerned with practical risks that would have a negative effect on completing your research, and in Table 8.4 we have listed some of the risks that we see commonly encountered during student research projects. Similar risks can arise in other research projects, but an important additional risk factor for research projects that are done for a commercial or other client face is the problem of scope creep as we discussed in Chapter 2. Do not let your project get out of hand as a result.

ID	Task Name	Start	Finish	Duration
1	Prepare and submit proposal	03/11/2025	11/11/2025	7d
2	Literature review	12/11/2025	10/12/2025	21d
3	Finalize sampling plan	11/12/2025	16/12/2025	4d
4	Questionnaire design	11/12/2025	19/12/2025	7d
5	Obtain ethical approval	11/12/2025	24/12/2025	10d
6	Questionnaire pre-test and pilot	25/12/2025	31/12/2025	5d
7	Administer the questionnaire	01/01/2026	20/01/2026	14d
8	Draft method section of report	01/01/2026	06/01/2026	4d
9	Data preparation	21/01/2026	22/01/2026	2d
10	Data analysis	23/01/2026	05/02/2026	10d
11	Draft analysis and findings	06/02/2026	11/02/2026	4d
12	Draft final report	12/02/2026	03/03/2026	14d
13	Final editing	04/03/2026	10/03/2026	5d
14	Printing, binding and submission	11/03/2026	16/03/2026	4d

FIGURE 8.2 Example Gantt chart time schedule

Once you have identified possible risks, you can prioritize them using a simple low/medium/high classification and develop strategies for avoiding or mitigating them, as we have shown in Table 8.4. Make sure that you continue to monitor risks as the project unfolds.

8.4 MANAGING YOUR RESEARCH PROJECT

Like any other project, research requires active management as well as careful planning. In particular you will have to pay careful attention to the management of time, risks, key stakeholders, and your data once your project is underway.

8.4.1 Keeping to time

Once you have started your project, you will need to monitor its progress according to your project plan. If you are the only researcher conducting your own project, then keeping the project to the time schedule is really down to your own time management skills and your ability to motivate other stakeholders to participate and support you as necessary. You may have to adjust your time schedule as the study progresses in the light of any changes that occur. Remain alert to any potentially serious disruptions to your schedule. If you are conducting the project for academic study, you should ensure that your assigned supervisor, as well as any sponsor you may be working with, is kept up to date with the progress of your study and any potential disruptions.

If you are working as part of a project team, then more formal project monitoring and reporting will be needed. You should provide regular updates of completion of elements

TABLE 8.4 Example risks in a student research project

Stage	Example risks	Example avoidance or mitigation strategies
Research design and planning	• Research proposal rejected • Ethical approval rejected	• Ensure you understand and adhere to the proposal guidelines • Discuss your ideas with potential supervisor or other tutors before submitting • Ensure that you understand and follow ethical guidelines; seek advice if unsure • Be prepared to make changes and resubmit
Literature review	• Unable to access suitable sources	• Read around the literature prior to starting the topic to confirm availability of and access to suitable literature
Data collection	• Unable to access research site, required sample and/or achieve required sample size • Loss or corruption of data	• Negotiate and agree access to research site at the planning stage • Identify target population and sampling frame early in the project • Pretest and pilot questionnaire or other data collection instrument to test access levels • Ensure you store data securely and have more than one secure backup copy
Data analysis	• Missing/poor-quality data • Unable to analyze the data as planned due to lack of skills • Data do not provide useful insights	• Pretest and pilot questionnaire or other data collection instrument to reduce missing data problems and ensure data quality • Ensure that you have or can develop the necessary analysis skills when deciding your research design • Choose research questions and a research design that will generate useful insights even if the results are not what was expected
Writing up	• Lack of information on procedures followed during data collection and analysis • Lack of time to write up before submission deadline	• Use a research diary to capture relevant details during your project • Begin drafting your report early during the project

of the study and identify any potential changes to the original schedule. Remember that managing expectations is an important aspect of a successful research project. Whichever type of project you are undertaking, use your Gantt chart (example at Figure 8.2) to track progress, identify upcoming problems when they start to arise and communicate with key stakeholders clearly and appropriately. Be prepared to take action if something is obviously going off track.

8.4.2 Managing risk

If you have carried out a risk assessment as part of your project plan, then you will be aware of the potential difficulties that may arise. Once the project has commenced you should regularly refer to your risk assessment and consider the level of threat that each item continues to pose to the success of your project. As the project progresses you should be able to remove or downgrade the threat posed by different risks. Nevertheless you may encounter a situation where a risk to your project, such as the failure to collect sufficient data, actually occurs. As soon as you are aware of such a problem, you should inform relevant stakeholder(s), such as your academic supervisor. Decisions will then need to be made in terms of alternative courses of action or, in the worst-case scenario, to halt the project pending more radical review of the problems and potential solutions. Whatever the case, ensure that you actively manage risk and do not just wait for things to go wrong.

8.4.3 Engaging stakeholders

Throughout your project, you must ensure that you manage your relationships with key stakeholders. Do not assume that a particular stakeholder will cooperate or be able to give you access when you need it. Engaging with stakeholders during your research is about fully understanding their expectations and managing these throughout your project. This is primarily done through close and accurate two-way communication at both the planning and implementation stages. The level of contact will vary, depending on the type of project and your own status as student researcher or insider researcher.

Managing your project as a student researcher

When managing a research project that forms part of an academic qualification, you will have one or more stakeholder(s) within the academic institution, such as your supervisor and perhaps other tutors or programme management, with whom you will interact. Your supervisor in particular will play a key role in your project. The relationship that you develop with your supervisor is therefore crucial to both the success of your research and your enjoyment of the process. The role and responsibilities of supervisors may vary from institution to institution, so we recommend that you make sure you familiarize yourself with any guidelines from your institution about the role of the supervisor. You should view your supervisor as a core resource in terms of knowledge and advice, who can become a close mentor and supporter during your research project. Take time to get to know your supervisor and agree at the outset how you wish to work together. Establishing a few ground rules at the start can ensure that you gain the maximum benefit from this important relationship.

When carrying out a project as a student researcher, it is essential that you make yourself familiar with all the academic requirements and institutional processes to which you must adhere. It is likely that the institution will provide you with this information in guidance documents, which you should consult regularly during the project. Key aspects of this guidance will be the research proposal, required format for reporting, criteria for assessment, and the time deadline for delivery. Failure to adhere to any such guidance may lead to failure to meet the requirements for your degree.

Managing your project as an insider researcher

If you are an insider researcher doing research in or on behalf of your own organization, you will need to take into account the potential challenges that can arise as a result of being both a researcher and an organizational member. These have been categorized as 'organizational, professional and personal' by Costley et al. (2010: 1), who recognize the effects that they can have on your role as a researcher as well as on the outcome of your project. From an organizational perspective, being on the inside as an employee of the organization means that you will have pre-existing relationships with others with whom you may have close working contact. This position will have advantages. It will mean that you have deeper knowledge of the organization (for example its personnel, structure, and products) and perhaps direct experience of the research problem itself. At the same time, as a researcher you will draw from your professional and personal life in terms of your past experiences, knowledge, skills, and personal values.

As a researcher on the inside of an organization, there will be other organizational members that you work with in your regular role and with whom you will interact and whose expectations you have to manage during the research project. In some cases, internal politics and power plays can create difficulties for the insider researcher. One way to avoid being caught up in all of this is to maintain an open and relatively neutral stance in relation to the viewpoints of others. This will in part be achieved by maintaining good communication and providing regular progress updates with relevant stakeholders. Even so, being an insider researcher can require strong interpersonal and communication skills to manage the ambiguities and tensions that your dual role as a researcher and organizational member can throw up. We give an example of a master's level student researching within her organization in Research in Practice 8.1.

Research in practice 8.1 Researching an internal development programme

The progression of women into senior leadership roles is of increased importance to many organizations today. One mechanism used to encourage this is for women to attend a dedicated women's leadership programme that enables women to come together to explore a range of issues that enable them to address both challenges and motivators to successful progression to leadership.

A large engineering-focused organization who used women's leadership development programmes was concerned as there continued to be a shortfall in women progressing to senior levels. They were particularly experiencing attrition of mid-management level before movement to senior positions. The programme was therefore targeted at women relatively early in their leadership careers. A senior member of the

HR Department responsible for the programme was at the same time studying for a master's degree in Coaching for Behavioural Change and was interested to explore in her research the perceived value of the programme by participants.

The internal programme was sponsored by a key senior leader, and internal senior female speakers were involved in the delivery. Attendance was voluntary. The research sample was all participants who attended one specific programme cohort. The data collection method consisted of a pre and post questionnaire to gain a consistent evaluation measure of the perceived value of the programme, as well as semi-structured qualitative interviews to obtain rich data on the participants' experiences.

Given that the researcher was also responsible for the design and delivery of the programme and attended it, it was important she ensured that participants felt able to consent freely to being involved in the research project. It was important that the participants did not feel coerced to be part of the research. At the same time confidentiality and anonymity were crucial so that the research participants felt able to express their views without worrying about any internal consequences. In order to be aware of her own reactions during both the programme delivery and research study which ran in parallel, the researcher maintained a personal journal in order to remain reflexive. This helped her to be aware of any personal bias she may have had when maintaining the dual role of programme leader and researcher.

Source: Colin (2022)

Managing a research project client or sponsor

Many management research projects involve working closely in conjunction with an organization, institution, or professional body that either acts as the client for your research or facilitates it, for example, by allowing access and providing practical support. In either case you will need to manage the relationships with the key stakeholders in that organization. If the organization is acting as the client for your research, ensure that you agree on the research objectives and deliverables, how you will carry out the investigation, and what support you require from the organization. If you are doing the research as part of an academic qualification, be aware that the client organization's expectations in terms of the format of any output may be quite different. It may, for example, prefer a shorter, consultancy-style report or an oral presentation to a lengthy academic dissertation. When the organization is acting in a sponsorship role by granting you access to its site, personnel, and data, you will need to agree on ground rules in terms of how the research will be carried out and any specific issues regarding confidentiality, access, and so on. No matter what your research situation is, ensure that you work to agreed rules and deadlines. Document your research activities and keep in regular communication with key stakeholders as the project unfolds.

8.4.4 Managing your data

A research project generates a huge amount of data which today is likely to be in digital format but may be paper based. Some of this will be the result of your literature review, much of it gathered as part of your data collection for your own research, and still more of it generated by you in the form of notes, analysis, and so on. At the outset of your project you should think carefully about how you plan to capture, store, and manage all of this. Set up a suitable, secure system for both digital and/or paper documents. As the project unfolds, make sure that you can identify different versions of documents that you produce, as it is very easy to lose track of what you are doing. Finally, make sure that you have secure backup of your data, kept separately from your working copies. Today use of cloud technology to store data is common with a backup kept separately. Loss of data or of a draft of the final report due to computer failure, theft of a laptop, or fire will require you to repeat many hours of hard work.

8.5 KEEPING A RESEARCH DIARY

One of the most valuable tools available to a researcher is a **research diary** (also known as a research journal or research log). This is not an appointments calendar but a working document in which you record relevant information as you proceed through your project. As well as factual information such as dates of interviews or notes from discussions with your supervisor, it should include the thinking behind your decisions, such as why you chose a particular research design and your personal observations and reflections on your research and your role in it. It can be difficult to remember these aspects of your research experience when you sit down to write up your work. A diary can also be a way of reflecting on your own development as a researcher. Engin (2011: 296), in discussing the role of her own research diary, proposes that it was 'scaffolding her own construction of research knowledge'. By looking back at thoughts and reflections, the novice researcher can build an understanding of their own learning and development.

Some of the aims of a research diary are (Jankowicz, 2005)

- to generate a history of the research project by recording a summary of all of the key decisions and activities you undertake and the outcomes of those activities;
- to record your thinking about the research process as it happens;
- to act as a place to record ideas as they occur to you and your thoughts as to future directions for the research;
- to act as a record of people, places, or documents that you encounter during the research process;
- to provide a place for reflecting on your own practices as a researcher and your research skills;
- to provide a record on which you can base a reflective account of the project and your participation in it.

There are several different ways you can keep a research diary. Some researchers prefer a conventional notebook, or others use a loose-leaf binder, while others may use a digital device. Whichever you use, you may want to use a preprepared template, as we show in Research in Practice 8.2.

Research in practice 8.2 Example research diary format

Although there is no standardized preset format for a research diary, it useful to think about the sort of information that you will want to record. The example here shows a possible layout for a diary using preprepared template. This version makes it easy to track activities and record them for future reference.

Date	Activity	People involved	Aim	Outcome	Personal observations and reflections
6 March 2024	First meeting with project sponsor	Client, self	Agree expectations and deliverables; agree access and timescale.	Draft terms of reference agreed with client. Outline project plan prepared. Follow-up meeting booked for 5 April 2024.	An exciting project. Client seems genuinely committed to finding a solution, but I am worried that the scope of the project might creep as we get further down the road. Timings look a bit tight – need to ensure that access is arranged quickly.
11 March 2024	Begin literature review	Self	Become familiar with online literature searching. Begin locating sources of relevant literature.	Much more confident with using online journals. Located ten relevant literature sources.	I have realized that my next action must be to set up a data storage system and build more time into my schedule for the literature stage. There is a lot out there, and it's going to take some time!
15 March 2024	. . .	. . .	. . .	. . .	. . .

You may prefer to record your ideas electronically on a laptop, tablet, or smartphone. The increased availability of note-taking software programmes and apps makes this a very attractive option. Regardless of the medium you use, do not feel constrained just to use plain text in your diary. Mind maps, sketches, diagrams, or voice recordings can be equally valuable. The use of voice-activated notes makes keeping a diary particularly easy. As you work on your project, capture an entry at regular intervals, even during periods when you are not actively working on the project. Your research diary will act as a mechanism for maintaining momentum in your project but will also be a valuable resource when you come to write up your project and reflect on your own performance as a researcher.

8.6 PREPARING A RESEARCH PROPOSAL

The research proposal is a document that provides an overview of the intended research. It sets out the purpose of the research and a plan for how it will be carried out. The proposal should contain a clear statement of your proposed design and the selection that you have made, with supporting rationale. Proposals are used in a variety of research situations, including the following:

- *Research as part of a qualification,* where the research proposal must usually be approved by the academic institution before the candidate can proceed with the research. Here approval requires meeting the terms of reference and academic judgement of a supervisor or reviewing committee.
- *Commercial research,* where the proposal serves as a formal statement of the intended research. The proposal may be in response to an invitation to tender from a potential client, and the researcher or research team may well be in competition with other potential providers.
- *Funded research,* where the research proposal is used in the application for funding support. As with commercial research, the researcher is likely to be in competition with other researchers for available funds.

Whether you are looking to win business, access a research grant, or get approval for a proposed dissertation, your proposal is an important document. As Maxwell (2013: 140) points out, 'the purpose of your proposal is to explain and justify your proposed study to an audience of non-experts'. Especially in competitive bidding situations, the proposal stage is also a key moment in deciding whether or not to bid, and if a submission is made, the proposal is also a statement of your own or your research team's abilities to carry out the research (Gray, 2018). The process of developing your research proposal also provides you with the chance to think about, develop, and refine your proposed research and to get formal feedback. The latter is particularly relevant in student research projects, where you should take every opportunity to present and discuss your emerging ideas with those more experienced in research practice. We illustrate an example of a research proposal required for external research funding in Research in practice 8.3.

Research in practice 8.3 A research proposal for external funding

Financial planning and investment by retail investors involves significant complexity and difficulty for them in part due to often poor knowledge of financial products and industry terminology. Whilst retail investors can receive independent financial advice to help decision-making, the process of assessing risk in investment recommendations has been criticised by both regulators and academics as it may not lead to appropriate financial outputs for clients.

Professor Chris Brooks from the International Capital Market Association (ICMA) Centre at the University of Reading was interested to explore this problem and applied in the role as principal investigator to the Economic and Social Research Council (ESRC) via UK Research and Innovation (UKRI) for funding to conduct a research project. The aim of the project was to undertake a comprehensive and wide-ranging investigation of the financial decision-making of retail investors. The researchers had identified through preliminary work that emotions played a part but that the interaction of these with cognitive biases on the decision-making process had not been investigated.

As part of the funding application process, the researchers were required to complete a detailed proposal that presented the research problem and rationale for the research to be conducted, the research methodology, and the contribution the research would make to stakeholders in the financial sector. The research method involved access to databases and the analysis of the responses of over 100,000 retail investors to psychometric risk profiling questions with chosen investments and demographic/lifestyle data as well as the collection of new survey data. The aim was to investigate specifically the process and the degree to which retail investors' responses incorporated a capacity for loss. The study also evaluated the impacts of different methods of presenting data and terminologies used upon the investments chosen. Given the complexity and detailed nature of the data analysis required and the limited resources of the research team, external funding was essential. The proposal enabled the allocation of funding by the ESRC, and the research outputs were disseminated via academic publications as well as to practitioners and regulators in the financial sector via the partner organizations.

Sources: Brooks et al. (2019) and UKRI (2023)

8.6.1 The structure of a proposal

The exact content of a proposal will vary according to its purpose. However, Table 8.5 summarizes typical components of a proposal and their contents, again with the relevant chapter in this book for further reading. Before writing your proposal, ensure that you are fully conversant with any specific format or template you are required to use, including any word-count restrictions. For some student projects, it may be possible to discuss your proposal with a supervisor or other tutor before writing it (this will be made clear in guidance documents provided). In other situations, you may have the opportunity to clarify any questions with a representative of the reviewing body or those in the organization.

TABLE 8.5 Typical structure and components of a research proposal

Component	Indicative contents	Relevant chapters in this book
Abstract or executive summary (if required)	A succinct summary of the proposed research	Chapter 15
Introduction	Explain the background to the research problem	Chapter 2
Purpose of the research	What the research aims to achieve	Chapters 1 and 2
Review of literature (if required)	Locate the proposed research in relevant literature	Chapter 3
Research objectives and questions	Identify the research questions that the project will answer (in some proposals, these might be stated as research objectives or hypotheses)	Chapter 2
Research design	Proposed research design, including proposed data collection, sampling strategy, and data analysis	Chapters 4, 6, 7 (design)Chapters 9–12 (sampling and data collection)Chapters 13–14 (data analysis)
Deliverables	Format and method of dissemination of the results	Chapter 15
Ethical considerations	Identify and address any ethical considerations involved in the research	Chapter 5
Timeframe, resources, and budget	The overall plan for administering the project, including outline timeframe, resource requirements, and where appropriate, budget breakdown.	Chapter 8
Reference list (if required)	Correctly formatted in line with the proposal requirements and identifying all references used	Chapter 3

If possible, review other proposals and talk to those who have previously submitted proposals to the same body. Proposals that have been successful are likely to be most helpful, but unsuccessful ones can also be useful, especially if the writer has received feedback on why the proposal was rejected. As well as the formal requirements, a proposal writer 'needs a feel for the unspoken customs, norms, and needs that govern the selection process itself' (Przeworski and Salomon, 1995: 1). This can be particularly important in competitive environments, where you should try to familiarize yourself with the types of project, the priorities, and other requirements of the funding or buying organization. Finally, be aware that whilst your proposal documents your intended research design at the outset, your research project may adapt or change as you progress, and therefore the final study may vary slightly from the original proposal. However, only if your study changes significantly in terms of the research problem and/or method are you likely to need to revisit your proposal, for example, if this is a formal requirement of any academic, funding, or commercial body with which you are working.

8.6.2 Developing a working title

As Saunders et al. (2019: 541) observe, the title 'is the part of the project report on which most of us spend the least time. Yet it is the only knowledge that many people have of the project'. The title is not just the main way of communicating to others what your project is about, it can also influence whether your research is located in online searches once you have completed it. Formulating your title also forces you to think carefully about how you will describe your research. For this reason it is worth developing a working title early so as to identify the real core of your project so that you can sum it up clearly and in a few words. In addition, you will often need to give your project a provisional title in the research proposal. You should revisit and refine your title as the work progresses to ensure that it still accurately captures the essence of the project. A good title has the following characteristics:

- conveys an accurate description of the research to the reader;
- is not too long (as a guide, not more than 10–15 words);
- contains no abbreviations, jargon or acronyms;
- is grammatically correct.

Opinions differ as to the use of humour or catchy phrasing in a title. As with other aspects of writing, it is important to know your target audience. Probably the best advice is to avoid doing so unless you are writing for a forum in which such usage is common. Even then, for the working title, keep it serious and focused on the contents of the study. We discuss the development of your final title in Chapter 15.

8.6.3 Developing an effective proposal

The process of developing a proposal is an iterative one. Where practical, we recommend that you seek feedback on drafts from colleagues or tutors or through seminars, meetings, or other discussions. As you craft your proposal, keep in mind the following characteristics of a good proposal (ESRC, 2021; Maxwell, 2013; Przeworski and Salomon, 1995):

- *Impact*. Your proposal should capture the reader's attention and sustain it throughout by demonstrating the significance and impact of the proposed research.
- *Coherence*. Whilst the structure of the proposal is usually fixed, it is still essential that the components are coherent in terms both of the underlying logic and of the way in which that logic is communicated through a consistent narrative.

- *Scope and scale.* The proposal should clearly indicate the scope and boundaries of your project. It should show what will, and what will not, be included in the project. At the same time it should enable the reader to assess the size or scale of the project and assess its feasibility.
- *Clarity.* Use plain language that communicates clearly. Many research proposals will be seen by people who are not specialists in the subject and your main argument should be accessible to them, even if some technical language is required to explain finer details. Ensure you check grammar and spelling before submission.
- *Credibility.* Your proposed research must be credible in terms of its ability to address your chosen research questions. It must also be feasible in terms of the time and resources available. Ensure that any timescales and budget data are credible and accurate.
- *Consistency with the brief.* As we have explained, research proposal requirements vary. Ensure that your proposal reflects the requirements of the brief.

On top of this, it is worth noting the advice offered by the Economic and Science Research Council, a UK research funding body:

> Convey to the panel your genuine interest, understanding and enthusiasm for the work.
>
> ESRC (2021)

CRITICAL COMMENTARY 8.1

Can my proposal change?

We write a proposal at the start of a research project based on our thinking and research design decisions at the time we set out on our research journey. A question that student researchers often ask is whether they can subsequently make changes to their proposal. It may often feel uncomfortable to be pinned down to decisions made before perhaps you have completed all of your reading of literature and while you are still exploring the wider topic.

The answer is that an academic research project proposal should be seen as a working document. It sets out the roadmap for your proposed research and represents an important thinking process for you to follow to support your decision-making. However as you proceed, particularly in the early stages, you may wish to make slight alterations to say the wording and semantics of your research questions (based on literature you find) or the methodology (based on information or resource implications that come to light). Such minor adjustments to your proposal should always be discussed and agreed with your supervisor. More major changes to your proposed research, such as a new topic, may require a rewriting of your proposal.

Be aware that changes to a proposal for funding or a commercial research proposal may be less flexible given the importance and formal nature of the proposal, and you should check with the funding/commissioning body before any changes are made. Note also that a proposal is distinct from an application for ethical approval. Consider ethical approval as more of a stated contract as to what you will be doing and how you will address ethical risks, and so any proposed changes will need to be reconsidered by the approving panel.

CHAPTER SUMMARY

- A research design lays out the way in which you are going to go about doing your research project. Your research questions are the bridge between your research problem and your research design. It is possible to map research questions to appropriate research designs.
- A number of factors should be considered at the selection of a research design. These include prior research and thinking, ethical factors, stakeholder expectations, access, resource availability, and researcher preferences and skills.
- At the planning stage a researcher should consider all potential risk factors and, ideally, develop a risk assessment log which is consulted periodically as the project progresses.
- A research diary can be a valuable mechanism for capturing relevant information as well as your thinking as you progress through your project.
- A research proposal is a document that provides an overview of the intended research. It is often the basis for subsequent approval of a project. The structure and content should make clear the purpose of the research, the intended design, data collection, analysis, and deliverables of the project.

NEXT STEPS

8.1 Selecting a research design. As a next step you need to finalize your research design in sufficient detail to provide a good basis for writing your proposal. Think about the research questions you have set and then look at Table 8.1 and decide on a specific research design that is appropriate for your project. Sum up your thinking by completing the following statements.

- I will adopt the following research design to investigate my research question . . .
- This research design is appropriate because . . .

8.2 Identifying key stakeholders. Identify the key people and/or organizations whose support will be important to the success of your project. Think here about how you are going to gain access to key stakeholders and keep their support.

8.3 Identifying key resources. Identify any key resources, such as software or access to a particular database, and make the necessary arrangements to ensure that they are available when you need them.

8.4 Risks. Look back at Table 8.4. Review the risks that you may encounter during your project and the degree of risk, taking into account how likely they are to happen and their potential impact, and decide how you intend to manage them. Record your assessment in writing and review it regularly as the project proceeds.

8.5 Record-keeping. Decide on a format for your research diary/log. If you are setting out on a research project, begin a research diary now. Note how you will keep information on your progress and your reflections on your experiences.

8.6 Key activities and outline project plan. At this point you should be able to identify key activities needed to complete your research and so prepare a project plan. You will need to make an estimate of how long each activity will take. Use the table here (or other format if you prefer) to develop an outline project plan, making due allowance for any turnaround times for drafts or review.

Project planning table

Activity ID number	Activity	Estimated duration	Start date	Finish date	Notes
1					
2					
3					
. . . n					

8.7 Time schedule. Using the data from the table, develop a graphical version of your time schedule for your project plan in the form of a Gantt chart for inclusion in your research proposal and to help you manage your project, and communicate its progress to yourself and others.

8.7 Research proposal. Review requirements for your research proposal. Building on the steps outlined, complete your proposal for review/submission.

FURTHER READING

For further reading, please see the companion website.

REFERENCES

Brooks, C., Sangiorgi, I., Hillenbrand, C. and Money, K. (2019). Experience wears the trousers: Exploring gender and attitude to financial risk. *Journal of Economic Behavior & Organization*, 163: 483–515.

Buchanan, D. A. and Bryman, A. (2007). Contextualizing methods choice in organizational research. *Organizational Research Methods*, 10(3): 483–501.

Colin, J. (2022). *An Exploratory, Organisation-Based Study of the Perceived Value Which a Group of Emerging Female Leaders Find in a Women Only Leadership Development Programme.* Master's dissertation, Henley Business School at the University of Reading, Henley-on-Thames.

Costley, C., Elliott, G. C. and Gibbs, P. (2010). *Doing Work Based Research: Approaches to Enquiry for Insider-Researchers.* London: SAGE Publications.

Engin, M. (2011). Research diary: A tool for scaffolding. *International Journal of Qualitative Methods*, 10(3): 296–306.

ESRC (2021). *How to Write a Good Proposal [Online].* Economic and Social Research Council. Available at: www.ukri.org/councils/esrc/guidance-for-applicants/how-to-write-a-good-proposal/ (Accessed 19 April 2023).

Gray, D. E. (2018). *Doing Research in the Real World.* 4th ed. London: SAGE Publications.

Jankowicz, A. (2005). *Business Research Projects.* 4th ed. London: Thomson.

Maxwell, J. A. (2013). *Qualitative Research Design. An Interactive Approach.* 3rd ed. Los Angeles, CA: SAGE Publications.

Przeworski, A. and Salomon, F. (1995). *On the Art of Writing Proposals.* Social Science Research Council. Available at: www.ssrc.org/publications/the-art-of-writing-proposals/ (Accessed 26 April 2023).

Saunders, M., Lewis, P. and Thornhill, A. (2019). *Research Methods for Business Students.* 8th ed. Harlow: Pearson Education.

UKRI (2023). *Understanding the Decision-making of Retail Investors [Online].* UK Research and Innovation. Available at: https://gtr.ukri.org/projects?ref=ES%2FP000657%2F1 (Accessed 26 April 2023).

PART III

Collect

The ability to collect good quality data is essential in any research project. In Part III we therefore take a close look at data collection. We start in Chapter 9 by examining sampling, the process of deciding where you will collect your data and how much you will need to collect. The remaining three chapters look at specific methods for data collection. Chapter 10 reviews questionnaire design and administration, while Chapter 11 examines in-depth individual and group interviews and the capture and storage of interview data. Chapter 12 looks at a range of other techniques for data collection including diaries, observation, documents, and artefacts. We also include the collection of data through social media and the use of big data, reflecting the growing importance of online data in business and management research.

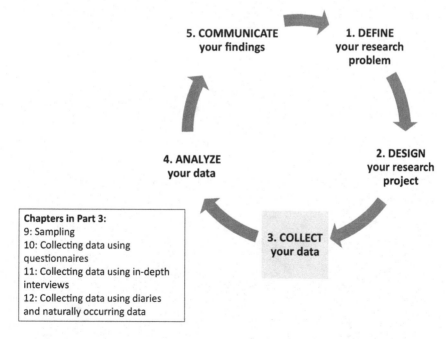

5. COMMUNICATE
your findings

1. DEFINE
your research
problem

2. DESIGN
your research
project

3. COLLECT
your data

4. ANALYZE
your data

Chapters in Part 3:
9: Sampling
10: Collecting data using questionnaires
11: Collecting data using in-depth interviews
12: Collecting data using diaries and naturally occurring data

DOI: 10.4324/9781003381006-11

Sampling

9.1 INTRODUCTION

A key step in the data collection stage of your research project is deciding where you will collect your data and how much you will need to collect. This is the process of **sampling**, and it has important implications for the quality, feasibility, and inclusivity of your research. Firstly, selecting an inappropriate or inadequate sample of data can reduce the quality of your research to the point where your findings are meaningless. Secondly, gaining access to a suitable sample can pose major practical challenges for your research and even determine whether a particular project is researchable. Thirdly, sampling decisions have ethical implications, including achieving inclusivity, which must be taken into account when designing your sampling approach. In this chapter we therefore take an in-depth look at the sampling process. We begin by defining what is meant by sampling before looking at different sampling methods. We then discuss how sampling procedures are applied in different research approaches, before looking at the important topic of sample size. We conclude the chapter with a look at how to access and recruit your sample.

DOI: 10.4324/9781003381006-12

9.2 WHAT IS A SAMPLE?

The starting point for thinking about sampling is the idea of a **target population**. In research, the term 'population' refers to the totality of elements that are of interest to the researcher as a source of data. These elements may be individuals (such as customers, employees, or managers), organizations (such as charities, schools, or retailers), events (such as hospital operations or product recalls), documents (such as customer records within a database or online blog posts), or artefacts (such as pieces of equipment or technology). Depending on the nature of your research problem, your target population may be exceptionally large, very small, or anywhere in between. If you were researching Internet users in the USA, for example, you would have a potential target population of around 312 million users (Internet World Stats, 2023). By way of contrast, if you were investigating the experiences of current US Supreme Court justices, the target population would be precisely nine named individuals (Supreme Court, 2023). If your research interest was in thoracic (chest) surgeons in the US, your target population would be 4,449 active physicians (AAMC, 2021). Each population varies in terms of size, how well it is defined in terms of membership, and how easy it is likely to be to access.

Census or sample?

Factors such as these all influence whether or not it is possible to carry out a **census** of the entire population. For some situations, such as small populations that are easily accessible, for example, employees in a small company, a census may be the best approach. In others, even if it is theoretically feasible, it may not be desirable from a cost, time, or efficiency point of view to collect data from everyone. In addition, if the population is very large, the amount of data may be overwhelming: imagine trying to process 312 million survey responses on your laptop or analyzing hundreds of hours of interview data. For all these reasons, researchers typically take a smaller subgroup, known as a **sample**, from their target population. The individual elements that make up the sample are referred to as **cases** or **observations** (Figure 9.1). For example, if you were carrying out a survey study amongst employees and had a sample of 500 who completed your questionnaire, each participant

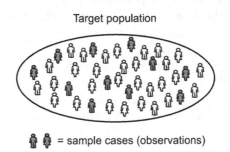

Target population

= sample cases (observations)

FIGURE 9.1 Target population and sample

would be a case or observation within your research sample. (Note that the word case is being used here differently from the way it is used in the context of a case study research design, as in Chapter 7.)

9.2.1 The sampling process

The precise details of the sampling process depend on the type of research you are carrying out and, in particular, whether you are using quantitative, qualitative, or mixed methods. Nevertheless, we can identify a series of steps that guide the sampling process. We show these in Figure 9.2 to set the scene for a more detailed discussion of particular aspects of sampling in the rest of the chapter.

Step 1: Determine the target population

The first step is to determine your target population. Here you should refer back to your original research problem to identify the people, documents, or other elements that are relevant to your investigation. At this stage it can be useful to use secondary data sources such as organizational data, industry reports, or government statistics to help you estimate the nature and size of the population and identify other relevant information that assists you in drawing up a population profile. Such information may also help you to decide how a sample within the population can be accessed.

Step 2: Identify the sampling frame

Next you need to identify the **sampling frame**, which is a listing of all the elements of your target population from which the sample can be drawn. So for example, if your target population was all employees in a specific organization, a suitable sampling frame would be a list of all employees and their contact details. In reality, a sampling frame may not be complete, either because records are not accurate or because no full listing is available. As a result, the sampling frame can be a source of bias in your sample, as we discuss when we look at sampling bias.

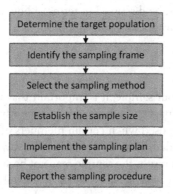

FIGURE 9.2 Generic sampling process

Step 3: Select the sampling method

Step three involves selecting a suitable sampling method. The selection depends on the research design you are using and is a key area of difference between quantitative and qualitative research methods. As a general rule, quantitative researchers look to use sampling methods that will generate a sample that is statistically representative, whilst qualitative researchers use methods that generate a sample that is theoretically relevant but without being representative in a statistical sense.

Step 4: Establish the sample size

The next step is to determine how big a sample you need. Here again we see some significant differences between quantitative and qualitative research in terms both of the sample size and how it is determined. As well as impacting on the quality of your findings, sample size has significant practical implications for data collection, so we discuss it in more detail in Section 9.5.

Step 5: Implement the sampling plan

Implementation of the sampling plan can take place only once all of the previous steps have been addressed. This is where sampling as a planning activity merges with data collection itself. At this stage you should be monitoring progress to make sure that your sampling plan is working and that you are getting a sample of sufficient quality and size. You will also need to make sure that you can establish and maintain access during data collection.

Step 6: Report the sampling procedure

The sampling process used in your study must be fully reported within your final research report in the section where you describe your research design. This should include reporting of the target population, the sampling frame, the calculation of the sample size and response rate and details of the sampling method used. Any particular difficulties or anomalies encountered should be discussed in terms of how they were addressed and the potential impact they may have had on your findings.

9.2.2 Sampling bias

In the process of obtaining your sample, it is important that you do not introduce bias in your selection, which will impact the subsequent quality of your research. **Sampling bias** (or selection bias) is the term used when certain members of the total population have a greater chance of being included, often as a result of the way in which the sampling process has been conducted. As a result, the sample may not be statistically representative in a quantitative project, and this can affect any statistical generalizations made from the data. Sampling bias is a key concern for quantitative research but may also occur in qualitative studies, where it can prevent a thorough exploration of a topic or introduce distortions by, for example, unintentionally excluding particular participants from the sample. Recognizing sources of sampling bias can help you to prevent this from adversely affecting your research.

There are three main sources of sampling bias. Firstly, it can occur when only part of the target population have the opportunity to be in the sample because we have somehow systematically excluded particular individuals via our sampling frame or access method. For example, if you use the Internet to access a group such as 'public transport users' and not all public transport users are also Internet users, then your sample will be biased towards 'public transport users who use the Internet' rather than public transport users as a whole.

Secondly, we may unintentionally include people in our sample who do not meet the sample criteria. For example, in order to determine whether someone should be included, we may use filter questions in a questionnaire or whilst arranging interviews. If such filter questions are not sufficiently precise, we may include participants who do not meet the criteria for the sample. Incentivization schemes in which people are rewarded for participation may also create bias in the sample, as we noted in Chapter 5.

Thirdly, problems may arise as a result of people declining to participate. The term **nonresponse bias** is used to refer to bias created because those who decline to take part are systematically different from those who do take part. Aspects of your research design (for example, the length or wording of a questionnaire) may deter certain people from wanting to take part. Nonparticipants may have different features, such as being employed or unemployed, and this may be relevant to your research project. Different groups may also be more or less likely to respond. A study by Jang and Vorderstrasse (2019), for example, found significant differences in Internet-survey completion according to race or ethnicity and education level of participants. Of course, being able to identify who does not take part or why they do not do so can be difficult. Techniques such as comparison of early versus late responders (who are assumed to be similar to non-responders) can be used to help to identify potential nonresponse bias (see Armstrong and Overton, 1977).

9.3 SAMPLING METHODS

A range of methods are available for choosing your sample. As we show in Figure 9.3, these fall into two groups, probability and non-probability methods, each with a number of different techniques. We will discuss each in turn before looking at how they are used in different research situations in the next section.

9.3.1 Probability sampling

Probability sampling methods use randomization or chance to select the sample, based on each member of the population having a known, although not necessarily equal, probability of being selected. Probability sampling methods are the preferred approach for quantitative research because they generate samples which can be analyzed using appropriate statistical techniques to make inferences about the population from which the sample was drawn. For example, based on data from a probability sample of customers' spending

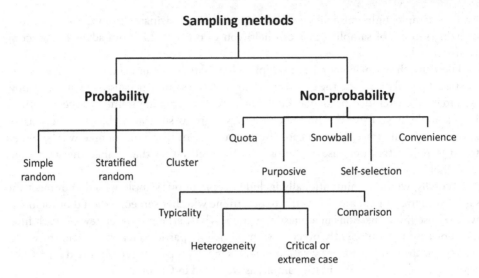

FIGURE 9.3 Probability and non-probability sampling methods

habits, we could draw conclusions about the spending habits of the overall customer population. A number of different probability sampling techniques can be used, depending on the target population and the research aims. These include the following.

Simple random sampling

In **simple random sampling** the required number of elements is simply drawn at random from the population so that there is a known and equal chance of selecting each one. This type of sampling relies on a complete and accurate sampling frame being available and assumes a degree of homogeneity within the target population. A workable procedure for randomized selection must also be available. This could be done manually by, for example, assigning each individual in the sampling frame a unique identification (ID) number, writing each ID number on a piece of paper, mixing them up in a container, and then drawing numbers at random until the required sample size is reached. The individuals whose ID numbers have been drawn then form the sample (the equivalent of drawing names out of a hat!). (Technically, what we have described is referred to as sampling without replacement; removing one individual ID changes reduces the remaining population and therefore changes the probability of selection. If the population is large, this change can usually be ignored.) In practice, particularly if the sampling frame is in a digital format (such as a spreadsheet listing all employees), the sample selection will best be done with computer assistance. The companion website gives guidance on how to do this using MS Excel.

Stratified random sampling

Sometimes the target population in our research contains a number of distinctly different subgroups or 'strata' within it, and we want to make sure that each subgroup is adequately represented in our sample. For example, a retail organization may have different types of outlet (hypermarket, supermarket, convenience store, petrol station etc.). Particularly if one of the subgroups is quite small, random sampling might result in one group not being adequately covered or even being omitted altogether. In this situation we can apply **stratified random sampling**, in which the population is divided (stratified) into separate subgroups, and sample sizes are calculated for each one. This may be done by proportionate stratified sampling, in which the sample for each subgroup is proportionate to its size within the total population. Alternatively, it may be disproportionate stratified sampling, in which case the size of each subgroup may be determined by other factors (for example, choosing equal group size). Disproportionate stratified sampling can ensure that each group is adequately represented, but the resulting overall sample will not usually be representative of the population as a whole.

Cluster sampling

Cluster sampling is often used in very large populations and where it may be difficult to accurately identify a sampling frame or it would be very costly to do so (Arnab, 2017). This may happen due to the geographic spread of the target population. Suppose, for example, that a research study was investigating healthcare delivery in hospitals within a particular country and needed to gain access to a representative sample of 1,000 nursing staff members. Given the size and geographic spread of nursing staff within the hospital network, it might be extremely difficult and costly to collect a sample based on the total population. Therefore, instead of selecting individual nursing staff from across the country, you could randomly select ten hospitals and then randomly select 100 nursing staff members from each to make up the sample of 1,000. This is the basis of cluster sampling: dividing the population into subgroups (clusters) from which a random sample is then chosen. It can facilitate data collection (collecting data from 100 nurses in each of ten hospitals, for example, may be much easier than collecting data from 1,000 nursing staff members selected from hospitals all across the country), but the resulting sample may be less representative than with other probability sampling methods.

9.3.2 Non-probability sampling

Non-probability sampling methods, as the term implies, do not use random selection for choosing a sample. Instead, the researcher uses alternative criteria such as theoretical relevance or convenience to choose the sample. Non-probability methods are particularly important in qualitative research, but they are also employed in quantitative research, especially where probability methods cannot be applied. As a result they are very widely encountered in research, so it is important to understand the options available and their relative advantages and disadvantages.

Convenience sampling

A **convenience sample** is one in which the elements from the population are accessed through some point of contact that is convenient and practical to the researcher. This is often done through personal contacts such as work colleagues, fellow students, neighbours or by accessing large groups such as student cohorts within a college or university. Today it is also possible to contact a convenience sample through your online network via social media platforms such as LinkedIn and Facebook. Convenience sampling can provide a quick and cost-effective option, but it can lead to bias in the selection process and therefore an unrepresentative sample. Care therefore needs to be taken to check the representativeness of the final sample and to discuss any resulting limitations when reporting your research.

Quota sampling

Quota sampling is a non-probability variant of stratified sampling in that the researcher sets out sample quotas for inclusion of specific subgroups within the population. For example, if you were investigating customer responses to a new store layout in a hypermarket you might wish to know the views of different customer groups. You would then identify the relevant customer subgroups (such as customers shopping with children and those shopping without) and calculate the desired quota (sample size) for each. Sample size could be proportionate to the size of each in the total population or based on some other factor, such as ensuring that each subgroup is adequately represented. Data are then collected using, for example, convenience or self-selection sampling, until the desired quotas are reached. Quota sampling gives some control over the final composition of the sample but, like convenience sampling, may not lead to a representative sample.

Purposive sampling

Purposive or **theoretical sampling** is an important form of non-probability sampling, widely used in qualitative research methods in which the researcher selects cases for the sample based on their theoretical relevance to the aims of the research. We will look at purposive sampling in more detail when we discuss sampling in qualitative research later in the chapter.

Snowballing

The **snowballing** approach to sampling is useful to researchers when a complete sampling frame is difficult to identify or access. The researcher starts with a few known members of the population who meet the sample characteristics, and these are approached to participate and also to identify others they know who also meet the desired sample characteristics. For example, research amongst people who attend music festivals could be conducted by approaching known festivalgoers who then put the researcher in contact with other festivalgoers or pass on a research questionnaire for other festivalgoers to complete. As with other non-probability sampling methods, careful thought needs to be given with respect to sampling bias in the resulting sample, but snowballing may be a particularly useful sampling approach when researching hard-to-access, relatively closed communities or groups.

Self-selection

Finally, if no prior sampling frame or access to potential participants exists, the researcher can use techniques to encourage relevant people to self-select for inclusion in a study. This can be done by placing announcements or advertisements online or placing posters in relevant locations where potential participants will see them. For example, a research study into children's behaviour could place posters in locations such as doctors' surgeries or child health clinics to ask for parents to volunteer to participate in research by scanning a QR code on their mobile phones to access an online questionnaire. Self-selection does raise concern about bias. It may be, for example, that parents who volunteer to discuss their child's behaviour may differ in terms of their attitudes or beliefs, in some systematic way, when compared to those who do not volunteer. As we discuss later in the chapter, self-selection is becoming an increasingly common method of sampling thanks to online recruitment.

9.3.3 Multistage sampling

Multistage sampling, as its name suggests, involves two or more stages in sample selection. A widely used example is multistage cluster sampling whereby, having selected the first set of subgroups (clusters), a further set of subgroups within those clusters is identified from which the sample is drawn. A sample of homeowners in a UK region, for example, could be selected by randomly selecting a sample of counties, then randomly selecting a sample of towns/cities within those counties, and finally randomly choosing a sample of households the owners of which form the final sample. This is an example of multistage random sampling (Onwuegbuzie and Collins, 2007), but in practice multistage sampling may involve a combination of both probability and non-probability sampling methods. We discuss multistage sampling further in the context of qualitative and mixed methods research in the next section.

9.4 SAMPLING IN QUANTITATIVE, QUALITATIVE, AND MIXED METHODS RESEARCH

Sampling is an important consideration in all forms of research, but the objectives and methods used varies according to the choice of approach. Quantitative and qualitative research varies in particular with respect to their preference for probability and non-probability sampling techniques and the extent to which the sampling plan is fully specified in advance of data collection or responds to emerging findings as the research proceeds. Table 9.1 summarizes these differences, which we then discuss in more detail before examining sampling in mixed method research.

9.4.1 Sampling in quantitative research

Sampling procedures in quantitative research typically emphasize the importance of being able to use the resulting sample data to make statistical inferences about the target

TABLE 9.1 Quantitative and qualitative sampling compared (adapted from (Flick, 2009: 119)

Sampling for quantitative research	Sampling for qualitative research
Selection on the basis of statistical representativeness of a wider population	Selection on the basis of theoretical relevance to the research question
One-shot collection of a sample following a plan defined in advance	Sampling plan responds to emergent findings during analysis
Sample size is defined in advance	Sample size may not be defined in advance
Sampling, data collection, and data analysis are sequential	Sampling, data collection, and data analysis may be iterative
Sampling is finished when the predetermined sample size has been reached	Sampling is finished when theoretical saturation has been reached
Preference for probability sampling methods	Preference for non-probability, purposive (theoretical) sampling methods

population. This, in turn, is a reflection of the interest in aggregate properties of populations and phenomena and the generalizability of any findings that characterizes much quantitative research. Consequently, a central aim of quantitative research sampling is to generate a sample that is statistically representative of the target population. Probability sampling methods are therefore the preferred approach because of their advantages in this respect. If non-probability methods are used, as they sometimes are in practice, care has to be taken regarding the generalizability of the findings and the extent to which they can be said to represent the target population.

In terms of sampling procedures, quantitative sampling is typically a sequential process in which the sample plan is decided in full in advance of data collection. Although, in practice, some adjustments may be made in response to problems in data collection, such changes should be avoided where possible, and if not, the consequences for sample quality should be assessed and reported in your findings. Particular concern is likely to be raised regarding possible sampling bias and the sampling plan, and the resulting sample should be carefully designed to minimize these. At the end of your report, you should provide explicit, detailed, and critical coverage of your sampling procedures and their implications for your findings.

9.4.2 Sampling in qualitative research

Sampling in qualitative research typically follows a very different logic to that in quantitative research, reflecting the different interests, such as investigation in depth and from the perspective of those involved, that characterize much qualitative research. In particular, qualitative research does not usually seek to make statistical generalizations so is less concerned with the need to achieve statistical representativeness in sampling. Instead, sampling focuses on choosing a sample that is able to offer rich and in-depth insights into the phenomenon under investigation and to help the researcher build a theoretical understanding of it. In fact writers such as Maxwell (2013: 97) go so far as to suggest that the term 'sampling' itself is problematic for qualitative research due to the assumptions in which it is rooted. Instead, he proposes that the term 'purposeful selection' is more appropriate to the way in which qualitative research proceeds.

Not surprisingly, qualitative researchers typically use non-probability sampling methods, particularly purposive or theoretical sampling techniques. Table 9.2 summarizes different approaches to purposive sampling that can be used. Other non-probability sampling techniques may also be employed in qualitative research. Maxwell (2013: 99), for example, points out the value of selecting on the basis of being able to develop 'the most productive relationships' that can help you gain access to the best data for your study. As with any non-probability sampling method, you should be careful about the extent to which your sampling approach may be introducing an element of sampling bias into your research.

The sampling process used in qualitative research can also differ from those used in quantitative designs. Some projects may adhere to a sequential process similar to that in Figure 9.2, in which a sample is fully decided in advance by identifying the target population, developing a sampling frame, and then choosing the sample members. Other qualitative research projects, however, take a more emergent approach to sampling, reflecting the developmental nature of some qualitative research designs. Here, sample membership and sample size are not fixed in advance of the project but instead respond to developments during data collection and analysis to allow the researcher to follow up new lines of inquiry, to probe more deeply into a particular topic area and to test the adequacy of emerging theory. To use the term from grounded theory, sampling continues until the point where **theoretical saturation** is reached, that is to say, no new insights are emerging from the data

TABLE 9.2 Approaches to purposive sampling in qualitative research (based on Maxwell, 2013: 98)

Approach	Purpose	Characteristic
Typicality	Ensuring that the sample incorporates typical examples which represent the phenomenon under investigation	Sampling amongst typical cases provides confidence to the researcher of the relevance of the data derived and that it is representative of the population
Heterogeneity or maximum variation	Ensuring that the sample captures a range of variation and differences within the population	Provides the researcher with less data from each case but provides maximum variation across sampling cases for capturing diversity and the range of the phenomenon
Critical or extreme cases	Sampling includes cases that are an extreme example of the phenomenon being investigated	Provides a critical test of a theory under development or provides more insights than would be achieved from a 'typical' case
Comparison	Sampling captures cases that can be compared across different settings or individuals	Used in multi-case designs to enable the researcher to make comparisons that help to show the reasons for the differences between settings or individuals

or, as Woolcott (quoted in Baker and Edwards, 2012: 4) puts it, 'you keep asking as long as you are getting different answers'. We illustrate the practical application of sampling methods in a qualitative interview-based research project in Research in Practice 9.1.

Research in practice 9.1 Home is where the new start is: emergent sampling in qualitative research

A key goal of criminal justice systems is to reduce reoffending by those leaving prison (UN, 2023). One of the factors that can decrease the chance of reoffending is having safe and suitable accommodation to move into. Provision of such accommodation can, however, be difficult in practice since it involves close and active collaboration between multiple agencies. Research suggests that this is particularly difficult in the case of individuals who have been in local authority care as children as they are less likely to have a family to return to and may be less prepared for living outside an institution.

Debbie McKay's masters research project (McKay, 2022) set out to investigate how to improve collaborative working to get better housing outcomes for care-experienced prison leavers. Her chosen research design was a qualitative interview study, involving participants from different agencies involved. She adopted a purposive sampling approach to identify the organizations and roles that would be appropriate and used her professional network to identify initial participants. She then used snowball sampling to get in contact with further individuals with experience in the topic area. These included staff from central and local government agencies, as well as third sector professionals who were involved in resettlement. As the research unfolded, emerging findings suggested a further group of resettlement specialists should be included so they were invited to participate as well. The final sample was 15 participants who were able to provide insights from multiple perspectives in understanding the complexities of multiagency collaboration.

Some qualitative research designs, such as case study and ethnography, can also feature multistage sampling, in which the researcher first has to begin by identifying one or more research sites where the research will take place and then has to develop a sampling plan for use within that site. If you were conducting an organizational ethnography, for example, you would first have to select a suitable organization and then identify your sample within that organization using appropriate sampling techniques. This can be thought of as an example of multistage purposive sampling, as opposed to the multistage random cluster sampling discussed earlier.

9.4.3 Sampling in mixed methods research

Sampling in mixed method research can use of wide combination of approaches (Collins, 2015). As Onwuegbuzie and Collins (2007: 290) note, 'In mixed methods research, sampling schemes must be chosen for both the qualitative and quantitative components of the study'. They go on to identify two relevant criteria in selecting a sampling design for mixed methods. The first they call 'time orientation' and refers to whether the sampling is concurrent or sequential. In concurrent sampling, the researcher may be seeking to compare the resulting findings; in sequential sampling, the sampling in the first stage will inform sampling in the next stage (i.e. multistage sampling). The second criterion relates to the relationship between the quantitative and qualitative samples. Here, Onwuegbuzie and Collins (2007) suggest four relationship options:

1. Identical, where the same sample is used in both the quantitative and qualitative phases.
2. Parallel, with different samples for the qualitative and quantitative phases, but drawn from the same population.
3. Nested, where the sample for one phase of the project is a subset of the sample used for the other phase.
4. Multilevel, where two or more samples are drawn from different populations.

Ultimately, the appropriateness of any given sampling approach will be driven by the overall research design, as discussed in Chapter 7. Research in Practice 9.2 gives an example of multistage sampling in a mixed methods research project illustrating a sequential time orientation (quantitative followed by qualitative) and nested, purposive sampling.

Research in practice 9.2 Multistage sampling in mixed methods research

Ramanujan et al. (2022) discuss multistage sampling in connection with a mixed methods evaluation project in rural India, looking at an intervention to raise different stakeholders' involvement in children's foundational learning in government schools. The project comprised a randomized control trial (RCT) involving 400 villages and qualitative case studies of four of the villages. The authors' focus is on the selection of the four villages out of 200 that were the subject of a community and school collaboration initiative. Ramanujan et al. (2022) describe a two-stage approach used when choosing the sample of four villages for the case studies:

- Stage 1 involved using senior programme staff as 'key informants' to nominate two 'responsive' (where there was positive engagement with teachers and community members) and two 'difficult' (where engagement was unchanged) sites based on their work with personnel in the field. This identified 25 'responsive' and 26 'difficult' sites.
- Stage 2 used quantitative data from the RCT to refine the selection to three 'responsive' and one 'difficult' site, whilst ensuring that the final sample remained diverse 'so that emerging conclusions could be triangulated across different contexts' (Ramanujan et al., 2022: 360).

In their write-up, the authors argue that their 'sampling process was enhanced by having data from diverse data sources and methodological perspectives' (Ramanujan et al., 2022: 361).

9.5 SAMPLE SIZE

A question asked at the outset of most research projects is 'how big does my sample need to be?' It is sometimes assumed that the larger the sample size, the better the quality of the findings. In practice, as we have already explained, issues such as selection of the population and sampling frame, the sampling methods used, and so on also affect the quality of your data. Nevertheless, sample size is important not only in terms of the implications for your analysis but also in terms of the cost, time, and effort required to reach a particular sample size. In this section we will take a look at the question of sample size for both quantitative and qualitative research; mixed methods research designs will typically require to select sample sizes appropriate to the designs being used and to 'enable appropriate generalisations and inferences' (Collins et al., 2007: 289).

9.5.1 Sample size in quantitative research

Sample size in a quantitative study, such as a survey, typically depends on four key factors.

1. The level of precision required. This refers to the maximum difference the researcher is prepared to tolerate between the estimated sample value obtained and the actual value that would be obtained in the population. In effect, this factor refers to the amount of error that will be accepted between the sample and population values. In general, the greater the precision required, the larger the sample that will be needed.

2. The homogeneity of the population. Different populations vary in terms of their homogeneity, that is, the degree to which members of the population share particular characteristics. The less homogenous (i.e. the more varied) the population, the larger the sample required.

3. The degree of confidence that you want in the accuracy of any generalizations you make about your population from your sample data. We explain this concept more fully in Chapter 13, but for now we will note that, everything else being equal, the higher the degree of confidence you want, the bigger the sample you will need to collect.

4. Method of analysis. Sample size should also take into account the type of analysis that is planned and the number of variables. In general, the more variables in your analysis, the larger your sample size will need to be.

One thing that might surprise you is that population size is not mentioned. It is the size of the sample, not the size of the population from which it is drawn, that matters most in the majority of situations. Only when the sample represents a significant proportion of the population is an adjustment necessary.

Deciding on your sample size

Several formulae are available for calculating sample size, and examples of these are provided on the companion website to help you decide on an appropriate sample size for your project. Although such formulae can help you to decide on your sample size, the decision is often influenced by practical issues such as cost, time, and access mentioned earlier. In addition, sample size also needs to conform to the proposed analysis techniques. Cohen (1992) provides guidance on sample sizes for different statistical techniques, and most statistics texts will make recommendations for specific analysis methods. We give further guidance in Chapter 13. Further guidance can also be had by looking at previous studies in your topic area to see what sample sizes have been used in the past.

So how big does your quantitative sample need to be? Sue and Ritter (2012) list some practical rules of thumb which can be a good starting point:

- Sample sizes typically should not be less than 30 (or more than 500).
- These sample sizes apply if you are wanting to look at subgroups within the sample (so sample size of not less than 30).
- If you are doing multivariate analysis, sample size should be at least ten times larger than the number of variables in the study.
- Larger samples are better than smaller samples.

We often give a (very rough) rule of thumb for a quantitative undergraduate or masters project of minimum of 50 responses, with 30 per subgroup if comparing groups, subject to meeting requirements of the proposed analysis approach.

9.5.2 Sample size in qualitative research

As we have seen, the logic of sampling in much qualitative research is different to that motivating quantitative research sampling, and the same applies to criteria for determining sample size, particularly if using theoretical saturation to guide your decision. An obvious difficulty with this approach, however, is that it is hard to know in advance when theoretical saturation will be reached. This makes it difficult to use as a basis for determining sample size in advance of the study. Whilst this is consistent with the flexible, emergent nature of much qualitative research, it does not help much with planning or budgeting for your project, especially if you have to declare your intended sample size in a proposal to a review board or supervisor. We discuss theoretical saturation in more detail in Critical commentary 9.1.

CRITICAL COMMENTARY 9.1

How much is enough? Theoretical saturation

Theoretical saturation has been suggested as a way of determining sample size in qualitative research in this chapter and is widely cited in the methods literature on sampling (Saunders et al., 2018). The notion that sampling in qualitative research should continue until you stop finding anything new seems entirely sensible. As Morse notes,

> If data are inadequate, lack of multiple examples and the scope is too circum-scribed, data are obvious and, therefore, difficult to conceptualize. There are too few examples in each category to identify the characteristics of concepts, to develop concepts, and to develop theory. In sum, research results are tentative, obvious, and uninteresting.
>
> (Morse, 2015: 588)

Theoretical saturation is, however, not without its limitations and critics.

One problem, as we note in Chapter 9, is that it is not possible to determine sample size in advance, with implications for planning the timing and cost of a project. Perhaps as a result, there is evidence from studies of published qualitative research that predetermined sample sizes are widely used in practice (Boddy, 2016). A second issue is that theoretical saturation is not applicable to all qualitative research approaches with different underlying epistemological and methodological assumptions (O'Reilly and Parker, 2013). A third issue arises because, it has been suggested, the concept of theoretical saturation is subject to different interpretations so exactly what it means or how it is achieved is not always clear. Saunders et al. (2018), for example, identify four different 'models' of saturation based on their analysis of how the term is used in practice. They suggest that researchers should be more transparent about how they are using saturation in practice, but also to ensure 'consistency between the theoretical position and analytic framework adopted' (Saunders et al., 2018: 1904). As always, specific research techniques must be used with due consideration to the broader context within which they are located.

So how big should your qualitative sample be? One option is to look at what other writers have done. In a study of 190 qualitative studies in high-grade academic journals that reported their sample size, Saunders and Townsend (2016) found a median sample size of 32.5, with lower and upper quartiles of lower quartile of 18.75 and 57.25 respectively. Based on this they suggest that 'a broad overall norm for practice likely to be considered sufficient of between approximately 15 and 60 participants' (Saunders and Townsend, 2016: 845). Guest et al. (2006) looked at when saturation was reached in terms of identifying new codes in their data analysis. They found that saturation was reached after 12 interviews, although, as they point out, it is hard to know how generalizable their findings are. Another option is to seek the advice and experiences of other qualitative researchers. Adler and Adler (in Baker and Edwards, 2012) suggest between 12 and 60, with a mean of 30, while Ragin (in Baker and Edwards, 2012) proposes 20 for a master's thesis and 50 for a PhD.

Your philosophical position and methodological approach are also important influences in deciding your sample size, as noted by King et al. (2019). They suggest that larger samples are more likely in post-positivist/realist studies compared to more interpretivist/phenomenological ones. In the context of interpretative phenomenological analysis, for example, Smith et al. (2022) suggest a sample size of five for a master's level study.

In addition, we can identify a number of factors to take into account when deciding on a likely sample size for a qualitative project (Morse, 2000; Baker and Edwards, 2012).

- Scope and complexity of the topic. The broader the scope and the greater the complexity of the topic, the bigger the sample that is likely to be needed to ensure that the topic is adequately explored.
- Population heterogeneity. As with quantitative research, the more variation there is in the population of interest, the bigger your sample should be. Sample size may also need to be higher if you want to compare the experiences of different groups.
- Quality of data. The depth and richness of data that you gather in qualitative interviews may vary greatly between participants. Such differences can influence the sample size needed.
- Stakeholder expectations. Although the research requirements should determine the decision on sample size, other stakeholders' expectations influence the final decision. In particular, those more familiar with the logic of quantitative sampling may find it difficult to accommodate the different requirements of qualitative research. Make sure that you are aware of the expectations of others when planning your sample size.

Remember that in qualitative research you will also need to allow for time to transcribe, analyze, and report your data. An hour-long interview can generate anything up to 10,000 words. If you are not careful, you may find yourself with more data than you can analyze thoroughly, especially if you are new to qualitative research (Smith et al., 2022). Ultimately, as with quantitative research, the final sample size will be a balance between theoretical desirability and practical feasibility. Our own guidance as a planning figure for final projects on master's programmes has been 12–15 in-depth interviews or three to five case studies using multiple sources of data. If you are doing an academic research project, your supervisor may also be able to offer advice on sample size.

9.5.3 Response rates

Finally, you will need to take into account likely response rates when setting your sample size. The **response rate** is the percentage of those contacted who respond and take part in your research. This can be relatively low, depending on the subject of the research, the data collection technique used, and the characteristics of the target population. A review of survey response rates reported in articles in organization and management journals between 2010 and 2020 by Holtom et al. (2022), for example, showed considerable variation over time and depending on the distribution method used. We show some of the findings in Table 9.3 to illustrate this variation. It is important to note, however, that the authors found different response rates according to the focus of the journal in which the article appeared, with much lower response rates for those concerned with firm-level or higher analysis. The study also found higher response rates among surveys with participants in China compared to the USA (78 per cent versus 65 per cent in 2020), with the authors concluding that 'country of origin has become a prominent influence on response rates' (Holtom et al., 2022: 1573). Also of interest in Table 9.3 is the growth in use of online data collection, representing 65 per cent of total surveys in 2020.

TABLE 9.3 Reported survey response rates by data collection medium (based on Holtom et al., 2022)

Data-collection medium	Number of surveys by year			Mean response rate (standard deviation) by year		
	2010	2015	2020	2010	2015	2020
In person	68	70	32	57 (21)	65 (20)	73 (21)
Mail	102	45	86	49 (24)	53 (26)	70 (21)
Phone	2	4	3	11 (01)	36 (19)	53 (21)
Online	84	148	223	55 (26)	54 (25)	65 (25)

In practice, you may find your response rates fall well below the figures given in Table 9.3. In consumer studies, for example, the response rate can come down to single figures. A study of online shopping by Rose and Samouel (2009), for example, achieved a response rate of 3 per cent (3 in every 100 contacted) from online shoppers. This may seem very low but is in fact typical of consumer research studies. In many cases it is possible to estimate the response rate in advance, either based on reporting in prior studies (found in the literature) or from your own experience in the relevant field. Estimation of the anticipated response rate is crucial because it enables you to calculate the level of overall selection from the sampling frame required in order to achieve your intended sample size. In the online shopping study, for example, an anticipated response rate of 3 per cent meant that a total of 4,800 online shoppers had to be contacted to achieve the desired sample of 144. Where available, response rates should be presented in your final report.

9.6 ACCESSING AND RECRUITING YOUR SAMPLE

Sampling must take account of practical as well as theoretical aspects of your research, in the sense that you must be able to access and recruit your intended sample. If you cannot do so, you will need to rethink your intended sampling plan and possibly your research design or even your entire research project. Frustratingly, some research problems can turn out to be unresearchable in practice due to access difficulties, so it is important to identify any potential access problems with your own project at the outset and to formulate strategies for dealing with them.

9.6.1 Access in quantitative research

Quantitative research typically requires fairly large samples made up of participants with particular characteristics. One of the challenges facing quantitative researchers is that, because of the sequential nature of the research, they do not know the viability of their sampling plan until data collection is underway, at which point it may be difficult or impossible to make changes. For that reason, it is important to learn as much as you can about the target population and its likely response rates before starting. Reviewing prior research, talking to subject experts and other researchers and a small pilot study can all be used to learn more about potential access problems and thereby reduce the risk of failure.

As you develop your sampling plan following the process in Figure 9.2, you need to work out how you will identify your sampling frame and how you will make contact with members of your sample, if they are human participants, or access documents or data stored on databases. Next we discuss various options.

Sponsorship

Engaging the support of a sponsoring or client organization can be a good way to gain access to a suitable target population and sampling frame, for example, a list of organizational members, employees, or customers. Depending on data protection and other confidentiality issues, you may not be able to get access to contact details directly and may instead have to ask the organization to distribute the data collection instrument on your behalf. In other cases, you may be able to include your questions in an existing survey being done by the organization or to have it invite participation through other channels such as employee newsletters, websites, and so on.

Online invitations

Another approach to recruiting a sample is to access online groups or forums and to invite members to take part by following a link to an online survey site where the questionnaire is hosted. Depending on the forum, this approach may require you to get agreement from the forum host. This is a form of self-selection sampling but can also be combined with snowballing by asking participants to pass the survey link on to others who fit the sample criteria. Alternatively, the Internet can be used for convenience sampling, where the survey is relayed to individuals within the researcher's own network of contacts, for example, through LinkedIn. These sampling approaches are, of course, non-probability, and so you need to be aware of the effect upon the representativeness of your sample and therefore potential sampling bias.

Online panels

Another Internet-based option is to use an online panel. An online panel is composed of a large group of people who have previously agreed to take part in online surveys. Panels are typically compiled by market research agencies or survey software providers that then use them to complete online surveys for clients. An online panel is therefore a set of pre-recruited members of a population from which a sample can be drawn for online research. The panel will be recruited according to a set of characteristics, most often relating to demographics such as age, gender, income, or location. Additionally, a panel may reflect certain behavioural characteristics such as working in a particular industry, belonging to a particular interest group, or using particular products or services. Online panels have become a very popular way to obtain quantitative samples with less effort on the part of the researcher, passing a lot of the detailed problems of sampling onto the agency running the panel. An example of using an online panel is given in Research in Practice 9.3

Research in practice 9.3 Using an online panel for research on service provision

Experienced academic researcher Dr Phil Davies reflects on his use of an online panel in a research project:

> The research was exploring transformation pathways for manufacturers shifting to service provision. A famous example of this transition is Rolls Royce Total Care Package for aeroengines, often known as 'power-by-the-hour'. The aim of our research was to challenge the unidirectional assumptions of this transition, showing manufacturers could take different pathways to the introduction of services. The research needed to sample manufacturing organizations to understand how their service offerings had evolved over time to identify transformation pathways.
>
> We used a popular survey platform and data collection service provider to collect data on our behalf. This decision was made due to our sample criteria and the level of access and effort needed to collect the sample size needed from this population. Our sampling criteria were as follows:

- US firms because they were advanced in service provision amongst manufacturers.
- >500 employees were needed as smaller enterprises were unlikely to be offering a range of service offerings.
- Firms needed to have a Standard Industry Classification (SIC) code between 35 and 37.
- Responses needed to be from managers with decision-making capability and above to ensure they had the broad overview and knowledge of their service provision this research needed.

> These details were provided to the survey service provider alongside the survey that was constructed on their platform. The survey service provider conducted final checks of the survey to ensure it had no errors before deploying it to the sample population. In this research, the primary lesson learnt was that it was essential we provided strict sampling criteria to ensure the organization collecting data on our behalf was collecting relevant data for our research. Challenges arose initially when we were less specific in our sampling criteria and the responses received were not of the expected standard (participants could not answer the questions, we had many leaving the survey early, etc).

Members of an online panel are often rewarded with financial payments, donations, or participation in lotteries, which can create bias. Researchers have identified potential problems arising from participants taking part only for financial reward, completing multiple versions of the same questionnaire, and misrepresenting demographic characteristics in order to be eligible to take part (Brüggen et al., 2011; Campbell et al., 2011; Chandler and Paolacci, 2017). The accuracy and honesty of such responses may therefore be questionable as the participant is motivated only by the monetary incentives.

You should therefore be aware that an online panel is a form of non-probability self-selection sampling because certain members of the population self-select to participate in the panel. Self-selection can bias a sample because we do not know if those who select to participate share the same characteristics as those who do not. In addition, since these are normally commercial services, their suitability will also depend on whether or not you have funding available. If you are considering using an online (or offline) panel, you need to do the following:

- Verify that the panel is representative of your target population. If you are dealing with a reputable market research agency, it will be able to provide details of the panel demographics and how the panel is recruited and maintained.
- Verify that the actual participants are representative of your target population. Again, the agency responsible for the panel should be able to provide details.

Personal network

A further option is to use your own personal and professional contacts through a combination of convenience and snowball sampling. You will have to pay particular attention to the problem of sampling bias if you use this route, but it can be an option if you have strong links to a particular group relevant to your research topic. It can be combined with online invitations (e.g. via LinkedIn or other social media sites).

9.6.2 Access in qualitative research

Similar options are available for qualitative researchers, but somewhat different considerations apply in gaining and maintaining access. Smaller sample sizes, direct contact with participants, and the emergent nature of sampling processes offer some advantages for qualitative researchers in that it is possible to monitor the progress of the sampling plan as it unfolds and to take actions to address any problems.

Nevertheless, qualitative researchers do face other challenges in gaining the appropriate depth of access and time commitment from participants. This can be a particular problem if the researcher is an 'outsider' in terms of the community under investigation. In such situations, it can be very useful to identify and secure the cooperation of a **gatekeeper** who is a member of the group being studied or who has insider status and can facilitate access. Gatekeepers may occupy a formal position, such as a senior manager (who may also be a formal sponsor) or an informal one, such as an influential individual in a group. Depending on their interest and role, gatekeepers may require information about the study, the rationale for choosing the site or individuals that you want to research, how disruptive the data collection is likely to be, and how the findings will be disseminated (including how the gatekeeper will benefit from the study).

In other situations, the researcher will have to establish contacts directly with potential participants. Your personal and professional network, or those of colleagues or others interested in the project, are very valuable here. The Internet also offers routes to contact potential participants through social media sites, professional forums, and other contact points. In Research in Practice 9.4 we give an example of sample access for an online participant observation study.

Research in practice 9.4 Sample access for participant observation within an online firm-hosted brand community

A research study undertaken by a PhD student (Shapiro, 2013) aimed to investigate what motivates an individual to participate actively in a firm-hosted online brand community. The research focused on the business to business (B2B) sector in the United States and specifically aimed to understand the individual-level consequences and personal values that are satisfied through such active participation. An ethnographic method was used in the study, which involved the researcher in collecting data via participant observation within an online community in order to gain access into the collective identity of the community.

Selection of the community for the study was based on four characteristics that would make the sample relevant to the research questions. These characteristics were as follows:

1. An active community: the community had to be active with regular and daily postings by the community members.

2. A community centred on a strong, globally known brand with most discussion being focused on brand issues and brand development.

3. Firm-hosted: the community to be hosted and managed by a B2B brand.

4. A community that had a distinct group of very active, 'evangelical' members. The involvement of these individuals was so significant that the host firm personally acknowledged them.

Contact was made with community managers and online consumer experience teams at various companies to explain the details of the study. However, during this process of searching for a relevant community, an approach was made to the researcher by a leading US firm in the software field that had become aware of the study and that had an online community that fitted all of the outlined requirements. The firm showed enthusiasm for the objectives of the research and how it could eventually be aligned with its own goals. Once access into the community has been negotiated, the researcher assessed the community through unobtrusive observation, which allowed the general culture and language of the community to be understood. During this phase, community activity and natural behaviour was not interrupted. The community was entered regularly by the researcher to look at salient activity and behaviour in the discussion forum. Field notes were recorded in a journal, which gave an understanding of the history, nature, and people of the community. Participant observation commenced after the unobtrusive observation had provided the researcher with a general understanding of the community and its characteristics. The researcher signed up as an official member of the community and posted an introductory letter to the community announcing the purpose of the research. Participant observation continued until such time as data saturation occurred.

9.6.3 Recruiting hard-to-reach and vulnerable populations

As discussed in Chapter 5 an important trend in research has been the growing recognition of the need for inclusivity in the research we undertake. This has significant implications for the sampling process. This may be because our research is seeking to work with a particular group, or more generally because we need to ensure our sample represents the broader, diverse population from which it has been drawn. In practice, this can be challenging when trying to recruit some groups. Reasons for this can include mistrust of the research process and goals by potential participants, concerns about risk of participation, constraints on time or other resources, and problems with 'labelling' potential participants (Ellard-Gray et al., 2015). The use of gatekeepers building rapport and trust may help with gaining access and recruiting potential participants. Snowballing sampling is one specific strategy that may work, although Ellard-Gray et al. (2015) suggest being ready to use multiple strategies to find the best approach. Research in Practice 9.5 provides an example of a student research project where a creative solution was needed to investigate a sensitive topic area.

Research in practice 9.5 Sampling in a sensitive research topic

Borrowing has an important and positive role in the modern economy. Excess debt, however, can be damaging for individuals. As well as impacting their immediate financial situation, research shows that problem debt can be associated with degradation of mental and physical health and impact the debtor's relationships with others and their own identity through the shame and stigma attached to indebtedness. Retail banks can play an important role in helping, but getting engagement from those in financial difficulty can be problematic. Laura Wallis's master's research project set out to gain a deeper understanding of factors influencing customer engagement with bank-led solutions in such situations using in-depth interviews.

Wallis's initial sampling strategy involved direct contact with those experiencing debt problems. Difficulty of access, the sensitivity of the topic, and the potential vulnerability of participants raised significant ethical concerns. Given the scope and time available for the project, she took the decision to work instead with debt advisors working for major UK-based debt advice charities or companies (DMC). Criteria for selection included that the interviewees must work directly with those in financial difficulty as part of their role. The final sample was 12 participants from four different DMCs who were able to give insights based on their personal experiences working with those in debt and also working with banks as partners in finding ways forward.

Source: Wallis (2022)

9.6.4 Factors affecting access

Regardless of the type of research you are doing, there are a number of factors that may influence your ability to gain access or to get individuals to participate in your research. These include the following:

- **Participant effort.** If participants (whether individually or at an organizational level) are expected to put considerable time and effort into the research, they are unlikely to agree to take part unless they can see a good reason for doing so. Such a reason may be in terms of some direct benefit to them or because they see the research as valuable in other ways, for example, in terms of solving a shared problem. Good explanation of the purpose and relevance of the research can help provide this.
- **Sensitivity.** A particularly sensitive topic may deter participation, especially in some contexts where people may be nervous about consequences or repercussions if they participate. Good briefing, including appropriate commitments, taking time to build up trust amongst potential participants, and the professionalism displayed by the researcher can help to overcome this barrier.
- **Confidentiality.** Topics vary in their degree of confidentiality, but in some business and management research projects, commercial confidentiality may be a particular concern for potential participants. This can be a particular deterrent in research that is highly sensitive (e.g. an employee satisfaction survey) or where the research is taking place in a very tightly bounded population in which a participant may be identifiable (e.g. a business-to-business qualitative research study within a small industry sector with limited numbers of competitor firms). In such cases, researchers may have to provide additional assurances regarding confidentiality. As a student researcher, for example, you may need to provide a copy of the confidentiality policy of your academic institution in addition to any other briefing documents. In some cases, particularly commercial research, it may be necessary to sign a non-disclosure agreement. Access will also be influenced by requirements of data protection, as discussed in Chapter 5. In other cases, it may be preferable to adjust the research focus so that the level of confidential disclosure required is reduced.

Gaining and maintaining access is likely to be one of the toughest practical challenges in any research project. Your ultimate success will very much depend on the appeal of your research topic, your negotiation skills, and your ability to build trust and credibility amongst stakeholders.

CHAPTER SUMMARY

- The target population is the totality of elements of interest to the researcher.
- As it is often difficult to access the total population, data from a sample, which is a subgroup drawn from the total population, is used for analysis. Sampling is the process by which we identify and access our sample data from the total population.
- The generic sampling process consists of six steps: determining the target population, identifying the sampling frame, selecting the sampling method, establishing the sample size, implementing the sampling plan, and reporting the sampling procedure.
- Sampling bias occurs when the sample is not representative of the population. Researchers should be aware of the sources of sampling bias when designing their sampling and data collection.

- There are two families of sampling method: probability and non-probability. Probability methods use some element of randomization in order to generate a statistically representative sample. Non-probability methods select on the basis of other criteria.
- Sampling in quantitative research aims to produce a statistically representative sample, with a preference for probability sampling methods to allow statistical generalization. Sampling in qualitative research aims to produce a theoretically relevant sampling, with a preference for purposive non-probability sampling methods to support theory building. Sampling in mixed methods research includes deciding on the time sequencing and relationship between the qualitative and quantitative elements.
- Sample size in quantitative research can be predetermined on the basis of the level of precision required, the homogeneity of the population, and the confidence level required by the researcher. Sample size in qualitative research will be influenced by any requirements for theoretical saturation and the need to achieve an appropriate balance between breadth and depth. When calculating sample size, it is important to take account of likely response rates.
- Access and recruiting your sample is an important practical task in any research project and should be considered at the planning stage.

NEXT STEPS

9.1 **Choosing a sampling method**. Identify your sampling method using the following questions as a guide:

   a. What is the population from which my sample will be taken?

   b. For quantitative research:

   i. What is my target population?

   ii. What sampling method (e.g. probability sampling, non-probability sampling) do I need to use? If probability, how will I conduct randomized selection?

   iii. What specific sampling method will I use?

   iv. What sample size will I need? Do I need to set any quotas?

   c. For survey studies: what response rate do I expect, and therefore how many questionnaires will I need to send out?

   d. For qualitative research:

   i. What sources of data are relevant to my inquiry?

   ii. Where will I find them?

   iii. What sampling method will I use?

   iv. What sample size should I use for planning purposes?

> **9.2 Gaining access**. How will you gain access to your intended sample? What potential barriers might you encounter, and how will you overcome them?
>
> **9.3 Describing your sampling plan**. Use the following prompts to describe your sampling plan:
>
> **a.** The proposed sampling method will be:
>
> **b.** This is appropriate because:
>
> **c.** The intended sample size is, or the following method will be used to determine the sample size:
>
> **d.** This is appropriate because:
>
> **e.** The limitations of my sampling plan are:

FURTHER READING

For further reading, please see the companion website.

REFERENCES

AAMC (2021). *Active Physicians in the Largest Specialties by Major Professional Activity, 2021*. Washington, DC: Association of American Medical Colleges. Available at: www.aamc.org/data-reports/workforce/data/active-physicians-largest-specialties-major-professional-activity-2021 (Accessed 25 March 2023).

Armstrong, J. S. and Overton, T. S. (1977). Estimating nonresponse bias in mail surveys. *Journal of Marketing Research*, 14(3): 396–402.

Arnab, R. (2017). *Survey Sampling Theory and Applications*. London: Elsevier.

Baker, S. E. and Edwards, R. (2012). *How Many Qualitative Interviews is Enough?* National Centre for Research Methods. Available at: http://eprints.ncrm.ac.uk/2273/ (Accessed 1 April 2023).

Boddy, C. R. (2016). Sample size for qualitative research. *Qualitative Market Research: An International Journal*, 19(4): 426–432.

Brüggen, E., Wetzels, M., de Ruyter, K. and Schillewaert, N. (2011). Individual differences in motivation to participate in online panels: The effect on response rate and reponse quality perceptions. *International Journal of Market Research*, 53(3): 369–390.

Campbell, C., Parent, M., Plangger, K. and Fulgoni, G. M. (2011). Instant innovation: From zero to full speed in fifteen years—how online offerings have reshaped marketing research. *Journal of Advertising Research*, 51(1 (50th Anniversary Supplement)): 72–86.

Chandler, J. J. and Paolacci, G. (2017). Lie for a dime: When most prescreening responses are honest but most study participants are impostors. *Social Psychological and Personality Science*, 8(5): 500–508.

Cohen, J. (1992). A power primer. *Psychological Bulletin*, 112(1): 155–159.

Collins, K. M. T. (2015). Advanced sampling designs in mixed research: Current practices and emerging trends in the social and behavioral sciences. In: Tashakkori, A. and Teddlie, C. (eds) *SAGE Handbook of Mixed Methods in Social & Behavioral Research*. 2nd ed. Thousand Oaks, CA: SAGE Publications.

Collins, K. M. T., Onwuegbuzie, A. J. and Jiao, Q. G. (2007). A mixed methods investigation of mixed methods sampling designs in social and health science research. *Journal of Mixed Methods Research*, 1(3): 267–294.

Ellard-Gray, A., Jeffrey, N. K., Choubak, M. and Crann, S. E. (2015). Finding the hidden participant: Solutions for recruiting hidden, hard-to-reach, and vulnerable populations. *International Journal of Qualitative Methods*, 14(5): 1609406915621420.

Flick, U. (2009). *An Introduction to Qualitative Research*. 4th ed. Los Angeles, CA: SAGE Publications.

Guest, G., Bunce, A. and Johnson, L. (2006). How many interviews are enough? An experiment with data saturation and variability. *Field Methods*, 18(1): 59–82.

Holtom, B., Baruch, Y., Aguinis, H. and Ballinger, G. A. (2022). Survey response rates: Trends and a validity assessment framework. *Human Relations*, 75(8): 1560–1584.

Internet World Stats (2023). *Internet Usage, Facebook Subscribers and Population Statistics for all the Americas World Region Countries July 31, 2022*. Internet World Stats. Available at: www.internet-worldstats.com/stats2.htm.

Jang, M. and Vorderstrasse, A. (2019). Socioeconomic status and racial or ethnic differences in participation: Web-based survey. *JMIR Research Protocols*, 8(4): e11865.

King, N., Horrocks, C. and Brooks, J. (2019). *Interviews in Qualitative Research*. 2nd ed. London: SAGE Publications.

Maxwell, J. A. (2013). *Qualitative Research Design. An Interactive Approach*. 3rd ed. Los Angeles, CA: SAGE Publications.

McKay, D. (2022). *Home is Where the New Start is: Improving Collaborative Working to Deliver Better Housing Outcomes for Prison Leavers with Care Experience*. Master's dissertation, Henley Business School at the University of Reading, Henley-on-Thames.

Morse, J. M. (2000). Determining sample size. *Qualitative Health Research*, 10(1): 3–5.

Morse, J. M. (2015). *Data Were Saturated*. Los Angeles, CA: SAGE Publications, 587–588.

O'Reilly, M. and Parker, N. (2013). "Unsatisfactory saturation": A critical exploration of the notion of saturated sample sizes in qualitative research. *Qualitative Research*, 13(2): 190–197.

Onwuegbuzie, A. J. and Collins, K. M. (2007). A typology of mixed methods sampling designs in social science research. *Qualitative Report*, 12(2): 281–316.

Ramanujan, P., Bhattacharjea, S. and Alcott, B. (2022). A multi-stage approach to qualitative sampling within a mixed methods evaluation: Some reflections on purpose and process. *Canadian Journal of Program Evaluation*, 36(3): 355–364.

Rose, S. and Samouel, P. (2009). Internal psychological versus external market-driven determinants of the amount of consumer information search amongst online shoppers. *Journal of Marketing Management*, 25(1–2): 171–190.

Saunders, B., Sim, J., Kingstone, T., Baker, S., Waterfield, J., Bartlam, B., Burroughs, H. and Jinks, C. (2018). Saturation in qualitative research: Exploring its conceptualization and operationalization. *Quality & Quantity*, 52(4): 1893–1907.

Saunders, M. N. K. and Townsend, K. (2016). Reporting and justifying the number of interview participants in organization and workplace research. *British Journal of Management*, 27(4): 836–852.

Shapiro, M. (2013). *An Exploration of Active Participation in a Firm-Hosted Online Brand Community*. PhD thesis, Henley Business School, University of Reading, Reading.

Smith, J. A., Flowers, P. and Larkin, M. (2022). *Interpretive Phenomenological Analysis: Theory, Method and Research*. 2nd ed. London: SAGE Publications.

Sue, V. M. and Ritter, L. A. (2012). *Conducting Online Surveys*. 2nd ed. Thousand Oaks, CA: SAGE Publications.

Supreme Court (2023). *About the Court.* Available at: www.supremecourt.gov/about/about.aspx (Accessed 25 March 2023).

UN (2023). *Open-Ended Intergovernmental Expert Group Meeting on Model Strategies on Reducing Reoffending, Working Paper E/CN.15/2023/13.* Vienna: United Nations Commission on Crime Prevention and Criminal Justice.

Wallis, L. (2022). *How do Customer Attitudes Towards Banks and Debt Influence Customer Engagement with Bank-Led Debt Solutions?* Master's dissertation, Henley Business School, University of Reading, Henley-on-Thames.

CHAPTER 10

Collecting data using questionnaires

CHAPTER LEARNING OUTCOMES

After reading this chapter you will be able to

- critically assess whether a questionnaire is a suitable data collection instrument for your research project;
- demonstrate the ability to design and structure a questionnaire, aligned with your research question(s) and conceptual model;
- define and apply robust procedures for pretesting, piloting, and administering a questionnaire.

10.1 INTRODUCTION

Almost everyone has some experience of questionnaires, whether in the form of employee feedback, customer satisfaction surveys, or as part of a formal research project. Perhaps because we are so familiar with them it is tempting to assume that they are an easy option for collecting data. In fact designing and administering a questionnaire requires careful thought and hard work if the resulting data are to be of any use in answering your research question. This chapter therefore takes a structured approach to using questionnaires for data collection. We begin by looking at situations in which it might be appropriate to use a questionnaire and review some strengths and weaknesses of questionnaires as data collection tools. Next we introduce a simple process to follow when designing and using them. We look at each step in turn, with particular emphasis on how to formulate appropriate questions and lay out the questionnaire itself. We conclude with a discussion of pretesting and piloting and a review of the options for distributing your questionnaire.

DOI: 10.4324/9781003381006-13

10.2 WHY AND WHEN TO USE A QUESTIONNAIRE

A **questionnaire** is a particular type of **data collection instrument** that uses a standardized, structured set of questions to measure variables, such as respondent attitudes, that are of interest to the researcher. Depending on the research, a questionnaire may be designed either for self-completion by the respondents themselves or for completion by the researcher on the basis of oral answers from participants given, for example, over the telephone. The data gathered by questionnaire are typically quantitative or easily quantifiable that can then be analyzed to answer our research questions.

Questionnaires are most obviously associated with survey research designs in which they are likely to form the primary, and often the only, data collection method, but in practice their use is much more widespread, as we show in Table 10.1.

10.2.1 Advantages and disadvantages of using questionnaires

Questionnaires are such a widely used method of data collection because they offer a number of advantages. Specific advantages include the following:

- Low cost. Questionnaires can enable us to reach a large sample at a relatively low cost in time and money, particularly if an online survey tool can be used for distribution.
- Speed of collection. Responses to questionnaires can be obtained in a relatively short period of time. Data preparation can also be relatively fast if data are collected electronically and can be transferred directly into a software programme for further analysis.
- Flexibility. Questionnaires can be used to measure a wide variety of variables and can be administered in a variety of ways.

TABLE 10.1 How questionnaires may be used in different research designs

Research design	Role of questionnaires in data collection
Survey study	Main or sole method used to measure relevant variables
Experiment and quasi-experiment	Used alongside other methods, such as observation, to measure relevant variables before, during and after the experiment
Nonexperimental explanatory research	Used alongside other methods, such as secondary data, to measure relevant variables
Case study	May be used alongside other data collection methods, for example, for triangulation purposes
Action research	May be used alongside other data collection methods

- Anonymity. Questionnaire distribution can be separated from subsequent data handling, so helping to ensure respondent anonymity and data confidentiality.
- Reach. Online questionnaires in particular open up great possibilities for reaching a geographically dispersed sample (although it is important to be aware that some potential participant groups may not be reachable online or have lower response rates).
- Reduced interviewer effects. In self-completed questionnaires, the role of the researcher in the data collection process is minimized, thus reducing the influence on the responses generated. If a questionnaire is administered face-to-face or by telephone, researcher training, and standardized procedures are used to reduce interviewer effects.

Many of these advantages have been intensified with the introduction of online survey tools which permit distribution and collection of questionnaires via the Internet, as we discuss later in this chapter.

There are, however, some disadvantages to using questionnaires of which you should be aware. These include the following:

- Variable response rates. Given the ubiquity of questionnaires, potential participants may be suffering from survey fatigue, leading to low response rates. Aspects of the questionnaire itself may also influence response rate, such as its length, how interesting it is to respondents or the relevance of the topic. Response rates can be improved by careful design and administration of the questionnaire (see also Chapter 9 for a discussion of response rates).
- Partial completion. Respondents may fail to complete questions appropriately or fail to answer them in full. There may be no opportunity to identify and clarify poorly completed responses until they are detected at the analysis stage, when they may have to be removed, leading to reduced sample size and potential bias as a result of the pattern of non-completed items.
- Limited range of responses for participants. Questionnaires are fixed in terms of the structure and format of the questions. Respondents are required to answer in a way that matches how the researcher has framed the questions. There is little opportunity for respondents to provide feedback, for example, where they feel that the response options offered do not fit their preferred response.
- Respondent literacy level. Completion of a questionnaire can often require good levels of literacy, which may be a problem for some groups of respondents such as young children. Use of questionnaires across different language groups can also be challenging and requires careful thought by the researcher in terms of translation.
- **Common method bias.** Use of the same questionnaire to measure both independent and dependent variables can contribute to common method bias, which may distort resulting statistical tests. Various options are used to address this where it is seen as a potential problem (Podsakoff et al., 2012).

These disadvantages are inherent in questionnaire design, but their impact can be minimized by good questionnaire design and by a well-thought-through process for administering the questionnaire and analyzing the data.

10.3 THE QUESTIONNAIRE DESIGN PROCESS

Your questionnaire must be able to generate valid and reliable data about the variables relevant to your investigation. At the same time it must be structured and laid out in a way that encourages participation and thereby a high response rate. It also needs to be in line with ethical requirements in terms of informed consent. Before it is sent out, it needs to be pretested and piloted. Finally, you will need to give careful thought to how you will distribute it to your sample. If you send out a poor-quality questionnaire you will get poor-quality data back. If it is a really poor questionnaire, you may get no data back at all. Good questionnaire design is therefore fundamental to the success of your data collection.

To help you achieve this, we recommend following a structured design process that we show in Figure 10.1. The remainder of the chapter is dedicated to examining each stage in turn to identify key points to consider and key decisions to be taken when using questionnaires for data collection.

10.4 IDENTIFY RELEVANT CONCEPTS/VARIABLES

Once you have confirmed that a questionnaire is an appropriate data collection technique for your research, the first, and crucial, step is to identify the relevant concepts that you wish to measure as variables in your questionnaire. They should relate to your research question and any theory that you wish to test in your research.

In descriptive surveys, for example, relevant concepts will be those aspects of the phenomenon or population that you wish to be able to measure, for example, customers' satisfaction levels or their shopping frequency. In analytical surveys, the concepts will be derived from the theory you wish to test and are included in your conceptual model and hypotheses.

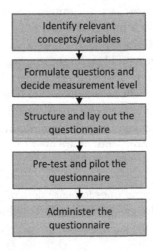

FIGURE 10.1 The questionnaire design process

Once you have identified the relevant concepts, you will need to define them. Based on your knowledge of the topic area and your review of relevant literature, you should define your concepts and the dimensions of them that you wish to measure in your questionnaire as variables. The dimensions can be derived from a range of sources, including previous studies, theoretical literature on the topic, or by carrying out exploratory research, for example, a qualitative interview study. Research in Practice 10.1 gives an example of the dimensions of a complex concept: service quality.

You can summarize your concepts/variables and their definitions in a data collection matrix as we discuss later in the chapter (see Table 10.4).

Research in practice 10.1 Dimensions of service quality

In a classic article, Parasuraman et al. (1988) reported their development of the SERVQUAL instrument, a questionnaire used to measure service quality. Prior exploratory research had identified ten dimensions used by customers in assessing service quality. These dimensions were tangibility, reliability, responsiveness, communication, credibility, security, competence, courtesy, understanding/knowing the customer, and access. These fed into the next stage of the research project, which resulted in the SERVQUAL instrument, which consists of five dimensions, defined by Parasuraman et al. (1988: 23) as follows:

1. Tangibility: physical facilities, equipment and appearance of personnel

2. Reliability: ability to perform the promised service dependably and accurately

3. Responsibility: willingness to help the customer and provide prompt service

4. Assurance: knowledge and courtesy of employees and their ability to inspire trust and confidence

5. Empathy: caring, individualized attention that the firm provides to its customers

Each of these dimensions is measured by a set of questions in the SERVQUAL instrument, allowing the researcher to gain an understanding of the different dimensions of service quality in the research situation.

10.5 FORMULATE YOUR QUESTIONS AND DECIDE THE LEVEL OF MEASUREMENT

The next step is to decide how you will measure the concepts you have identified as relevant to your research. To do this you will have to develop what are known as **indicators** that can be used as measures of those concepts. If, for example, you wanted to measure the concept of success in the context of a project, one possible indicator might be whether or not the project was completed on time. In questionnaires, of course, indicators will take the form of questions or statements to which participants can respond.

10.5.1 Formulating your questions

Formulating your questions is probably the hardest part of questionnaire design, at least for those new to research. It is our experience as tutors and supervisors that the weakest feature of most questionnaire-based student research projects is the questions they use to collect their data. So how do you formulate suitable questions? There are, in principle, two options.

First, you can use or adapt well-established measures from prior research. Suitable measures can often be found in academic journal articles. In some cases, the scale will be reproduced directly in the article (or in an appendix). In other cases, only the original source may be indicated and this will then need to be located to find the full scale. Alternatively, handbooks such as Bearden et al. (2011), Brunner (2019), and Roth et al. (2008) provide listings of previously used questions from a wide range of studies. It is likely that you will need to adapt or tailor existing questions to fit the context of your own research.

Aside from saving you the time of developing your own measures, the big advantage of using existing measures is that information regarding their validity and reliability will be available in the referenced work. Note, however, that just because a set of questions appears in print does not automatically mean that they are a good measure of your chosen concept. Ensure that you check the source for information on the quality of the proposed measure. Be aware also that some measures may be subject to commercial or other restrictions, so you should check before using them. Wherever existing measures are used, their source should be fully acknowledged and referenced in your final report.

If no previous measures are available to use, you will need to develop your own questions to collect your data. Pay close attention to literature discussing the definitions and dimensions of the concepts you are intending to measure. Designing your own questions is a demanding task if you are trying to measure a complex construct, so ensure that you are thoroughly familiar with your topic, consult more specialist texts on question development, and seek advice from your supervisor or other subject matter expert if possible.

Wherever possible, use existing validated, reliable scales rather than inventing your own. For these reasons, we strongly recommend completing your literature review before designing your questionnaire. Whatever you do, try to make sure the questions you include in your questionnaire represent the best possible measures of your research variables.

10.5.2 Levels of measurement

As you develop your questions you will need to decide what level of measurement to use for each of your variables. Measurement, as we are using the term here, is the process of assigning a number to an observation to facilitate analysis. In management research we often need to measure many different types of variable, including things like nationality, gender, employee satisfaction, and share price. It is fairly obvious that using a number to 'measure' gender is not the same thing as using a number to measure share price. Therefore we need to be able to recognize different levels of measurement that we can use in our research. Conventionally we do this by distinguishing between **nominal**, **ordinal**, **interval**, and **ratio** measurement levels.

Nominal data

The nominal or categorical level of data is the lowest level of measurement and is used when numbers are applied to distinguish different categories such as employment status of employees (e.g. full-time/part-time) or geographic location (e.g. different office sites).

Membership of the categories must be comprehensive and mutually exclusive, and categories have no natural rank order.

Ordinal data

Ordinal data can be placed in rank order from highest to lowest but do not allow us to measure how much difference there is between the categories. For example, measuring how often people drive, using the categories 'every day', 'at least 3 times per week', '1–2 times per week', and 'less than once per week' allows us to place respondents in rank order, but we cannot specify exactly the difference between them in terms of the number of times they drive their car.

Interval data

Interval data can be placed in rank order, but it is also possible to measure the size of the difference between the values. Interval data do not have a naturally occurring zero point, so whilst we can add or subtract values, it makes no sense to multiply or divide them. Temperature, measured in degrees Celsius, is an example of an interval scale. We can calculate the difference between 24°C and 12°C but cannot say that one is twice as warm as the other. Similarly, 0°C does not represent an absence of temperature.

One of the most commonly encountered rating scales in management research is the Likert scales. In response to a statement such as 'statistics is fun', for example, a Likert scale requires the respondent to indicate their degree of agreement or disagreement. Such an agreement scale usually ranges from 'strongly agree' to 'strongly disagree', and conventionally, a five- or seven-point scale is provided. The data generated by Likert-type rating scales are often treated as interval data for analysis in managerial research, but this use is contentious, as we discuss in Critical Commentary 10.1.

CRITICAL COMMENTARY 10.1

Likert scale data: interval or ordinal?

The Likert-type rating scale has become an established technique for measuring responses to statement items in social science questionnaires. Typically these will be statements regarding attitudes, perceptions, or feelings to which the respondent indicates their level of agreement or disagreement. The output generated by Likert scales is often treated as interval data and analyzed using the techniques appropriate to that measurement level.

Despite this, there is debate over whether or not Likert scale data can really be considered as interval level. The alternative view is that Likert scale data should be treated as ordinal: responses can be placed in rank order, but the intervals between the values cannot be assumed to be constant (Jamieson, 2004). As a result, only those analysis techniques suitable for ordinal data should be used.

In management research it has become accepted practice to assume that 'people treat the intervals between points on such scales as being equal in magnitude' (Hair et al., 2020: 243) and therefore to treat Likert scale data as interval data. We follow that approach in this book. Nevertheless, this remains a contentious issue and it is important to be aware of the debate and to decide how you will treat Likert-type rating scale data in your project.

Ratio data

Finally, ratio data is the same as interval data, with equal distance between measurement intervals, but this time with a meaningful zero point. Height and age are two examples of ratio scales. Ratio data is the highest level of measurement

Implications of the different measurement levels

The level of measurement which you choose has implications for your subsequent data analysis because certain statistical techniques require a particular level of measurement. Decisions that you make at the questionnaire design stage therefore have serious implications for later stages of your research, and so as part of your research design, you should identify your intended analysis techniques to ensure that you collect appropriate data. We discuss the selection of statistical techniques by data type in Chapter 13, but as a general rule, the higher the level of measurement, the more options you have from an analysis point of view. We summarize levels of measurement and their features in Table 10.2.

10.5.3 Question format

Alongside deciding on your measurement level, you will also have to decide on what question format to use. We now present a range of options from which to choose. As we explain, different formats generate data at different levels of measurement, so it is

TABLE 10.2 Levels of measurement

Level of measurement	Frequency counts	Place in rank order	Quantify difference between each value and add and subtract values	Multiply and divide values	Level of measurement
	Allowable operations				
Nominal	√				Lowest
Ordinal	√	√			
Interval	√	√	√		↕
Ratio	√	√	√	√	Highest

For what purpose do you use the Internet? (please select as many as applicable)

a) Work/business ☐

b) Leisure ☐

c) Search for information about products and services ☐

d) Buying products and services ☐

FIGURE 10.2 Example checklist question

important to consider your choice of question format alongside your required measurement level.

Checklist

In checklist-format questions the respondent is presented with a list of options from which they select as many as apply (Figure 10.2). This generates nominal data, but as respondents may select multiple options, it does not result in each respondent being in one, and only one, category. This may complicate analysis because it is less easy to categorize respondents, so it is important to decide how the data will be analyzed if you are intending to use this question format.

Categorical scales

In this question format the respondent is presented with a list of options from which they select one, and only one, category. The categories chosen must be meaningful to the respondents, mutually exclusive, and exhaustive (i.e. cover all options). For some questions it may be necessary to provide an 'other' category; this is sometimes accompanied by an open-ended question for the respondent to provide additional details. The data from such open questions may be hard to analyze, and if the 'other' option is heavily used by respondents, it may indicate poor choice of categories. When the topic is a potentially personal or sensitive one (such as gender or ethnicity), it is good practice to include a 'prefer not to say' option.

This is an important question format for gathering demographic data on your respondents. Variants include as follows:

- Binary choice (Figure 10.3a). The respondent has two options, such as yes/no or part-time/full-time, and must choose one. This type of question generates nominal data.
- Multiple choice (Figure 10.3b and c). The respondent has multiple options and must select only one. The categories can be nominal (such as marital status) or ordinal (such as age groups).

Rank preference scale

In this question format, respondents are presented with a list of items and must arrange them in rank preference (Figure 10.4). This produces ordinal-level data for the items that have been ranked. Note that because the resulting data are ordinal there are constraints on using this type of data to calculate an overall ranking for each of the options. As a

```
(a) What is your employment contract status?
                        ☐  Full-time
                        ☐  Part-time
(b) What is your age?
                        ☐  18-24
                        ☐  25-34
                        ☐  35-44
                        ☐  45-54
                        ☐  55 +
(c) What is your marital status?
                        ☐  Married

                        ☐  Single (never married or never
                            registered a same-sex civil partnership)

                        ☐  Divorced or formerly in a same-sex civil
                            partnership which is now legally dissolved

                        ☐  Widowed or surviving partner from a
                            same-sex civil partnership

                        ☐  Separated (but still legally married or still legally
                            in a same-sex civil partnership)

                        ☐  In a registered same-sex civil partnership
```

FIGURE 10.3 Example categorical scale questions

```
Please rank the following forms of exercise in terms
of your preference  where 1 = lowest and 5 = highest



        Jogging              ☐
        Cycling              ☐
        Swimming             ☐
        Strength training    ☐
        Yoga                 ☐
```

FIGURE 10.4 Example rank preference question

result the data generated may not be easy to interpret in practice. Respondents may also find it hard to rank a large number of items and may be unable or unwilling to differentiate between items. In our experience, rank preference scales are popular with novice researchers but can create problems later in the project if the analysis options have not been properly considered.

Numeric rating Likert-type scale

The Likert-type rating scale is often used to measure the strength of attitudes, feelings, or opinions. Typically, respondents are presented with a five- or seven-point scale on which they express the intensity of their views about a statement, as we show in Figure 10.5. The more scale points, the greater the potential to discriminate between respondents'

Please indicate below the degree to which you agree or disagree with the following statement:

'Online is an easy way to find out about products'

Strongly disagree		Neither agree nor disagree			Strongly agree	
☐	☐	☐	☐	☐	☐	☐

FIGURE 10.5 Example single-item Likert-type rating scale

Using the rating scale below please indicate the feelings you had following your most recent online shopping experience:

1. UNHAPPY	1 2 3 4 5 6 7	HAPPY
2. ANNOYED	1 2 3 4 5 6 7	PLEASED
3. CALM	1 2 3 4 5 6 7	EXCITED
4. RELAXED	1 2 3 4 5 6 7	STIMULATED
5. GUIDED	1 2 3 4 5 6 7	AUTONOMOUS
6. INFLUENCED	1 2 3 4 5 6 7	INFLUENTIAL

FIGURE 10.6 Example semantic differential scale (based on Rose and Samouel, 2009)

opinions, but this has to be balanced against their ability to answer to that level of precision. Data are treated as either interval or ordinal (see Critical Commentary 10.1).

Semantic differential scale

Semantic differential scales are another type of numeric rating scale that can be used to measure attitudes or feelings and again can utilize a five- or seven-point scale. The key feature of this type of scale is that it utilizes statements at each end of the scale that describe the attitude or feeling using opposite adjectives such as good/bad or happy/sad. Respondents circle numbers or place a mark along a continuum to indicate their own position. The example in Figure 10.6 is taken from an investigation into the various emotions generated during online shopping and shows eight different items (Rose and Samouel, 2009). Numbers are assigned to each opposite emotion. The data generated are typically assumed to be interval.

Summated rating scale

The rating scale in Figure 10.5 is a single-item scale because it uses one question (item) to measure the underlying variable. An alternative approach is to use what is known as a

summated scale or multi-item scale. As the names suggest, this is a scale which consists of several questions (items) that are combined (summated) in some way to produce a single measure for the chosen variable. Summated scales can capture more of the complexity of a concept and provide greater measurement precision, thereby giving a more valid measure than a single-item scale.

The number of items in a summated scale and how they are combined can vary. In Research in Practice 10.2 we show an example of a summated scale used to measure affective commitment. In this case there are six items that would be included as six Likert-style rating questions in the questionnaire. Determining the level of affective commitment for a respondent involves calculating the arithmetic mean (average) score of the six responses by that particular respondent to give a single figure which can then be incorporated into further analysis. In addition, it would be standard practice when using multi-item scales to check the reliability of the scale, which we discuss in Chapter 13. Developing valid and reliable summated scales is a demanding task and can easily form a research project in its own right. This is one of the reasons why we strongly encourage you to use existing scales, suitably adapted if necessary, where possible.

Summated scales are very common in business and management research for measuring complex constructs. Single-item scales may be used where a well-established measure exists or when measuring self-reported intentional behaviour (such as intention to repeat purchase). Examination of prior research in your topic area can help you to decide what type of scale is appropriate for your project.

Research in practice 10.2 Measuring affective commitment

The extent to which employees are committed to their organizations is of interest to both academics and practitioners. One dimension of commitment is what Meyer et al. (1993: 539) refer to as 'affective commitment'. 'Employees with a strong affective commitment', they suggest, 'remain with the organization because they want to' (Meyer et al., 1993: 539).

In order to measure this dimension of commitment, Meyer et al. have developed and tested a multi-item scale. The scale consists of six items shown in the next section. Each item is measured on a 1–7 rating scale (where 1 = strongly disagree; 7 = strongly agree). Those items marked (R) are negatively worded and need to be reverse-coded (i.e. a rating of 1 becomes 7, 2 becomes 6, etc.) before analysis (see Chapter 13). The final measure of affective commitment is calculated by taking the arithmetic mean (average) of the six items.

1. I would be very happy to spend the rest of my career with this organization.

2. I really feel as if this organization's problems are my own.

3. I do not feel a strong sense of 'belonging' to my organization. (R)

4. I do not feel 'emotionally attached' to this organization. (R)

5. I do not feel like 'part of the family' at my organization. (R)

6. This organization has a great deal of personal meaning for me.

Open questions

The formats we have been looking at so far are examples of closed questions, in which the respondent is provided with a set of predefined responses from which they must choose one or more options. Closed questions are the most common format in questionnaires. The limited number of response options and their structured nature makes it easier to analyze the answers using quantitative analysis techniques. On the other hand, while the answer format provides structure for the respondents, it also constrains their responses to the researcher's view of the topic. The alternative is to adopt an open question format. Open questions do not have a fixed set of optional answers but invite the respondent to answer in their own words. You might, for example, ask respondents to explain in their own words their reasons for answering a closed question in a particular way. Open questions enable the capture of richer and more in-depth data that may provide insights or responses beyond the researcher's initial framing of the research problem.

Open questions can vary in their complexity and degree of 'openness'. The simplest format is that of a single item response in which the respondent is asked to provide a single response to a specific question. This might be numeric (such as age or length of time in the organization) or textual (such as favourite colour or city of residence). In Figure 10.7 we show an example requiring a numeric response in the form of the respondents' annual household income. Although this type of question offers the possibility of eliciting an exact answer, in some cases, for example a sensitive subject like income, respondents may be unwilling or unable to provide the required degree of precision. In such situations a categorical scale offering a set of broader categories (e.g. of different household income levels) and a 'prefer not to say' option may be more suitable.

Alternatively, the question may be phrased more openly to invite a longer answer from the respondent. Figure 10.8 gives an example of open questions adapted from a workshop evaluation form that provides delegates the opportunity to make suggestions to the tutor for future workshops.

We recommend caution when using open questions in questionnaires. Response rates are likely to be much lower than for closed questions and responses can vary greatly in terms of the amount of information provided by each respondent. Perhaps most importantly, open-ended questions create additional complexity when it comes to analysis. Even an apparently simple question such as 'what is your job role?' can elicit many different sorts of answer, as the question may be understood in different ways by respondents and, with variations in spelling, language, and local practice regarding how jobs are described, the resulting data can be very difficult to analyze. If you are really interested in capturing the respondents' own perspectives in their own words, you should perhaps consider a different research design such as a qualitative interview study.

What was your household income during the last tax year?

£ [   ]

FIGURE 10.7 Example single-item response open question

In future workshops, what should the tutor:

(a) Continue doing?

(a) Do differently?

FIGURE 10.8 Example open question

10.5.4 Evaluating the quality of your questions

It is important that the data collected by your questionnaire are valid and reliable, and good questions are central to this. In Chapter 4 we reviewed a range of criteria for judging quality in quantitative research and you should review them to help you assess the quality of your questions. Less technically, McGivern (2022: 405) offers the following checklist for the wording of any question to help to ensure reliability and validity.

- It measures what it claims to measure.
- It is relevant and meaningful to the respondent.
- It is acceptable to the respondent.
- It is understood by the respondent (and the interviewer, if using one).
- It is interpreted in the way in which you intended.
- It is interpreted in the same way by all respondents.
- It elicits an accurate and meaningful response.
- The meaning of the response is clear and unambiguous.

This means paying careful attention to how you word your questions. We give some examples of common mistakes in questionnaire wording in Table 10.3 to help you avoid basic errors. Ultimately, however, the most important thing is to ensure that the questions make sense to your respondents. This is something that requires a sound knowledge of your target population in terms of their level of literacy or degree of understanding of the research topic, along with careful pretesting and piloting, as we discuss later in the chapter.

10.5.5 Using a data collection matrix to manage your questions

Most questionnaires will contain numerous questions measuring several variables. To help you manage these and to make sure that you do not leave any vital questions out of your final questionnaire, we suggest that you set up a data collection matrix. This is a simple table as shown in Table 10.4 that you can use to keep track of the measures that are needed in your questionnaire. It provides a way of systematically linking research question, variables

TABLE 10.3 Common mistakes in questionnaire wording

Mistake	Example	Possible remedy
Double barrelled questions or statements	'I enjoy watching soccer and cricket on television'	Split into two questions.
Double negatives	'The project was not unsuccessful'	Change the wording so the statement is worded positively, combined with a rating scale.
Leading questions	'We should spend more money on welfare to ensure that no child goes hungry'	Adopt neutral wording; in this case if the researcher is interested in a possible link between attitudes to welfare spending and attitudes to child poverty, they could be measured separately and then the relationship investigated statistically.
Technical language or jargon	'Do you make use of Extensible Messaging and Presence Protocol applications online?' 'Do you have a strong sense of affective commitment to your organization?'	Ensure question wording is appropriate to your audience. In example (a) everyday language description plus an example could be offered. Example (b) is more difficult. Here the researcher is trying to measure a complex abstract concept (affective commitment) directly. A multi-item rating scale is likely to be more suitable as a measure.

TABLE 10.4 Example data collection matrix

Research question(s)	Concept/ variable to be measured	Concept definition (including source)	Questions to be included in the questionnaire	Number of items in the scale	Source(s) of questions	Question numbers in questionnaire

to be measured, details of the questions you will use to measure the variable, and where the questions appear in the questionnaire. As well as helping you to prepare your questionnaire, the data collection matrix provides a very useful guide during your analysis. A version of it can also be included in your final report when describing your questionnaire. In Research in Practice 10.3 we illustrate a data collection matrix in use as part of a student project.

Research in practice 10.3 Developing questions to measure variables in a conceptual mode

For his final MBA project on factors influencing mobile shopping by smartphone, Davin MacAnaney developed a conceptual model that identified several variables that existing theory suggested could be relevant influential factors. To test the model, it was decided to use an analytic survey study, with data being gathered by questionnaire. Designing the questionnaire involved identifying the relevant variables in the model and formulating suitable scales to measure them. The researcher did this by building on previous work that had looked at factors influencing technology adoption all the way back to Davis' (1989) work in the area. In the next section we present a simplified version of the model, containing only two of the independent variables that were used in the final study, along with examples of the questions used to measure the variables captured in a data collection matrix similar to that in Table 10.4 (MacAnaney, 2013).

Variable	Number of items in the scale	Questions to measure variable	Sources	Question numbers in questionnaire
Perceived usefulness (PU) (independent variable)	5	1. Shopping online through my smartphone would improve my efficiency in my ability to shop. 2. Shopping online through my smartphone would enable me to do my shopping conveniently. 3. Shopping online through my smartphone would enhance my effectiveness in my ability to shop. 4. Shopping online through my smartphone would save me time. 5. In general, I believe shopping online through my smartphone would be useful.	Taylor and Todd (1995), Khalifa and Cheng (2002), Wang and Barnes (2007), Kurnia et al. (2006) and Wong and Hiew (2005)	Q 6–10
Perceived ease of use (PEOU) (independent variable)		1. It is easy to learn to shop online through your smartphone. 2. Shopping online through your smartphone is understandable and clear. 3. Shopping online through your smartphone is/might be easy to use.	Wang and Barnes (2007), Luarn and Lin (2005), Chew (2007) and Lin and Wang (2005)	Q 11–13
Online shopping adoption via smartphone (SSA) (dependent variable)		1. I have adopted online shopping through my smartphone. 2. I believe I will continue to shop online through my smartphone in the future. 3. I believe my interest towards online shopping through my smartphone will increase in the future.	Davis (1989), Bhattacherjee (2001), Mallat et al. (2006), Kurnia et al. (2006), Luarn and Lin (2005), Liao et al. (2007), Khalifa and Shen (2008), Moon and Kim (2001) and Shin (2007)	Q 31–33

Note: The sources presented are examples only and are not included in our reference list.

10.6 STRUCTURE AND LAY OUT THE QUESTIONNAIRE

Even the best questions will not produce the desired results if your questionnaire is compromised by poor layout or a confusing structure. As part of the questionnaire design process, you will also need to decide on the structure and layout of your questionnaire. You should order your questions so that respondents find the questionnaire structure both logical and easy to follow. This will improve the potential response rate by encouraging respondents to feel involved and engaged in the process of completing the questionnaire. Figure 10.9 provides a suggested structure for your questionnaire.

10.6.1 Briefing and consent

The questionnaire should begin by briefing the respondent about the nature of the research and requesting their informed consent in line with the ethics guidelines discussed in Chapter 5. The briefing information should start with a short statement informing the respondent of the purpose of the research and what it is seeking to investigate. It should confirm procedures regarding respondent anonymity and data confidentiality and include an informed consent disclaimer along these lines:

> By completing and returning this questionnaire, it will be understood that you give consent for your responses to be used for the purposes of this research project.

If your research project is part of a course of study, ensure you conform to your institution's requirements regarding evidencing informed consent in questionnaire research.

10.6.2 Opening questions

Your opening questions should get the attention of the respondent and help to build rapport. They should be uncomplicated and immediately relevant to the respondents, thereby building their confidence and interest in participating. Leave more complex or probing questions until later in the questionnaire. Opening questions can also be used as filter questions to screen respondents to establish that they do meet required sample characteristics. For instance, in consumer experiences with a particular product, a filter question might be included to confirm that respondents have used that product. Filtering

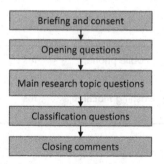

FIGURE 10.9 Suggested questionnaire structure

will, however, impact on the ultimate sample size and is not a substitute for a properly targeted sampling plan. Research in Practice 10.4 gives an example of filter questions from a study of online search behaviour.

Research in practice 10.4 Example filter questions

For a study on online search (Rose and Samouel, 2009) the sample consisted of frequent online shoppers who were using the Internet to search for product information related to small electrical goods. Here we show some of the filter questions used at the start of the questionnaire to identify relevant respondents for the sample.

Q1: How frequently do you use the Internet? (please select one only)

a) Daily	☐
b) Weekly	☐
c) Monthly	☐
d) Less than once a month	☐

If you have selected c) or d), please do not complete the questionnaire

Q2: For what purpose do you use the Internet? (please select as many as applicable)

a) Work/business	☐
b) Leisure	☐
c) Search for information about products and services	☐
d) Buying products and services	☐

If you have selected a) and/or b) only, please do not complete the questionnaire

Q3: Please indicate if you have ever searched for information online for any of the following items:

a) Small electronic goods (e.g. mobile phone, sports watch, digital tablet)	Yes	☐	No	☐
b) Electrical white goods (e.g. washing machine, microwave, refrigerator)	Yes	☐	☐	No

c) Larger electronic goods (e.g. laptop, printer, television, games console)	Yes	☐	No	☐
d) Computer accessories (e.g. software, hardware accessories, upgrades)	Yes	☐	No	☐

If you have answered No to all, please do not complete the questionnaire

10.6.3 Main research topic questions

The main body of your questionnaire contains the majority of the questions that you have identified in your data collection matrix and that will provide the bulk of the data needed to answer your research questions. Questions should be grouped together by general topic and should build logically in terms of the sequence of the questioning. The order of the questions should be such that you begin broadly and slowly to funnel into more specific questions. This gives the respondent a general understanding of the topic being investigated before moving on to more detailed questioning. In sequencing the questions, you should also be aware that answers to earlier questions may influence responses to later ones. For example, questions about a respondent's attitude to risk-taking by others might influence their answers to subsequent questions about their own risk-taking behaviours.

A number of aspects of the structure and layout will contribute to an effective response rate. Firstly, think about the relative importance of your questions. If there are questions that are not compulsory or critical to the analysis, put them at the end so that if the respondents give up you still have some potentially usable data. Secondly, think about the ways in which respondents are asked to indicate their answers. Consistency is helpful for respondents, so try to keep questions with similar response formats together (e.g. all rating scale questions) and use the same response mechanism (such as ticking a box, circling an option or entering a number) as much as possible. Thirdly, consider the visual aspects such as the amount of space between questions, size of the typeface, or use of colour. These decisions should always be made with regard to the characteristics of your respondents and then tested in the pretest and pilot stage. Finally, make sure that you proofread your questionnaire. Spelling errors and grammatical mistakes are unlikely to impress potential respondents. Online survey platforms can be very helpful here, but it is still essential that you check your questionnaire thoroughly.

'Don't know' and conditional routing questions

In some questionnaires not all questions will be relevant to all respondents. For example, respondents will not be able to answer questions about their experiences of a product they have never used, and it would make no sense to force them to give a response. Indeed, if they did, it would potentially distort the findings.

One solution is to include a 'don't know', 'not applicable', or similar option as part of the question response choices (note that 'don't know' is not the same as 'neither agree nor disagree' as the mid-point of an odd-numbered Likert-type scale). Inclusion of a 'don't know' option creates the risk that respondents will choose it as the default because they are not motivated to fill in the questionnaire correctly. To some extent this can be assessed, along with the need to include the 'don't know' option, during the pretest and piloting of the questionnaire.

Another option which can be useful if there is a large section of questions that do not apply to certain respondents is to use conditional routing questions. These allow you to direct people to relevant areas of the questionnaire. Conditional routing questions take the general form: 'if you have answered X then go to question A, if not go to question B'. If they are included, they should be clearly signposted throughout the questionnaire to aid accurate completion. Most online survey tools contain routines to support routing questions, but for other forms of self-completed questionnaires, conditional routing adds complexity and needs to be carefully tested. In addition, any form of routing question will affect the sample size for the questions within the questionnaire. If responses that are critical to your research project are given by only a small proportion of respondents, you may find yourself without enough data. Like filter questions, routing questions are not a substitute for a well-executed sampling plan. Nevertheless, used appropriately, they can help to ensure that respondents are required only to answer questions within their experience, and thereby they support completion rates and reduce the risk of spurious data as a result of inappropriately answered questions. Figure 10.10 gives an example of conditional routing questions.

10.6.4 Classification questions

In most research projects you will need to collect demographic and socio-economic information, such as age, employment status, or income, from your participants. Classification questions are used to collect this kind of data. In some projects this information will be central to your research question, for instance, if you were investigating the association

---

Question 9. Have you purchased online in the last 10 days?

      ☐ Yes

      ☐ No

If you answered No, please go to **Question 13**

If you answered Yes, was the purchase for personal use, work use or a gift?

      If personal use, go to **Question 10**

      If work use, go to **Question 11**

      If a gift, go to **Question 12**

FIGURE 10.10 Example of conditional routing

between age and use of mobile phone for personal banking or the difference in satisfaction levels between part-time and full-time employees. In other cases it is needed so that you can describe the sample from which your data has been obtained and compare it to the target population. To develop your classification questions, you should first draw up a list of the relevant classification variables, based on your research questions and the characteristics of the target population. To do this you may need to look at secondary data, such as organizational records or government statistics, that give more details on the characteristics of your target population.

You should be aware of the personal nature of some classification data, such as salary, and, therefore, how the sensitivities of respondents may affect their willingness and ability to provide a response. In order to overcome this, consider using categorical scales with a range of options (as shown in Figure 10.3 for age) rather than asking for exact numbers. Willingness to provide classification data can be strongly linked to the respondent's belief in the anonymity of the questionnaire and therefore the ability of the researcher to link specific data to specific respondents. A clearly worded briefing and informed consent statement will help in this regard. It is also common practice to place classification questions at the end of your questionnaire, by which time the respondent should be more comfortable about the nature of the research and providing personal data. In any case, consider including a 'prefer not to say' option for particularly sensitive questions as discussed earlier.

10.6.5 Closing comments

Closing comments can include any instructions for return and submission if these have not already been dealt with, along with any courtesies such as thanking respondents for their time.

10.6.6 Questionnaire length

As tutors, we often get asked how long a questionnaire should be. This is not an easy question to answer. Whilst a questionnaire that would take hours to complete would probably deter many potential participants, the actual evidence on the relationship between questionnaire length and response rates is mixed. As de Vaus (2014) explains, it is difficult to disentangle the impact of questionnaire length from other factors such as layout, topic, and sample type. So how long should your questionnaire be? On balance, we agree with de Vaus' (2014) guidance not to be obsessed with the length of your questionnaire but not to make it longer than it needs to be.

10.6.7 Language and accessibility

When designing and laying out your questionnaire, give thought to your target audience in terms of readability and visual accessibility of the text and any graphics being used. Factors to consider include font size, colour contrast, and layout. If your questionnaire is to be used across different languages, careful thought needs to be given to translation. For some widely used scales, different language versions may be available. If translation required, a common approach is known as back translation where the questions are translated into the required language and then translated back to the original language to verify the precision of the translation. Whatever approach you use, ensure that all language versions are pretested and piloted.

10.7 PRETEST AND PILOT THE QUESTIONNAIRE

Before sending out your questionnaire, it is essential that you test it to identify any problems while there is still time to correct them. We recommend a two-stage approach. Firstly, carry out a **pretest** of your questionnaire with a small group of people (ideally similar to, or familiar with, your intended sample) in order to check that the questions are clear and they understand them. Ask them to complete the questionnaire. Time how long it takes and ask for feedback on their experience of completing it. Do the questions make sense? Is the language and wording appropriate? Is the structure and layout clear and easy to follow? You can also include subject matter experts in your pretest as they can give more detailed insight into the questions themselves. If you are a student researcher we strongly recommend that you get feedback from your supervisor as well. The pretest stage provides you with guidance and feedback for improvements and changes during the early design stage.

Secondly, you should conduct a full test of the questionnaire by carrying out what is called a pilot study. A **pilot study** is conducted amongst a small subgroup of the target population and using the same administration method as the full survey will use. The purpose is to identify any problems or difficulties with the questionnaire and to test the administration of the questionnaire under operational conditions. In addition, if a sufficient sample is acquired it may be possible to run preliminary data analysis, although this will depend on the sample size required for the test(s) being used. In some cases, it may be possible to ask some respondents for feedback on how they experienced completion of the questionnaire. A pilot study should happen at a point where it is still feasible to make meaningful changes prior to full data collection and analysis. While pretesting and piloting can be time consuming, they will help to ensure that your questionnaire is fit for purpose.

10.8 ADMINISTER AND DISTRIBUTE THE QUESTIONNAIRE

The design process should also consider the administration method that you will use for your questionnaire. In this final section, we look at different distribution options, beginning with online.

10.8.1 Online questionnaires

The Internet is probably now the most important channel for questionnaire administration. Online distribution can reduce turnaround times and costs and allow the researcher to involve participants who would be difficult or impossible to reach using more traditional distribution methods such as post or telephone. Online questionnaires can also reduce data collection and entry errors that can arise through manual data handling. In addition, an online questionnaire may appeal to particular groups of respondents, thanks to their familiarity with the online environment, speed of access, and ease of completion and return.

Choosing an online survey platform

The popularity of online questionnaires, at least amongst student researchers, is partly due to the widespread availability of user-friendly proprietary online survey tools, such as SurveyMonkey and Qualtrics. These support the researcher in creating and distributing the questionnaire and collecting the resulting data. Working online can also enable you to enhance the layout, appearance and usability of the questionnaire. If you are considering using an online survey tool we suggest that you review the different options available. Based on our own experiences we recommend that you confirm the following points before making a decision.

- Does the survey tool support the question formats and any special requirements (such as conditional routing) that are needed?
- How easy is the design interface to use and is support available if there is a problem?
- What policy does the site have regarding data security, and is this adequate for the project?
- What file formats are available for exporting data on completion of the project? (For analysis you will need to be able to export the raw response data in a suitable format such as a Microsoft Excel-readable file.)
- Are there any limitations regarding, for example, the number of questions or the number of respondents?

In many cases the answers to these questions will depend on the package purchased. Often the free or trial options place restrictions on the options available, number of respondents/ questions, output file formats and so on, so make sure that you understand these when evaluating different providers' offerings. You should also check whether you have access to a suitable online survey tool via your academic institution or organization. Although they have less capability than some online survey tools, MS Forms and Google Forms can also be useful in some contexts, for example, organizations where they are used for internal surveys.

Survey access device

Alongside choice of online survey platform, you should also consider what types of device potential respondents are likely to use to access the questionnaire. These can range from desktop PC and laptops to mobile devices, including tablets and smartphones. In fact, mobile devices are increasingly likely to be the preferred option for many respondents (Antoun et al., 2017). Brace and Bolton (2022: 172) suggest that, when designing your questionnaire, 'you should always check to see how your questions will appear on a mobile'. Fortunately, most online survey platforms support a range of devices, typically offering previews for smartphones. Options such as QR codes can facilitate access by mobile device.

10.8.2 Distributing your questionnaire

In practice an online questionnaire can be distributed in a number of different ways for self-completion by the participant, including the following:

- Online, where access to the questionnaire is via a URL link or QR code posted on a website such as a social media site or online community.
- Email or other messaging channel, where a URL link is delivered to the sample using an existing distribution list.
- Via QR code (or shortened URL) on an advertising/recruiting poster or other physical means of distribution.

If you are using a hard copy, paper-based questionnaire, other distribution options for self-completion include the following:

- Post, or internal mail, where the researcher distributes the questionnaire in hard copy and it is self-completed by the respondent, who returns it in a similar way. Note that if a public postal service is used, consideration needs to be given to how to manage return postage using prepaid envelopes or a similar arrangement.
- Researcher delivery and collection, where the researcher (or assistant) delivers a hard copy of the questionnaire to respondents, who fill it in for later collection by the researcher. A variant of this can be used in studies such as experiments where a participant may be asked to complete a questionnaire prior to, during, or after the experiment.

Questionnaires can also be administered by an interviewer who may also be involved in helping to recruit potential respondents (e.g. as part of quota sampling). Options include the following:

- Face-to-face interview, where the respondents is asked questions by the interviewer, who completes the questionnaire via an electronic device such as a tablet or on paper.
- Telephone interview, where the interviewer contacts the respondent by telephone and administers the questionnaire via a preprepared script.

Professional interviewers may be used in commercially funded research, but for most student projects the researcher will be the interviewer.

10.8.3 Choosing a distribution method

The method selected for questionnaire distribution is in part dictated by the nature of the sampling frame being used, and the type of contact details you have (e.g. whether you have access to email, telephone, or other contact details) as well as the sampling method (e.g. some form of probability sampling method versus self-selection, snowballing, etc.). Other considerations in the choice of questionnaire distribution will be the characteristics of the sample and the method to which they are most likely to respond. A further consideration is the nature of the research topic and the degree of sensitivity or complexity involved. In some instances, there may be value in having an interviewer present in person who can ensure that the respondent both understands and is comfortable with the questions. In others, the greater anonymity of self-completion may be preferred. Where a questionnaire is administered by a team of fieldworkers, it is important to provide clear briefing to them regarding their role and involvement in the questioning of respondents. Finally, consider likely response rates for your chosen sample, given your intended distribution method as discussed in Chapter 9.

CHAPTER SUMMARY

- Questionnaires use standardized, structured questions to gather quantitative or quantifiable data on variables of interest to the researcher. As a data collection technique they can offer low cost, speed of collection, flexibility, anonymity, and reduced interview effects. Potential disadvantages include variable response rates, partial completion, the limited range of responses offered, and requirement for respondent literacy.
- A structured approach should be taken to questionnaire design, including identification of relevant concepts (variables), formulation of appropriate questions, structuring the questionnaire, pretesting and piloting, and questionnaire administration.
- The choice of concepts to be measured as variables in the questionnaire should be driven by the research question, prior theory and research, and any conceptual model/hypotheses to be tested.
- Question formulation involves selecting appropriate question wording, deciding a suitable level of measurement (nominal, ordinal, interval, or ratio) and choosing an appropriate question format. For measuring more complex concepts, a multi-item, summated scale is often used. Questions should be evaluated against appropriate quality criteria.
- Structure and layout of the questionnaire are also important. Questionnaire structure may include the following elements: briefing and consent, opening questions, main research topic questions, classification questions, and closing comments.
- Questionnaires should be thoroughly pretested and piloted before being distributed.
- Distribution options depend on the target population, sampling frame, and nature of the characteristics of the sample. Online is increasingly the default distribution channel, but other administration methods including face to face, telephone, and post can also be used.

NEXT STEPS

10.1 Identifying relevant concepts/variables. Draw up a data matrix (see Table 10.4). Return to your research questions and any conceptual model/ hypotheses you are using. Identify the key concepts that you are investigating in your research project and list them in your data matrix. How are the concepts defined in the literature you have studied?

10.2 Questionnaire administration. Decide how you will administer your questionnaire so that you can make arrangements regarding distribution and return and, if using online survey, design your survey using an appropriate online survey tool.

10.3 Formulating your questions. Review your literature; identify any scales or questions that already exist from prior research that can be used for the measurement of your own variables. Ensure that the prior variables do match the definition of your own variables. Note the wording of the questions and consider any adaptation you will need to make. Note the references in your data collection matrix. If no existing measures are available, decide how you will develop your own measures. Select an appropriate measurement level and question format for each question and record them in your data collection matrix.

10.4 Preparing your questionnaire. Begin to draft your questionnaire by using the structure provided at Figure 10.9. Use each of the five boxed headings to create five sections for your questionnaire and use your data collection matrix to populate each section. Once you have done that, review your questions and the overall questionnaire for completeness and accuracy.

10.5 Pretesting and piloting. Carry out a pretest and pilot of your questionnaire. Incorporate any required changes, recording what was done and the reasons for doing so in your research diary or journal.

FURTHER READING

For further reading, please see the companion website.

REFERENCES

Antoun, C., Couper, M. P. and Conrad, F. G. (2017). Effects of mobile versus PC web on survey response quality: A crossover experiment in a probability web panel. *Public Opinion Quarterly*, 81(S1): 280–306.

Bearden, W. O., Netemeyer, R. G. and Hawks, K. (2011). *Handbook of Marketing Scales: Multi-Item Measures for Marketing and Consumer Behavior Research*. 3rd ed. Thousand Oaks, CA: SAGE Publications.

Brace, I. and Bolton, K. (2022). *Questionnaire Design: How to Plan, Structure and Write Survey Material for Effective Market Research.* 5th ed. London: Kogan Page.

Bruner II, G. C. (2019). *Marketing Scales Handbook: Multi-Item Measures for Consumer Insight Research, Volume 10.* Fort Worth, Tx: GCBII Productions.

Davis, F. (1989). Perceived usefulness, perceived ease of use, and user acceptance of information technology. *MIS Quarterly,* 13(3): 318–340.

de Vaus, D. (2014). *Surveys in Social Research.* 6th ed. Abingdon: Routledge.

Hair, J. F. J., Page, M. and Brunsveld, N. (2020). *Essentials of Business Research Methods.* 4th ed. New York, NY: Routledge.

Jamieson, S. (2004). Likert scales: How to (ab) use them. *Medical Education,* 38(12): 1217–1218.

MacAnaney, D. (2013). *An Investigation into the Factors that Drive Online Shopping Through Smartphones in the United Kingdom.* MBA dissertation, Henley Business School, University of Reading, Henley-on-Thames.

McGivern, Y. (2022). *The Practice of Market Research: From Data to Insight.* 5th ed. Harlow: Pearson Education.

Meyer, J. P., Allen, N. J. and Smith, C. A. (1993). Commitment to organizations and occupations: Extension and test of a three-component conceptualization. *Journal of Applied Psychology,* 78(4): 538–551.

Parasuraman, A., Zeitmahl, V. A. and Berry, L. L. (1988). SERVQUAL: A multiple-item scale for measuring customer perceptions of service quality. *Journal of Retailing,* 64(1): 12–40.

Podsakoff, P. M., MacKenzie, S. B. and Podsakoff, N. P. (2012). Sources of method bias in social science research and recommendations on how to control it. *Annual Review of Psychology,* 63(1): 539–569.

Rose, S. and Samouel, P. (2009). Internal psychological versus external market-driven determinants of the amount of consumer information search amongst online shoppers. *Journal of Marketing Management,* 25(1–2): 171–190.

Roth, A. V., Schroeder, R., Huang, X. and Kristal, M. (2008). *Handbook of Metrics for Research in Operations Management: Multi-Item Measurement Scales and Objective Items.* London: SAGE Publications.

CHAPTER 11

Collecting data using in-depth interviews

CHAPTER LEARNING OUTCOMES

After reading this chapter you will be able to

- assess whether interviews are suitable data collection tools for your research project, either on their own or in conjunction with other data sources;
- appraise the suitability of different types of interviews for the research project;
- plan interviews, from selecting interviewees and a setting, to structuring the interview and deciding whether and how to use technology;
- define robust procedures for recording and storing the data collected.

11.1 INTRODUCTION

In this chapter we look at how to gather qualitative data by interviewing research participants. We can obtain verbal accounts of behaviours, events, thoughts, or emotions by interviewing research participants individually or in a group setting, for instance through focus groups. Although interviews have traditionally been done face to face, there is currently much interest in the potential of the Internet, including social media, for data collection. We therefore include a discussion of the issues emerging when using technology to conduct interviews. Interviews can generate a lot of data, so you also need to develop protocols for recording and storing the data that you collect. We discuss how to do this in the final section of the chapter.

Interviews are a widely used data collection method in many research designs, as summarized in Table 11.1.

11.2 INDIVIDUAL INTERVIEWS

An interview consists of the researcher talking directly to research participants. This may take various forms. Fully structured interviews with closed-ended questions are

DOI: 10.4324/9781003381006-14

TABLE 11.1 The role of interviews in different research designs

Research design	Role of interviews in data collection
Ethnography	Used alongside observational methods
Grounded theory	Alongside observations and, possibly, analysis of documents
Case study	Used alongside other qualitative or quantitative methods
Action research	Alongside analysis of documents and, maybe, observations
Interview study	Primary data collection method
Mixed methods	Used alongside quantitative methods, to initiate, corroborate, or elaborate on quantitative findings

characteristic of the interviewer-administered surveys discussed in Chapter 10. In this chapter we focus on in-depth interviews, which are generally semi-structured or even completely unstructured, and are useful for deriving detailed information or to get insights into the lived experience of participants.

Features of in-depth interviews include (Legard et al., 2003: 141–142)

- combination of structure and flexibility, to enable coverage of desired topics and follow-up of issues emerging during the interview;
- interaction between the researcher and the participant;
- use of a range of techniques to achieve depth in the responses;
- sensitivity to the participant's own language as a way of understanding meaning.

Denzin and Lincoln (2018: 519) describe in-depth interviews as 'the art of asking questions and listening'. Nevertheless, simply launching into questions because you happen to have access to someone is likely to result in irrelevant data, along with a lost opportunity to address topics that later turn out to be central to your research question. Instead, careful planning is essential to increase the level of insight and the credibility of your study. The following sections will help you to plan your interviews.

11.2.1 Choosing your interviewees and scheduling interviews

When choosing whom to interview, you should follow the guidelines on sampling set out in Chapter 9. As interviews typically form part of a qualitative study, non-probability methods are generally preferred, particularly purposive or theoretical sampling. The decision as to how many interviews are needed should take into account the type of research design adopted, the philosophical orientation of the research and what other data sources are being used. One approach, noted in Chapter 9, is to continue interviewing until you reach theoretical saturation. This requires that you reflect on the insights generated during the data collection process so that you can identify when you do not need additional interviews.

Elite interviewing

One type of interview that is common in business research is elite interviewing. According to Marshall and Rossman (2011: 155), 'elite individuals are considered to be influential, prominent and/or well-informed people in an organization or community; they are selected for interview on the basis of their expertise in areas relevant to the research'. Examples can include chief executives and senior managers, the leaders of employer or labour organizations, or industry analysts and commentators.

Elite interviewing can be useful in exploratory research, as it taps into the experiences of individuals with specific expertise, and therefore, it can help identify the key issues of interest in a specific area. However, you should always consider carefully whether such potentially partial, privileged accounts provide the insight that you need for your research questions. Table 11.2 presents some of the potential benefits and problems of this method.

Access to elite interviewees may be difficult. For instance, they may have a gatekeeper who filters access to the interviewee or they may travel regularly because of their job. Conversely, sharing a professional or personal background, being interested in the topic of the research, or having a personal introduction from a trusted contact, are all factors that can help with access to elite interviewees (Liu, 2018).

Scheduling your interviews

Data collection through interviews may take much longer than anticipated, particularly if you are interviewing people with busy schedules or who are geographically dispersed. You should make sure that you allow sufficient time for each interview, and if you are conducting your interviews face to face, include time for travelling to and from the site. You will also need time to organize the logistics of the meeting such as preparing the room for the interview and to follow up with research participants, for example, to request clarification of points raised in the interview.

Interviewing also requires considerable energy and mental focus. For instance, you may need to adapt your terminology or style to the interviewee, or you may need to change the order of the questions, as a result of something that the interviewee has said. Therefore, you should avoid scheduling too many interviews for the same day, or without intervals between each, as you will be too tired to get the best out of each one.

TABLE 11.2 Potential benefits and problems of elite interviewing

Potential benefits	Potential problems
• Extra knowledge, due to the informant's position and experience • Broad overview of issues • Retrospective accounts • Draw upon informant's tacit knowledge • Explanation of complex situations – 'why' and 'how' questions	• Establishing the expertise of the informant • Control of the interview process • Partial perspective • Philosophical concerns about privileged accounts • Ensuring confidentiality and anonymity may be difficult, when reporting findings

If you are new to interviewing, allow yourself plenty of time between sessions so that you can reflect not only on the content of the interview but also on your own interviewing skills, and if relevant, make changes.

11.2.2 How much structure?

While unstructured interviews may be useful for certain types of research such as those that look at the interviewee's life story (e.g. a CEO's path to their current role), Easter-by-Smith et al. (2021) warn against the assumption that less intervention from the interviewer will lead to more insight into the interviewee's perspective. On the contrary, the lack of structure may lead to misunderstandings about what is being discussed or about the meaning of what is being said. Very unstructured interviews can be hard to relate to the underlying research question, make comparisons between different interviewees and, therefore, to analyze. The result of too little intervention, they argue, is poor-quality data being gathered. On the other hand, too much structure risks restricting the chance for participants to express their views and feelings, turning an open-ended interview into a researcher-delivered questionnaire. In most cases in business and management research, you are therefore likely to be using a semi-structured approach, with a limited number of key questions or discussion topics, but with scope to probe each topic area.

11.2.3 The interview guide

Of vital importance is the **interview guide** (also known as an **interview schedule** or **interview protocol**), which is the list of questions to explore during the interview. The open-ended questions in a semi-structured interview will be more like discussion topics that aim to investigate the experiences and understandings of participants than the sort of closed-ended questions that you see in the typical quantitative survey. Nevertheless, you need to ensure that your interviews gather data relevant to your research questions, so designing the interview guide is an important part of carrying out interview-based data collection. The choice of specific topics for discussion will be informed by your research questions as well as the results of your literature review, your own prior knowledge and experience of the topic area or preliminary discussions with those knowledgeable in the area.

As you develop your interview schedule, you should be careful with the wording of the questions. You want to avoid technical or ambiguous language, which may lead to misunderstandings. You also want to avoid language that is non-inclusive or discriminatory. Be aware that relatively few topics can be covered in a semi-structured interview because you need to allow time to probe and explore emerging issues. In an hour-long interview you can expect to address between six and ten main topics. As you design your interview schedule, it is helpful to create a simple table in which you list your research questions and your proposed discussion topics to make sure that nothing is left out and that the schedule is not crowded with questions that will simply take up interview time to the detriment of core themes.

A feature of in-depth interviewing is that it is usual to refine topics/questions, or to include new ones, as the research proceeds. For instance, you may change the wording of a question that keeps being misunderstood by interviewees or replace topics that fail to elicit interesting questions with new ones that emerged during the first interviews. Be aware, however, that the more changes you make, the more difficult it will be to compare interviews and, hence, analyze the resulting data. In some cases, changing or adding questions may also mean that you need to reapply for ethical approval, as discussed in Chapter 5.

11.2.4 Types of interview question

It can be difficult to elicit opinions, perceptions, or feelings that are deeply held by the individual because of sensitivity or lack of internal awareness of them. We can apply specific techniques, within the interview setting, to address these challenges and improve the quality of the output, as shown in Table 11.3.

Project techniques

You can see from the examples in Table 11.3 that there are likely to be points of sensitivity of which the researcher would need to be aware when formulating interview questions. In some situations, even simple requests for information about background experience

TABLE 11.3 Types of interview question	
Type of question	*Example question*
Background/demographic *Establish key facts and serve as warm-up*	• What is your role in the organization? • What were your experiences of volunteer work before joining the organization? • Tell me about your career prior to joining the organization.
Descriptive *Directive and factual questions; responses are likely to be somewhat constrained by the question*	• What new development projects are currently in progress? • What activities are you undertaking in social media? • How is the department organized?
Open *Opportunity to explore the topic and scope for the participant to develop their own views*	• Tell me about your experience of the firm's employee retention policies. • How do you go about preparing for a new overseas assignment? • How do you feel when you are doing a coaching session? • What does sustainability mean to you?
Probing *Follow up on previous question(s) to gain a fuller understanding, clarify points that are unclear, obtain additional details, gather examples, understand the participant's reasoning and own explanations, etc.*	• What do you mean? • Can you give me an example of that? • Why do you think this is the case? • What was the result of that? • What makes you say that? • What did you mean by it being a typical example of . . . ? • How was that different from other situations you have experienced? • How did you feel about that?

may make interviewees feel that the researcher is questioning their suitability for their job if they are not handled sensitively by the researcher. You may also find that participants struggle to answer some questions, particularly those relating to deep feelings and motivations, or about topics that they have not really explored or articulated before. In such circumstances, researchers can use **projective techniques**. These involve the use of stimulus material such as preprepared pictures, cartoons, examples of products, or simple self-complete activities such as asking someone to place a list of items in their order of preference. You can also ask participants to bring photographs or other materials along to the interview as a way of helping them talk about complex issues that they may be reluctant or unable to explore through direct questioning.

Critical incident technique

Another useful interview approach is the **critical incident technique** (CIT). This technique, which was introduced by Flanagan (1954), can be used to investigate significant happenings, such as a particular event, intervention, process or problem identified by the interviewee, and why they happened, who was involved, how they were managed, what the consequences were, and so on. For instance, if the subject was 'effective project meetings', the researcher might ask the participant to think of a project meeting that was particularly effective (or ineffective) in which they had been involved. This incident then forms the basis for probing questions such as the following:

- What happened?
- Why did it happen?
- Who was involved?
- What were the outcomes?
- How did you deal with the situation?

CIT can help participants focus on their own experiences and generate a rich data set based on experiences and perceptions, thereby supporting an inductive approach.

Problem questions

There are some question styles that should generally be avoided (King et al., 2019; Smith et al., 2022), including the following:

- Questions that make presumptions about the topic or the participants' experience of it, such as 'what discriminatory behaviour have you seen in your time in the organization?'
- Closed questions such as 'do you believe that current recruitment policies are effective?', which may put participants under pressure to choose a particular position, whereas they may not see the issue in such terms.
- Manipulative questions such as 'given all of the poverty in the world, do you think that bonuses should be cut for senior managers?', as these can create a situation where a particular type of answer is likely.

- Overly complex, multiple questions such as 'can you tell me a bit about your background, educational qualifications, job experiences and how you came to be here?' These can be confusing for the interviewee, as well as make it hard for the interviewer to keep track of whether all points have been covered in the answer.

When formulating your questions, you should be aware of the potential problem of social desirability bias. This refers to the tendency of participants to give answers that protect the participant's ego or that are deemed to be correct or be socially acceptable. For example, participants might exaggerate their reported use of eco-friendly products because it is socially desirable to adopt sustainable behaviours.

Language and terminology

As you develop your questions, make sure that the language and terminology is appropriate for your interviewees. Where possible, interview in the native language of the participant. It is also important to make sure that you share a common understanding of the terms being discussed. For instance, managers may use the term 'marketing' to refer specifically to advertising, public relations, and other communication initiatives, whereas academics tend to use that term in a broader sense. You should also avoid asking the research question(s) directly and using overly theoretical terminology. As Flick puts it:

> Discovering theoretical concepts and using scientific concepts is something for the data analysis process; using concrete everyday wording is what, in contrast, should happen in your questions and the interview.
>
> Flick (2023: 205)

When preparing your interview guide, King et al. (2019) note that writing out your questions in full can help you focus on how you have worded them and can help to avoid the problem question styles we have identified here. This may be particularly useful if you are new to qualitative interviewing. The potential downside, however, is that can reduce flexibility and make the interview very directive.

11.2.5 Sequencing the interview

Careful thought needs to be given to the sequencing of the interview. At the start, briefly describe the research, indicate the aims of the interview, and explain why the participant has been asked to take part. You should also assure the participant of confidentiality and obtain their agreement to the interview being recorded, if relevant. This is the point at which you would collect the signed informed consent form (see Chapter 5 for an example).

It is usually best to open the interview with an 'ice breaker' question on a topic that engages the participant but is not too challenging. The background/demographic questions in Table 11.3 are appropriate for this. More complex or controversial topics should be raised later in the interview.

As you come towards the end of the time agreed for the interview, you can signal that you are reaching the final topic, to allow the interviewee time to return to a more conversational mode. It is good practice to avoid ending the interview on a negative or stressful note. Invite the interviewee to add any comments or to address issues that they feel are important before concluding. Finally, you should thank the participant for their time, inform them of the next steps, and if appropriate, confirm their willingness to take part in additional data collection.

11.2.6 Interviewing skills

Brinkmann and Kvale outline the characteristics of a good interviewer:

> A good interviewer knows the topic of the interview, masters conversational skills and is proficient in language, with an ear for his or her subjects' linguistic style. The interviewer must continually make on-the-spot decisions about what to ask and how; which aspects of a subject's answer to follow up, and which not; which answers to comment and interpret, and which not. The interviewer should have a sense for good stories and be able to assist the subjects in the unfolding of their narratives.
>
> Brinkmann and Kvale (2018: 93)

There are several skills you should develop, to become a good interviewer, including the following:

- Really listen to what the person is saying and respond with a question that is useful to you. It is all too easy to focus on the next question and not really listen to the person at all.
- Put the participant at ease by opening with simple, ice-breaking questions, or even by spending a few minutes just chatting before you start recording or taking notes.
- Phrase questions sensitively so that your interviewee is not put on the defensive.
- Practise your observation skills, and note particular voice tones, body language, silences, or obvious discomfort.
- Check your understanding throughout the interview by summarizing what has been said and seeking clarification.
- Avoid judgemental responses to interviewee comments, such as 'that's very interesting' or 'that must have been annoying', because that may be interpreted by the interviewee as encouragement for certain types of answers.

It is difficult to acquire all these skills at once, especially when you are trying to take notes as well. So before embarking on your data collection, you should conduct one or two pilot interviews. The pilot interview gives you an opportunity to practise your skills and allows you to check whether the interview guide works as you intended and determine how long the interview is likely to take. After the pilot interview, you should reflect on your interviewing skills, the type of data generated and the appropriateness of the interview guide.

Discussing with the participant how the pilot interview went may provide additional useful feedback.

11.2.7 Technology-mediated interviews

Using technology to conduct in-depth interviews enables you to interview people in locations that are distant, difficult, or dangerous to access. It also reduces the cost and time required to reach participants and increases flexibility in scheduling. Indeed, using technology to conduct interviews may make research more accessible and inclusive for both researchers and participants. We distinguish between technological options for **synchronous** (i.e. real-time) and those for **asynchronous** (i.e. nonsimultaneous) interviewing.

Video conferencing and telephone-based (synchronous) interviewing

Conducting interviews by telephone or video conferencing services such as MS Teams or Zoom can speed up and reduce the cost of data collection. It can even be the only feasible way to reach participants in a broad geographic region. Some participants may actually prefer telephone interviews, as they offer flexibility, are easy to reschedule in case of an emergency, do not require the interviewee to host the interviewer, and may help interviewees feel more at ease discussing sensitive matters. Technology-based interviews are particularly useful for extended projects or those aiming to capture the participants' views in real time, as the researcher can check the participants' thoughts and experiences at key stages in a process. Most video conferencing platforms also offer recording and closed caption capture, subject to participant agreement to be recorded as discussed in Chapter 5. This means that, when you finish the interview, you will have a rough transcript of the conversation ready.

Technology-based interviews work better when there is a reasonable level of trust between researcher and participant, which may be difficult to establish if the participant is not used to being interviewed in this way. If you are using telephone and, thus, only hearing each other, it may be difficult to establish rapport, and this limits the opportunity to probe topics in depth or access to non-verbal data such as gestures or facial expressions. Another disadvantage is that access to digital technology is still unequal across society, which may limit your ability to include certain groups in your sample.

Message-based (asynchronous) interviewing

When using message-based interviews, the exchange between interviewer and participant still follows a question-answer structure, but these are done via email, direct messaging on social media, instant messaging or other asynchronous forms of communication. Gruber et al. (2021), for example, found that using WhatsApp to conduct interviews with migrants during the Covid-19 pandemic could actually have advantages over face-to-face interviews:

> They easily allow the sending of photos and videos. Another point to consider is that many mobile applications allow sending voice messages. Therefore, participants' ability to write or type is not necessarily a default selection criterion with respect to the sample.
>
> Gruber et al. (2021)

Message-based interviews are particularly suitable for sensitive topics, where interviewees may prefer to not talk face to face. Asynchronous interviews also allow participants to respond when it is most convenient for them, as opposed to the time and location determined by the interviewer. Kaufmann (2020) argues that giving this flexibility to interviewees reduces issues of power asymmetry between interviewer and research participant. Another advantage is that it makes it easy to continue the conversation at a later date, for instance, if an interesting thread emerges during analysis of the data.

However, as with telephone interviews, there is loss of visual data, and it may be difficult to establish rapport with the participants. It may even be difficult to confirm the identity of the participants. Asynchronous interviewing also requires flexibility from the part of the interviewer, as well as additional care to ensure privacy and data protection. It also requires that the participants have access to the technology and are familiar with it. Research in Practice 11.1 looks at one example of using email to conduct asynchronous interviews in a sensitive topic area in healthcare.

Research in practice 11.1 Interviewing using emails

For her doctorate, Bhatti (2019) conducted email-based interviews with adolescents suffering from alopecia, a dermatological condition where individuals lose some or all of their hair. She sent participants one question a week over a period of six weeks. To protect the participants' privacy 'all interviews were conducted on a secure university email. During data collection, all data was anonymised. This was done by copying the emails to a separate word document and any names and locations were changed. These documents were password protected and access to the system also required a password' (Bhatti, 2019: 96).

Bhatti opted for emails because the available literature suggested that adolescents prefer to talk about their experiences with alopecia over the Internet, rather than face to face, given their familiarity with the medium and because of the stigma associated with alopecia. Bhatti also felt that adolescents might answer her questions more truthfully because online interviews offer a sense of anonymity. Moreover, interviewees could answer her questions when it was most convenient for them, and they could do so at their own pace which would result in thoughtful and detailed responses to her questions. She said that 'the repeated interactions within email interviews allows a greater degree of rapport to be developed in comparison to synchronous interviewing. Alopecia is a highly sensitive and emotional topic. I felt this would be more appropriate because it allows me to build a relationship with the participants were they would feel comfortable disclosing their experiences' (Bhatti, 2019: 82–83).

In addition, conducting interviews over email was less time-consuming and more cost-effective than face-to-face interviews, allowing Bhatti to recruit from a broad geographical area and to conduct multiple interviews at the same time.

Source: Bhatti (2019)

11.3 GROUP INTERVIEWS

Group interviews are used for topics that benefit from exploration within a social group setting, where the group dynamic generates more insight than would have been the case with individual interviews. For example, when inputs from one participant could inspire others to come up with their own contributions. Group interviewing also helps dissipate power imbalances between interviewer and interviewees and encourages participation. The moderator or facilitator 'promotes an interaction and ensures that the discussion remains on the topic of interest' (Stewart and Shamdasani, 1998: 505) and is key to a successful group interview.

Group interviewing can take a variety of forms, including completely informal unstructured 'conversations' with groups of people during field research. The best-known variant of group discussions is, perhaps, the focus group. A **focus group** brings together participants to discuss a focal topic and is particularly suitable to explore emergent issues from the perspective of the participants. Commercially, they are often associated with market research. Focus groups can be a time-effective approach to the collection of qualitative data, and the group dynamics should help the generation of new thinking and insights. They are an important method with participants who may be more comfortable in a group setting, such as children. However, it is not suitable to explore issues that require individual introspection, or for topics where privacy or commercial confidentiality are likely to inhibit open discussion in the group. It is also possible that social pressure limits the expression of views that diverge from the majority, a phenomenon known as compliance. This leads the group to reach a consensus decision that results from the desire for group harmony and acceptance, rather than the critical consideration of alternative perspectives. More introverted or less confident members may also find it difficult to express their views in front of others, while in certain cultural or organizational settings it may be deemed impolite or unwise to disagree publicly with others. Focus groups may also be of limited value with elite interviewees as it may be impractical to bring together several executives in the same room at the same time.

Group interviews should not be seen as a way of conducting several individual interviews at the same time.

11.3.1 Composing the focus group

Who takes part in a focus group is important both to group dynamics and to the credibility and usefulness of your findings. Clearly one criterion is the participants' knowledge of the topic itself. Another one is the homogeneity of participants. The presence of people from different positions in the organizational hierarchy may be a particular issue here. People from similar backgrounds may find it easier to discuss some topics, but lack of diversity may reduce fresh thinking. A balance is probably needed, although you may convene groups with different members precisely to compare those differences. Another issue to decide is whether to bring together complete strangers or to use people who already form a natural group (e.g. an existing project team). The former may require more socialization time at the start of the meeting, taking time away from discussion. However, the latter may give problems if the group works with hidden assumptions of which you, the researcher, are not aware.

Recruitment by intermediaries

Researchers will sometimes use intermediaries to recruit focus group participants in specific locations or close-knit communities, and where there are language barriers. However, Parker and Tritter report the following problems arising from using intermediaries to recruit participants for a study of diabetes in South Asian women:

> [T]oo little was known about those who attended the focus group in relation to those who might have attended and little, if anything, was known about those who were actually approached but refused to attend . . . recruitment can drift into a process of 'convenience' sampling, whereby people whom we know little about are selected simply because of their accessibility.
>
> (Parker and Tritter, 2006: 29)

Focus group size and number

Recommendations as to the size of a focus group vary. The smaller the group, the easier it is to manage the discussion, and more opportunity there is for depth and probing. For example, in a group with ten participants, each would contribute only an average of six minutes' input in a one-hour meeting. Large groups may also result in 'social floating', which is when some participants rely on others to 'do the talking' (Cronin, 2008: 235). If you do not have experience of facilitating group discussions, you should start with fewer participants. The authors' own experience is that five to eight is a manageable number for most topics.

In terms of how many focus groups to hold, Krueger and Casey (2000) advise conducting three or four focus group interviews with each type of participant. This number should be enough to reach theoretical saturation.

11.3.2 Planning the focus group

Running a focus group can be very challenging, so good preparation is essential. If possible, you should conduct a pilot focus group, particularly if this is your first time interviewing in a group setting. It is advisable not to conduct more than one or two focus groups per day, particularly if you lack prior experience. In some cases, it may be possible to use a focus group moderator, allowing you as the researcher to act as an observer, which should be reported in your method write-up. Other points to consider when planning a focus group include the following.

Timing and recording

Plan on one and a half to two hours for the session, which should give you about one to one and a half hours' actual discussion time. During this time, there will be a multitude of ideas discussed and interventions to manage, so it will be very difficult to take notes at the same time. We therefore recommend recording the meeting if you have informed consent from all participants.

Choosing the setting

The setting of the group interview can influence the quality of the data generated, for example, whether it is 'home' territory for the participants or outside their normal environment. You should therefore take into account the nature of the location, the level of formality required, lighting, seating, the ambient noise level, and the level of security and privacy.

Choosing the location

The location should allow for the non-obtrusive observation and recording of the participants and the discussion. So for instance, recording equipment or note-takers may be beyond a one-way mirror. There are commercial service providers that offer facilities that meet all these requirements, which you may prefer to use, depending on your requirements and budget.

Selecting the topics

The actual topics to be discussed will depend upon the purpose of the focus group. Do not overestimate the number of topics you can cover in a single session. You should prepare an interview guide based on the research questions and containing a checklist of the points that ought to be covered in the discussion and in which order. Table 11.4 provides an outline for a focus group conducted to test a new brand of diet breakfast cereals.

11.3.3 Conducting the focus group

Running a focus group can be a real challenge for the novice researcher. Next are some issues to keep in mind for each of the five stages of the focus group meeting, as identified by Finch et al. (2013).

The first stage is about scene setting and clarification of ground rules. At this stage it is vital to put people at their ease. You should introduce the topic in nontechnical language, indicate the aims and objectives for the meeting, and outline the ground rules. You also need to ensure that you have the fully informed consent of all participants, including permission for any recording, and ask participants to confirm this by signing a suitably worded consent form (see Chapter 5).

The second stage is to introduce each participant. The aim here is to get people thinking of themselves as a group and encourage discussion and interaction. Use name cards if appropriate.

In the third stage, you should introduce the opening topic, to get everyone engaged and to act as a scene setter for later topics. Try to encourage interaction within the group. If someone seems to be dominating the discussion, you should bring others in. You can try a general approach, such as 'What do other people think about this?' or 'What does [name] think about this suggestion?'

Once the rules and scope are clear, and everybody feels relaxed and reassured, we can move on to the fourth stage, the discussion of the main topic areas for the focus group.

TABLE 11.4 Example of a discussion outline for a focus group

Stage	Topics
Welcome and ground rules	Welcome • Purpose of meeting • Recording of interview • Expectations regarding confidentiality • Informed consent • Discussion rules Introductions
Ice breaker	The perfect breakfast cereal • Characteristics • Associations
Discussion	General attitudes towards breakfast cereals General purchase and consumption of breakfast cereals • Probe for specific types and brands of cereals Purchase and consumption of breakfast cereals when trying to lose weight Attitudes towards diet breakfast cereals • Probe for specific brands • Specific experiences and satisfaction • Brand perceptions
Testing and conclusions	Show and discuss packaging concepts Show and discuss advertising concepts Reactions to sample product
Closing	Thank participants for their time Inform them of the next steps

You must find the right balance between intervening to keep the group on topic versus allowing flexibility to explore interesting areas. You also need to keep everyone involved, probe for fuller responses on key topics, and prevent the group discussion dissolving into simultaneous dialogue.

The fifth and last stage is to conclude the discussion. You should select the final topic in advance and signal the ending of the meeting by introducing it as the final topic. At the end, offer people the chance to raise any issues they feel have been left out. Finally, close with the normal courtesies.

11.3.4 Technology-mediated focus groups

There is a growing interest in the use of technology such as Zoom, WhatsApp, or online discussion groups to bring together geographically dispersed participants. There are also commercial service providers that offer platforms for conducting online focus groups. Again, technology-mediated focus groups can be synchronous or asynchronous, using audio/video or only text.

Particular advantages of technology-mediated focus groups are ease of participation and cost reduction. They are easier to organize than physical meetings and therefore can be conducted at shorter notice than traditional focus groups. As well as helping to overcome problems of geographical location, online focus groups can be effective for participants who are hard to reach, for instance, frequent travellers, and for people with mobility problems. It is possible that participants give more honest answers as they do not feel inhibited by the close presence of the moderator and the other participants. In the case of text-based focus groups, there is the advantage of not needing to transcribe the responses, which saves time and money and reduces mistakes. However, there may be a loss of visual data and other non-verbal inputs, such as body language. There may be limited interactivity. It is also difficult to expose the participants to external stimuli, such as a product sample, unless these are sent ahead of the group interview (which is not always possible for logistical, cost, or commercial-sensitivity reasons).

Synchronous, text-based focus groups are recommended for projects covering simple, straightforward issues, for instance, following up a previous meeting or experience. However, it is very difficult to keep the momentum going as you will have to read the various comments while typing probing questions or prompts to move the discussion along. A good tip is to have a number of pre-typed standard sentences such as 'thank you for that contribution; could you elaborate on that point?' which you can then copy and paste into the discussion platform. Research in Practice 11.2 gives an example of using a synchronous, text-based focus group.

Asynchronous text-based focus groups may run over several days. Participants are asked to log in a certain number of times per day and register their responses to particular questions or prompts. The moderator reads the comments and probes on specific issues or asks the next question on the discussion guide. This type of focus group tends to generate more content than the synchronous one. It also allows time for deeper reflection by each participant and for the researcher to introduce a variety of online or offline prompts, such as asking the participants to visit a website, try a product sample, or reflect on comments made earlier in the process. However, in this format, there is a heightened risk of participants dropping out between interactions.

Research in practice 11.2 Using online group chats to collect data

Doctoral researcher Silvia Lang reflects on the use of online chats to conduct focus groups for her research into electronic word of mouth:

> Online focus groups worked well for me because my participants were familiar with [the platform]. It was cost-effective and I could include participants from a broad geographical area.
>
> To ensure privacy, I set up accounts specifically for the project, changing passwords and deleting the conversation history between sessions.
>
> When I posted a question, they all replied at the same time. So, typing skills were important. I had sentences prepared for the welcome, the introduction, the questions and the end. And I had an assistant checking that I replied to all

comments and alerting me if someone was silent for too long. I used two computers simultaneously. If someone was silent or dropped out, I used the second computer to reach out to them, by email or on their private account.

I had the content of the discussions right there, with no need for transcriptions. But the answers tended to be short because that's how people chat online. And they used smiley faces and emoticons, so I had to keep asking people to explain what they meant by those. I could not check their body language, so I lost that dimension. Also, people kept jumping to other topics that they thought were related, for instance online shopping, and I had to redirect the conversation.

I felt that the participants were more relaxed than in a traditional setting. They were not concerned with language issues because no one heard their accents, and many were joining in from their sofas, a café or other relaxed place.

11.4 CAPTURING AND STORING YOUR INTERVIEW DATA

Whether you are interviewing the research participants individually or in a group, you need to ensure that you record and store all the data. You also need to make notes of the context and process of the data collection, such as if there were any interruptions or there was loss of eye contact after a particular question. In this section, we discuss general principles of data collection in interviews.

11.4.1 Recording the data and your notes

The field notebook has been the traditional means of capturing fieldwork data, contextual information, and other notes, such as descriptions of people whom the researcher met, events related to the fieldwork, or key conversations, as well as the researcher's own actions and working hypotheses. You can create paper copies of your interview guide with plenty of blank space in which to write down participants' answers and your notes. Alternatively, you can enter relevant information in a notetaking app on your phone or laptop. After the interview, if you are using a digital notebook, you may be able to dictate notes, capturing quite detailed observations or reflections. Dictation is a common feature of popular text editing software such as MS Word or Apple Notes and worth considering.

In practice, trying to write down everything that is being said during an interview is not possible. Extensive note taking can be distracting as your attention is divided between what is being said, what should happen next, and what you are trying to write. It is particularly difficult to keep accurate notes in a group setting. For instance, if you are conducting a focus group with six users of a particular product, it would be hard to capture what is being said, by whom, and with what effect, in addition to reflections on how the use of product samples impacts on the interactions between individuals.

The preferred option in most situations is therefore audio or video recording. This allows you to focus on what is being said or what is happening rather than taking notes.

Often, when you go back to your recordings you will notice subtle elements such as shifts in the vocabulary or changes in tone that you may have missed during the actual interview; you can also use your recording to clarify exactly what happened, in what order and in reaction to what. Digital recording devices are particularly useful if recording in-person interviews. The resulting files can easily be transferred (e.g. by email), backed up, and edited. In addition to specialist recorders, most smartphones and video conference platforms offer a recording facility which may be suitable. For online video conferencing, you can normally use the platform's in-built recording capability.

Points to consider when selecting a recording device include the following:

- Test the recording quality in a real-life interview situation. Check that your recorder can cope with a reasonable level of background noise and with the layout of the room. This can be a particular problem with focus groups.
- Check that the device has adequate battery life and storage space and that recording will not be interrupted or terminated by incoming calls or messages if you are using a smartphone or similar device.
- Ensure that the file is easily exportable to other platforms for playback, storage, and analysis.

Where possible, use some sort of backup during the interview, for example, by taking notes as well as recording, or by having more than one recorder.

Whatever recording method you use, always ask for permission from the research participant when the interview is scheduled, and remind them again when it comes to the actual interview as part of the informed consent procedure. You also should offer to stop the recording at any time, if needed. See Chapter 5 for more details.

11.4.2 Storing the data and your notes

You will need to file your data and notes thoroughly and systematically to ensure that you can access them at a later stage and, if relevant, to make them accessible to other members of your research team. It also provides an evidence trail to show that your work was completed legitimately. Detailed records also help with micro-level analysis and understanding of your data, because they allow you to review all of the issues that were raised during the data collection, to look for discussion on topics the salience of which only becomes evident in later stages of the project, and to study details such as hesitations or the specific vocabulary used in particular exchanges. Above all, keeping extensive records allows you to extract quotations in the participants' own words, which can be used when presenting your findings.

You need to make sure that you adhere to any ethical or legal requirements regarding data protection, both general (e.g. masking the identity of the participants) and specific to your institution (e.g. regarding saving documents online). Finally, you need to consider how you are going to destroy the data collected, namely, when you are going to do so and whether you need to use specialist services to handle the destruction of confidential data. See Chapter 5 for more details.

CRITICAL COMMENTARY 11.1
The nature of interview data

Interview data fall into the category of researcher-instigated data: it is the interviewer that decides the questions, asks them, follows up on some answers, and usually, decides when to terminate the interview. Moreover, the way the interview setting is organized and the techniques used in the interview may help the interviewee feel more or less relaxed and talk about things that they had not planned to. Taking this position to an extreme, it can be argued that what is said and how it is said is a product of the social context of the interview and the interactions within it. That is, that interviews do not capture some underlying external reality and that they are not simple reports or snapshots of the subject matter. Rather, that interviews are created in the interactions between the interviewer and the interviewee. 'Thus', as Denzin and Lincoln (2018: 519) observe, 'the interview is a negotiated text, a site where power, gender, and class intersect'. For instance, Bhatti (2019), reflecting on her PhD investigation of adolescents with alopecia described in the Research in Practice box 11.1, writes about how, at times, she felt conflicted about how to react to what the interviewees were telling her:

> I was grateful that I had formed a level of trust with my participants, especially because I engaged with them online. It felt like a double-edged sword; whilst on some levels, this may have helped them to be confident and open up to me more, the way I could respond to them was limited.
>
> (Bhatti, 2019: 187)

From this perspective, the interview changes from being a 'resource' for finding about the world outside the interview to a 'topic' where the research focus is on investigating the ways in which meaning is actively constructed during the interview by the participants. Discuss the following questions:

- How might elements of the setup (e.g. location, venue, time of day) impact on the interviewee's emotions, behaviour, and ultimately, the responses that you get?
- How might your own characteristics (e.g. gender) and behaviours (e.g. your attire) impact on the interviewee's emotions, behaviour, and ultimately, the responses that you get?
- Would you include these factors in your reporting of the study and its conclusions? Why/why not?
- How would you discuss these factors in your report?

CHAPTER SUMMARY

- In-depth interviews may be conducted individually or in a group setting, either face to face or mediated by technology, and synchronously or asynchronously. A semi-structured approach offers advantages for analysis.
- Preparing for an individual interview involves developing a suitable interview guide including relevant questions in an appropriate sequence. Careful thought needs to be given to the number of topics that can be adequately covered in the time available.
- Focus groups are a form of group interview. Preparation for a focus group involves deciding on the group composition, the venue, and the topics to be discussed.
- Technology can be used for interviews. Applications include telephone and video conferencing services for synchronous, voice-based interviews, and email and messaging for asynchronous, text-based interviews.
- Data capture and storage need careful planning. Audio and video recording are recommended, but the researcher should always gain participant agreement. Field notes provide an opportunity to capture additional details, including the thoughts of the researcher. Storage needs to be well organized and secure.

NEXT STEPS

11.1 The role of interviews in the research design. Revisit the key research articles from the literature that you have reviewed and identify how they use interviews to collect data. For instance, is it the only tool to collect data, or is it used in conjunction with others? Reflect on how the use of interviews helped the authors to answer their research questions.

11.2 Assessing the advantages and disadvantages of interviews as a data collection approach. List the advantages and disadvantages of interviews as a data collection approach for your project. Consider a broad range of factors, including the cost or time required for data collection.

11.3 Addressing limitations. Identify the limitations arising from using interviews in your study.

11.4 Technology-mediated data collection. Decide if you are going to use some form of technology interface to conduct your interviews. Ensure that you know how to use the technology and deal with technical problems. Check that participants are comfortable with the technology, as well.

11.5 Set up your data collection. Negotiate access and clarify expectations regarding how long you can stay on the site, what you can access, and what you will be providing in return. Decide the type of instructions and the level of structure that you need to provide to the research participants. Construct the interview guide and prepare appropriate briefing and informed consent documents (Chapter 5). Organize logistical aspects such as booking rooms or creating online discussion forums. If relevant, set up anonymized online accounts and passwords. Carry out a pilot interview.

11.6 Recording your data. Decide how you are going to record and store the data and your notes. Obtain authorization to record the interviews, as relevant.

FURTHER READING

For further reading, please see the companion website.

REFERENCES

Bhatti, A. (2019). *I Wouldn't Wish Alopecia on My Worst Enemy "—Adolescents" and Parents' Experiences of Alopecia*. PhD thesis, University of Huddersfield, Huddersfield. Available at: http://eprints.hud.ac.uk/id/eprint/35166/.

Brinkmann, S. and Kvale, S. (2018). *Doing Interviews*. 2nd ed. Los Angeles, CA: SAGE Publications.

Cronin, A. (2008). Focus groups. In: Gilbert, N. (ed) *Researching Social Life*. 3rd ed. London: SAGE Publications.

Denzin, N. K. and Lincoln, Y. S. (eds) (2018). *Handbook of Qualitative Research*. 5th ed. Thousand Oaks, CA: SAGE Publications.

Easterby-Smith, M., Jaspersen, L. J., Thorpe, R. and Valizade, D. (2021). *Management and Business Research*. 7th ed. London: SAGE Publications.

Finch, H., Lewis, J. and Turley, C. (2013). Focus groups. In: Ritchie, J., Lewis, J., McNaughton Nicholls, C., et al. (eds) *Qualitative Research Practice: A Guide for Social Science Students and Researchers*. 2nd ed. London: SAGE Publications.

Flanagan, J. C. (1954). The critical incident technique. *Psychological Bulletin*, 51(4): 327.

Flick, U. (2023). *An Introduction to Qualitative Research*. 7th ed. Los Angeles, CA: SAGE Publications.

Gruber, M., Eberl, J. M., Lind, F. and Boomgaarden, H. G. (2021). Qualitative interviews with irregular migrants in times of COVID-19: Recourse to remote interview techniques as a possible methodological adjustment. *Forum Qualitative Sozialforschung/Forum: Qualitative Social Research*, 22(1).

Kaufmann, K. (2020). Mobile methods: Doing migration research with the help of smartphones. In: Smets, K., Leurs, K., Georgiou, M., et al. (eds) *The SAGE Handbook of Media and Migration*. Thousand Oaks, CA: SAGE Publications.

King, N., Horrocks, C. and Brooks, J. (2019). *Interviews in Qualitative Research*. 2nd ed. London: SAGE Publications.

Krueger, R. A. and Casey, M. (2000). *Focus Groups: A Practical Guide for Applied Research*. 3rd ed. Thousand Oaks, CA: SAGE Publications.

Legard, R., Keegan, J. and Ward, K. (2003). In-depth interviews. In: Ritchie, J. and Lewis, J. (eds) *Qualitative Research Practice*. London: SAGE Publications.

Liu, X. (2018). Interviewing elites: Methodological issues confronting a novice. *International Journal of Qualitative Methods*, 17(1): 1–9.

Marshall, C. and Rossman, G. B. (2011). *Designing Qualitative Research*. 5th ed. Thousand Oaks, CA: SAGE Publications.

Parker, A. and Tritter, J. (2006). Focus group method and methodology: Current practice and recent debate. *International Journal of Research and Method in Education*, 29(1): 23–37.

Smith, J. A., Flowers, P. and Larkin, M. (2022). *Interpretive Phenomenological Analysis: Theory, Method and Research*. 2nd ed. London: SAGE Publications.

Stewart, D. W. and Shamdasani, P. N. (1998). Focus group research: Exploration and discovery. In: Bickman, L. and Rog, D. J. (eds) *Handbook of Applied Social Research Methods*. Thousand Oaks, CA: SAGE Publications.

CHAPTER 12

Collecting data using diaries and naturally occurring data

12.1 INTRODUCTION

In this chapter we look at methods of gathering data that do not rely on asking participants questions about the phenomenon of interest. The first method covered in this chapter is the writing of diaries or other records, prompted by the researcher. The second is observation in which, rather than ask people what they do, we observe their behaviours. The third is the collection of data on social media, and the fourth one is the collection of pre-existing documents and other records. The fifth method is big data, and the sixth and final one is the collection of artefacts: objects such as pieces of technology, clothing, or products that people use in their everyday or organizational lives and that might inform our research.

12.2 DIARIES AND OTHER RESEARCHER-INSTIGATED DOCUMENTS

One way of collecting data for qualitative research projects is to ask participants to keep records at particular points in time, or following certain events, by creating and maintaining

DOI: 10.4324/9781003381006-15

a diary. When using diaries, 'participants are the agents of the data collection' (De Meulder and Birnie, 2021: 220).

Participants may be asked to keep data concurrently with particular events that they are involved in. One example is Pebdani et al.'s (2022) investigation of time use by academics during the Covid-19 pandemic, where participants were prompted to record what they were doing, at different times of the day, over the course of one week. Alternatively, participants may be asked to enter the data retrospectively, for example, at the end of the day or at the end of specific event, such as a meeting. The former offers enhanced spontaneity and detail, but the latter may be more practical, less taxing, and make it easier to ensure confidentiality (for instance, where diaries focus on aspects of the workday or workplace). Traditionally, diaries were written by hand into a notebook, but nowadays, such records may be captured through blogs, status updates on social networks, text messages, or mobile apps. You will have to decide the degree of structure that you provide to participants when asking them to keep a diary. Keeping instructions to a minimum allows participants maximum creativity in terms of the content and the form of what they write. Alternatively, you may wish to specify what elements to include, how often to write, and so on. A more structured approach, where you specify how often to write, what elements to include, and so on, can help to ensure that you collect data on all aspects of your research questions. A structured format generates data that is less open-ended and idiosyncratic than the nondirective approach, which may be easier to analyze.

When designing your diary study, it is worth taking into account Bowey and Thorpe's (1986) advice.

- Consider the participants' ability to express themselves well in writing.
- To sustain interest and reduce drop-out, maintain regular contact with the participants, providing continuous encouragement and reassurance.
- Think about how best to ensure confidentially in the collection process.

Research in Practice 12.1 gives an example of a diary study.

We have concentrated here on written diaries, but text-based diaries are not the only format that you can use. Photographs and drawings can also be a form of participant-generated data that has potential application in the study of organizations and management. They are particularly useful in contexts where participants are highly mobile or illiterate.

Research in practice 12.1 Using diaries for data collection

For her PhD, Constança Monteiro Casquinho studied whether mindfulness practice increased interpersonal and self-trust, within organizations, using a mixed methods research design, consisting of an experiment, in-depth interviews, and observation.

For the experimental part of her study, the researcher split participants into two randomly assigned groups. One group attended an in-person mindfulness course, followed by audio-guided daily practice sessions. As well as a self-assessment questionnaire, both groups maintained diaries during the experiment. Monteiro provided prompts such as this one to the nearly 500 participants:

> Listen to this guided mindfulness practice and afterwards please register in the space below your daily journal entries answering the following questions:

1. How did you feel during the practice?
2. What do you recall from your day/previous days that may be related to your practice?
3. When you think about your mindfulness practice, what comes to mind?

Analysis of the diary entries allowed the researcher to put the questionnaire results in context. For example, it was found that psychological safety was significantly stronger in the treatment than in the control group. Based on the diary entries, the researcher proposed that the reason for this difference was that participants in the treatment group were focused on actual experiences rather than imagined dangers, as illustrated by this entry:

> Today we experimented with food again. I couldn't help but notice that the sission was exactly the same one of the 4th day. No judgement. I did experiment with a piece of apple this time, and found it very interesting. I think that the methaphor of the dxperiences is very on point and lies at the core of mindfulness. Many things often we just pass by, and the anticipation often is more intense that the experience itself. Living in the now, and experiencing experiences to the fullest with all our emotions is a practice i have only recently started doing and it makes me appreciate life much more, so i see why this point needs to be stressed and repeated.
> (Participant from Treatment Group, daily journal day 9,
> typos as per the diary entry)

12.3 COLLECTING DATA BY OBSERVATION

Observation of what people do can help us understand both individual behaviours as well as how people interact with each other and with their environment. As a data collection method, it involves the purposeful observation, recording, and analysis of behaviours in an organized way. For example, we may employ observational techniques to learn how customers navigate a store. The key advantage of observation is its potential to generate first-hand data about people's behaviour instead of relying on their memory and descriptions of it. It can be particularly useful when you cannot ask questions of the research participants or they cannot explain their behaviour, for instance, if you were studying how young children react to a new toy. Observation may also be the only way of capturing some types of interaction or very transient behaviours in sufficient detail to allow further investigation, for example, in conversation analysis. However, it can be a slow way of gathering data because data can only be collected at the pace at which the phenomenon occurs. Where researcher time is limited, it may be possible to concentrate on behaviours of relatively short duration such as observing business partners in a negotiation process, rather than observing how the partnership relationship evolves over time.

Observation is feasible only if the phenomenon that you are studying is actually observable or can be inferred from exhibited behaviour. For example, observation may be useful to study queuing behaviour but it does not help us understand the motivations or thought processes of those involved. It also has limited application in the study of private behaviours, such as personal habits or certain types of interactions to which the researcher is unlikely to have access.

Creswell (2016) identifies the following steps in collecting data by observation.

- Choose the site for the observations, secure access, and get the necessary permissions. You may need to identify a gatekeeper to help you access.
- Develop your observation protocol. Decide how you will capture your observations, as well as your reflections on them.
- Start with limited objectives. You may not be able to get much insight into behaviours, in the first few sessions. Focus on observing, rather than taking notes.
- Decide on your role as observer, but be prepared to change it, over time, if required.
- Record what you are observing in your field notes, as per your observation protocol.
- Withdraw slowly from the site once the observation is finished, ensuring that you thank participants. Confirm how the data will be used and the findings disseminated.

12.3.1 Forms of observation

Observation can take different forms according to the requirements of the research project and the preferences of the researcher.

Covert versus overt

You can either make your presence known to the participants or observe them covertly. This decision is often influenced by the concern that knowledge of being observed, and what the researcher is interested in, will influence the behaviours of those whom you are observing, leading to bias. This is called the **observer effect**. For instance, employees may want to present a particular image of how they conduct daily tasks, if they know they are being observed. However, there are serious ethical issues to consider when making the decision between covert and overt observation, as discussed in Chapter 5. A possible solution is to tell participants that you are observing, for instance, their interactions but not mention what you are specifically interested in, for example how interactions vary with gender. Alternatively, if you are able to spend a prolonged period in the social setting, your presence may become accepted to the point where it is no longer a factor in people's behaviour, although this can still raise ethical issue in cases of extreme or illegal behaviour. Prior to undertaking any observational study, ensure you are compliant with any ethical requirements and discuss with your supervisor/tutor if you have one.

Participation versus observation

Your role as an observer may vary in terms of participation in the setting being studied. Gold (1958), in a seminal article, identified four roles.

1. *Complete observer.* You are simply a spectator to events as they happen. For example, observing a meeting.

2. *Participant-as-observer.* You participate in the social setting whilst simultaneously adopting the role of observer. This is the role typically adopted in a long-term ethnographic study.

3. *Observer-as-participant.* You enter the social setting primarily as an observer but participate to a limited extent. This may be suitable if you are spending a short time in the field, for example, observing a sales team.

4. *Complete participant.* You act as a full participant (for example, by becoming a group member), and observation is covert. This role has been used in some ethnographic studies but clearly raises ethical concerns regarding informed consent since a measure of deception is involved (see Chapter 5).

Natural versus artificial setting

You may study the behaviour as it occurs in its natural setting. For example, you might observe project teams working in their normal office environment. Alternatively, you may use a contrived setting, where you manipulate the conditions under which the behaviour takes place. This manipulation can be as limited as changing the layout of the office environment to observe staff's reactions or go as far as conducting observation in a laboratory. Using a contrived approach may speed up the data gathering process and allow control of extraneous variables in an experiment, however the behaviour observed may differ from what would occur naturally.

Structured versus unstructured

At the design state you need to decide how structured your observation should be. You can approach the research setting with a prior list of characteristics and behaviours that you want to observe. This approach, known as structured observation, is associated with quantitative research designs such as experiments. Alternatively, you can record events as they unfold without deciding the focus of your observations beforehand. This approach, referred to as unstructured observation, is typical of qualitative observational studies such as ethnography.

12.3.2 Qualitative approaches to observation

The goal of a qualitative approach to observation is, typically, to generate a thick description of the situation being investigated. Observation may be covert or overt but will generally be done in a natural setting. Observation is likely to be relatively unstructured, with the researcher deciding what to record as events unfold rather than beforehand. An example of a qualitative approach to observation is given in Research in Practice 12.2.

Research in practice 12.2 An observational study of a recycling hub in China

For his PhD, Yvan Schulz (2018) studied e-waste management and treatment, in the People's Republic of China. He spent a total of 18 months living in China, conducting observations of the recycling facilities, the workers, and the electronic products as they were dismantled and processed for recycling. This included living with a plastic recycling family for a week.

In the early stages of his research, Schultz visited the recycling hub relatively unencumbered. However, over time, security at the park increased:

> Some of them wished to protect what they saw as proprietary information. But most of them simply sought to avoid publicity and the risk of being exposed as having possibly not entirely legal activities.
>
> (Schulz, 2018: 53)

To overcome this limitation, Schultz resorted to covert observation techniques:

> In some cases, I became a simple resident wanting to acquire or discard (electric and electronic equipment), in others a professional merchant looking to buy or sell such devices.
>
> (Schulz, 2018: 54)

Despite the ethical concerns, Schultz feels that this approach improved his findings:

> It is one thing to collect information on prices for DEEE* but quite another to try to buy or sell DEEE at those prices, for instance. If one studies trade, then one must trade – at least a little or attempt to do so – in order to understand the famous 'native's point of view'.
>
> (Schulz, 2018: 54)

*Disposal of electric and electronic waste

Source: Schulz (2018)

You need to make sure that you capture and store all the data needed. The simplest way of recording your data is to make notes in your field notebook, which may be complemented with audio or video recordings or photography. Emerson et al. (1995) offer the following advice for taking field notes.

- Note your initial impressions of the situation, then focus on key events of incidents. As observation proceeds, try to move beyond your personal reactions as the researcher to develop an understanding of what is important or significant from the perspective of the participants.
- Start broadly, then focus your observations as your own knowledge of the situation develops. Be alert to patterns or regularities in what is happening, and also to exceptions that can deepen your understanding of the phenomenon.
- Use brief written notes to capture points of interest. Later, write them up as a fuller set of field notes.

If it is not possible to make notes during observation, you should try to record your thoughts as soon as possible afterwards. This will aid recall and avoid the writing task becoming too burdensome.

12.3.3 Quantitative approaches to observation

Quantitative approaches to observation typically take a structured approach, with the aim of producing quantifiable data for subsequent numerical analysis. The researcher role must allow adequate time and scope for detailed recording, so a complete observer role may be most suitable. Structured observation has a long tradition in management practice. For example, in a well-known study on the nature of managerial work, Henry Mintzberg (1973) carried out structured observation of five chief executives to find out what they actually did.

Structured observation involves the coding of the observed behaviour according to a defined coding schedule specifying which actions are to be recorded and how they will be categorized. The contents of your coding schedule are determined by the research questions you are trying to answer. For example, if you were investigating factors causing high levels of customer complaint in a supermarket, your coding schedule would capture behaviours relevant to the in-store experience, such as cleanliness, waiting tomes at the counter, or the behaviour of sales staff. Research in Practice 12.3 gives an example of coding schedules for structured observation.

For your own project, you may be able to use or adapt an existing coding schedule that has been used in prior studies. If you develop your own, you should consider the following.

- Identify the focus of your observation. As with developing a questionnaire, you need to be clear on what you want to measure in your observation, using prior theory to help you define the coding scheme.
- Determine the behaviours or activities that you wish to observe during your study. Define each one so that it can be understood by the coder or explained to the reader in the final report.
- Formulate a code for each element and decide what format you will use for recording, for example, event frequency, time sampling, or duration of activity.
- Develop your coding schedule document so that it is easy use in the conditions under which the observation will be carried out.

You should be aware of the issues that can affect data quality. There may be observer effects that influence participants' natural behaviour. Moreover, there can be selectivity or inconsistencies in either the sampling or the coding process, leading to bias. Problems can also arise due to inattention by the coder, misinterpretation of the coding schedule, or inconsistencies in coding if more than one observer is used. Measures of inter-rater reliability can be used to assess the consistency of multiple observers/coders.

Research in practice 12.3 Example of structured observation coding schedule

If we were undertaking observation in a supermarket in order to understand the underlying causes of customer complaints regarding checkout service, we could create an observation schedule that included factors believed to influence satisfaction levels. In Example 1 we show a simple coding schedule to capture the frequency of events. In Example 2 we show a coding schedule used to record each occurrence that is observed during an interval of time. The latter technique, referred to as time sampling, has the advantage of preserving the sequence of events.

Example 1: Event frequency

Observed behaviour	Number of observations Date/hour
One or more checkout tills not staffed	////
Sales staff talking to one another	/////////
Sales staff ignoring customers	///////
Queue of more than two customers at a checkout till	//////////////
Untidy checkout till	//

Example 2: Time sampling

Observed behaviour	1st (10 mins)	2nd (10 mins)	3rd (10 mins)	4th (10 mins)	5th (10 mins)	6th (10 mins)	Date Hour observed
One or more checkout tills not staffed	/	/				//	
Sales staff talking to one another		/	/			/	
Sales staff ignoring customers						/	

Observed behaviour	1st (10 mins)	2nd (10 mins)	3rd (10 mins)	4th (10 mins)	5th (10 mins)	6th (10 mins)	Date Hour observed
Queue of more than two customers at a checkout till		/					
Untidy checkout till	/			/			

12.3.4 Technology-mediated observation

Video can be used to study behaviours in the physical world, for instance to record private behaviours in the home. This has the advantage of making the presence of the observer less obvious, particularly if the cameras are positioned in a non-intrusive way. It can also speed up data collection, as various individuals, groups, or sites can be 'observed' simultaneously and across diverse geographic locations. Video also provides a permanent record that can be studied more closely and revisited as required during analysis. Audio recording may be easier to use than video and is a particularly important source of data for conversation analysis. Some of the first work in conversation analysis was actually done using data from taped telephone calls (Wooffitt, 2005). Any recording requires appropriate permissions and ethical clearance (see Chapter 5).

The Internet can also be an important environment in which to conduct observations. This can take the form of monitoring discussion forums, studying the participants' social media presence, or observing their browsing behaviour, among others. Observing online behaviour, sometimes described as netnography, goes beyond recording what people write and focuses on behaviours or actions (Kozinets, 2002). This includes how often users interact with each other, what social norms guide their interactions, whether there is a formal or informal hierarchy, among others. Research in Practice 9.4 (in Chapter 9) gives an example of participant observation in an online community, and in Chapter 5 we discuss ethical issues that can arise in this type of online research.

12.3.5 Choosing your approach to observation

In making the decision about whether and what type of observation is appropriate for your study, you should consider the following:

- Purpose of the research. Consider how observation will answer the research question and be integrated into your intended research design.
- Access. A key consideration is where the research setting will be and how you will gain access to it. It may take some time to organize and to negotiate access.

- Comfort in the role. Think about your skills to carry out the observation and how you feel about the role, such as participant-observer, that you will adopt.
- Time available. When setting the schedule at the outset of your research, ensure that you have sufficient time available for the planned observation.
- Cost implications. Consider any likely costs in accessing and participating in different types of observation.

12.4 COLLECTING DATA THROUGH SOCIAL MEDIA

Social media are now part of everyday life, and as a result, there is a growing interest in using social media data in management research, such as when investigating consumer behaviour online. Researchers can collect the data that social media users create whenever they post a message on Facebook or Weibo, share a video on TikTok or Douyin, message each other on WhatsApp or Telegram, or publish a blog post on Wordpress or Medium. These data can tell researchers about the users themselves, as well as about their interests and their behaviours. For example, comparison of X (formerly known as Twitter) posts before and after Covid-19 was declared a pandemic shows an increase in disclosure of personal and sensitive information (Blose et al., 2020). Alternatively, researchers may focus on the structure of the networks in those platforms: how users relate to each other, and how content spreads among those networks. Research in practice 12.4 presents an example of this type of research.

If you have decided that you are using social media data for your research project, you should consider Flick's (2023: 363) advice.

- Consider whether you should focus on one platform versus following a multi-platform approach.
- Choose which social media platform or platforms are most suitable for your research question.
- Decide what the criteria for selecting data from this platform are, including how much data you need.
- Think about how collecting data on social media may create bias, both in terms of the groups that you are reaching, and the phenomenon that you are studying.

As with observations, you need to decide if you will collect data overtly and participate in the community. Remember that while social media data may be in the public sphere, that does not mean that they are available for public use. You will need to consider the ethical implications of using social media for your project, particularly those around informed consent and privacy.

Some academic institutions require you to create an account or username specifically for your research project. This is both to be transparent about your identity as a researcher, and to separate your researcher identity from your other identities as much as possible, for instance, in case research participants want to contact you afterwards. You should be aware that your online personas are searchable, and that content shared in one platform or account could find its way to others. Kerrigan and Hart (2016) refer to this as social media leakage. Thus, the creation of a different account for the project does not guarantee complete separation between identities.

12.4.1 Setting up your social media data collection

Most platforms allow you to create a developer account and collect data in real time via an application programming interface (API), a software interface that allows you to access and search the social media platform's data. While some platforms allow free API access for research purposes, many do not, or they may impose restrictions on the data that you can collect. You will need to consult the terms of your chosen platform carefully to assess what data you can use, for what purpose, and how much it may cost you. Understanding terms of access and obtaining permission to collect data is time-consuming, and you will need to factor that in your project planning.

The process for collecting data from blogs is a bit different. Hookway and Snee (2017) offer the following suggestions:

- Searching: Use general search engines to find posts containing words or phrases relevant to your research questions.
- Trawling: Use the search facilities within a specific blogging platform (e.g. Wordpress) to find bloggers and posts with specific characteristics relevant for your sampling criteria.
- Solicitation: Recruit bloggers that meet your sampling criteria, and agree directly with them how you are going to collect the data that you need for your project.

Yet another option is to use commercial social media scraping tools. These software products search various social media platforms (including blogs) according to the terms that you specify. The data can then be exported, for instance, to a spreadsheet. Scraping tools vary significantly in terms of what data they extract and how. So you will need to decide carefully which is most suited for your project. Many tools offer free trial periods.

12.4.2 Challenges in social media data collection and use

You are likely to face several challenges specific to this type of data collection tool:

- Finding relevant data for your project. With so many people using social media platforms, and so much content being generated every day, it can be difficult to find the material that is relevant for your study.
- Contextualizing the data. Short social media inputs (e.g. a tweet or a meme) often exist in a certain context. To fully assess its meaning, you may need to collect data about that context. You will need to decide, for instance, whether to also include retweets, treat retweets as separate units of analysis, or look at conversations rather than individual tweets.
- Verifying the identity of the social media user. There are numerous cases where social media users assume false identities. For example, they may lie about their gender,

age, or location or pretend to suffer from a serious illness. If your research question requires you to know exactly who is posting the social media content, you will need to check and validate the identity of the social media users in your sample.

- Storing your data. This can be an issue both in terms of the size of the data set that you end up collecting as well as the variety of the type of data collected.
- Processing your data. Social media data may include text, photos, videos, links, hashtags, and metadata. This presents challenges in terms of the format for storing the data set and how to analyze it.
- Platform changes. Social media platforms regularly change their features. Some of these are purely cosmetic, but others change what data you can access or how, or prevent you from continuing to collect data. This is a significant risk if you are conducting a longitudinal project.

Research in practice 12.4 Studying a social movement

A research study was undertaken by Md Hassan Zamir to investigate how activists behave online and how they develop social networks. The focus of the research was the Shahbag movement, in Bangladesh. Zamir's project addressed research questions such as 'Who were the central activists of the Shahbag movement on X (formerly known as Twitter)?' and 'How was information diffused during the Shahbag movement?'

Zamir used an authorised data reseller, which provided both real time and historical data, which enabled Zamir to study topic shifts and network formation, longitudinally. Zamir decided to focus on the hashtag #Shahbag, only, which had been the most commonly used. This meant that tweets using other hashtags, or no hashtags, were excluded.

Zamir collected a total of 116,314 tweets and associated hashtags, usernames, timestamps, mentions, geolocation, and platform information. The data collected were saved in Excel and CSV file formats. As the data set included tweets in two different languages (Bangla and English), but most automated analysis tools can process content in one language, only, Zamir decided to retain the English language tweets, only. He analyzed whose content was retweeted and who was mentioned in the tweets, in order to identity opinion leaders and networks of Shahbag supporters and detractors.

Source: Zamir (2017)

12.5 COLLECTING DOCUMENTS AND OTHER RECORDS

So far we have looked at ways of collecting data by asking people or watching how they behave. We now turn our attention to another important source of data in management research: documents and other written or electronic records. These fall under the broad heading of secondary data. In this chapter we define 'documents' as written, printed, or electronic matter which can include textual, visual, or even audio formats. The data contained may be verbal, such as meeting notes, numeric, such as sales statistics; or non-verbal, such as images from advertisements. This broad definition aims to capture the ways individuals and organizations may use documents to express themselves or to achieve their goals.

Documents and records can be the object of research in their own right, for example, in content analysis or critical discourse analysis. More often, researchers use such data to find out about something external to the document itself, for instance, such as an organization's sales performance. Their diversity and richness mean that documents and other records have many potential applications in different research designs, as we show in Table 12.1. These data sources can also be relevant at other points in your research project (for example, for background information or as part of the literature review), but in this chapter we are focusing on their use in the empirical stage of your research.

Advantages of documents as data sources

One of the most important advantages of documents as data sources is that they are a form of naturally occurring data. They represent an unobtrusive, non-reactive form of data collection (Webb et al., 1966), avoiding some of the problems of social desirability bias. Documents can also be useful in retrospective longitudinal research since they provide a

TABLE 12.1 The role of documents and other records in different research designs

Research design	Role of documents and other records
Ethnography	May be used as a supporting data source
Case study	May be used alongside other methods; may be particularly useful in retrospective studies
Grounded theory	May be used as a supporting data source
Action research	May be used alongside other data collection methods, either as part of the action research project cycle or for the researcher's thesis cycle
Content analysis (both quantitative and qualitative)	Primary data source; may be in the form of text, pictures, video or other visual media
Critical discourse analysis	Primary data source may be in the form of text, pictures, video, or other visual media
Experiment and quasi experiment	Secondary data may be used alongside other methods to measure relevant variables before, during, and after the experiment
Nonexperimental explanatory research (quantitative)	Secondary data may be the primary data source or be used alongside other data collection methods, such as questionnaires, analysis, other visual media to measure relevant variables

contemporary record of past events that can be reviewed by the researcher. You might, for example, use customer complaint emails to trace how the reason for complaining has changed over time. More generally, documents can be an important source for triangulation, complementing other sources, such as interviews, or as part of a mixed methods research project. In some situations, documents and other records may offer a lower-cost and quicker data collection method than alternative methods, depending on the type of documents and their accessibility. Moreover, they can allow us to research topics that would not otherwise be researchable, for example, events for which there are no participants available or accessible.

Limitations of documents as data sources

Documents also have limitations. Coverage of a topic is likely to be partial, leaving gaps that may have to be filled by other data collection methods. Partial coverage may arise from a combination of practical, ethical, and legal reasons, as would be the case if you wanted, for example, to access an organizational database containing confidential data. Archived collections of documents, such as the files that have been kept on a particular project, can also represent a partial viewpoint, depending on the criteria used to decide what documents should be kept and what should be destroyed. The quality of documents can also vary and, in some cases, be difficult to ascertain; documents reflect the purpose for which they were created, rather than our research needs. Neither are they necessarily an accurate representation of their subject. For instance, company policy guidelines may not reflect what is done in practice. Similar concerns arise when looking at secondary data such as government statistics or previous research projects.

12.5.1 Finding and obtaining documents

Several factors will influence the way you go about collecting documents for your project.

Sampling plan

Your research questions may require you to collect the whole population of a particular type of document or just those documents relevant to a specific event or organization (Lee, 2012). For instance, a study of changes in how public companies have discussed environmental sustainability in their annual reports, over time, could use the complete set of annual reports for the target population or take a random sample from a predefined sampling frame.

Either way, you will have to define your target population, identify a suitable sampling frame, and decide a sampling approach, as discussed in Chapter 9. If your focus is on specific events or organizations, for instance, studying environmental reporting by a specific company, you would have to identify and obtain documents that relate to that scenario. However, if your focus is on broad subjects, such as television advertising, there may be no suitable listings available, and you will have to develop your own to help you identify relevant documents.

Are the documents in the public or private domain?

Documents in the public domain are available to any member of the public to view. If they are online, they may also be downloadable, which will make collection and storage easier. In Table 12.2 we identify a range of different data sources. Data may or may not require some form of payment to gain full access. Locating public domain documents will require similar techniques to those you will have used for your literature review, such as online searching, as discussed in Chapter 3.

Privately held documents, such as those held internally by organizations, will not be so easy to identify or obtain are likely to require consent from the organization. At this point it is useful to distinguish between the formal 'official' documents and records in an organization and the less official, 'grey materials'. Examples of official documents include company newsletters, human resource records, company reports, customer satisfaction surveys, or employee handbooks. These are the documents that are created, and acknowledged, by the activities of an organization. You will need to contact the respective owner of these documents to negotiate access. Less official 'grey' documents include emails, memoranda, notes from team meetings, and personal working notes. These may reside with individuals within the organization, often in their own laptops or files, and not stored centrally. Such data may be difficult to locate, and the researcher may not even be aware of its existence unless it is mentioned by the holder. Although such documents may generate important insights, their ownership status may be unclear, and they may be easily lost, for example, if

TABLE 12.2 Example sources of online secondary data

Type of data	Example sources
National census data	• UK National Census by the Office of National Statistics (www.ons.gov.uk/ons/index.html) • US Census Bureau (www.census.gov)
Government surveys and statistics	• UK Office of National Statistics (www.statistics.gov.uk) • National Archives and Records Administration of the United States (NARA) (www.nara.gov) • Eurostat (http://epp.eurostat.ec.europa.eu/)
Large-scale surveys	• OECD statistics (http://stats.oecd.org/) • Euromonitor (www.euromonitor.com/) • IPUMS (www.ipums.org) • PEW Research Centre (www.pewresearch.org)
Longitudinal studies	• British Household Panel Survey (www.iser.essex.ac.uk/bhps) • UK Millennium Cohort Study (www.cls.ioe.ac.uk/) • Inter-university Consortium for Political and Social Research (ICPSR) (www.icpsr.umich.edu/web/pages/)
Qualitative secondary data archives	• UK Data Archive (also includes quantitative data) (www.data-archive.ac.uk) • The Qualitative Data Repository (https://qdr.syr.edu)

an individual leaves the organization. Gaining access to organizational documents is likely to be easier if you are an insider researcher or if you are conducting action research inside the organization. Whatever your status, you should ensure that you have permission to access and use any documents or records and that you respect your ethical obligations, as well as any legal or other restrictions relating to their use.

Location

In some cases, it may be possible to find relevant material online, using conventional search techniques. Research in Practice 12.5 gives an example of such a study. If you want to capture everything that has been written about a particular organization or issue, across a range of different online locations, a web crawler may be helpful. Note that such technology can still require extensive researcher input to set up the search and to filter the results. In addition, it raises some complex ethical issues regarding the use and reporting of online material, as discussed in Chapter 5.

In other cases, it will still be necessary to visit an archive such as a library or record office in person either to negotiate access or to view the documents themselves, even if they are open to public access. The same applies to private documents which may not exist in digital format or may be held in electronically or physically secured areas that cannot be accessed from outside. You may have to travel and spend time on site studying documents, which will have time and cost implications for your project.

Document format

Whilst many documents will be in electronic format, some may be printed or even hand-written. If you are collecting documents in electronic format, make sure that you have the technology to read them and that the document is in a format that can be read directly by your chosen programme. In the case of documents that are available only in printed or written format, you may be allowed to copy, scan, or photograph the document. If not, you will have to rely on field notes. If original documents are loaned to you, you will need to arrange for their safe return on completion of the project.

Research in practice 12.5 Capturing newspaper stories about female leaders

A research study was undertaken for an undergraduate research project, to study how women that hold top business and leadership roles are represented in the media (Anon, 2014). They analyzed articles in the leading national newspapers in the UK and the US as they were deemed to represent the mainstream views in those countries. The sample was restricted to articles published in March, as this is when International Women's Day takes place and, therefore, when special attention might be given to women in those newspapers.

The student researcher used the database Nexis to search for newspaper articles in the chosen publications, using the search terms 'Wom*n OR Female*' AND 'Leader* OR manage* OR executive*', and the exclusion 'politic*'. A further search was conducted for the term 'glass ceiling', within the chosen publications. The search identified 164 articles, from which 30 newspaper articles were deemed relevant for the research project and selected for content analysis.

12.6 BIG DATA

The digitalization of many of our personal and professional activities has resulted in the generation and availability of ever larger digital data sets. For instance, our physical activity is monitored by our smartphones, our home appliances are connected to the Internet, and many of our communications take place over the Internet or a phone. There has also been a popularization of the publication of government and other public data, generating what is called as open data. At the same time, there have been impressive developments in computing power and analytical tools, enabling management researchers to collect and analyze very large digital data sets about human behaviour and organizational processes. For instance, Bradley et al. (2020) used project development data stored in the public repository GitHub to study relationships and organizational dependencies among software developers in the Open Source Software community.

This type of source of research data is usually referred to as big data. In addition to being large in volume, big data is 'characterized by being generated continuously, seeking to be exhaustive and fine-grained in scope, and flexible and scalable in its production' (Kitchin, 2014: 2). Fosso Wamba et al. (2015), following a systematic review of the literature on big data, identify five characteristics of big data that both describe the attributes of this source of data and its usefulness in research. The five proposed characteristics are 'volume' to capture the magnitude of the data sets; 'variety' to refer to the range of data sources and data formats in the data set; 'velocity' to describe the speed at which data are constantly becoming available; 'veracity' to depict the importance of assessing the quality and trustworthiness of the data source; finally, 'value' refers to the evidence-based insight that may be derived from the data, once it has been processed (Fosso Wamba et al., 2015).

Big data research may be exploratory in nature, looking for trends and patterns in the data set as discussed in Chapter 6. Alternatively, research may focus on the analysis of correlation between two or more selected variables, as is typical of quantitative research. However, when using big data, researchers tend to follow an inductive approach, starting from data rather than theory (Kitchin, 2014). Big data may be used on its own, or as a starting point for understanding a digital phenomenon. In that case, analysis of the data sets may be complemented with other data collection methods, such as interviews or document analysis, a process that Flick (2023: 379) calls 'thickening of data'.

12.6.1 Collecting big data for your project

Quinton and Reynolds (2018) list four sources of big data.

1. Data collected and stored by commercial firms, such as product usage data. This type of data may be difficult to access because of its commercially sensitive nature. Access will need to be negotiated directly with the firm.

2. Data held by public bodies and government agencies, such as public health data. This type of data may be accessible, subject to permission from the data holder.

3. Data held by service providers, such as text message history. This type of data is sometimes shared with the public.

4. Data uploaded by individuals to online, public platforms such as discussion forums or content sharing websites. This type of data tends to be accessible by API, subject to the platform's terms and conditions.

Projects may use data from just one of those sources, or multiple ones. Quinton and Reynolds (2018) advise that integrating multiple data sets is time-consuming and complex as you will need to master the methods for matching cases across the databases. You will also need to carefully consider the characteristics of the database. You will need to know how the data were collected, which data fields are included in the data set, how they are recorded, and in which format. You will also need to clean the data set. For instance, if you are collecting product reviews, it may be advisable to identify and remove fake accounts. You will also need to remove duplicates and identify missing data. Or if your study involves analysis of religious affiliation, you should be aware that countries such as France and Rwanda do not include that information in their official statistics.

12.6.2 Challenges of using big data for your project

Using big data is likely to face three big challenges:

- *Skills and resources to access and process large data sets*. Data sets are not only very large, but they may also include unstructured data such as sound or images. Significant technical skills and technological resources, including computing power, are likely to be needed. You may need to use the services of a commercial firm to extract the data set and access specialist analysis technology and additional storage capacity.
- *Partial topic coverage*. Even though the data set may include a large number of entries, the actual coverage of the topic that interests you may be limited. The data sets were created for a specific purpose, and their content reflects the interests and goals of the organization that created the data set, rather than those of your research project. Popular data sets also tend to originate from a small number of countries (Koch et al., 2021).
- *Ethical concerns*. The lack of visibility of data collection in some cases (e.g. smart home technology), or the lack of complete understanding of how the data are going to be used (e.g. loyalty card data), means that may not be possible to be sure that the people about whom the data were collected have given informed consent for the data to be used in your research, as discussed in Chapter 5. There have also been cases where

analysis of presumably anonymized data has resulted in the identification of specific individuals and their behaviours, violating their privacy.

12.7 ARTEFACTS

Artefacts can include the tools that employees use to perform a particular work task, the clothes that job applicants may wear for an interview, the packaging of the products that are produced by an organization, or the type of furniture in an office. Spennemann's (2021) project *Cultural Heritage in the Age of Covid-19*, for example, collected face masks, hand sanitizer dispensers, public education posters, social distancing signage, and other artefacts associated with the Covid-19 pandemic. Artefacts may be an important data source in research because so much of our communication is done by means other than words. Moreover, aspects of the physical environment, such as tools or furniture, influence our behaviour through their material presence and their symbolic meaning.

It is rare to see a management research project that relies exclusively on artefacts. Instead, artefacts tend to be analyzed as a complement to other data. For example, a study of new technology implementation could include investigation of the physical system (i.e. the artefact), as well as observation of how it is used by operators. Alternatively, a diary study of consumer shopping habits could be supported by the collection of artefacts such as shopping lists, carrier bags, and so on.

Artefacts are likely to belong to an organization or to an individual as their private property. They have financial and/or sentimental value for their owners. Artefacts may be housed in a secure site such as a museum or library or be in the possession of private individuals. If they cannot be moved, or are stored in a secure site, you may gain access to them for only a specific period of time. You will have to rely on your field notes, along with photographs or video, if permitted. If you are asking research participants to gather artefacts for your research, you may wish to restrict the size, type, and number of objects that participants can produce. Otherwise, you risk ending up with material that is cumbersome to store or difficult to compare. You will also need to consider the safekeeping of any items that are loaned to you and the arrangements to return them, if relevant.

CRITICAL COMMENTARY 12.1

Observer effects and unobtrusive measures

In this chapter we have mentioned observer effects and their potential influence on research data. Observer effects arise when participants' awareness that they are being researched influences their behaviour. Webb et al. (1966) suggest four dimensions of what they called 'reactive effects':

1. Awareness of being tested or 'the guinea pig effect', as a result of which

participants behave in ways other than normal, for instance to create a particular impression.

2. Role selection, in which the participant tries to adopt a particular role within the research, for example, in response to their expectations about what the researcher is looking for.

3. Measurement as a change agent, in which the mere fact of being part of the research project induces change.

4. response sets in self-report measures such as questionnaires in which participants' answers exhibit a pattern that is clearly unrelated to the questions actually asked, for example, consistently choosing one position on a scale, irrespective of the question.

Webb et al. (1966) propose what they call unobtrusive measures as a counter to these problems. Naturally occurring data, covert observation, and artefacts are examples of such measures.

CHAPTER SUMMARY

- Diaries and other researcher-instigated documents, such as drawings and photographs, may be a valuable source of data in management research. The degree of structure and guidance given for the diary entries should reflect the focus of the research.

- Observation involves the purposeful observation, recording and analysis of behaviours and other activities in an organized way. Designing an observation study requires decisions about the researcher's role, whether the observation will be covert or overt, whether the setting should be natural or artificial, and the degree of structure required. Observation can also be carried out in online environments.

- Social media data can provide insight into participants, their interests and behaviours with no interference from the researcher. Particular care is needed in terms of contextualizing the data, false identities, ensuring informed consent, and protecting the privacy of participants.

- Documents are written, printed or electronic materials that contain verbal, numeric, or non-verbal data. The collection of documents for a research project is influenced by the sampling plan, whether the documents are in the public domain, their location, and the format they are in. Access will have to be negotiated with document holders and appropriate permission and ethical clearance gained.

- Big data refers to large digital data sets, generated through individual or organizational activities, and which are exhaustive in nature and fine-grained in scope. They can offer insight about human behaviour and organizational processes, but this may be partial. Using big data requires sophisticated technical skills and resources and raises informed consent and privacy concerns.
- Study of physical artefacts and their use can offer valuable insights into the ways in which material things are used, as well as the meanings they hold for people. There are practical limitations regarding accessing and storing this type of data.

NEXT STEPS

12.1 The role of non-verbal accounts in your research design. Revisit the key research articles from the literature that you have reviewed and identify any that have collected data by means other than survey or interviewing the research participants. What collection methods have been used?

12.2 Assessing the advantages and disadvantages of the selected data collection methods. With reference to your specific research project, list the advantages and disadvantages of the data collection methods discussed in this chapter. Consider a broad range of practical, technical, and ethical factors.

12.3 Addressing limitations. Consider possible ways of minimizing the limitations identified in the previous step.

12.4 Technology-mediated data collection. Decide if you are going to use some form of technology interface to collect your data. Ensure that you know how to use that interface and deal with technical problems.

12.5 Set up the empirical exercise. Think about how you will negotiate access to the research site and clarify expectations regarding how long you can collect data, what you can access, and what you will be providing in return. Decide the type of instructions and the level of structure that you need to provide to the research participants and construct the coding schedule, if relevant.

12.6 Capturing your data. Decide how you are going to capture and store the data and your notes.

FURTHER READING

For further reading, please see the companion website.

REFERENCES

Anon (2014). *A Critical Discourse Analysis of How Women in Top Business and Leadership Roles Were Represented within The Times and The New York Times During March 2013*. BSc dissertation, Leeds University Business School, Leeds. Available at: http://resources.library.leeds.ac.uk/final-chapter/dissertations/lubs/3305example6.pdf.

Blose, T., Umar, P., Squicciarini, A. and Rajtmajer, S. (2020). Privacy in crisis: A study of self-disclosure during the Coronavirus pandemic. *arXiv preprint arXiv:2004.09717*. https://arxiv.org/abs/2004.09717

Bowey, A. M. and Thorpe, R. (1986). *Payment Systems and Productivity*. Basingstoke: Palgrave Macmillan.

Bradley, R., Mockus, A., Ma, Y., Zaretzki, R. and Bichescu, B. (2020). Coordinating interdependencies in an open source software project: A replication of Lindberg, et al. *AIS Transactions on Replication Research*, 6(14). https://doi.org/10.17705/17701atrr.00057.

Creswell, J. W. (2016). *30 Essential Skills for the Qualitative Researcher*. Thousand Oaks, CA: SAGE Publications.

De Meulder, M. and Birnie, I. (2021). Language diaries in the study of language use and language choice: The case of Flemish sign language and Scottish Gaelic. *Language Awareness*, 30(3): 217–233.

Emerson, R. M., Fretz, R. I. and Shaw, L. L. (1995). *Writing Ethnographic Fieldnotes*. Chicago, IL: The University of Chicago Press.

Flick, U. (2023). *An Introduction to Qualitative Research*. 7th ed. Los Angeles, CA: SAGE Publications.

Fosso Wamba, S., Akter, S., Edwards, A., Chopin, G. and Gnanzou, D. (2015). How "big data" can make big impact: Findings from a systematic review and a longitudinal case study. *International Journal of Production Economics*, 165: 234–246.

Gold, R. L. (1958). Roles in sociological field observations. *Social Forces*, 36(3): 217–223.

Hookway, N. and Snee, H. (2017). The blogosphere. In: Fielding, N. G., Blank, G. and Lee, R. M. (eds) *The SAGE Handbook of Online Research Methods*. London: SAGE Publications.

Kerrigan, F. and Hart, A. (2016). Theorising digital personhood: A dramaturgical approach. *Journal of Marketing Management*, 32(17–18): 1701–1721.

Kitchin, R. (2014). Big data, new epistemologies and paradigm shifts. *Big Data & Society*, April-June: 1–12.

Koch, B., Denton, E., Hanna, A. and Foster, J. G. (2021). Reduced, reused and recycled: The life of a dataset in machine learning research. *arXiv preprint arXiv:2112.01716*. https://arxiv.org/abs/2112.01716

Kozinets, R. V. (2002). The field behind the screen: Using Netnography for marketing research in online communities. *Journal of Marketing Research (JMR)*, 39(1): 61–72.

Lee, B. (2012). Documents in organizational research. In: Symon, G. and Cassell, C. (eds) *Qualitative Organizational Research*. London: SAGE Publications.

Mintzberg, H. (1973). *The Nature of Managerial Work*. New York, NY: Harper and Row.

Pebdani, R. N., Zeidan, A., Low, L.-F. and Baillie, A. (2022). Pandemic productivity in academia: Using ecological momentary assessment to explore the impact of COVID-19 on research productivity. *Higher Education Research & Development*. https://doi.org/10.1080/07294360.2022.2128075.

Quinton, S. and Reynolds, N. (2018). *Understanding Research in the Digital Age*. London: SAGE Publications.

Schulz, Y. (2018). *Modern Waste: The Political Ecology of E-scrap Recycling in China*. PhD thesis, University of Neuchâtel.

Spennemann, D. (2021). *Collecting COVID-19 Ephemera: A Photographic Documentation of Examples from Regional Australia*. Albury, NSW: Institute of Land Water and Society, Charles Stuart University.

Webb, E. J., Campbell, D. T., Schwartz, R. D. and Sechrest, L. (1966). *Unobtrusive Measures: Nonreactive Research in the Social Sciences*. Chicago, IL: Rand McNally.

Wooffitt, R. (2005). *Conversation Analysis and Discourse Analysis*. London: SAGE Publications.

Zamir, M. (2017). *Anatomy of a Social Media Movement: Diffusion, Sentiment and Network Analysis*. Doctoral thesis. Available at: https://scholarcommons.sc.edu/etd/4229.

PART IV

Analyze

The purpose of data analysis in research is to move from a set of raw data, such as the responses to a questionnaire or recordings of in-depth interviews, to knowledge that helps you to answer your research question. In the process you need to turn the raw data into something that provides meaning in relation to the research questions that you are trying to answer. In doing so you want to be confident that any conclusions you reach are justified by your data. You will also need to be able to communicate your findings, so an important aspect of data analysis is preparing output that is meaningful to others.

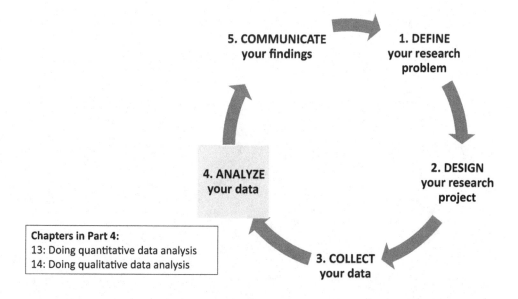

Chapters in Part 4:
13: Doing quantitative data analysis
14: Doing qualitative data analysis

DOI: 10.4324/9781003381006-16

These activities are the focus of Part IV. In Chapter 13 we look at quantitative data analysis, including the use of descriptive and inferential statistics, as well as how to report your analysis. In Chapter 14 we review qualitative data, explaining the coding process as a way of identifying themes in your data. We also look at the use of visual display techniques to help your analysis along with how to report your findings. Both chapters are supported on the companion website by guides on how to use software to support the analysis process.

Analyzing quantitative data

13.1 INTRODUCTION

The focus of this chapter is quantitative data analysis, and we begin by setting out a simple process to follow when carrying it out. We then look at how to get your data ready for analysis before introducing techniques for exploring and describing your data using tables, summary statistics, and graphs. Next, we introduce some more advanced analysis techniques, including how to use inferential statistics to test hypotheses and estimate population parameters. We conclude with a brief look at presenting your findings.

This chapter is designed to be used in conjunction with the book's companion website, which covers analysis techniques introduced here in more detail and shows how to carry them out using popular software packages.

Note: unless otherwise stated, the data used in this chapter are fictitious.

13.1.1 Using a computer

Quantitative data analysis is going to involve using statistics. Fortunately, quantitative data analysis software packages are widely available, which largely removes the need for you to be able to perform statistical calculations yourself. These programmes range from basic

DOI: 10.4324/9781003381006-17

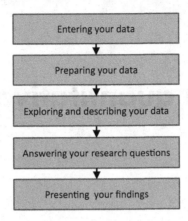

FIGURE 13.1 The quantitative data analysis process

statistical functions within spreadsheet packages to bespoke statistical analysis software. Choice of programme depends on the analysis you are doing. Whilst spreadsheet-based software will be adequate for many simple projects, a specialized statistics package will be needed for more advanced analysis. In this chapter and on the companion website, we refer to two programmes that represent different ends of the spectrum in terms of specialization:

- Microsoft Excel (hereafter MS Excel) as an example of a popular spreadsheet software programme.
- IBM SPSS Statistics (hereafter SPSS) as an example of a specialist statistics programme that is widely used in social science research.

The companion website gives further information on using these two packages for the analysis techniques introduced in this chapter.

13.1.2 The analysis process

Figure 13.1 presents the key steps in quantitative data analysis. It is essential to begin with careful data entry, followed by thorough preparation prior to analysis including data cleansing to remove data entry errors. The next step is data exploration and description. In this step, you get a feel for, and generate descriptive statistics of, your sample data. This provides the platform from which to answer your research questions. Throughout the process you need to think about how you will present your findings, so it is important to save your output as you work and keep a record of the decisions that you make and actions that you take.

13.2 ENTERING YOUR DATA

The first step in the analysis process is to get your data into a format that can be analyzed by your chosen software programme.

	A	B	C	D	E
1	Respondent ID	Employment status	Age (years)	Job satisfaction	Affective commitment
2	1	0	28	6	5
3	2	1	46	5	4
4	3	1	19	4	4
5	4	1	33	3	4
6	5	1	45	5	6
7	6	1	23	6	5

FIGURE 13.2 Example data matrix created in MS Excel

13.2.1 Creating a data matrix

A standard format for preparing quantitative data is to set up a case-by-variable **data matrix**. Figure 13.2 shows a typical example that was created in MS Excel and is laid out as follows.

- The first column contains a unique numerical identifier (ID) for each case. This allows you to refer to individual cases and, if required, recover the original layout if it is changed during the analysis process.
- Columns after the first one represent individual variables. In a data matrix for a questionnaire, for example, each question would have its own column.
- Rows contain the data for a particular case or observation, such as an individual respondent's answers to a questionnaire.

An individual cell in the grid therefore represents the unique data for a particular variable for a particular case. In Figure 13.2, for example, cell C3 represents case number 2's age in years (46).

If your data were captured electronically (e.g. using an online survey tool), data entry should be a straightforward process of exporting the file in an appropriate format and then opening it in your chosen software. If you have collected your data on paper, you will probably have to enter your data by typing it directly into your analysis software. Further details on setting up data matrices in MS Excel and SPSS are given in the companion website.

13.2.2 Coding

Data that are already in numerical form can usually be entered directly into your data matrix. Other data may need coding prior to entry. In the context of quantitative data analysis, **coding** is the process of assigning meaningful numerical values to non-numerical responses to facilitate analysis. The most common coding task is the allocation of numbers to categories of nominal variables (such as gender or occupation) so that they can be

TABLE 13.1 Example codebook entry for a single question in a questionnaire

Question number	15
Variable name	Licence
Question wording	What type of driving licence do you hold?
Categories and codes	Full driving licence = 1 Provisional driving licence = 2 Do not hold a driving licence = 3
Special instructions	Leave missing values blank

analyzed using appropriate statistical techniques. For example, rather than entering the words 'full-time' or 'part-time' in the data matrix for a variable recording employment status, you would allocate each response category a number (e.g. full-time = 0, part-time = 1) and enter the number instead, as shown in column B of the data grid in Figure 13.2. For variables where there are more than two categories each category is similarly allocated its own unique number. The resulting coding scheme should be carefully recorded by building up a codebook that contains the question number, question wording, the variable to which it refers and the coding structure used, as shown in Table 13.1. The details can also be added to your data collection matrix if you have created one (see Chapter 10).

Where data are captured using Likert-type scales, the responses should be coded and entered as numerical values rather than statements. A five-point response scale, for example, labelled 'strongly disagree' to 'strongly agree' could be coded 'strongly disagree' = 1 to 'strongly agree' = 5, with the mid-point 'neither agree nor disagree' being coded 3.

13.2.3 Managing your data

Good data management is essential in any research project to guard against potential data loss and data corruption as well as manage version control and maintain data security, so make sure that you

- create a backup of your master data, stored in a secure environment separately from your working copy of the data on your laptop or PC hard drive;
- save your work regularly, making backups of your working files, including any analysis output;
- record any changes you make to your master data set and store a fresh backup copy in a secure environment;
- update your research diary/log, recording any changes, insights, or conclusions from your analysis;
- store and/or destroy the data securely at the end of the project in accordance with relevant data protection rules and any agreements made with respondents or other stakeholders as part of data collection.

If you are carrying out a project for an academic qualification you will probably be required to keep a copy of your data until your award is confirmed. Make sure that you understand the requirements of your institution regarding data handling, storage, and disposal.

13.3 PREPARING YOUR DATA FOR ANALYSIS

Once your data have been entered, you can start final preparation for analysis, beginning with **data cleansing**. This involves the following steps:

- checking for errors
- dealing with missing values
- transforming your data to facilitate analysis
- checking scale reliability

13.3.1 Checking for errors

Errors can occur during data collection or data entry. Error checking takes time and can be boring but needs to be done; it is also better to do it early rather than wasting time analyzing faulty data. Actions to take include the following.

- Check that the responses fall within the valid range for the variable. A score of 55 on a five-point Likert-type rating scale, for example, is obviously wrong.
- If filter questions have been used in a questionnaire, confirm that the rules have been applied correctly. For example, if someone indicates in response to a filter question that they have not used a particular service, they should not then go on to rate the quality of that service.
- Look for logical inconsistencies in responses. A person who responds that they are 20 years old in one question should not report that they have 30 years' work experience in another.
- Confirm that respondents fall within the target population.

Correct errors where possible; cases with errors that cannot be corrected should be removed from the data set. Where a case should not have been included in the sample, it should also be removed. Note any changes and the reasons for them in your research diary/log.

13.3.2 Dealing with missing values

For some observations in your data matrix, there may be no data entered in a particular cell. This might be because the question did not apply to that particular case, because the respondent failed to answer, or because the data could not otherwise be obtained. These cells represent **missing values**. It can be useful to code such missing values in a consistent way to distinguish, for example, between failure to respond, non-applicability, or other data problems. SPSS allows you to predefine a number of missing values. (If using MS Excel, you can leave the cell blank and use the comments function to record the reason for the missing value.)

Missing values in a data matrix are a fact of life in many research projects and need to be dealt with as they can affect your analysis by reducing sample size, distorting summary statistics, and potentially introducing **bias** if there is a systematic pattern to the missing data. One option is deletion. Hair et al. (2020) suggest exclusion of a case or variable if the missing data points exceed 15 per cent of the total. Alternatively, cases with missing values may be excluded on a variable-by-variable basis; otherwise they remain in the data set (this could apply, for example, when question did not apply to a particular respondent). A third option is substitution, in which another value (such as the sample mean) is substituted for the missing value. Whatever decisions you make regarding missing values should be reported in your final write-up.

13.3.3 Transforming your data to facilitate analysis

Data transformation is the process of changing your original data to a new format to facilitate analysis or reporting. This can include recoding data into new categories, such as recoding nominal data into a smaller number of groups. For example, information about a respondent's town or city of residence might be recoded according to the county, state, or province in which the town or city is located in order to reduce the number of categories. Recoded data may be easier to report, or recoding may be needed if the number of cases in each original category is too small for analysis. If recoding, always ensure that the original data are kept for checking or further analysis.

Negatively worded questions

Another common data transformation task is **reverse coding** any questions with negatively worded statements (see Chapter 10). This is often needed if you are intending to combine both positively and negatively worded questions in a summated scale, but it can also be useful if you are comparing results from both negatively and positively worded questions. For a five-point Likert-type scale, for example, reverse coding involves changing a rating of 5 to a rating of 1, 4 to 2, 2 to 4 and 5 to 1 (3 does not need to be changed). Specialist software such as SPSS includes routines to facilitate recoding, and it can be done easily in MS Excel.

Summated scales

If your research involves using summated, multi-item scales to measure certain concepts you will need to calculate the combined scale. Table 13.2 shows an example of a summated scale where the mean of the responses to five questions (PU1 to PU5) is calculated to give an overall measure of Perceived Usefulness (PU) for each respondent. If you are using existing scales, you should check to see what summation method is appropriate for your chosen scale.

TABLE 13.2 Example summated scale (PU = perceived usefulness)

Respondent ID	PU1	PU2	PU3	PU4	PU5	PU (Mean of PU 1–5)
1	3	2	3	3	3	2.8
2	5	5	5	5	3	4.6
3	3	3	5	4	3	3.6
4	3	3	2	3	2	2.6
5	4	4	5	5	4	4.4

13.3.4 Checking scale reliability

If you are using summated scales to measure a concept you need to ensure that respondents' answers to the items (questions) are consistent. If they are not, it may indicate that the scale is not a reliable measure. A common test of scale reliability is Cronbach's coefficient alpha (or just **Cronbach's alpha**), which returns a score between 0 and 1. The higher the score, the higher the reliability of the scale. A common rule of thumb is that an alpha of 0.7 is an appropriate threshold to indicate a reliable scale, although scores between 0.6 and 0.7 may also be accepted (Hair et al., 2019). Cronbach's alpha can be generated in SPSS and calculated in MS Excel. See the companion website for more details.

13.4 EXPLORING AND DESCRIBING YOUR DATA

Once your data are ready for analysis, the next stage is data exploration using summary statistics and graphical display techniques. The initial goal is to get a feel for your data set and what it is telling you about your sample. Throughout the data exploration stage, you should be alert to anomalies or other interesting or unexpected features of your data that warrant further investigation, whilst also keeping your research questions in mind. Ensure that you record what you have done by saving appropriate output and noting your emerging thoughts in your research diary/log.

Begin by exploring each variable individually, a process known as **univariate analysis**. Once you have a sound understanding at the univariate level, you can then investigate any differences or associations between variables or groups. Is there, for example, an association between customer satisfaction and loyalty? Do full-time employees differ from part-time employees in their level of engagement? Analysis of two variables simultaneously is known as **bivariate analysis**; analysis of more than two is known as **multivariate analysis**.

The culmination of this stage of analysis is to finalise a set of descriptive statistics that will summarize your sample and key variables in your data set for inclusion in your final report. When you reach this point, you are should be ready to start working on the next level of analysis: answering your research question.

We will now look at techniques for analyzing and describing sample data, beginning with univariate analysis.

13.4.1 Univariate data exploration techniques

Univariate analysis techniques can be used to describe and summarize each variable in your sample, typically in terms of four main characteristics:

- frequency distribution
- central tendency
- dispersion
- shape of the distribution

Choosing an analysis technique

The choice of analysis technique is strongly influenced by the measurement level of your data (i.e. nominal, ordinal, interval or metric as discussed in Chapter 10). Table 13.3 lists techniques for exploring and summarizing data, along with the measurement level with which they are most compatible. For some analysis techniques, data may need recoding into a smaller number of categories if the number of categories is too large to be handled easily.

13.4.2 What is the frequency distribution of a variable?

One of the first things you will want to know is how much of your sample falls within different categories or ranges of values for each variable. This is referred to as the variable's **frequency distribution**. Tabular and graphical techniques can be used to explore and present this information.

Frequency tables

Frequency tables provide a very useful way of investigating the frequency distribution of nominal and ordinal variables, as shown in Figure 13.3. Metric (interval or ratio) data will often need to be recoded into a smaller number of range bands, in which case they can be treated as ordinal data. Where there are missing values in the data set, as here, an additional column can be included to report valid per cent. This is the percentage of the total of non-missing values for each category in the sample. This is the fourth column in Figure 13.3. Rows represent categories, with the last row providing totals for the columns. Note the use of the letter n in the caption, to indicate sample size.

    Frequency tables allow you to see whether responses are fairly evenly distributed across the categories by checking whether the percentages for each category are similar. When presenting frequency tables in reports, a simplified format is often used. These contain only the category frequency counts and valid per cent information, as shown in Table 13.4.

TABLE 13.3 Common univariate descriptive statistics and graphical presentation techniques

Category	Typical applications	Summary statistic/ descriptive technique	Measurement level of data		
			Nominal	Ordinal	Metric (interval/ ratio)
Frequency distribution	Examine and report the frequency distribution of responses	Frequency tables	Yes	Yes	Yes (may need recoding)
Measures of central tendency	Identify and report a typical response value for the variable	Mode	Yes	Yes	Yes (may need recoding)
		Median		Yes	Yes
		Mean			Yes
Measures of dispersion	Measure and report the extent to which the responses are spread out	Minimum/ Maximum/Range		Yes	Yes
		Interquartile range			Yes
		Variance/standard deviation			Yes
Shape of the distribution	Measure and report the extent to which the variable conforms to a normal distribution	Skewness			Yes
		Kurtosis			Yes
Graphical techniques	Examine and report the distribution of responses graphically	Pie chart	Yes	Yes	Yes (may need recoding)
		Bar chart	Yes	Yes	Yes (may need recoding)
		Histogram			Yes
		Box plot			Yes

Exploring and presenting frequency distributions graphically

Bar charts can be used to depict the data in frequency tables and to explore the frequency distribution of nominal and ordinal variables in a more visual way. Each bar represents a particular category or value of the variable and the height or length of the bar represents the frequency count or valid per cent of the observations in that category. Example horizontal and vertical bar charts are shown in Figure 13.4 using the data in Table 13.4. (Note that M Excel refers to vertical bar charts as column charts.)

Bar charts can be used with any level of measurement, but **histograms** are commonly used for showing the frequency distribution of a metric variable and for spotting potential

Employment Status

		Frequency	Percent	Valid Percent	Cumulative Percent
Valid	Full time	17	28.3	29.3	29.3
	Part time	41	68.3	70.7	100.0
	Total	58	96.7	100.0	
Missing	System	2	3.3		
Total		60	100.0		

FIGURE 13.3 Frequency table of respondent employment status (n = 60) (created in SPSS)

TABLE 13.4 Simplified frequency table showing frequency of car driving (n = 1220)

Car driving frequency	Count	Per cent
Every day	783	64.2
At least 3 times per week	264	21.6
1–2 times per week	127	10.4
Less than once per week	46	3.8
Total	1220	100.0

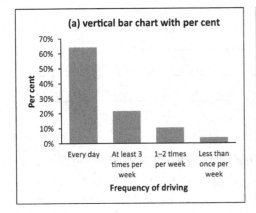
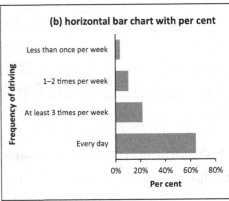

FIGURE 13.4 Bar charts showing frequency of car driving (n = 1220)

extreme values. They are normally drawn vertically as a series of bars with no gaps in between, as shown in Figure 13.5. When creating a histogram, the range of observed values in the variable is divided into class intervals or bins. These intervals, which are usually equal, are known as the bin range and are shown on the horizontal axis. In the example

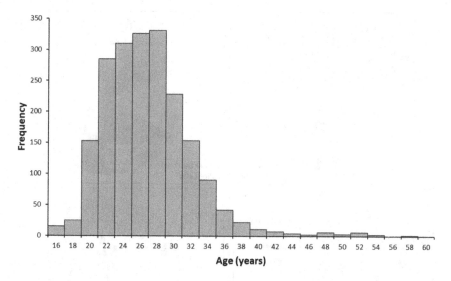

FIGURE 13.5 Histogram showing the age of medal winners in the 2016 Olympic Games (data from Griffin, 2018)

in Figure 13.5 the intervals are set at two years. The height of the bar represents the frequency of cases in the class interval.

Pie charts can be used to depict the data in a frequency table in a more visual way by representing each category as a slice of a pie. The relative size of each slice indicates the proportion of the whole represented by each category. Pie charts can be used with any measurement level but are primarily useful where the aim is to show differences in proportions. Figure 13.6 shows different examples of pie charts based on the same data set.

What is a typical value for a variable?

Measures of **central tendency** (or location) can be used to identify a typical value or average response for a variable. The three most commonly encountered are:

1. The **mode**, which is the most frequently occurring value for the variable. It can be used for any level of measurement (metric data may need to be grouped) but is the only measure of central tendency applicable to nominal data.

2. The **median**, which is the value that is in the middle of the distribution, i.e. has 50 per cent of the observed values lying below it and 50 per cent above it (Figure 13.7). It can be used for ordinal and metric data. An advantage of the median is that it is relatively insensitive to extreme values.

3. The arithmetic **mean**, which is the arithmetic average of the data set. The mean is the most commonly encountered measure of central tendency for metric data, but it is influenced by extreme values.

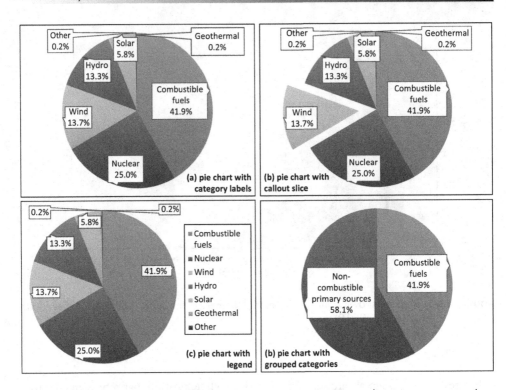

FIGURE 13.6 Example pie charts showing European Union EU27 net electricity generation by source, 2021 (Eurostat, 2023)

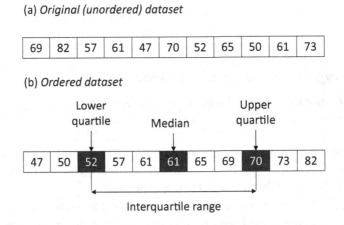

FIGURE 13.7 Calculating the median and interquartile range for a data set

13.4.3 How spread out are the responses?

Measures of dispersion (or spread) provide a way of summarizing the level of agreement between cases for a particular variable and indicate how well your chosen measure of central tendency typifies the variable. Common measures include:

- The **range**, which is the spread of data from the minimum to the maximum value for the variable. Range is a simple measure of spread, applicable to ordinal and metric data. The maximum and minimum values can also be reported along with the range.
- The **interquartile range**, which is the range between the bottom and the top 25 per cent of the observations, known as the lower and upper quartiles (Figure 13.7). It can be applied to ordinal or metric data. The smaller the inter-quartile range, the better the median is as a summary of the data. The interquartile range can be shown graphically on box plots.
- The **variance** and **standard deviation**, which are both measures of how far the distribution is spread out from the mean. Although variance is an important measure, we often report the standard deviation (which is the square root of the variance), since this is measured in the same units as the mean, which makes it easier to interpret. The lower the standard deviation, the better the mean is as a summary of the data. Both are applicable to metric data only.

Looking for outliers or extreme values

An **outlier** is an observation with characteristics that are distinctly different from other observations in the sample, such as a very high or very low value for a particular variable. Outliers may arise as the result of data collection or data entry errors that have not been detected during data cleansing; these should be corrected as described earlier. Others may be accurate observations for which you have an explanation but which still strongly influence the findings. Outliers may also be observations for which you have no explanation; these may indicate some aspect of the population of which you were not aware and warrant further investigation. Outliers can exert a strong influence on some statistical measures such as the arithmetic mean, as we show in Research in Practice 13.1.

Looking for outliers is an important part of the data exploration process. Frequency tables and graphical displays and minimum/maximum values can be used to help identify potential outliers, following which they should be thoroughly investigated before you decide what action to take. One approach is to employ analysis techniques that are less sensitive to outliers (such as using the median rather than the mean). In extreme cases you may need to remove outliers from your analysis, but this should be a last resort. Any action that you take regarding outliers should be discussed and justified in your final report.

Research in practice 13.1 Outlier or not?

To illustrate the potential problem that outliers can cause, Hair et al. (2020) cite the example of the impact of US businessman and founder of Amazon Jeff Bezos' personal net worth on calculations of the average (mean) net worth of households in Medina, Washington, where he lives. According to their calculations, the average net worth of Medina households including Jeff Bezos was just over US$82 million in 2018. Removing Bezos (net worth US$112 billion at that time) from the calculation brings the average net worth of the remaining households down to just over US$21.5 million. Removing two other very wealthy individuals (one of whom is Bill Gates) with a combined net worth of US$92 billion brings the average household net worth down to US$222,000. But what figure provides the most representative picture of household net worth in Medina? Should Bezos (and others) be excluded from the analysis? Should a different analysis technique be selected, one that is less sensitive to extreme values? 'The answer', as Hair et al. (2020: 349) put it, 'depends on the research objectives'.

13.4.4 Exploring the shape of a variable's distribution

Examining the shape of the frequency distribution of your ordinal and metric variables will give you a better understanding of how well your summary statistics capture relevant features of the data. It will also help you to identify any outliers and to check whether or not your data meet any assumptions required by statistical tests that you plan to use later. In particular, you may need to check whether or not your data conform to a normal distribution.

Is a variable normally distributed?

Some statistical tests require that your data are normally distributed. The **normal distribution** (also known as a Gaussian distribution) can be identified by its characteristic bell shape (Figure 13.8). It is symmetrical about a single central peak, which represents the most frequently occurring value of the distribution (i.e. the mode), with the mode, median, and mean all being identical. Another interesting property of the normal distribution is that almost all of the distribution (99.73 per cent) lies within ± 3 standard deviations (σ) of the mean (μ).

A variable may differ from a normal distribution in one of three main ways:

1. *The number of peaks* (modes). The normal distribution has a single peak and is therefore **unimodal** (i.e. it has one mode). Data with more than one peak is described as **bimodal** (two peaks) or **multimodal** (more than two peaks) and may suggest subgroups within the data that are worth further investigation (Figure 13.9).

2. *Lack of symmetry.* Asymmetrical data are said to be skewed (Figure 13.10), and **skewness** can be identified visually by the longer 'tail' of values to one side or the other. If

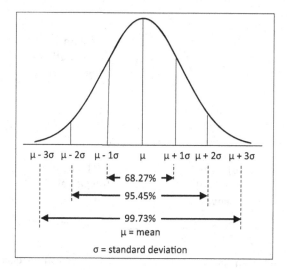

FIGURE 13.8 Normal distribution

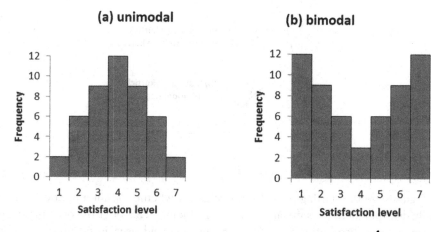

FIGURE 13.9 Unimodal and bimodal data

the tail runs in the direction of the higher values, it is right tailed or positively skewed. In the opposite direction it is left tailed or negatively skewed. The mean of skewed data will tend to be pulled in the direction of the skew. Extreme skewness may indicate the existence of outliers.

3. *Relative 'peakiness'.* **Kurtosis** is the term used to describe the extent to which a distribution is peaked or flat (Figure 13.11). A 'flat' distribution exhibits negative kurtosis and is said to be platykurtic. A 'peaked' distribution shows positive kurtosis and is described as leptokurtic. Extreme kurtosis is an indication that the distribution of the data is non-normal.

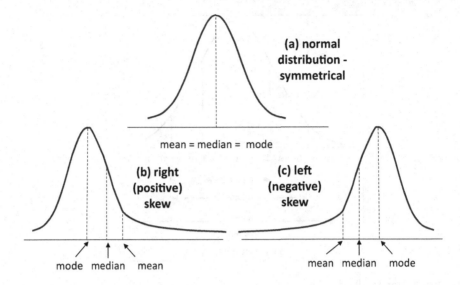

FIGURE 13.10 Skewness

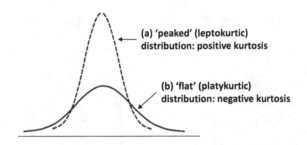

FIGURE 13.11 Kurtosis

Histograms are the starting point for investigating whether or not a metric variable is normally distributed. Some software packages, including SPSS, offer the option of superimposing a normal distribution curve over a histogram to aid visual inspection. In addition, you can calculate summary statistics that measure skewness and kurtosis. For both measures, a perfectly normal distribution should return a score of 0. Otherwise:

- A positive skewness value indicates positive (right) skew; a negative value indicates negative (left) skew. The higher the absolute value, the greater the skew.
- Similarly, a positive kurtosis value indicates positive kurtosis; a negative one indicates negative kurtosis. The higher the absolute value, the greater the kurtosis.

Further details on interpreting skewness and kurtosis statistics can be found on the companion website, along with a discussion of the **Kolmogorov-Smirnov** and the **Shapiro-Wilk** statistical tests that can be used to test the assumption that your sample data are drawn from a normally distributed population.

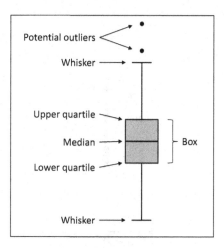

FIGURE 13.12 Components of a typical box plot

A **box plot** can be used to identify potential outliers and to explore the shape of the variable's distribution. A box plot (also known a box-and-whisker plot) consists of a box-shaped area that shows the interquartile range and contains a bar indicating the median. Attached to the box are two 'whiskers' which represent more extreme values. Conventions vary regarding the whiskers. In SPSS, for example, the box plot whiskers extend to the smallest and largest values that are within one and a half lengths of each end of the box. Values beyond that are individually flagged. Figure 13.12 shows the components of a typical box plot.

Figure 13.13 gives an example box plot created in SPSS using the Olympic medal winner age data set shown in the histogram in Figure 13.5. Note the potential outliers. Each one has been individually numbered to make it easier to identify in the data set for further checking. SPSS also highlights observations with values more than three times the height of a box with an asterisk or star (*).

13.4.5 Describing your data

You should now be ready to generate a structured description of your sample data using appropriate descriptive statistics and graphical techniques. This will typically include the following:

- A summary of your sample and its demographics characteristics
- Univariate descriptive statistics for key variables (see Table 13.5 for an example)

Regardless of whatever further analysis is required, these will normally be included in your research report. Sample demographics will typically appear in the research design section and univariate descriptive statistics early in the results and findings section.

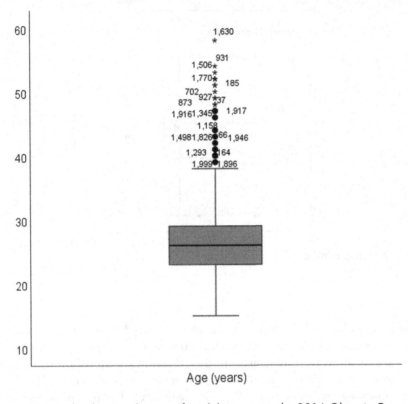

FIGURE 13.13 Box plot showing the age of medal winners in the 2016 Olympic Games (data from Griffin, 2018)

TABLE 13.5 Example of univariate descriptive statistics for key variables in a small study

Measure	n	Mean	Standard deviation	Range	Skewness	Kurtosis
Effective communication	72	6.0	1.04	5.7	−2.12	5.90
Genuineness of relationship	72	5.6	1.14	5.0	−1.53	2.42
Would recommend to others	72	5.7	1.42	5.0	−1.10	0.41

13.4.6 Exploring more than one variable at once

Many interesting problems in quantitative analysis can be addressed only by combining data from two or move variables simultaneously. For instance,

- to investigate whether or not there are differences between groups with respect to their scores on variables of interest;
- to investigate whether or not two or more variables are associated.

TABLE 13.6 Techniques for exploring more than one variable

Purpose	Statistic/ technique	Measurement level		
		Nominal	Ordinal	Metric (interval/ ratio)
Compare different groups or different variables with respect to their scores on metric variables of interest	Tables of means	Yes (as a grouping variable)	Yes (as a grouping variable)	Yes
	Bar chart of means	Yes (as a grouping variable)	Yes (as a grouping variable)	Yes
	Box plot	Yes (as a grouping variable)	Yes	Yes
Explore the association between two nominal or ordinal variables	Contingency tables	Yes	Yes	
	Clustered bar chart	Yes	Yes	
	Stacked bar chart	Yes	Yes	
Explore the association between two metric variables	Scatter plot			Yes

This is the domain of bivariate and multivariate analysis, and in Table 13.6 we summarize a range of techniques that can be used for exploring your data.

Exploring differences between groups

Tables offer a simple way of comparing the means of different groups in your sample, as shown in Table 13.7. In addition, if the categories are ordinal, the table can be inspected to see if there is any direction to the relationship. In Table 13.7, for example, you can see that the mean level of satisfaction decreases with age; this suggests that there is a negative association between customer age and customer satisfaction levels in the sample data.

Group means can also be presented visually using bar charts. Each bar represents a category within the categorical variable, and the height or length of the bar represents the mean of the metric variable, as shown in Figure 13.14a. Where the values of the metric variable fall within a very narrow range, it may be desirable to truncate the scale used for the metric variable rather than show the full range of the scale (Figure 13.14b). Truncating the scale will tend to emphasize visually any differences between the groups but can also be misleading, so always ensure that you clearly indicate the axis scale.

TABLE 13.7 Table of mean satisfaction levels by customer age group (n = 175)

Age group	Mean (1 = highly dissatisfied, 7 = highly satisfied)	Standard deviation	Min.	Max.	Range	n
18–29	5.10	.898	3	7	4	30
30–39	4.72	1.108	2	7	5	35
40–49	4.19	1.055	2	6	4	38
50–59	3.91	.969	2	6	4	41
60 and over	3.70	.961	2	6	4	31
Total	4.30	1.111	2	7	5	175

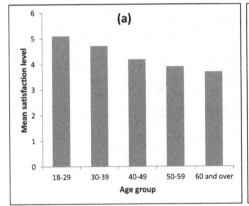 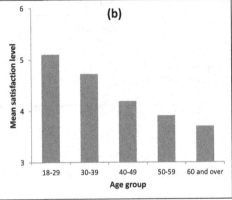

FIGURE 13.14 Bar charts of mean satisfaction levels by customer age group (data from Table 13.6)

If you have ordinal or metric data as one variable and categorical data as the other, multiple box plots can be used to compare different categories, with each box plot representing the scores for one group of the categorical variable as shown in Figure 13.15. Note how the box plot, by combining information about dispersion and central tendency, reveals that there is considerable overlap between adjacent age groups. Multiple box plots can also be used to compare two or more metric or ordinal variables.

Exploring associations between categorical variables

Researchers are often interested in exploring associations between categorical variables. Is there, for example, an association between how often people drive and their level of

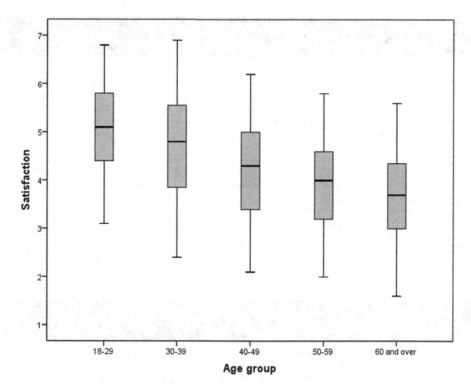

FIGURE 13.15 Multiple box plots of mean satisfaction levels by customer age group (data from Table 13.6)

income? **Contingency tables** provide a starting point for answering such questions. The basic layout is illustrated in Table 13.8, which shows a contingency table created using data relating to frequency of driving and household income. Contingency table layouts can be described using the format: number of rows × number of columns (r × c), so this is a 3 × 4 contingency table. The numbers in the cells are frequency counts, showing how many observations fall into each. Totals are also given for each row and each column. These are referred to as marginal totals. In addition there is a grand total (i.e. the total sample size) in the bottom right-hand corner of the table.

Frequency counts are not always easy to interpret, especially if the group sizes are different, so it is common practice to convert them to percentages. If one of the variables is assumed to be the independent variable, it is conventional to use the total number of observations in each category of that variable to calculate the percentages. In Table 13.9 we have selected household income as the independent variable because we believe that it may affect driving frequency. Percentages are therefore calculated as row percentages (if column totals had been used, then the percentages of each column would have summed to 100).

From the percentages for each income category for each driving frequency category in Table 13.9, you can see that there appears to be an association between income and driving frequency. Looking at the first column of the table, you can also see that the

TABLE 13.8 Contingency table showing driving frequency of licence holders aged 17 and household income, showing counts (n = 1220)

	Driving frequency				
	Every day	At least 3 times per week	1–2 times per week	Less than once per week	Totals
Annual household income					
Up to £20,000	205	110	55	23	393
£20,000 to £35,000	228	72	36	13	349
Over £35,000	350	82	36	10	478
Totals	783	264	127	46	1220

TABLE 13.9 Contingency table showing driving frequency of licence holders aged 17 and household income, showing per cent of row totals (n = 1220)

	Driving frequency				
	Every day	At least 3 times per week	1–2 times per week	Less than once per week	Totals
	(%)	(%)	(%)	(%)	(%)
Annual household income					
Up to £20,000	52	28	14	6	100
£20,000 to £35,000	65	21	10	4	100
Over £35,000	73	17	8	2	100
Totals	64	22	10	4	100

proportion of those driving every day increases with household income, suggesting a positive association between household income and driving frequency (73% > 65% > 52%): driving frequency increases as household income rises. Note how much easier it is to interpret the percentages as compared to the simple counts, given the unequal group sizes and larger number of cells.

Clustered bar charts can be used to display the data from contingency tables graphically. Figure 13.16 shows the data from Table 13.9 presented in this way. Driving frequency is used for the horizontal axis and the bars in each cluster represent the percentage of observations for each category of the household income variable. Notice how the chart underlines

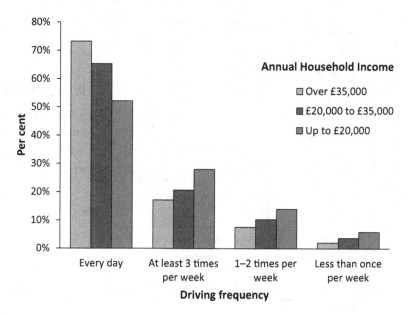

FIGURE 13.16 Clustered bar charts of driving frequency by annual household income (n = 1220)

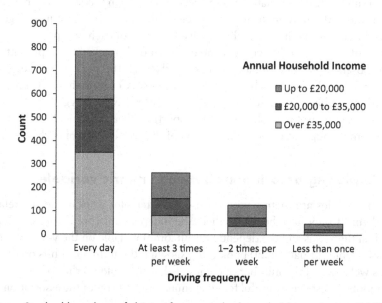

FIGURE 13.17 Stacked bar chart of driving frequency by household income (n = 1220)

the association in the sample data between income and driving frequency and that inspection of the two outside driving frequency groups confirms that the relation is positive.

Another way of presenting contingency tables is to use a **stacked bar chart** as shown in Figure 13.17. This time the observations from the household income category groups are

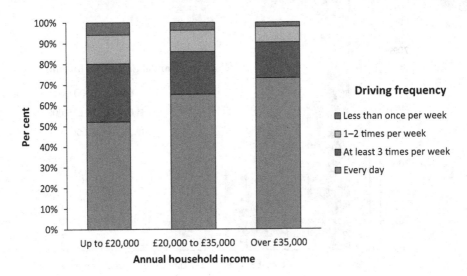

stacked in a single bar rather than clustered side by side. Each section of the bar represents the proportion of the household income category for that driving frequency group. The overall height of each bar indicates the relative total size of each group.

A variant of the stacked bar chart is one in which each stacked bar represents 100 per cent of the observations for that bar (MS Excel calls this a 100 per cent stacked bar chart). As shown in Figure 13.18, each bar represents a category of household income, and each section within the bar represents the per cent of each driving category in that bar. This layout is particularly useful for showing the proportion of each driving frequency category for each income group but loses any indication of the relative size of each income group.

13.4.7 Exploring associations between metric variables

When both variables are metric, you can use a **scatter plot** to examine the relationship between them. If they have been specified, the independent (predictor) variable should be plotted on the x-axis and the dependent (outcome) variable on the y-axis. Figure 13.19 shows a scatter plot of data on 30 book titles, showing the number of hits on each title in the seller's website and the number of copies of that title sold on the website.

Scatter plots are especially useful for examining four features of the association between two metric variables.

- *Whether the association is positive or negative*. If the association between two variables is positive, a high score on one variable is associated with a high score on the other; in a scatter plot this is shown when the line of points run upwards from left to right (Figure 13.20a). A negative association, on the other hand, is indicated when the slope runs downwards from left to right (Figure 13.20b).

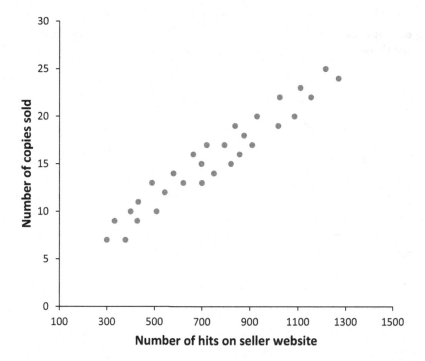

FIGURE 13.19 Scatter plot of number of hits on seller website and the number of copies sold online for 30 different book titles

- *Whether or not the relationship is linear.* A linear relationship is characterized by the data points lying in roughly a straight line. Departures from linearity can take many different forms. One possibility is a curvilinear relationship, as shown in Figure 13.20c. Some statistical measures of association (such as the Pearson correlation coefficient) make the assumption that the relationship is linear; this can be checked using scatter plots.
- *The strength of the relationship.* The more concentrated the points, the stronger the relationship between the variables; conversely, the more scattered they are, the weaker the relationship. Summary statistics of relationship strength are available, but visual inspection of a scatter plot is the starting point.
- *Identifying outliers.* Observations with unusual combinations of values may constitute outliers from the overall pattern, as we show in Figure 13.20d, where two points in the lower right corner are distinctly different from the general pattern. Such outliers can affect the assumption of linearity and exert a strong influence on some analysis techniques. They should be examined closely and, if appropriate, removed from the analysis.

In the example in Figure 13.19, there is clearly a positive association between book sales and website hits (sales go up as the number of hits increases); the relationship is fairly linear and looks quite strong with no outliers.

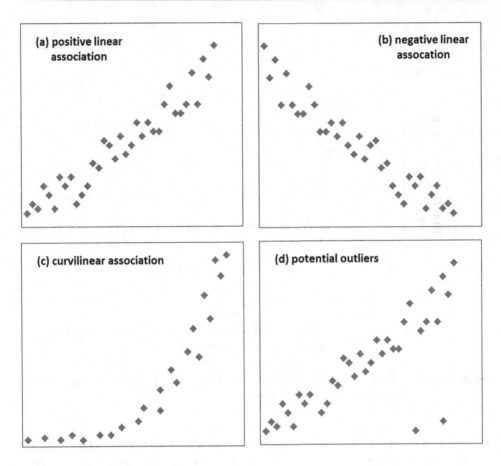

FIGURE 13.20 Example scatter plots

13.4.8 Exploring time series data

A **time series** is a form of longitudinal data that consists of a sequence of observations over time. Usually the observations are of a single entity (such as a firm, industry, or country) at regular intervals (such as monthly or yearly) over a fairly long period. Time series are very common in business and management, whether dealing with aspects of the organization such as its sales, staffing levels, and numbers of customers, or of the broader economy such as national income, unemployment, or retail sales. Visual inspection is important for analyzing time series, so one of the first things that you should do is plot your time series as a line chart. Time is plotted along the horizontal x-axis, the values for the variable on the vertical y-axis. Figure 13.21 shows two plots of the same time series. The visual difference is due to the differences in the scaling of the vertical axis. Figure 13.21b chart has a much higher resolution which emphasizes the change over time; in Figure 13.21a the change is barely discernible. As with any other graph, care needs to be taken both when drawing and interpreting time series plots.

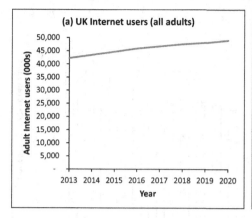 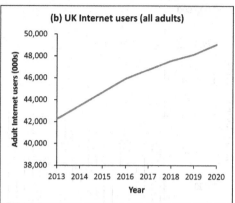

FIGURE 13.21 UK Internet users (all adults), thousands 2013–2020 (ONS, 2021)

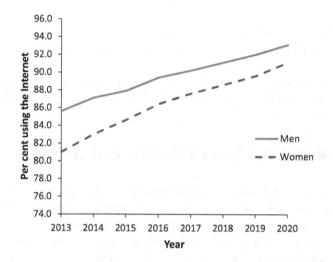

FIGURE 13.22 Time series plot showing per cent adult Internet users by sex, UK 2013–2020 (all adults) (ONS, 2021)

Two or more sets of time series data can be plotted for comparison of trend and other features. Figure 13.22, for example, compares the use of the Internet by sex over a seven-year period.

If the time series are measured in different units, it can be useful to use index numbers. Alternatively, different scales can be used on the vertical axes. In some cases it is clearer to use a different chart type (such as a bar chart) to emphasize differences in scale. Figure 13.23 shows this by presenting changes in total US retail sales between 2000 and 2021, plotted as a bar chart with the scale on the right, and the per cent of total sales represented by electronic shopping and mail-order houses, plotted as a line graph with the scale on the left.

Further details on time series analysis can be found on the companion website.

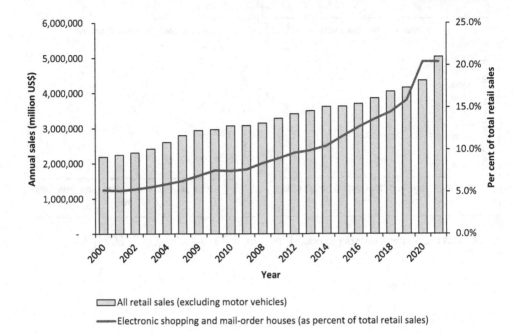

FIGURE 13.23 Time series plot showing total retail sales (excluding motor vehicles) and electronic shopping and mail-order house sales as per cent of total retail sales, USA 2000–2021 (US Census Bureau, 2021)

13.5 ANSWERING YOUR RESEARCH QUESTIONS

We have called the next step in the analysis process 'answering your research questions', to stress the need to focus your analysis on achieving your research objectives. This stage involves applying appropriate analysis techniques to your data and interpreting the results. Choice of technique depends upon your research questions. It is also heavily influenced by the level of measurement used and how many variables are being analyzed at once.

13.5.1 Descriptive and inferential statistics

Before looking at specific statistical techniques, we need to explain the crucial difference between descriptive and inferential statistics. **Descriptive statistics**, such as the sample mean or standard deviation, are used to analyze, summarize, and simplify your sample data. **Inferential statistics**, on the other hand, are used to make inferences about the population based on the sample data. To illustrate this distinction and the reason we need to make use of inferential statistics, suppose that you were investigating whether or not there is a difference between full-time and part-time employees in terms of their level of engagement. You use descriptive statistics to explore your sample data and find that the mean engagement level is higher for full-time employees than it is for part-time employees. But does this difference hold for the population of all company employees or only for those in your sample? Here you run into a problem: **sampling error**.

Sampling error refers to the naturally occurring difference between a sample statistic and the true measure for the population. As part of your analysis, you will want to know whether the difference between the engagement levels of the two groups in your sample may be due to sampling error rather than to an underlying difference between full-time and part-time employees. This is where inferential statistics come in. You could use a suitable inferential statistical test to see whether it is likely that the difference in engagement levels found in your sample reflects an underlying difference in the overall population or has come about as a result of sampling error. Note that because of sampling error even inferential statistics do not allow us to be absolutely certain, but they do give us an indication of how confident we can be in our findings in relation to the population.

Inferential statistics have two critical applications in quantitative research projects:

1. to estimate population parameters
2. to test hypotheses

We will begin by looking at how to use inferential statistics to estimate population parameters, before examining hypothesis testing in more detail.

13.5.2 Estimating population parameters

The characteristics of the sample are known as **sample statistics**; the characteristics of the population are known as **population parameters**. For example, the mean of the sample data is a sample statistic, but the mean of the population from which the sample came is a population parameter. Sample statistics, such as the sample mean, provide a **point estimate** of the corresponding population parameter (i.e. the population mean), but in practice a point estimate cannot be expected to provide an exact value of a given population parameter due to sampling error. You can, however, use inferential statistics to provide an estimated range of plausible values for the unknown population parameter. Such **interval estimates** are called **confidence intervals** and have the general form:

Point estimate ± Margin of error

The point estimate is normally the relevant sample statistic (e.g. the sample mean) and the margin of error is calculated according to a desired confidence level. The result is two numbers which are the lower and upper boundaries for the confidence interval, either side of the point estimate, as we show in Figure 13.24.

It is common to calculate confidence intervals at the 95 per cent confidence level (although 90 per cent and 99 per cent intervals are also used). What this 95 per cent means is that if we took 100 samples at random from the population, 95 of them would fall within the boundaries of the confidence interval. The higher the confidence level, the wider the interval that will be calculated, so a 99 per cent confidence interval will be wider than a 95 per cent confidence interval for the same data. Interval width is also affected by the variability in the sample (higher variability increases interval width) and by sample size (higher sample size reduces interval width). Research in Practice 13.2 shows confidence intervals in use.

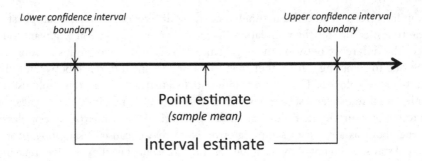

FIGURE 13.24 Point and interval estimates

Research in practice 13.2 How satisfied are the customers?

You have been asked to investigate satisfaction levels among a company's customers. A survey of a random sample of customers shows a mean satisfaction level of 4.25, measured on a seven-point multi-item scale, where 1 is highly unsatisfied and 7 is highly satisfied. Local managers are relieved. Maybe the score is not great – they hoped it would be closer to 6 – but at least it looks positive: the average is just the 'right' side of the scale's midpoint of 4. For your report, you decide to include not just a point estimate of the customer population mean but also confidence intervals, so as to give managers a better idea of the range of plausible values for the true population mean based on the sample data. The table here shows 95 per cent and 99 per cent confidence intervals for the population mean. The 95 per cent confidence interval shows that the lower confidence level is 3.80 and the upper confidence level is 4.70; for the 99 per cent confidence interval, the figures are 3.68 and 4.82, respectively. Note that the 99 per cent confidence interval is wider than the 95 per cent confidence interval. Note also that both confidence intervals include values below 4, indicating that the true population mean may plausibly be below the scale midpoint. Perhaps the local managers will not be so satisfied with their customers' satisfaction levels when they see the final report.

Table of confidence intervals for the mean

Confidence interval	Sample mean	Lower confidence level	Upper confidence level
95%	4.25	3.80	4.70
99%	4.25	3.68	4.82

Confidence intervals are particularly useful for estimating and reporting parameters such as the population mean, and we recommend that they are used and reported when describing a population on the basis of suitable sample data. They are not difficult to calculate using a computer and in SPSS are routinely included as part of the output

TABLE 13.10 Customer satisfaction levels by age group showing confidence intervals for the mean (n = 175)

Age group	n	Mean	Standard deviation	95% confidence interval for mean	
				Lower bound	Upper bound
18–29	30	5.10	0.898	4.76	5.44
30–39	35	4.72	1.108	4.34	5.10
40–49	38	4.19	1.055	3.84	4.53
50–59	41	3.91	0.969	3.60	4.21
60 and over	31	3.70	0.961	3.35	4.06
Total	175	4.30	1.111	4.13	4.46

from a number of different tests. Confidence intervals can also be used to compare the mean scores of different groups, as shown in Table 13.10. If any of the groups' confidence intervals overlap, it cannot be assumed that their population means are different. Confidence intervals can also be plotted visually using a confidence interval chart as shown in Figure 13.25. The chart suggests a negative association between customer age and satisfaction levels but also shows that there is considerable overlap in the confidence intervals between adjacent groups. Further statistical tests can be used to confirm these findings.

13.5.3 Testing hypotheses

In Chapter 4 we introduced deductive research designs that involve formal hypothesis testing. Although it is not always explicitly stated, hypotheses are normally statements about the population being examined, not just the sample. This is important because if you have collected sample data, you face the problem of sampling error. As a result, you cannot simply take the sample statistics as reflecting the true picture for the population, so inferential statistics are used to carry out hypotheses tests. A general procedure for doing so is shown in Figure 13.26, and each step is described in more detail later.

Formulate null and alternative hypotheses

The starting point is to formulate clear, testable hypotheses. Although this is here shown as part of the analysis process, your hypotheses are normally formulated much earlier, as discussed in Chapter 4. They should be closely linked to your research question and to existing theory or prior research. Formulating a hypothesis involves developing two statements, the research (or alternative) hypothesis and the null hypothesis. The **research hypothesis** (typically written as H_1) is a statement of what you expect to find in the data. The **null hypothesis**

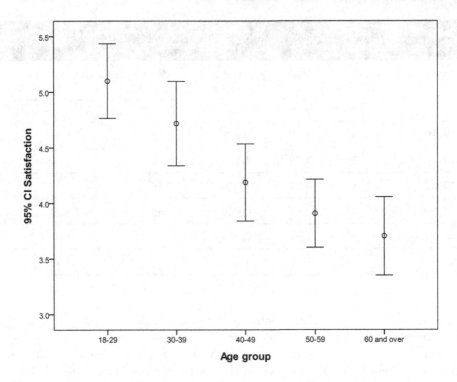

FIGURE 13.25 Chart of confidence intervals (CI) for mean satisfaction levels by customer age group (data from Table 13.9)

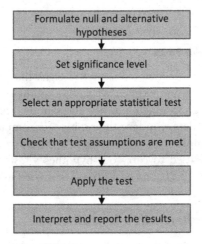

FIGURE 13.26 Hypothesis testing procedure

(written as H_0) is usually a statement that there is no difference or no association between the variables of interest. For example, if you were testing a research hypothesis that there is a difference between full-time and part-time employees' engagement levels, the null hypothesis would be that there is no difference between the two groups.

If you are new to hypothesis testing, the need for a null hypothesis may seem rather strange. It is important, however, because the hypothesis test is actually to see whether the evidence is sufficiently strong for you to be confident in rejecting the null hypothesis. If the null hypothesis is rejected, the research hypothesis is accepted in its place. For this reason, the research hypothesis is also commonly referred to as the **alternative** (or alternate) **hypothesis**.

Table 13.11 shows two examples. The first is about expected differences between two groups. It is what is known as a **nondirectional hypothesis** because it does not specify in which direction the difference should lie, just that they will not be the same. The second example concerns an expected association between two variables. In this case it is formulated as a **directional hypothesis** because the expected direction of the association (i.e. positive) is stated. Where there is more than one research hypothesis to be tested, it is common to number them consecutively (e.g. H_1, H_2, H_3, and so on). (Note that in business research reports, it is standard practice to show only the research hypotheses, with the null hypotheses being implied but not explicitly stated.)

Set the significance level

The next step is to decide on the criteria for rejecting or accepting the null hypothesis. This is done by setting what is called a **significance level**. Referred to by the Greek letter α (alpha, not to be confused with Cronbach's alpha), the significance level is expressed as a probability and specifies the level of risk of committing what is known as a **Type I error** (Figure 13.27). Type I errors occur when you reject the null hypothesis when it is in fact true. In business and management research, α is usually set at 0.05 (i.e. 5 per cent). What this means is that we are prepared to take a 5 in 100 (i.e. 1 in 20 or 5 per cent) chance of rejecting a null hypothesis when it is actually true. If safety were at stake, for instance, in a drug trial, a higher significance level such as 0.01 (1 in 100 chance of a Type I error) might be preferred.

Another possible error is known as a **Type II error** (Figure 13.27). This occurs when the null hypothesis is accepted when it is actually false, so we fail to detect something that is

TABLE 13.11 Example hypothesis statements	
Example 1	
H_1:	There is a difference between the mean level of engagement of full-time employees in Company A and the mean level of engagement of part-time employees in Company A.
H_0:	There is no difference between the mean level of engagement of full-time employees in Company A and the mean level of engagement of part-time employees in Company A.
Example 2	
H_1:	There is a positive association between the number of years working at Company A and level of engagement of employees at Company A.
H_0:	There is not a positive association between the number of years working at Company A and level of engagement for employees at Company A.

	H₀ is true	H₀ is false
Reject H₀	Type I error (α)	Correct
Accept H₀	Correct	Type II error (β)

FIGURE 13.27 Type I and Type II errors

really there. The probability of doing so is referred to as β (beta) error. There is a trade-off between the two types of error. Reducing the probability of a Type I error (by making α smaller) increases the probability of a Type II error.

A related concept is the statistical power of a test. Power refers to the probability of correctly rejecting the null hypothesis when it should be rejected and is equal to $1 - \beta$. In other words, power determines the probability of finding an effect if one is there. It is influenced by the chosen α, but also by the sample size (larger sample sizes give greater power), by the degree of variation in the population (the larger the variation in the population, the lower the power), and by the size of the effect (for example, the magnitude of difference) that you are trying to detect (the smaller the size of the effect, the lower the power).

Select an appropriate statistical test

Selection of an appropriate statistical test depends on what you are testing for and the type of data being analyzed. A useful categorization of statistical tests distinguishes between parametric and nonparametric tests. **Parametric tests** can be used with interval or ratio data and make certain assumptions about the distributional properties of the data. Where those assumptions are not met, or where the data are nominal or ordinal, **nonparametric tests** may be used instead. We present a range of test options later in the chapter. We indicate whether tests are parametric or nonparametric; other test assumptions are discussed in the relevant section for each test on the companion website (see Table 13.13).

Check that the test assumptions are met

Once you have selected your test, you need to check that your data meet any assumptions required by the test. These vary according to the particular test, and we list them when discussing different statistical tests in the companion website. In some cases further testing of assumptions is needed after the test has been run. If the assumptions of the test cannot be met, a different test may have to be applied.

Apply the test

Applying the test is the moment where software programmes come in really handy because they do all (or most) of the number crunching for you, so rather than formulae and lots of calculations, you will usually be presented with the output from the test. To illustrate the process, we present a simplified example test output shown in Table 13.12. It is taken from an independent 2-sample t-test, which tests for the difference in mean scores between two groups. The hypotheses being tested are as follows:

H_1 There is a difference between the mean level of engagement of full-time employees and the mean level of engagement of part-time employees.

H_0 There is no difference between the mean level of engagement of full-time employees and the mean level of engagement of part-time employees.

The table shows that the mean engagement levels for full- and part-time workers are 4.8 and 2.9, respectively, and there are 30 respondents in each group. There is clearly a difference in the mean engagement levels in the sample. You now need to interpret the test results to see whether this difference is likely to apply to the population. There are two key values that you need to check. The first is the **test statistic**, which is calculated as part of the test routine and used to determine the degree to which the sample data are consistent with the null hypothesis. The second is the **p-value** (probability value), which is the probability of observing a test statistic that is at least as extreme as the one that has been observed, assuming that the null hypothesis is true. You can think of the p-value as the probability that your null hypothesis is correct. It will take a value between 0 and 1. In this case the test statistic (t) is 5.584, and the p-value is 0.000.

The output also includes the **degrees of freedom** (df) for the test. Simplifying somewhat, this number represents the number of values that are free to vary when calculating some common test statistics (such as the t-test). Where relevant, it is normally included in the test output, and it is standard practice to report the degrees of freedom in your write-up.

Interpret and report the results

You now compare the p-value from your test results against your pre-specified significance level (α). If the p-value is less than your chosen significance level, you can reject the null hypothesis (H_0) and accept the research (or alternative) hypothesis (H_1). The test result, as shown in Table 13.11, gives $p = 0.000$. Since 0.000 is less than 0.05 (i.e. p is less than α), you reject the null hypothesis (H_0) and accept the research (alternate) hypothesis

TABLE 13.12 Example statistical test output (independent 2-sample t-test)

	Full-time employees	Part-time employees
Mean engagement level	4.8	2.9
Variance	1.84	1.60
Observations	30	30
Degrees of freedom (df)	58	
Test statistic (t)	5.584	
Significance (two-tailed) = p-value	0.000	

(H₁). You conclude that there is a statistically significant difference in the mean level of engagement of full- and part-time employees.

If p had been greater than 0.05, you would have accepted the null hypothesis (H₀) and rejected the research (alternate) hypothesis (H₁). You would have concluded instead that there is no difference in the mean level of engagement of full- and part-time employees.

To sum up the procedure:

- if $p < \alpha$ then reject H₀ and accept H₁;
- if $p \geq \alpha$ then accept H₀ and reject H₁.

Testing directional hypotheses

In the example just given, the research hypothesis (H₁) was nondirectional: it did not specify whether full-timers' level of engagement was more or less than that of part-timers, merely that they were different. The required test therefore just looks for difference, regardless of the direction of that difference. Such tests are known as **two-tailed tests**. Had the research hypothesis been directional (e.g. that part-timers' engagement levels were higher), a **one-tailed test** would have been required. The basic procedure remains the same, but you may need to adjust the p-value if the statistical software you are using reports only the p-value appropriate for a two-tailed test. Further details on running one-tailed tests are given on the companion website.

How significant is significant?

The output of a hypothesis test tells us whether our results are statistically significant but does not tell us much about the practical implications. Remember that the power of a statistical test is influenced by sample size, so a very small difference might therefore turn out to be statistically significant if a large enough sample is used. When interpreting your results, you therefore should evaluate their practical significance as well as their statistical significance. Reporting relevant descriptive statistics, confidence intervals, sample sizes, and full p-values can also help you to communicate the practical significance of your research to readers. In addition, there are a number of standard measures of effect size that can be reported to indicate the magnitude of any observed effect. Further details can be found in Cohen (1992).

13.5.4 Significance tests (1): tests of difference

A very wide range of significance tests are available. We introduce some common ones in this section, grouped into two categories, starting with techniques used for tests of difference, for example, between two or more groups. Tests of this type are important in experimental designs (for example, in comparing pre- and post-test results), for comparing groups in natural experiments and in descriptive studies for testing for differences between demographic groups. These are summarized in Table 13.13.

TABLE 13.13 Significance tests (1): tests of difference

Purpose	Name	Measurement level of variables
Significance test of whether the sample comes from a population with a specified mean (parametric)	One-sample *t*-test	Interval or ratio
Significance test of the difference between the means of two paired samples (parametric)	Paired two-sample *t*-test	Metric (dependent)/categorical with two paired groups (independent)
Significance test of the difference between the means of two independent (not related) samples (parametric)	Independent two-sample *t*-test	Metric (dependent)/categorical with two non-paired groups (independent)
Significance test of the difference between the means of three or more groups (parametric)	One-way, independent analysis of variance (ANOVA)	Metric (dependent)/categorical with more than two groups (independent)
Significance test for difference between two groups (nonparametric)	Mann-Whitney test	Ordinal or metric (dependent)/categorical with two non-paired groups (independent)

Is the sample mean different from a known population mean?

A **one-sample *t*-test** is used to test whether the population mean from which your sample is drawn is the same as a comparison mean specified as part of the test. You could use it, for example, to test whether the level of customer satisfaction in one particular retail store is different from the company's target customer satisfaction level. The one-sample t-test requires interval or ratio data from a single probability sample. The data should be normally distributed, although the test is reasonably robust provided the data are unimodal and fairly symmetrical. The test can be run in SPSS.

Differences in means between two related groups: paired 2-sample *t*-test

The **paired** (or **dependent**) **2-sample** *t*-test is appropriate where the groups are related or paired. A typical example is an experimental design where the same individuals are measured pre- and posttreatment and the researcher wishes to test for differences in the mean of the two scores. The test assumes that the differences between the scores for the two samples are normally distributed. This can be checked by computing the differences (for example in MS Excel or SPSS) and examining for normality. The paired sample *t*-test can be run in MS Excel or SPSS.

Differences in means between two independent groups: independent 2-sample t-test

An **independent 2-sample** *t*-test can be used to compare the mean scores of two independent groups. You might wish to compare, for example, the full-time and part-time employees in your sample in terms of their average age to see whether any difference between them is likely to hold at the population level. The independent 2-sample *t*-test requires a categorical independent variable with two independent groups and an interval or ratio dependent variable. The dependent variable should be normally distributed, and the variance of the two groups should be approximately equal. If the variances are not equal, a version of the test that adjusts for inequality of variance can be used. Both versions of the test can be run in MS Excel or SPSS; the latter also includes the option of testing the assumption of equal variance as part of the test and gives output for the *t*-test adjusted for unequal variance. An example is given in Research in Practice 13.3.

Research in practice 13.3 Independent 2-sample *t*-test

An independent 2-sample *t*-test is being used to determine whether there is a statistically significant difference in levels of customer satisfaction (measured on a seven-point summated scale where 7 is 'highly satisfied') between customers of convenience stores and customers of megastores. The tables in the next section show sample output from SPSS.

The first table (Group Statistics) reports descriptive statistics for the two groups showing that the mean satisfaction level of convenience store shoppers in the sample is higher than that of megastore shoppers (4.79 > 3.33). The sample size (*n*) of each group is 28 and 24 respectively (note that sample sizes do not need to be equal to run this test).

The second table (Independent Samples Test) contains the test results. The first two columns report the results of Levene's test for equality of variance. The null hypothesis for this test is that the variances of the two groups are equal. If the result of this test is significant (i.e. $p < 0.05$), we would conclude that variances are significantly different. In this case it is not significant (0.530 > 0.05), so we would accept the null hypothesis and conclude that the variances of the two groups are equal. This allows us to use the output in the row marked 'Equal variances assumed' when reporting the results of the test. (If the variances are not equal, the results from the row marked 'Equal variances not assumed' should be used instead.) The results of the *t*-test are shown in the columns headed '*t*-test for equality of means'. The test statistic (*t*) is 5.693 with 50 degrees of freedom (df). The two-sided *p*-value is <.001, which is less than the significance level of 0.05; we would therefore conclude that the difference is statistically significant.

The SPSS output also reports the difference between the two means, which is 1.452 (i.e. 4.79–3.33) and includes a 95 per cent confidence interval for the difference. The latter does not include zero, which suggests that zero (i.e. no difference) is not a plausible value for the mean difference at the 95 per cent confidence level, something confirmed by the results of the *t*-test.

Group Statistics

	Store format	N	Mean	Std. Deviation	Std. Error Mean
Customer satisfaction	Convenience store	28	4.79	.917	.173
	Megastore	24	3.33	.917	.187

Independent Samples Test

		Levene's Test for Equality of Variances		t-test for Equality of Means							
						Significance		Mean Difference	Std. Error Difference	95% Confidence Interval of the Difference	
		F	Sig.	t	df	One-Sided p	Two-Sided p			Lower	Upper
Customer satisfaction	Equal variances assumed	.400	.530	5.69	50	<.001	<.001	1.452	.255	.940	1.965
	Equal variances not assumed			5.69	48.8	<.001	<.001	1.452	.255	.940	1.965

RIP 13.3 Independent 2-sample t-test (SPSS output)

Differences in means between three or more groups: one-way independent ANOVA

If you want to compare the means of more than two independent groups, you can use **one-way independent ANOVA** (analysis of variance). You might wish to compare, for example, the mean level of employee satisfaction at different locations to see whether any differences were statistically significant. One-way independent ANOVA requires a categorical independent variable with three or more independent groups and an interval or ratio dependent variable. The dependent variable should be normally distributed, and the variance of the groups should be approximately equal. The test can be run in MS Excel or SPSS; the latter can also run a test for equality of variance.

Mann-Whitney test

If you wish to compare two independent groups but your data do not meet the assumptions of the independent t-test, for example, because the dependent variable is ordinal rather than metric, the **Mann-Whitney** test may be used instead. This is a nonparametric test that tests for differences in the ranked scores of two independent groups. The null hypothesis is one of no difference between the groups. The test can be run in SPSS.

13.5.5 Significance tests (2): measuring and testing associations between variables

Contingency tables and scatter plots are very useful for exploring potential associations between variables but, as with other findings from sample data, they should be subject to further examination and testing. Here we look at some widely used techniques for doing so for different levels of measurement (Table 13.14).

Nominal and ordinal variables: chi-squared test of association

If you have created a contingency table of two categorical variables, the **chi-squared test of association** (also referred to as chi-square or χ^2, using the Greek letter chi) can be used to

TABLE 13.14 Measures and tests of association

Purpose	Name	Measurement level of variables
Test of association between two categorical variables (nonparametric)	Chi-squared (χ^2) test of association	Nominal or ordinal
Test of association between two categorical variables (nonparametric)	Fisher's exact test	Nominal or ordinal (small samples and 2 × 2 contingency tables)
Measure the strength of association between two categorical variables (nonparametric)	Cramer's V	Nominal or ordinal (for two ordinal variables with a large number of categories, use Spearman's rho or Kendall's tau)
Measure the strength of association between two categorical variables (nonparametric)	Phi	Nominal or ordinal (2 × 2 contingency tables)
Measure the strength and direction of association between two metric variables (parametric)	Pearson's correlation coefficient (r)	Metric
Measure the strength and direction of association between two ordinal variables or between one ordinal and one metric variable (nonparametric)	Spearman's rho (ρ)	Ordinal or metric
Measure the strength and direction of association between two ordinal variables (nonparametric)	Kendall's tau (τ)	Ordinal or metric
Predict the value of a dependent variable from knowledge of the value of one or more independent variables	Linear regression	Metric (dependent), metric (independent)

test whether there is a statistically significant association between the two variables. The test works by comparing the observed frequencies of the cells in the contingency table with the frequencies that would be expected if there was no association between the variables, in order to calculate a test statistic that is compared to an appropriate chi-squared distribution for significance. The chi-squared test is a nonparametric test and is very flexible, but it does require that the samples are independent (i.e. each case can appear in only one cell) and that the data are frequency counts, not percentages. If used for a 2 × 2 table the frequency of each cell in the expected frequency table should be at least 5. For larger tables, no more than 20 per cent of cells should have less than an expected frequency of 5 and none below 1. The test can be run in MS Excel (with some manipulation of the data) or in SPSS. An example is given in Research in Practice 13.4.

Research in practice 13.4 Chi-squared test of association

The chi-squared test allows us to test whether or not the association between household income and driving frequency that we saw in Table 13.9 is statistically significant. The test output, generated in SPSS, is shown later. The first table (Case processing summary) provides a summary of the cases included in the analysis. The second table (Annual household income * Driving frequency cross-tabulation) is the contingency table of the data, showing counts and per cent of row totals (this is the same data as in Table 13.9). The third table (Chi-square tests) contains the test result. The relevant one is marked Pearson chi-square and gives a test statistic of 43.685 with 6 degrees of freedom (df) and a p-value (labelled Asymptotic significance) of <0.001. This is below 0.05, so we would therefore conclude that the association between annual household income and driving frequency is statistically significant.

(Note that below the table, SPSS advises you that the assumption regarding the number of cells with an expected frequency below 5 is satisfied by your data.)

Case Processing Summary

	Cases					
	Valid		Missing		Total	
	N	Percent	N	Percent	N	Percent
Annual household income * Driving frequency	1220	100.0%	0	0.0%	1220	100.0%

Annual household income * Driving frequency Crosstabulation

			Driving frequency				Total
			Every day	At least 3 times per week	1 - 2 times per week	Less than once per week	
Annual household income	Up to £20 000	Count	205	110	55	23	393
		% within Annual household income	52.2%	28.0%	14.0%	5.9%	100.0%
	£20 000 to £35 000	Count	228	72	36	13	349
		% within Annual household income	65.3%	20.6%	10.3%	3.7%	100.0%
	Over £35 000	Count	350	82	36	10	478
		% within Annual household income	73.2%	17.2%	7.5%	2.1%	100.0%
Total		Count	783	264	127	46	1220
		% within Annual household income	64.2%	21.6%	10.4%	3.8%	100.0%

Chi-Square Tests

	Value	df	Asymptotic Significance (2-sided)
Pearson Chi-Square	43.685[a]	6	<.001
Likelihood Ratio	43.714	6	<.001
Linear-by-Linear Association	38.408	1	<.001
N of Valid Cases	1220		

a. 0 cells (0.0%) have expected count less than 5. The minimum expected count is 13.16.

RIP 13.4 Chi-squared test of association (SPSS output)

Nominal and ordinal variables: Fisher's exact test

If you have a 2 × 2 contingency table with a small sample or cells with expected frequencies below 5, you can use Fisher's exact test instead of chi-squared. It can also be used for larger tables and bigger samples, but in such situations the chi-squared test is usually adequate. Fisher's exact test can be run in SPSS.

Nominal and ordinal variables: measures of association (Phi and Cramer's V)

Phi and **Cramer's** V can be used to provide a direct measure of the strength of the association between the variables in a contingency table. Phi is used for 2 × 2 contingency tables, whilst Cramer's V can be used for any size of contingency table (including 2 × 2). Both statistics take a value between 0 and 1, where 0 shows no association and 1 shows perfect association. They can be calculated in SPSS when carrying out chi-squared or Fisher's exact test and SPSS also reports the statistical significance for each test. Note that the value of Cramer's V cannot be compared reliably between different-sized tables (de Vaus, 2014). If both your variables are ordinal with a large number of categories, you can use Spearman's rho or Kendall's tau as a measure of association instead of Cramer's V.

Association between metric variables: Pearson's correlation coefficient (Pearson's r)

Pearson's correlation coefficient or **Pearson's r** (also referred to as the Pearson product–moment correlation coefficient) is a measure of the strength of the linear association between two metric (interval or ratio) variables. It takes a value between -1 and 1, where -1 is perfect negative correlation and 1 is perfect positive correlation. In practice, perfect correlation is highly unlikely, and the resulting value of r will lie somewhere between the two extremes, as shown in Figure 13.28.

To interpret Pearson's correlation coefficient, first check whether the association is positive (positive values of r) or negative (negative values of r). Next assess the strength of the association. Table 13.15 offers rules of thumb for doing so on the basis of the value of r. In addition, Pearson's r can be tested for statistical significance where the null hypothesis is that there is no association (i.e. that $r = 0$).

Pearson's correlation coefficient should be used only if the association between the two variables is linear, so check this using a scatter plot. In addition, if you are testing for statistical significance, the data should come from normally distributed populations. Pearson's correlation coefficient can be calculated in MS Excel or SPSS; its statistical significance can be calculated in SPSS, as shown in Research in Practice 13.5.

Association between ordinal variables: Spearman's rho and Kendall's tau

Spearman's rank-order correlation coefficient, also known as **Spearman's rho**, is a nonparametric summary statistic for measuring the association between two ordinal variables. Like

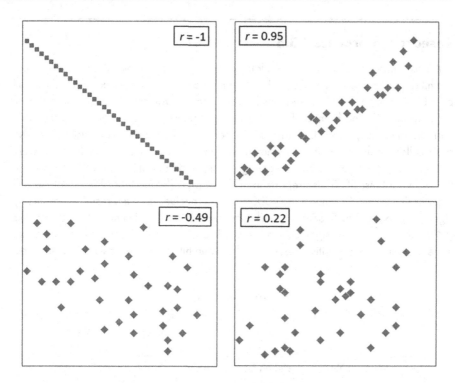

FIGURE 13.28 Scatter plots illustrating the strength of Pearson's correlation coefficient (r)

TABLE 13.15 Descriptors for correlation coefficient strength (Cohen, 1992: 157; de Vaus, 2002: 272)	
Absolute value of correlation coefficient	Descriptor
0.10 to 0.29	Low
0.30 to 0.49	Medium
0.50 to 0.69	High
0.70 and above	Very high

Pearson's r, Spearman's rho returns a value between −1 and 1. It can be run in SPSS, which can also perform a significance test of the null hypothesis of no association between the variables. An alternative to Spearman's rho is Kendall's rank correlation coefficient, more commonly known as **Kendall's tau**. You can use Kendall's tau in preference to Spearman's rho when there are many tied ranks, for instance as a result of having a low number of categories in the ordinal variables.

Research in practice 13.5 Pearson's correlation coefficient

In this example, SPSS is used to calculate Pearson's r for the book sales and seller website hit data from Figure 13.19. It is in the form of a correlation matrix, which shows all possible combinations of correlations between the two variables. The cells in the leading diagonal running from top left to bottom right report the correlation between each variable and itself, hence the correlation coefficient (Pearson's correlation) of 1. The other cells give the correlation coefficient (r) between sales and hits on the seller website. The coefficient is 0.954, indicating a very strong positive correlation between the two variables. SPSS also reports the p-value (Sig. (2-tailed)) for the test of the null hypothesis that r = 0. Since p = 0.000 we can conclude that the result is statistically significant. Note that SPSS also marks the correlation coefficient with two asterisks (**) to show that this is significant at the 0.01 level. Overall, we would conclude that there is a very strong positive association between hits on the seller website and sales.

Correlations

		Hits on sellers website	Sales (copies)
Hits on sellers website	Pearson Correlation	1	.964**
	Sig. (2-tailed)		<.001
	N	30	30
Sales (copies)	Pearson Correlation	.964**	1
	Sig. (2-tailed)	<.001	
	N	30	30

**. Correlation is significant at the 0.01 level (2-tailed).

RIP 13.5 Pearson's r for the correlation between website hits and online sales (SPSS output)

Predicting the value of one variable from another: linear regression

Regression analysis can be used to predict the value of a dependent (or outcome) variable from knowledge of the value of one or more independent (or predictor) variables. Regression analysis can therefore be used for forecasting based on the knowledge of independent variables. Regression analysis is also used for testing hypotheses about the expected relationship between independent and dependent variables in explanatory research. As a result, regression is a very important analysis technique in quantitative research. In this section we will introduce bivariate (or simple) linear regression applied where we have one metric dependent variable (Y) and one metric independent variable (X), using the example of book sales and website hits. The expected relationship is shown visually in Figure 13.29.

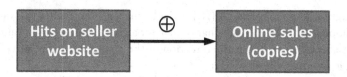

FIGURE 13.29 Conceptual model of the relationship between website hits and book sales

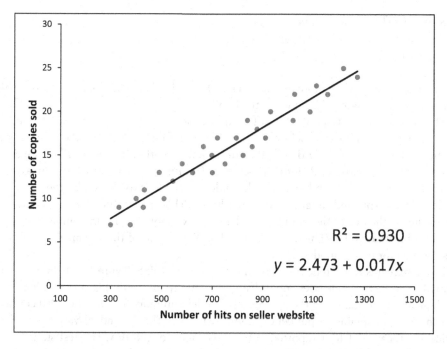

$$R^2 = 0.930$$

$$y = 2.473 + 0.017x$$

FIGURE 13.30 Scatter plot, regression line, and regression equation for website hits and online book sales (n = 30)

The data used are the number of hits on the seller's website and the number of copies sold on the website for 14 book titles, introduced earlier and used in Research in Practice 13.5. In bivariate **linear regression** the software will find a straight line that best summarizes or 'fits' the data points in the scatter plot, as shown in Figure 13.30. Rather than relying on guesswork, regression analysis of this kind uses a technique called least squares to generate the line. Any straight line such as this can be described by a simple formula, which you can think of as a mathematical model that summarizes the relationship between website hits and sales in the data. The basic formula is as follows:

The two parameters (b_0 and b_1) are referred to as **regression coefficients** and are shown in the formula in Figure 13.30. The first, b_0, is the intercept ($b_0 = 2.473$), which is where the line crosses the y-axis where $X = 0$. It gives the value that the dependent variable (Y) will have when the independent variable (X_1) has a value of zero. The second coefficient, b_1, is the slope (gradient) of the line ($b_1 = 0.017$). It shows how much the dependent (Y)

variable changes as the independent (X_1) variable changes: the higher the value of b, the steeper the slope and the bigger the change in Y for a given change in the value of X_1. The b_1 coefficient also tells you about the direction of the change: if it is positive, the slope is positive; if it is negative, the slope is negative.

We can use the equation to calculate an expected value of Y for a given value of X. Using the website hit data, for example, we can predict the number of copies sold (Y) if there are 1,000 website hits (X_1) as follows:

$$\text{Sales} = b_0 + b_1 \times \text{website hits}$$
$$= 2.473 + (0.017 \times 1000)$$
$$= 19.47$$

Our regression model therefore predicts that if the book seller achieves 1,000 website hits, it will sell approximately 19 copies of the book.

This regression line is a line of best fit, but it is not a perfect fit; some of the points in the scatter plot lie above or below the line. We therefore need a measure of how good the fit is. This is provided by the **coefficient of determination**, known as R^2 (R squared). By converting the value of R^2 into a percentage (multiply by 100), you get a measure of what per cent of the variability in the dependent variable is explained by the regression model. The unexplained variance is due to other variables not included in the model. The higher the R^2, the better the fit of the model. We have shown R^2 for the online book sales in Figure 13.30. It is 0.930, which indicates that 93 per cent of the variance in book sales is accounted for by the model.

Bivariate regression can be run in both MS Excel and SPSS. Figure 13.31 shows output from SPSS using the book sales and website hits data. To interpret this, start by identifying the R^2, which is contained in the box marked Model Summary. The R^2 ($= 0.930$) confirms that the model explains 93 per cent of the variability in the dependent variable. The statistical significance of R^2 is reported in the table labelled ANOVA. The test statistic is in the column marked F ($= 369.378$) and the resulting probability is given in the column marked Sig. ($<.001$). Since this is below 0.05, you would conclude that R^2 is statistically significant. Next look at the regression coefficients in the B column of the table labelled Coefficients. Here you see the intercept (labelled Constant) is 2.473, and the b^1 coefficient for Hits on sellers website is 0.017. The statistical significance of the coefficients is given in the same table in the column marked Sig. and the test statistics for each in the column marked t. You can see that both are below 0.05, showing that the coefficients are significantly different from zero.

Overall, on the basis of the output in Figure 13.31, you would conclude that there is a statistically significant relationship between website hits and book sales. As well as checking statistical significance, you should also consider the practical significance of your findings. For example, is the impact of website hits on sales large enough to make the information practically relevant and useful? Linear regression also requires some assumptions to be met for its use to be appropriate. We discuss these in more detail on the companion website. Despite these limitations, regression analysis offers us greater insights into a bivariate relationship than the correlation coefficient alone.

Model Summary

Model	R	R Square	Adjusted R Square	Std. Error of the Estimate
1	.964[a]	.930	.927	1.353

a. Predictors: (Constant), Hits on sellers website

ANOVA[a]

Model		Sum of Squares	df	Mean Square	F	Sig.
1	Regression	676.115	1	676.115	369.378	<.001[b]
	Residual	51.252	28	1.830		
	Total	727.367	29			

a. Dependent Variable: Sales (copies)

b. Predictors: (Constant), Hits on sellers website

Coefficients[a]

Model		Unstandardized Coefficients		Standardized Coefficients		
		B	Std. Error	Beta	t	Sig.
1	(Constant)	2.473	.725		3.412	.002
	Hits on sellers website	.017	.001	.964	19.219	<.001

a. Dependent Variable: Sales (copies)

FIGURE 13.31 Regression analysis for book sales and website hits (selected SPSS output)

Multiple linear regression

Bivariate regression can be extended to include more than one independent variable by using multiple regression, thereby allowing the testing of more complex conceptual models. Multiple regression analysis generates a value for R^2 for the overall model and a regression equation with a regression coefficient for each independent variable:

$$y = b_0 + b_1 X_1 + b_2 X_2 + \cdots + b_n X_n$$

where b_0 is the intercept, $b_1 X_1$ is the contribution of independent variable X_1, $b_2 X_2$ is the contribution of independent variable X_2, and so on, holding the effects of the other variables constant. It also allows the researcher to assess the relative importance of each independent variable in predicting the dependent variable. This can help us to answer the question of which independent variable makes the greatest contribution in the prediction of the dependent variable, as shown in Research in Practice 13.6. We discuss multiple regression, including test assumptions, in more detail on the companion website.

Research in practice 13.6 Factors influencing smartphone shopping adoption

In this Research in Practice we revisit MBA student Davin MacAnaney's study of factors influencing online shopping by smartphone. Here we present a fuller version of his conceptual model, this time with three independent variables and one dependent variable. All variables are measured on a multi-item seven-point rating scale.

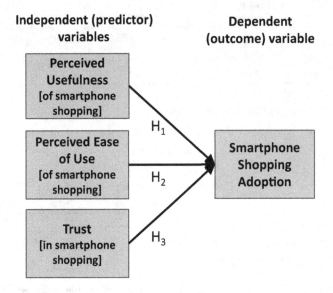

H₁: Perceived Usefulness has a positive impact on Smartphone Shopping Adoption

H₂: Perceived Ease of Use has a positive impact on Smartphone Shopping Adoption

H₃: Trust has a positive impact on Smartphone Shopping Adoption

RIP 13.6 Conceptual model of factors influencing smartphone shopping adoption

Multiple regression analysis generates a value for R^2 for the overall model and a regression equation with a regression coefficient for each independent variable:

$$y = b_0 + b_1X_1 + b_2X_2 + \cdots + b_nX_n$$

where b_0 is the intercept, b_1X_1 is the contribution of independent variable X_1, b_2X_2 is the contribution of independent variable X_2, and so on, holding the effects of the other variables constant.

The results of the regression showed that the R^2 was 69 per cent with a p-value of 0.000. The b coefficients for the independent variables were as shown in the table.

Summary of *b*-coefficients for independent variables

	b-coefficient	p-value
Perceived usefulness	0.841	0.000
Perceived ease of use	0.103	0.067
Trust	0.323	0.000

As a result, H_1 and H_3 were accepted at the 5 per cent significance level, whilst H_2 was rejected: perceived usefulness and trust both have a statistically significant impact on smartphone shopping adoption. Further inspection of the test output showed that perceived usefulness has a greater relative impact than trust. Perceived ease of use had a much lower relative impact and was not statistically significant. In his final report Davin went on to discuss the practical significance of his findings.

Source: MacAnaney (2013)

Inferring causality

Tests such as chi-squared, correlation, and regression can help us to establish whether variables co-vary. As we explained in Chapter 4, however, you cannot infer causality on this basis alone since other criteria need to be met as well. It is important, therefore, to be careful when interpreting the results of such tests.

13.5.6 Taking it further

There are many more multivariate analysis techniques available to the researcher. Hair et al. (2019) classify these into dependence and interdependence techniques:

- Dependence techniques, such as multiple regression, in which one or more variable is identified as a dependent variable to be explained or predicted by two or more independent variables.
- Interdependence techniques, such as **cluster analysis** and **factor analysis**, in which there is no dependent variable. Instead, the aim is to analyze the underlying pattern structure in the variables or cases being analyzed. Such techniques are an important element of data-driven research, as discussed in Chapter 6.

The companion website gives guidance about where to learn more about multivariate analysis techniques.

> ## CRITICAL COMMENTARY 13.2
>
> ### The *Cult of Statistical Significance*
>
> The *Cult of Statistical Significance* is the title of a book by Ziliak and McCloskey (2008) that criticizes the emphasis placed on statistical significance testing in many branches of science. Ziliak and McCloskey are not alone in their criticisms of the central role played by significance testing. We will pick up two concerns that relate to our discussions of significance testing in this chapter.
>
> The first is that, as we have noted, statistical significance is not the same as practical significance. With very large samples, tiny effects can be statistically significant. Whether such effects are of practical relevance depends on the context. That is why we have stressed the need to discuss effect sizes and practical significance along with statistical significance when reporting your results.
>
> The second is that significance testing can encourage what Field (2018: 99) calls 'all or nothing thinking', where researchers use a pre-specified significance level in a very dogmatic way, treating a result where $p < 0.05$ as significant and dismissing one where $p > 0.05$ as insignificant, even if the differences between the two observed p-values might be tiny and both be very close to 0.05. Avoiding such apparent arbitrariness is one of the reasons we have suggested that you report full p-values and use confidence intervals rather than simply mark some results as 'significant' and others 'non-significant'. Providing more information in this way allows the reader to make an informed judgement about your results.

13.6 PRESENTING YOUR FINDINGS

Having completed your analysis, you will need to present your findings. In doing so, you should use a combination of tables, charts, and figures. Make sure that you integrate them into your text by applying the 'hamburger' or 'sandwich' technique of (1) introducing the material, (2) presenting it, and (3) interpreting and commenting on it. Your write-up will typically include the following:

- An overview of the sample and its demographics using descriptive statistics
- Descriptive statistics for key variables
- Results of further analysis and hypothesis tests

When reporting the results of your hypothesis tests, we recommend that you clearly indicate the hypotheses being tested, the relevant sample statistics, the appropriate test statistic, and the exact p-value from the output. You should then interpret the result, commenting on both the statistical and practical significance of your findings. Reporting conventions vary, particularly when describing significance levels. One alternative is to report p-values as a range, for example $p < 0.05$ or $p < 0.01$, rather than give the exact p-value. Another method is to use asterisks (*) to indicate the level of significance. A common practice is to use one asterisk (*) to show that $p < 0.05$ and two asterisks (**) indicate that $p < 0.01$. Our view is that exact p-values convey more information and therefore are to be preferred, but in the literature you will probably see all three methods being used.

Chapter 15 gives further guidance on presenting your findings.

CHAPTER SUMMARY

- The aim in quantitative data analysis is to move from raw data to knowledge that will help you to answer your research questions.
- The process of quantitative data analysis involves data entry, data preparation, data exploration, using the data to answer your research question and presentation of your findings.
- In data entry you get your data into a format that can be analyzed by your chosen software package.
- Data preparation includes checking for data entry or other errors, dealing with any missing values, carrying out any data transformation such as creating summated scales, and checking scale reliability.
- Data exploration uses summary statistics and tabular and graphical analysis techniques to identify the main features of your sample data.
- Univariate exploratory analysis involves looking at variables individually, typically in terms of four characteristics: frequency distribution, central tendency, dispersion, and the shape of the distribution.
- Bivariate exploratory analysis examines two variables simultaneously in order to answer more complex descriptive questions, to investigate differences between groups or to see whether or not two variables are associated.
- Time series are a form of longitudinal data that consists of a sequence of observations over time.
- Answering the research question in quantitative analysis involves the use of descriptive statistics to analyze, summarize, and simplify your sample data and the use of inferential statistics to draw conclusions about the population from which the sample data were drawn.
- Inferential statistics can be used to generate confidence intervals which represent a range of plausible values for a population parameter such as the mean or population proportion.
- Inferential statistics can be used to carry out significance tests of hypotheses. Hypothesis testing entails formulating null and research (alternative) hypotheses, deciding on a significance level for acceptance of the test, selecting an appropriate test, checking assumptions, applying the test, and interpreting the results.

NEXT STEPS

13.1 Getting ready to start your analysis. Before you start your analysis, review your research questions and your conceptual model and hypotheses (if you are using them in your project). If you have not already done so, ensure you have access to your intended analysis software on a suitable laptop or PC.

13.2 Entering your data. Follow the guidance in Section 13.2 to enter your data into your chosen software package. Make sure that you create a secure backup copy of your data.

13.3 Preparing your data. Follow the guidance in Section 13.3 to prepare your data for analysis. Make notes of all your actions, ensuring that you create new master and backup copy of your data if you make any changes.

13.4 Exploring and describing your data. Follow the guidance on data exploration in Section 13.4. The following sequence is suggested.

   a. Calculate final sample size after all data preparation.

   b. Describe your sample demographics.

   c. Explore and describe other variables in your data set.

   d. Test any assumptions required by statistical tests you plan to run.

13.5 Answering your research questions. Now apply your proposed analysis techniques.

   a. If you are carrying out hypothesis testing, are the results statistically significant?

   b. Are your findings of practical significance?

   c. What conclusions do you draw in relation to your research questions?

13.6 Presenting your findings. Review your analysis, your notes, and your saved output. Decide which tables, charts, etc. should be incorporated in your final report and/or presentation. Ensure that they are securely stored, ready for preparing your report.

13.7 SUMMARY OF CHART TYPES USED IN THIS CHAPTER

Chart	Name	Description	Typical applications
	Pie chart	Plot of the proportion of the whole represented by each category or value of a variable	Showing the relative proportions of the categories within a nominal or ordinal variable. Best used with a smaller number of categories
	Bar chart	Plot of the frequency of each category or value of a variable	Comparing the frequency of each category within a nominal or ordinal variable. For ordinal data the categories can be arranged in rank order to make it easier to spot patterns
	Clustered bar chart	Plot of the frequency of each category or value of a variable for different groups placed side by side	Comparing the frequency of each category of a nominal or ordinal variable for each group in the grouping variable. If the grouping variable is ordinal, the groups can be arranged in rank order to make it easier to spot patterns
	Stacked bar chart	Plot of the frequency of each category or value of a variable for different groups stacked in a single bar	Comparing the total of each group in the grouping variable and the relative frequency of each category within each group. If the grouping variable is ordinal, the groups can be arranged in rank order to make it easier to spot patterns
	100 per cent stacked bar chart	Plot of the proportion of each category or value of a variable represented by each group stacked in a single bar representing 100 per cent of the observations	Comparing the relative proportions of each category of a normal or ordinal group between different groups in the grouping variable. If the grouping variable is ordinal, the groups can be arranged in rank order to make it easier to spot patterns
	Bar chart of means	Plot of the means of a variable for different groups	Comparing and showing differences in means between different groups. If the grouping variable is ordinal, the groups can be arranged in rank order to make it easier to spot patterns

Chart	Name	Description	Typical applications
	Histogram	Plot of the frequency distribution of a metric variable	Inspecting the shape of the distribution to check for multimodality, outliers, skewness, and kurtosis
	Box plot	Plot of summary statistical measures of an ordinal or metric variable	Inspecting the shape of the distribution and particularly for identifying potential outliers
	Multiple box plot	Box plots for more than one variable or for the values for different groups in a single chart	Comparing the distribution of a variable for different groups or for different variables in a single chart
	Scatter plot	Plot of multiple observations of two variables set as the x- and y-axes	Visual inspection of the association between two variables to investigate the strength of the association, whether it is positive or negative, whether or not it is linear and identifying potential outliers
	Line chart	Plot of values for one or more variables over time	Visual inspection of time series data to identify trends and to compare variables over time
	Confidence interval chart	Plot of confidence intervals for groups or variables	Comparing the confidence intervals for different groups or for different variables in a single chart

13.8 SUMMARY OF STATISTICAL TESTS USED IN THIS CHAPTER

Type of test   **Analyst's question**   **Test or measure**

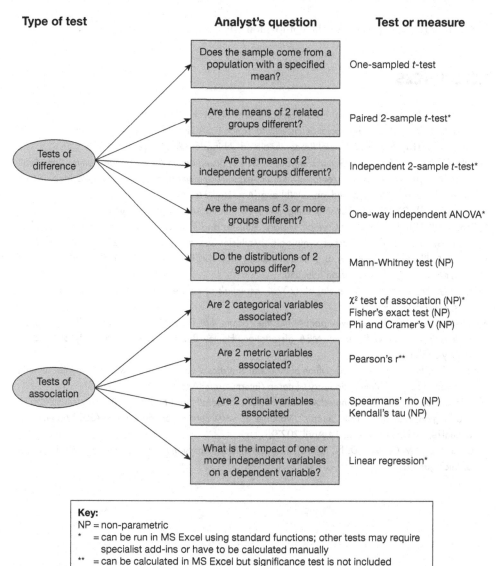

	Analyst's question	Test or measure
	Does the sample come from a population with a specified mean?	One-sampled t-test
	Are the means of 2 related groups different?	Paired 2-sample t-test*
Tests of difference	Are the means of 2 independent groups different?	Independent 2-sample t-test*
	Are the means of 3 or more groups different?	One-way independent ANOVA*
	Do the distributions of 2 groups differ?	Mann-Whitney test (NP)
	Are 2 categorical variables associated?	χ^2 test of association (NP)* Fisher's exact test (NP) Phi and Cramer's V (NP)
	Are 2 metric variables associated?	Pearson's r**
Tests of association	Are 2 ordinal variables associated	Spearmans' rho (NP) Kendall's tau (NP)
	What is the impact of one or more independent variables on a dependent variable?	Linear regression*

Key:
NP = non-parametric
*   = can be run in MS Excel using standard functions; other tests may require specialist add-ins or have to be calculated manually
**   = can be calculated in MS Excel but significance test is not included

FIGURE 13.32 Summary of statistical tests

FURTHER READING

For further reading, please see the companion website.

REFERENCES

Cohen, J. (1992). A power primer. *Psychological Bulletin*, 112(1): 155–159.

de Vaus, D. (2002). *Analyzing Social Science Data*. London: SAGE Publications.

de Vaus, D. (2014). *Surveys in Social Research*. 6th ed. Abingdon: Routledge.

Eurostat (2023). *Net Electricity Generation, EU, 2021 (%, Based on GWh)*. European Commission. Available at: https://ec.europa.eu/eurostat/statistics-explained/index.php?title=File:Net_electricity_generation,_EU,_2021_(%25,_based_on_GWh).png (Accessed 16 April 2023).

Field, A. (2018). *Discovering Statistics Using IBM SPSS*. 5th ed. London: SAGE Publications.

Griffin, R. (2018). *120 Years of Olympic History: Athletes and Results*. Available at: www.kaggle.com/datasets/heesoo37/120-years-of-olympic-history-athletes-and-results (Accessed 23 April 2023).

Hair, J. F. J., Black, W. C., Babin, B. J. and Anderson, R. E. (2019). *Multivariate Data Analysis*. 8th ed. Upper Saddle River, NJ: Pearson Education.

Hair, J. F. J., Page, M. and Brunsveld, N. (2020). *Essentials of Business Research Methods*. 4th ed. New York, NY: Routledge.

MacAnaney, D. (2013). *An Investigation into the Factors that Drive Online Shopping Through Smartphones in the United Kingdom*. MBA dissertation, Henley Business School, University of Reading, Henley-on-Thames.

ONS (2021). *Internet Users 2020*. Office of National Statistics. Available at: www.ons.gov.uk/businessindustryandtrade/itandinternetindustry/datasets/internetusers (Accessed 14 April 2023).

US Census Bureau (2021). *Estimated Annual Sales of U.S. Retail Firms by Kind of Business: 1992–2021*. Washington, DC: US Census Bureau. Available at: www.census.gov/data/tables/2021/econ/arts/annual-report.html (Accessed 14 April 2023).

Ziliak, S. T. and McCloskey, D. N. (2008). *The Cult of Statistical Significance*. Ann Arbor, MI: University of Michigan Press.

CHAPTER 14

Analyzing qualitative data

CHAPTER LEARNING OUTCOMES

After reading this chapter you will be able to

- define robust procedures for organizing, preparing, and coding your data;
- demonstrate the ability to create and use memos to support qualitative data analysis;
- appraise the issues that are likely to arise when analyzing qualitative data, including regarding the use of CAQDAS;
- select and apply visualization techniques to interpret the data and communicate your research findings;
- draw and verify conclusions from qualitative data.

14.1 INTRODUCTION

In this chapter we introduce a set of analysis techniques that can be applied in a wide variety of qualitative research projects built around the simple process depicted in Figure 14.1. We begin by looking at how to prepare your data for analysis. We then explain how to use coding to identify the key themes in your data. The coding-based approach described fits here broadly within the tradition of 'thematic analysis', which can be thought of as 'a method for developing, analyzing, and interpreting patterns across a qualitative data set, which involves systematic processes of data coding to develop themes' (Braun and Clarke, 2022: 4). We move on to present three types of visual display techniques, matrices, networks, and graphical displays and show how they can help you describe and interpret data for different research questions. Afterwards, we consider ways of verifying your findings and drawing conclusions so that you can be confident that they give a trustworthy account of the problem under analysis. Then, we explain how you ensure that your findings are answering the research question(s) that guide your project, before offering guidance on how to present qualitative analysis in your final report. You will see that the approach to

DOI: 10.4324/9781003381006-18

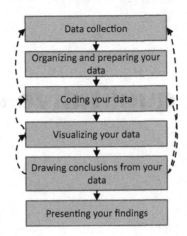

FIGURE 14.1 Steps in the qualitative analysis of data

qualitative data analysis may vary depending on the research design, the types of data, and the philosophical orientation.

As Figure 14.1 shows, qualitative data analysis may proceed in an iterative manner. Preliminary data analysis usually begins during data collection, because the size of the sample (e.g. the number of interviews) may be influenced by when you reach theoretical saturation. Also, preliminary conclusions may point to the need to add or modify elements of the data collection (e.g. ask participants a clarifying or follow-up question). The steps in Figure 14.1 are consistent with an inductive approach to research, where the aim is to build theory from the data; although, as we shall see, it is also possible to incorporate a preliminary conceptual framework into this process.

14.2 PREPARING AND ORGANIZING YOUR DATA

Following data collection in a qualitative study, you will typically have a large, semi-structured, or unstructured data set consisting of numerous audio and text files, images, or objects, in addition to field notes. You need to store and organize these data so that you can easily find and access specific data inputs when you need to.

14.2.1 Getting organized

As soon as data collection begins, it is crucial to organize your data. Digital files such as text, video recordings, or illustrations should be organized into computer folders, clearly named to identify the content of each file. Physical items such as objects need to be stored in boxes or other suitable containers. Moreover, handwritten observation notes and other data that exist in physical format only may need to be copied or scanned. Files should be organized in a way that best reflects your thinking about the project in question, and this can change as the process evolves. For example, if you have collected data from more than one location, you may initially have a folder for each location, but later you may prefer to organize the folders around themes from your analysis.

Ensure that you store your data securely to prevent theft or unauthorized access, and to protect against accidental loss or damage. Create a backup copy of your master data plus copies of your work as you proceed; store these securely, separately from your laptop or PC.

14.2.2 Preparing your data

Data preparation should begin while data collection is underway. We recommend that you type out your field notes while they are still fresh in your mind and store them along-side the raw data to which they refer. Practical tips for managing your notes include the following:

- Details of the data source—Ensure that you can identify the source of your data by including relevant details, such as the name and job position of the research partici-pant and the time, date, and location of data collection.
- Page layout—If you are working with paper copies, make one page margin extra wide, or use double spacing, for annotations.
- Page numbering—Ensure that each page is clearly numbered.
- Line numbers—Numbering each line of notes helps to record the location of key bits of data.

14.2.3 Transcribing your audio and video recordings

We recommend that you transcribe your recordings, if possible. The benefits of transcrip-tion, as compared to audio or video recordings, include the following:

- It is easier to analyze textual than audio data.
- It is quicker to revisit and review textual data following initial analysis.
- It is easier to cross-reference and refer back to previous analysis.
- It facilitates the use of verbatim quotations when writing up your final report.

You will have to decide whether you are going to do your own transcriptions or work with a professional transcriber. Doing your own transcriptions will save money, guarantee confi-dentiality, and enable you to immerse yourself in the data. However, it is time-consuming. It can take between four and eight hours to transcribe a one-hour interview, depending on the number of people speaking, your skills, and the quality of the recording. Moreover, the time that you invest in transcription is time that you cannot spend in collecting further data or analyzing what you have collected already, delaying the conclusion of your project.

If you decide to do your own transcriptions, there are various options available. If you used a stand-alone digital recorder or your smartphone to record your interviews, you can use specialist transcription software, such as Otter.ai (https://get.otter.ai/interview-transcription/) for playing back and reviewing recordings. You can also use voice recog-nition software, such as Dragon (www.nuance.com/en-gb/dragon.html). Another option is to record your interview directly on a video conferencing platform such as Zoom or MS Teams, which offer the option of generating transcripts, automatically. Dictation and transcription functions in MS Word can also be used. None of these options offer completely correct and reliable transcriptions. In particular, they may struggle with strong accents, acronyms, and technical or new terms (such as 'Covid', which one software that we used would transcribe as 'coffee'). In addition, some of these options may not be available in the language that your participants are using. However, if it works for you, this type of software can be very helpful to get a first draft transcription for your recordings, and it is less expensive than using a professional transcriber.

When transcribing, create a new paragraph every time a person starts speaking. If relevant, identify each speaker at the beginning of each paragraph, for example, interviewer, participant 1, and so on. If you are using transcription software, you can bookmark sections of the file to mark important points for review. You can add notations to your transcript in order to signal pauses, noticeable changes in pitch, and other details of the conversation.

14.3 CODING YOUR DATA

Within the data set that you have collected, some data will have more significance for your study than others. Hence, you need to select and focus on the data that is relevant to your research questions. To do so, you need to read through all the material collected to get a sense of the whole data set. Once you have familiarized yourself with the data, you can begin **coding**. In qualitative data analysis, coding involves looking at the data, identifying themes, and marking them. You can think of coding as applying a selective filter to your data set to funnel a mass of raw data into meaningful concepts or themes (Dey, 1993). In this context, a code is 'a word or short phrase that symbolically assigns a summative, salient, essence-capturing, and/or evocative attribute for a portion of language-based or visual data' (Saldaña, 2021: 5). These portions might relate to events, statements, objects, or actions/interactions in the data that appear to be significant to your research questions. The sections sharing common characteristics or with related meanings are grouped under a common code. The code acts as a marker or flag, allowing you to bring together similarly coded data as your analysis progresses.

14.3.1 What to code?

What makes portions of data significant will be determined by your research questions. For instance, if your question related to individuals' motivations to help as volunteers, you would look for data that referred to reasons, beliefs, and other factors that drove them to volunteer. One approach to coding can be thought of as 'inductive'. In this case, the researcher does not have any codes in mind before starting the analysis. As relevant themes are identified in the data, the researcher decides upon a suitable code and allocates it to that particular portion. Alternatively, coding can follow a more 'deductive' approach. Here the researcher starts coding with codes already identified from the literature or the research questions. Such a priori codes serve as sensitizing concepts (Blumer, 1954) that can help structure the initial analysis. In practice, qualitative researchers typically adopt a mixed approach. They may start with an initial list of codes but are prepared to revise, add to, or reject initial codes as the analysis proceeds.

14.3.2 The coding process

The example provided in Research in Practice 14.1 illustrates the coding process.

Research in practice 14.1 Example of the coding process

In this interview extract, a manager talks about a new role leading the start-up division of a large corporation. The researcher asked about obstacles faced in the new role, to which the interviewee replies:

First of all we face the scepticism. I think when I took the job on, nine months ago now, the reaction of my peers was probably 'that's great, sounds very exciting – they'll never let you do it'. I think we've overcome that to a large extent. Then there is resistance, not because people don't like the idea but because inevitably it means we need resources, we need skills, we need cooperation from other business units and it's not necessarily at the moment been proved to them that by giving us those things it helps them towards their objectives at all.

Here, we see the same extract after coding has begun. The researcher has high-lighted relevant parts of the text and allocated each a code, which is written in the margin.

Scepticism First of all we face the scepticism. I think when I took the job on, nine months
Resources ago now, the reaction of my peers was probably 'that's great, sounds very
Conflicting exciting – they'll never let you do it'. I think we've overcome that to a large
objectives extent. Then there is resistance, not because people don't like the idea but
  because inevitably it means we need resources, we need skills, we need
  cooperation from other business units and it's not necessarily at the moment
  been proved to them that by giving us those things it helps them towards
  their objectives at all.

When coding, you work line by line, image by image, or audio/video segment by segment, highlighting appropriate segments of data and noting the name of the code. If you are coding by hand, this can be done by writing in the margin with a pencil and highlighting the text using different-coloured highlighter pens. Coding can also be done using word processing or specialist software as we discuss later in the chapter. As you work through the next transcript, image, or recording, you look for further occurrences of those codes. As you progress you are likely to create other codes. In the case of the study reported in Research in Practice 14.1, subsequent interviewees might identify obstacles not mentioned before (e.g. jealousy), which need to be labelled using another appropriate code.

Naming and defining your codes

You need to think carefully about how you will name and define your codes. Names may come from the language of the participants, in which case they are called **in vivo codes** (e.g. 'scepticism' in Research in Practice 14.1). They may also come from your own interpretation of what is happening (as in the case of 'conflicting objectives'), or from theory. Whatever the source of the name, you need to be consistent in how you apply the code, so you will need to develop working definitions of your codes as you proceed. As coding is the start of the process of theorizing about your data, developing definitions for your codes is an important part of that process.

Managing your codes

As you proceed, you will need to keep a record of what you have coded and where so that you can retrieve coded segments later, and look at all the data belonging to a particular code.

If you are coding on paper, you can create an index card or digital file for each code, noting the name and definition of the code at the top of the card. Then, cut the corresponding data from a copy of the original data source and paste it onto the relevant card or file, recording where each extract came from, as illustrated in Figure 14.2. As you add codes, you can create new index cards or files, and because each card or file is separate, it is easy to rearrange them for later analysis.

Another option is to create a table or spreadsheet cross-tabulating your data sources with your codes, as illustrated in Figure 14.3. As coding proceeds, add columns for

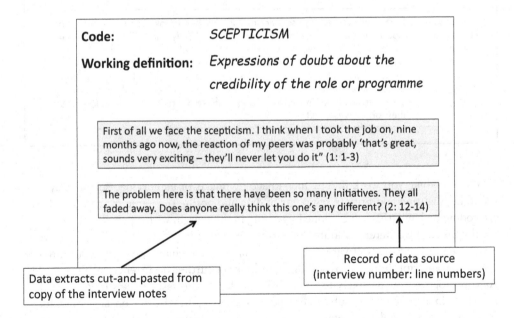

Code: SCEPTICISM

Working definition: Expressions of doubt about the credibility of the role or programme

First of all we face the scepticism. I think when I took the job on, nine months ago now, the reaction of my peers was probably 'that's great, sounds very exciting – they'll never let you do it" (1: 1-3)

The problem here is that there have been so many initiatives. They all faded away. Does anyone really think this one's any different? (2: 12-14)

Data extracts cut-and-pasted from copy of the interview notes

Record of data source (interview number: line numbers)

FIGURE 14.2 Using index cards for coding

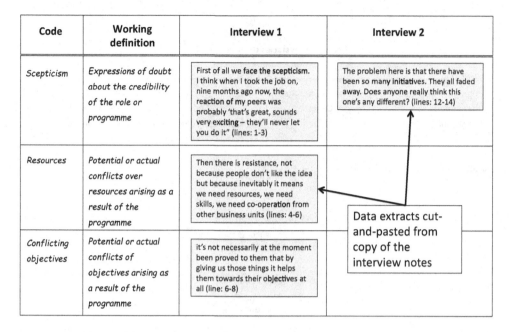

Code	Working definition	Interview 1	Interview 2
Scepticism	Expressions of doubt about the credibility of the role or programme	First of all we face the scepticism. I think when I took the job on, nine months ago now, the reaction of my peers was probably 'that's great, sounds very exciting – they'll never let you do it" (lines: 1-3)	The problem here is that there have been so many initiatives. They all faded away. Does anyone really think this one's any different? (lines: 12-14)
Resources	Potential or actual conflicts over resources arising as a result of the programme	Then there is resistance, not because people don't like the idea but because inevitably it means we need resources, we need skills, we need co-operation from other business units (lines: 4-6)	Data extracts cut-and-pasted from copy of the interview notes
Conflicting objectives	Potential or actual conflicts of objectives arising as a result of the programme	it's not necessarily at the moment been proved to them that by giving us those things it helps them towards their objectives at all (line: 6-8)	

FIGURE 14.3 Using tables to manage coding

each data source (e.g. interview) and rows for each code you create. This also allows you to compare responses and look for patterns in the data as we discuss later in the chapter.

14.3.3 Coding hierarchies

The codes generated in this first stage are your initial or level 1 codes (Hahn, 2008). If some of your level 1 codes share common features, you should group them under one theme. In our start-up example, the four codes identified could be grouped under the theme 'obstacles to success', as shown in Figure 14.4.

Furthermore, as 'scepticism' and 'jealousy' seem to be dimensions of the same type of phenomenon, you could create a label showing that these codes are related, as in Figure 14.5. This is called a level 2 code (Hahn, 2008).

The process of creating levels of codes reduces the number of blocks you are working with. It can be thought of as a form of **hierarchical coding**, which has the following benefits:

> Hierarchical coding allows the researcher to analyse texts at varying levels of specificity. Broad higher-order codes can give a good overview of the general direction of the interview, detailed lower-order codes allow for very fine distinctions to be made, both within and between [interviews].
>
> King (2004: 258)

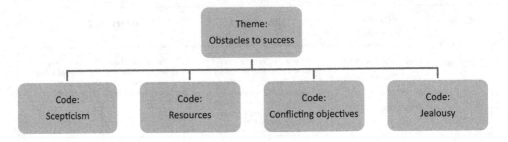

FIGURE 14.4 Emerging themes

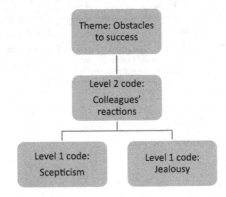

FIGURE 14.5 Level 1 and 2 codes

If you find that you have created a code that is too 'broad' and which needs detailed analysis, you can split it into subcategories. For instance, you could split the code 'resources', as illustrated in Figure 14.6. Here, you are creating a hierarchy in reverse, starting with the broad, higher-order category and adding lower-order, fine-grained codes. When you create a new code, you must revisit your earlier data to see whether there is any other case that should be relabelled with the new code.

You may also find cases that contradict what you found earlier; for instance, the new role was met with enthusiasm, leading to unrealistic expectations, and thus becoming an obstacle to success. If so, you need to create a new level 1 code. Moreover, because this reaction is so different from the others, you need to create a level 2 code that reflects this difference. You also need to create an even higher-level code, a level 3 code, to show how the existing level 2 codes are related. Figure 14.7 illustrates the expanded coding scheme.

As this example shows, codes relate to each other at increasing levels of abstraction. Multiple level 1 codes are aggregated into a level 2 code reflecting the interconnectedness of the codes under it. In turn, related level 2 codes are aggregated into a level 3 code, and so on, in an iterative process, until you reach a level that represents your results in a coherent manner, as illustrated in Figure 14.8. Variations on hierarchical coding are very widely used in thematic analysis. Terminology for different levels varies

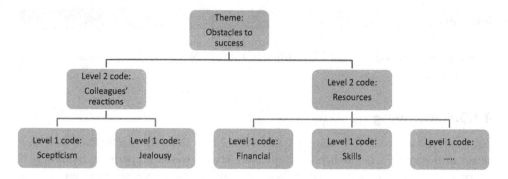

FIGURE 14.6 Creating subcategories

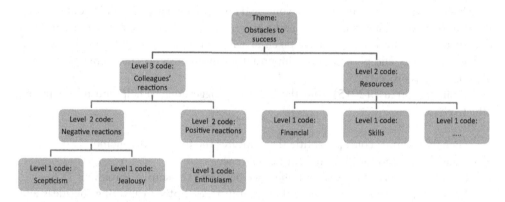

FIGURE 14.7 Examples of a revised coding scheme

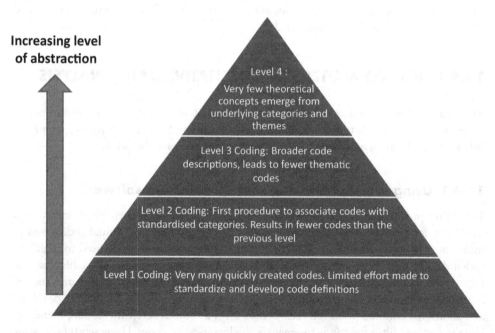

FIGURE 14.8 Coding hierarchy (adapted from Hahn, 2008: 172)

by methods used and proposed by different authors. Nevertheless, the basic process is often similar.

14.3.4 Memoing

As you reread and code your materials, you will see how things fit together and how they relate to theory. In a research project spanning several weeks or, perhaps, months, it is nearly impossible to remember all of those 'aha!' moments. So you need to capture your thoughts before they are lost, using a technique known as **memoing**.

A **memo** may be a short phrase, a sentence, or even a paragraph recording your ideas as they happen. You can capture them in your field notes, in a separate file, or in your research diary, to help you draw conclusions and write up your analysis. Memos can be used to document any actions that you have taken or will need to take, record your thoughts on codes and themes, and perhaps most importantly, capture insights about emerging theory as your analysis proceeds.

Corbin and Strauss (2015) offer the following suggestions to help you use memoing effectively:

- Give the memo a conceptual title that captures the topic of the memo.
- Date each memo for filing and future reference.
- Include extracts of raw data and reference details of the source, if relevant.
- Make your memos conceptual rather than just descriptive; capturing the ideas and insights emerging.

As with field notes, capture your memos as soon as they occur. You can return to them and expand on your original ideas as needed.

14.4 USING COMPUTERS IN QUALITATIVE DATA ANALYSIS

Although coding is a process of **data condensation**, it may generate a large number of codes needing further interpretation and analysis. Coding therefore requires a considerable amount of data management, which is what computers are good at.

14.4.1 Using word processing and spreadsheet software

The coding process can be supported by using word processing or spreadsheet software. In MS Word, for example, the comment function can be used for your initial coding and to make short memos on sections of text. Text highlighter colours can be used to highlight coded data as well. Programmes like MS Word can also be used to create tables such as Figure 14.3. Larger data sets are more easily managed in a spreadsheet programme, such as MS Excel, as shown in Figure 14.9. Additional rows can be added as the coding develops, and additional columns used for each coding level as you develop the coding hierarchy. Use the sort and filter functions to organize the lower-order codes. Using word processing

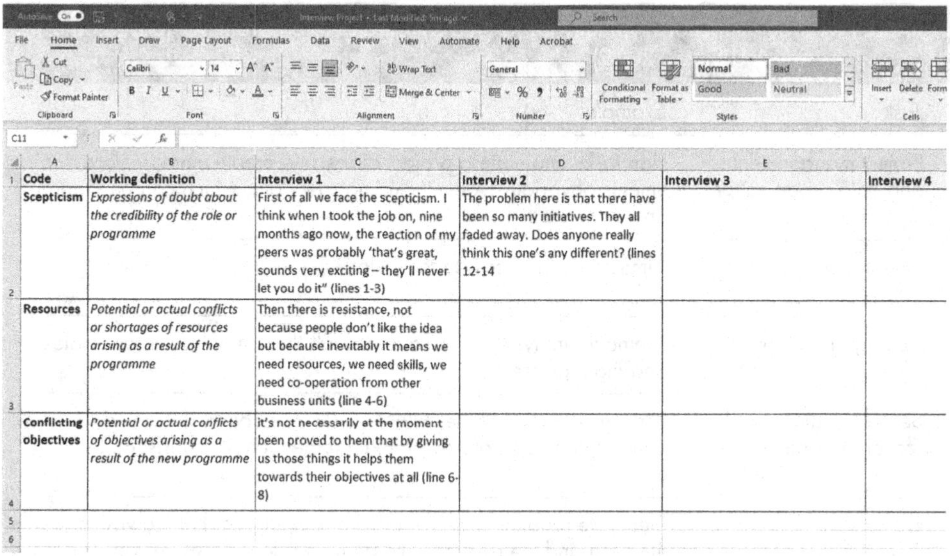

Code	Working definition	Interview 1	Interview 2	Interview 3	Interview 4
Scepticism	*Expressions of doubt about the credibility of the role or programme*	First of all we face the scepticism. I think when I took the job on, nine months ago now, the reaction of my peers was probably 'that's great, sounds very exciting – they'll never let you do it" (lines 1-3)	The problem here is that there have been so many initiatives. They all faded away. Does anyone really think this one's any different? (lines 12-14		
Resources	*Potential or actual conflicts or shortages of resources arising as a result of the programme*	Then there is resistance, not because people don't like the idea but because inevitably it means we need resources, we need skills, we need co-operation from other business units (line 4-6)			
Conflicting objectives	*Potential or actual conflicts of objectives arising as a result of the new programme*	it's not necessarily at the moment been proved to them that by giving us those things it helps them towards their objectives at all (line 6-8)			

FIGURE 14.9 Coding table created using a spreadsheet (MS Excel), used with permission from Microsoft

and spreadsheet software can also facilitate writing up as it is easy to extract relevant data from the tables for inclusion in the final report.

14.4.2 Using CAQDAS programmes

There are specialist software packages designed to support code-and-retrieve activities in qualitative analysis. They are known as computer aided qualitative data analysis software (CAQDAS) and include packages such as NVivo, MAXQDA, and Atlas.ti. Table 14.1 outlines some of the functionality that a CAQDAS programme may offer. As noted in Chapter 3, CAQDAS packages can also be used to support literature reviewing.

CAQDAS programmes have several advantages and disadvantages, as summarized in Table 14.2. You will also need to consider the characteristics of specific CAQDAS programmes, such as its availability at your institution, if access is cloud-based and compatible with your machine's operation system, what type of files it can process, where the data is stored, backup and sharing/collaboration options, or data visualization capabilities.

CAQDAS, like other software packages, can help with the manipulation and management of the data, but there is no replacement for the researcher's skill and judgement in data exploration and interpretation. You can learn more about using CAQDAS on the companion website for this book, which also contains an introduction to using NVivo for qualitative data analysis.

TABLE 14.1 Some functions typically performed by CAQDAS programmes (based on Lewins and Silver, 2009)

Task	Example
Project management and data organization	Plan tasks, maintain a project diary, and create memos; store documents of various types, including raw data, which can be tagged and annotated
Keeping close to the data	Almost instant access to the data
Coding and analysis	Thematic analysis of the data through the use of codes; generate and manage memos
Searching and visualization of data	Perform searches of the data sets, retrieve coded data, and where visualization tools are available, create models, charts, and other diagrams
Outputs	Generate reports, charts, and other outputs that help to visualize the data and the relationships being made, and share with other members of the research team

TABLE 14.2 Advantages and disadvantages of CAQDAS programmes

Advantages	Disadvantages
• Helps with project management, data organization, generation, and manipulation of codes • Can accelerate the process of data analysis, particularly with large amounts of data • Can produce reports and charts that assist visual analysis as well as reporting • Helps the sharing of data within the team • Can improve the study's 'trustworthiness' because it enables you to show the coding and analysis processes	• May encourage narrow range of analysis techniques • May lead to an emphasis on frequency counts, to the detriment of understanding the underlying meaning • Can distance you from the data through reliance on word search and other functions • Can give you a false sense of security • The tools have their own learning curve, and small projects may not justify the investment of time to acquaint yourself with the software

14.5 USING VISUALIZATION TO MAKE CONNECTIONS

During coding we start to see connections between data segments, building abstract and inclusive conceptual categories. But we still need to understand how emerging concepts are connected, before answering our research questions. For instance, you may want to compare the experiences of different participants, understand the chronological sequence of events in your data or the mechanisms influencing those events.

Relying on text alone to derive conclusions has several limitations, as Miles et al. point out:

> (Text) is cumbersome because it is dispersed over many pages and is not easy to see as a whole. It is sequential rather than simultaneous, making it difficult to look at two or three variables at once. Comparing several texts carefully is very difficult. It is usually poorly ordered, can get very bulky, and can make us feel monotonously overloaded. . . . Showing rather than telling can make a more effective and memorable impact on our audiences.
>
> Miles et al. (2020: 106)

Visual displays can give a systematic, visual representation of the data. They can be used to depict differences, relationships, and interconnections within the overall data set, such as how job roles changed over time and the impact those changes had on staff morale. They can also help depict the relationships between your codes and categories, for example, in a causal pathway. Visualization techniques can be applied to a single unit of analysis, such as one document or interview, or to several units at once to help in comparative analysis. In addition, they can be used both during the analysis process and as a presentation device in the final report. Like other analysis techniques, of course, visual data displays have limitations; we review some of these in Critical Commentary 14.1.

Visual displays may be broadly classified into one of three types: data matrices, networks, and general graphics (Miles et al., 2020).

14.5.1 Data matrices

A data matrix is basically a cross-tabulation, with data displayed in rows and columns. The headings for the rows and the columns reflect the dimensions that you want to capture in your analysis and may come from a prior conceptual framework or emerge as coding gets underway. The data entered in each cell of the matrix is driven by the matrix headings and can vary in abstraction. You may start by entering all the relevant data in the corresponding cell. Then, at a higher level of abstraction, select a word or phrase that captures the idea that you want to convey. You may also condense your findings into symbols which convey information in a non-textual manner.

Table 14.3 shows the extract of a data matrix from a multiple case study of online banks. The researcher was interested in how banks differed in their patterns of interaction, internally as well as with outside stakeholders. The columns represent the concepts being analyzed (internal versus external interactions) and the rows show the different companies studied (here, the original names have been replaced by fictitious ones). The cells display summaries of the data coded around the concepts studied.

Data matrices can help you spot patterns in the data. For example, do certain types of bank follow similar practices? Do certain practices occur together? In this way, data matrices can help you answer focused questions about your data. We show this in action in Research in Practice 14.2.

TABLE 14.3 Example of a data matrix

Company	Internal interactions	External interactions
Bargain Bank	• Open communication with direct access to top management • Relatively small number of employees located close together	• Frequent contact with customers emphasized as part of the company's culture
The People's Bank	• Cross-functional and cross-subsidiary project teams used to improve internal knowledge sharing and learning • Use of mobile apps to connect more often with customers	• Use of partnerships to share expertise (e.g. Partner A)
Big Bank	• Open communication • Non-dictatorial management style • Need for feedback mechanisms	• Knowledge sharing across the company's network of business partners • Cooperation to develop new product offerings

Research in practice 14.2 Using a data matrix to display comparisons

When studying the data from the online banking project, the researcher noticed that start-up banks and established ones had different approaches to internal interactions and created a table to capture that difference. This time, the banks have been grouped into two categories, start-ups vs established banks, and are shown in the columns rather than in the rows.

Informal routines used by online banks

	Start-up banks	Established banks
Informal routines	• Small teams on a single site easily able to communicate • Open communication culture to bring forward new ideas • Use of new brand to communicate need for innovation to staff	• Long-established periods of idea mobilization characterized by informal networking • Ideas kept 'covert' until workable to avoid their being crowded out • Use of fairs to generate support for new ideas

At this point, the researcher returned to the data to look for further evidence confirming or disconfirming the emerging findings.

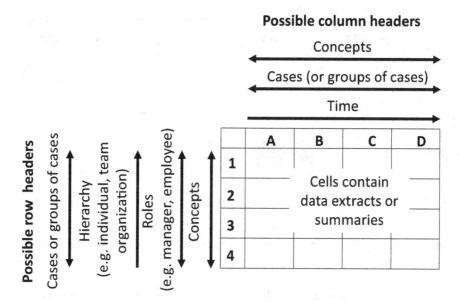

FIGURE 14.10 Possible column and row headers for data matrixes

Data matrices are not limited to cross-tabulating cases with concepts identified in the coding process. They are much more flexible. Figure 14.10 shows some possible column headers that could be used when developing data matrices. You might, for example, create a table using a dimension of time (such as months) as the column headers and different cases (which might be individual interviewees) as the row labels to display how they changed or developed over time. The cells contain relevant data extracts or summaries that relate to each case and time period. Alternatively, you might investigate the relationships between different concepts by using them as column headers and rows in your matrix, for example, by cross-tabulating dimensions of customer satisfaction with dimensions of service quality to investigate whether they are related. We will take a further look at different ways in which matrices can be used later in the chapter.

14.5.2 Networks

A network is a form of visual display using nodes and lines. The nodes can be concepts from your coding, events, or entities (e.g. organizations or people). The lines show connections between them. You can convey additional information about the links by using arrows to indicate directionality or effect (such as causal influence), symbols such as '+' or '−' to indicate whether an effect is positive or negative, and different widths to reflect the intensity of the link. Further information can be incorporated by exploiting the vertical and horizontal dimensions of the network display. For example, if you are depicting a process, you can show the progression of time along the horizontal axis and the various actors involved on the vertical axis, as in Figure 14.11.

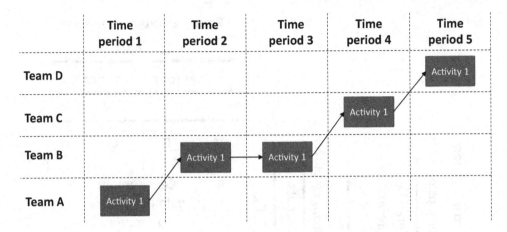

FIGURE 14.11 Example of a network display incorporating vertical and horizontal dimensions

The focus of your network and what to use as nodes depend on the purpose of your display. A network display of communication patterns between members of a virtual project team, for example, might have individual team members as the nodes with the links representing the direction, strength and frequency of interaction. A network display of the development of a start-up business, on the other hand, might use critical events (such as an injection of capital) as the nodes and use the lines to represent the sequencing of those events.

A very practical application is to depict the relationships between the concepts that you have coded in your data, in the form of a concept map or conceptual framework. We have already encountered this use of visual display in the form of conceptual models in Chapter 3. The concept map may draw on existing theory or be developed entirely from the data.

14.5.3 Graphic displays

Graphic display is the term Miles et al. (2020) use to describe visual displays that are neither networks or matrices. Whilst a graphic display can take many different forms, Miles et al. (2020: 110) argue that graphic representation 'is an act of imaginative data concensation and analysis that, at its best, evokes from its reader an at-a-glance understanding of the entire study'. One type of graphical display that is widely encountered is the thematic map or network (Attride-Stirling, 2001; Braun and Clarke, 2006). These are similar to the mind maps we described in Chapter 3. They are very flexible but can be used to map out visually the emerging coding hierarchy, working from high-order codes at the centre of the map, out to lower order codes.

14.5.4 Choosing a visual display format

The choice of visual display format depends on what you are trying to understand or communicate. Developing the displays is likely to raise further questions, requiring you to revisit your data to clarify meanings or steps in the process, or even collect more data to fill in the gaps, which is why it is useful to start analyzing your data early in the research process.

Give each display a meaningful title and date it, keeping a record of the criteria used to produce and populate your displays, for instance, why you chose particular nodes in a network. Use memos and your research diary to record your thoughts as you work, to support your final write-up.

CRITICAL COMMENTARY 14.1

Limitations to data display techniques in qualitative research

It is important to be aware of the limitations and pitfalls of using visual data displays in qualitative analysis. They include the following:

- Imposing an unsuitable display format onto your analysis. This is a risk early on in the analysis process, or when using a priori framework that forces your analysis in a particular direction.
- The approach may be too reductionist, oversimplifying a complex reality. A related risk is that the display becomes increasingly detached from the data as the analysis proceeds.
- The displays may be too complex or too large to share with others, particularly in written reports where physical space is limited. This requires careful thought and the redrawing of displays to make them suitable for sharing with others.
- Visual displays may be unsuitable for some research designs, such as conversation analysis.
- Visual displays may appeal to some individuals more than others. Your own preferences also influence the choice of analysis technique.

14.6 ANSWERING YOUR RESEARCH QUESTION

In this section we look at the use of coding and visual displays to answer your research questions. This is not an exhaustive set of instructions but, instead, a way to help you develop your understanding of the tools themselves and how to use them effectively in your project.

14.6.1 Answering 'what' questions

Qualitative answers to 'what' questions typically aim to give a detailed description of a phenomenon. The focus of coding will depend on what aspects of the phenomenon are relevant to the aims of the study, and these may not be clear at first. So your initial coding may simply be aimed at identifying what is going on in your data. Further rounds of coding then start to focus on key aspects of the phenomenon and its context. Early in the coding process, it can also be helpful to apply what Saldaña (2021: 112) calls 'attribute coding', which uses features of the sources such as demographics (gender, age, etc.), the setting (location, organization, etc.), or other aspects of the context. Attribute codes can help subsequent analysis by facilitating the comparison of groups or the description of different settings or contexts.

Data matrices can be used to display the various components of a phenomenon and explore the range of variations for each of these components within and between cases. A further use of matrices is to develop a descriptive taxonomy of your cases. Careful inspection of a data matrix cross-tabulating cases and relevant concepts from your coding may reveal that cases cluster together in different groups in terms of shared characteristics, as we saw in Research in Practice 14.2.

Network displays can be used to depict the network of relationships in which individuals or social units (e.g. teams) are located. The result is a simplified form of social network diagram, as shown in Figure 14.12, which depicts the actors involved in the award of research grants. While members of the network interact with each other, not every node interacts with all the others. The specific pattern of relationships between nodes results in different network forms. Social networks can be drawn from two perspectives: whole-network views depict the entire network within a defined boundary such as an organization; person-centred networks depict the network around the focal member (such as a particular individual). Simple network diagrams can be useful to capture the context of the issue that you are studying, depicting not only the key actors but also the roles that they play, what is exchanged (e.g. applications, grant funding, reviews, and so on), positive or negative attitudes, and other contextual information.

14.6.2 Answering 'why' questions

If your study focuses on 'why' questions your goal is to explain why something is happening. As explained in Chapter 4, this is a controversial area, but we can nevertheless suggest two key applications for qualitative research methods: investigating causal mechanisms

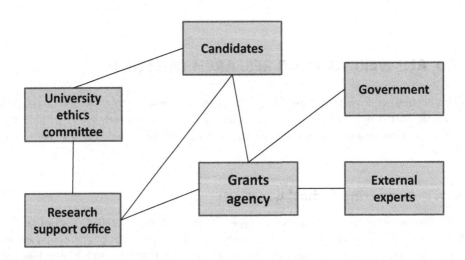

FIGURE 14.12 Example of a simple social network display

and understanding actors' reasons and beliefs in a particular situation. One approach is to apply what Saldaña (2021: 245) calls 'causation coding', which attempts to identify the mental models people use to make sense of cause-and-effect questions, placing the emphasis on actors' reasoning in a particular situation. Saldaña (2021: 243) suggests that words and phrases in the data such as 'because', 'so', or 'and that's why' may indicate causal attribution by a participant.

Data matrices can help us explore patterns of potential causes, causal mechanisms, and outcomes. Miles et al. (2020: 230) suggest starting with an 'explanatory matrix' as an 'initial first step to answer why certain outcomes were achieved and what caused them'. To illustrate this type of matrix, suppose that we were investigating the impact of an advertising campaign on customers' brand perceptions. During the coding process, the researcher classified participants according to their status as customers, their overall assessment of the campaign, their views on the campaign, and their resulting intentions. Subsequently, the researcher started to build an explanatory matrix, as shown in Table 14.4, to bring together these different dimensions.

To get a deeper understanding of causal factors we can use cross-case comparisons to investigate the relationship between influencing factors and outcomes of interest to the research. Data matrices can be very helpful here since they facilitate such comparisons.

You can also depict causal relationships using network displays, which can take the form of the sort of causal diagrams typically associated with quantitative explanatory research. This format is particularly suitable if the subsequent model is to be further tested using quantitative methods, for instance, as part of a mixed methods study, as exemplified in Research in Practice 14.3. In other situations, it may take the form of systems diagrams, incorporating feedback loops and other mechanisms.

TABLE 14.4 Example of an explanatory matrix (numbers in brackets indicate interview number: line number)

Customer type	Overall assessment (0 = neutral, + = positive, – = negative)	Short-run effects (e.g. belief state of viewers)	Longer-run consequences (e.g. intentions of viewers)	Researcher explanation
Prospective customer	0	'Sounds great but would they really do that?' (4: 8) 'All companies say that sort of thing' (6: 23)	No examples of intention to change current behaviour	Advertising campaign seen as not credible
Existing customers (satisfied)	+	'They go to the end of the world to help the customer' (1: 11)	. . .	. . .
Existing customers (dissatisfied)	–	'This never happens in reality. It is all a lie' (3: 36) 'It's not like that at all' (7: 12)	. . . . . .	. . .

Research in practice 14.3 Using a diagram in an investigation of service abandonment causes

In this project, researchers conducted 27 face-to-face interviews to identify factors that may cause customers to abandon interactions with chatbots. The coding process resulted in the identification of problems experienced during interactions with chatbots, the consequence of those problems for customers, and who they blamed for the problem experienced. The cause-effect links detected were represented in a network diagram.

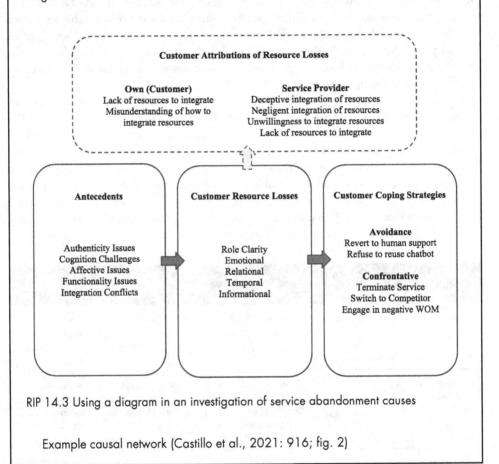

RIP 14.3 Using a diagram in an investigation of service abandonment causes

Example causal network (Castillo et al., 2021: 916; fig. 2)

Miles et al. (2020) caution against trying to develop a causal network too early in your analysis and then imposing that network on the analysis that follows. Instead, they emphasize the need for thorough coding and concept development, giving a sound basis on which to build any causal model. Even then, as we have repeatedly emphasized, you should be cautious about making causal claims.

14.6.3 Answering 'how' questions

A study focusing on 'how' questions aims to explain what happens by taking a process view, such as the sequence of events or activities that lead to a particular outcome. Qualitative methods are particularly well suited to investigating process and building theory about change, as we pointed out in Chapter 4. Coding plays an important part in process research, even when subsequent analysis is done quantitatively, because of the need to identify events that are relevant to the process being analyzed. Event types can vary according to the purpose of the study. Poole et al. (2000), for example, suggest six categories for coding events in the context of innovation research:

1. Activity events, such as administrative reviews, strategy meetings, and budgeting cycles
2. Idea events, when a significant change in ideas about the innovation occurs
3. People events, when there is a change in personnel or roles
4. Transaction events, when there is a change in the legal or social contracts linked to the innovation
5. Context events, when there is a change in the external or organizational environment of the innovation
6. Outcome events, when there is a change in the criteria by which the innovation is judged

When coding participant accounts from a process perspective, Saldaña (2021: 145) suggests that expressions such as 'if', 'then', 'and so' may indicate a sequence or process.

A time-ordered visual display can be particularly useful for the study of processes. You can create a matrix in which you cross-tabulate events, arranged in time order, against other dimensions of your topic, such as who is involved. For a study of the spread of innovation, for example, you might use the column headers in the matrix to record the key stages (events) in the process and the rows to represent hierarchical levels such as individual, team, organization, and so on. The cells are then populated with relevant data; for instance, details of what happened and why. Again, you can add symbols or use formatting to emphasize aspects of the data, such as their relative importance or a change of direction. This type of matrix is called an events listing, and we show an example in Research in Practice 14.4.

You can also produce an edited version of the event listings matrix called a critical incidents matrix (Miles et al., 2020). In a critical incidents matrix you present the data organized by time and type of event, but you display information only for those events considered important for the issue that you are studying, either by you as the researcher or from the perspective of the participants, for example, an economic inducement, an educational initiative, or a change in the environment. Critical incident matrices can be produced at varying levels of detail. The focus on specific incidents helps us to gauge the chain of events that lead to a particular outcome and facilitates the comparison across research settings. However, it requires you to manipulate the data, making decisions on what to include and what to leave out. What seems important at one stage may seem less so later in the analysis. Conversely, information that seemed unimportant early in the analysis process may acquire heightened importance in the light of additional data or further analysis. Hence, it is important to keep an open mind when preparing this type of chart and revisit it as you collect and analyze more data. You should start with a full events chart before producing the version that focuses on critical events only. Moreover, you should keep detailed notes about why you kept specific events in the chart or excluded them.

Research in practice 14.4 Visualizing events and processes

The figures in the next section were produced for a study of customer monitoring processes at a UK bank, labelled as BFI (Canhoto, 2007).

Customers' banking behaviour is scrutinized by customer-facing staff and the automated transaction monitoring system. Behaviour that does not match existing prototypes of 'legitimate behaviour' is categorized as 'unusual' and reported to the MLRO unit. The analysts in this unit investigate the alert, alongside other input such as previous transaction history. If they agree that the behaviour is not legitimate, the case is referred to an external entity (the FIU) using a form known as 'SAR'.

The sequence of events is illustrated in matrix form. Time is shown on the left-hand side, from top to bottom, mirroring how text is read in the UK, where the work was published. Other variables deemed important for the analysis are captured as column headers.

The display here shows the same monitoring process but in network format. Time is represented on the vertical axis and agents on the horizontal one. Other elements of the process are captured within the network. Symbolic elements are used to aid in the communication of the findings, such as boxes to represent inputs, diamonds to represent decisions, and triangles to represent decision outcomes.

Step	Agent	Activity	Input	Category	Output
#1	• BANK staff (e.g., branch) • ATMS • External sources (e.g., victim of fraud)	Scrutiny	Observed banking behaviour	Unusual behaviour	Referral to MLRO team: Alert
#2	• Analysts	Analysis	• Alert • Client history • Specific intelligence re: client or transaction	Suspicious behaviour	Referral to FIU: SAR

RIP 14.4A Events listing matrix for the detection of financial crime at BFI

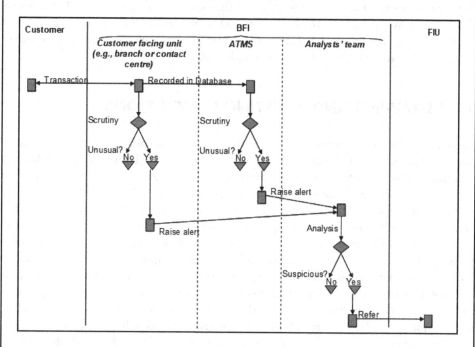

RIP 14.4B Network display for the detection of financial crime at BFI

You can also use networks to visualize processes. Networks are better than matrices for communicating the idea of flow, capturing complex or long processes, representing recurring events, and emphasizing how individual events reinforced each other, as illustrated in Figure 14.13. Networks are also very effective to represent decision processes. Flow charts, in particular, are very useful to depict key decisions to be made, the alternatives available at each point, and the consequences of the various decisions. Research in Practice 14.4 shows a network display used in this way. Despite the benefits of network displays to visualize processes, they offer limited opportunities to provide detailed information about

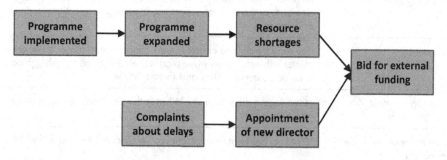

FIGURE 14.13 Example of an events network

the events depicted, the agents involved, and the outcomes of those events. To overcome this, you can use additional visual elements such as the shape of the boxes, the width of lines, colours, and various symbols to convey more information; for instance, events may be depicted by rectangular boxes and actions by circles.

14.7 DRAWING AND VERIFYING CONCLUSIONS

As you code your data, prepare memos, and create visual displays, you begin to identify significant parts of the data, key themes and how they are related, and to draw conclusions. We presented some tactics to help you make sense of qualitative data in Table 14.5, to be used in conjunction with the tools we have introduced so far.

The process you follow to reach conclusions will be shaped by the extent to which you are taking an entirely inductive approach versus using a prior theoretical framework. In the former, you identify emerging themes and develop propositions about the relationships between them as analysis unfolds. In the latter, you use existing theory to focus on particular themes and their possible relationships. Either way, you should adopt an iterative approach to your analysis, alternating between data and (emerging) theory in a process of constant comparison between the two. Iteration can deepen our understanding and provide a basis for drawing robust and rigorous conclusions. In our experience this is the most difficult stage of any qualitative analysis project, demanding a combination of creative yet rigorous thinking.

14.7.1 Counting in qualitative research

Counting can help you generate insight from qualitative data. We are not referring here to the use of quantitative methods (such as quantitative content analysis) to analyze non-numeric data, or a mixed methods study, but instead, the use of counting (such

TABLE 14.5 Tactics for getting meaning out of data (based on Miles et al., 2020)

Tactic	Comments
Noticing patterns	Look for patterns of similarities and differences between categories and/or patterns of processes, involving connections in time and space
Clustering	You may be able to cluster coded concepts into larger categories, cluster subjects (interviewees/cases, etc.) into meaningful groups, and/or cluster activities and events into sets
Making contrasts/comparisons	How does X differ from Y? What is the practical significance of any difference?
Noting relations between concepts	What sort of relationships can you envisage between X and Y?

Neighbourhood A   Neighbourhood B

FIGURE 14.14 Example word clouds

as the number of times a code occurs in a particular source) to check our own under-standings of what is happening in the qualitative data. For instance, counting can be used as a form of preliminary analysis, identifying patterns in the data and providing inspiration for further, in-depth investigation. It can also be used to verify our findings and interpretations, checking for negative evidence or ensuring that we are not relying on some informants to the exclusion of others. In addition, when reporting results, exact counts may be preferable to using vague expressions such as 'many interviewees' or 'the majority of participants'. Counting is done automatically, in the case of CAQ-DAS. If using text processing or spreadsheets, you can tally the number of entries for a particular code.

You can also use word clouds to visualize, or present, the frequency of different words in your data, or to contrast the dominant words across different groups. Figure 14.14, for example, shows word clouds for how people in two different London neighbour-hoods described the area where they lived. People in neighbourhood A used the word 'home' more often than the other group and emphasized education opportunities. People in neighbourhood B, on the other hand, mentioned the multicultural nature of the area, with its markets and festivals, and emphasized the transport links.

McNaught and Lam (2010) highlight the following limitations of word clouds:

- It is not possible to trace the words back to the original text. For instance, we cannot know from the word cloud what the term 'different' refers to, in the case of the word cloud for neighbourhood B, in Figure 14.14.
- Word clouds treat each word as the unit of analysis, rather than phrases. As a result, it fails to record or represent multi-word expressions such as 'Notting Hill' (neighbour-hood B). We would need to remove the space between the words in such expressions (e.g. 'NottingHill') for them to be considered together.

Remember, however, that the basis of qualitative analysis is interpretation and the under-standing of the diversity of a phenomenon, not its frequency. Something that occurs only once in your data may be analytically as important as something that occurs many times. Moreover, we cannot use counting to draw conclusions in qualitative analysis because neither the sample sizes nor the non-probability sampling methods typical of qualitative research would permit reliable statistical inference beyond the sample. Counting only has a supporting role in qualitative analysis.

14.7.2 Determining the trustworthiness of your findings

Rigorous and disciplined thinking must be carried through into the final stages of your analysis, in the way you determine the credibility of your findings. In Chapter 4 we discussed the question of quality in research. We recommend that you reread that section carefully, noting the methods suggested there. In addition, Table 14.6 offers a number of suggestions for testing or confirming your findings.

14.8 REPORTING QUALITATIVE DATA ANALYSIS

In this final section of the chapter we look at aspects of presenting the results of your qualitative data analysis. Whilst you should follow the general guidelines and structure for a research report discussed in Chapter 15, there are some points to bear in mind when reporting qualitative research.

Preserving confidentiality and anonymity

In-depth analysis, small sample sizes, and the use of direct quotations from sources can make it especially difficult to preserve the anonymity and confidentiality of participants when writing up. A single data extract may be enough to reveal the identity of a participant or an organization to the reader. Ensure that you carefully screen all direct quotations, paraphrases, or summaries to guarantee that any identifying references are removed or changed so as to preserve anonymity. In addition, as discussed in Chapter 5, you should use pseudonyms (e.g. Big Bank, Pharmco, etc.) or other designators (A, B, etc.) when referring to particular participants. Alternatively, you can use generic descriptions, such as job role. This requirement can make it difficult when describing your sample since some level of detail may be need for the credibility of your research and to provide relevant contextual or demographic background. Table 14.7 gives an example of how participant anonymity can be balanced with the inclusion of background and contextual details.

14.8.1 Presenting quotations

Verbatim quotations from interviews or other sources play an important part in your write-up. They can be employed to show the language people use in connection with a particular topic, to illustrate the meanings they attach to what is going on, to indicate how

TABLE 14.6 Testing and confirming your findings

Tactic	Explanation
Triangulation	Triangulation is based on the idea that multiple perspectives on a research situation can be compared to see whether findings can be confirmed. Options include the following: • Data triangulation, comparing multiple sources of evidence (such as different interview participants or types of data) • Theory triangulation, comparing different theoretical perspectives of the same data • Researcher triangulation, checking for agreement between evaluators (see inter-rater reliability on the companion website) • Methodological triangulation, comparing findings using different research methods in a multi-method study
Participant validation	You can use participant validation (or member checking) at different points in the research, for example, to give participants an opportunity to comment on interview transcripts or to gain feedback on emerging and/or final findings of your research. Feedback may give additional insight into the research findings from the perspective of those involved in the situation rather than as a validation of the 'truth' status of the findings. In applied research projects, you may seek feedback from potential users of the output in terms of its practical relevance.
Checking that we have not been biased in our selection or interpretation of the data	It is easy to be influenced by a particularly compelling account or be biased in our selection of data, for example, during coding. Common mistakes include the following: • Overreliance on easily accessible informants • Overweighting dramatic events • Overweighting evidence that fits the researcher's emerging explanation rather than contradicting it
Weighing the evidence	We may need to weigh the evidence collected, for example, to resolve conflicting factual accounts. Factors to consider include the following: • Nature of the informants/data sources – how well informed are they about a particular aspect of your topic? • Circumstances of data collection – do these impact on the quality of your data? • Can you validate the data in some way (e.g. through triangulation)?
Looking for negative (disconfirming) evidence	Look out for evidence that contradicts emerging explanations (the term 'deviant case' is sometimes used to refer to such evidence). How does such evidence affect those explanations? What modifications are necessary to your emerging conclusions?
Checking out rival explanations	Think about rival explanations that may account for what you are finding in your data. Perhaps there is an alternative explanation that is stronger than the one you had developed initially. Here, looking for negative evidence can be helpful
Reflecting on our own role and its influence on the research process	As discussed in Chapter 1, as researchers we are active agents in the research process, including the analysis and our final account. You can consider including a reflexive account as part of the final report, where you reflect on your role in the research process.

TABLE 14.7 Example table showing participant details		
Case	*Type*	*Participants*
CONCO	Construction company	1 senior manager 3 project managers 1 project management office staff member
SOFCO	Software engineering company	1 senior manager 2 project managers 3 SCRUM masters
DESCO	Design consultancy	2 senior managers 2 project managers 1 project management office staff member

they express their views, and to portray the richness of individual accounts. Silverman (2022: 544) offers the following advice on presenting verbatim quotations:

- Make one point at a time.
- 'Top and tail' each extract to show how it fits into your analysis, in what we call the 'hamburger' technique.
- Acknowledge any limitations of your data and your analysis of them.
- Convince the reader of the soundness of your interpretation.

Silverman (2022) also suggests numbering your data extracts, if you are referring to an extract several times and at different points in your write-up.

Quotations should typically be no longer than two or three sentences for most qualitative data analysis (longer extracts may be used in specific techniques such as conversation analysis). Very short extracts can be incorporated into the body of the text; longer ones are best presented as separate blocks of text, indented to make their status as quotations clear to the reader.

You should note, however, that if you include quotes from publicly available data such as social media posts, it will be possible to identify who has said that. Depending on the focus and terms of your study, this may represent a violation of the principles of informed consent and anonymity discussed in Chapter 5. As a result, it may not be possible to include verbatim quotes of your online data in your report.

14.8.2 Presenting data using visual data displays

Visual data displays can be a very effective way of presenting aspects of your findings. It is important not to overuse them and to remember that they do not constitute analysis on their own. The 'hamburger' method described for presenting quotations should also be used to introduce visual displays and explain their significance. As with verbatim quotes, you need to assess whether it is ethical to use visual data collected from social media and other online platforms. You will also need to make sure that they are clear and easy to follow.

CHAPTER SUMMARY

- The process of qualitative analysis of data includes organizing, preparing, coding, and visualizing your data, as well as drawing conclusions and presenting your findings.
- Qualitative data analysis is typically iterative in nature and may begin during the data collection to support sampling.
- You may accumulate data sources in different formats that require systematic organization prior to analysis. Preparation includes transcribing audio and video recordings.
- Coding helps you to reduce the data and move from raw data to meaningful themes. Hierarchical coding helps you to analyze data at varying but related levels of abstraction.
- Memoing provides a way of capturing your thoughts with respect to coding, emerging theory, and operational issues in your analysis.
- Software can help you manipulate and visualize the data. For larger projects, you may consider using a CAQDAS programme, although you should be aware of the strengths and weaknesses of such software.
- It can be difficult to analyze large sections of text and cumbersome to communicate your findings using just words. Visual displays help to overcome these limitations.
- Matrices display data in the form of cross-tabulations, whereas networks display data using nodes and links. You can use additional dimensions to represent time and level of analysis and formatting and symbols to increase the amount of information conveyed.
- Coding and visual displays can be used together to help you answer your research questions. Matrices and networks help you to identify and compare key concepts, actors, and contextual factors when answering 'what' questions. Visual displays also help to explain the effects observed, or why things happened the way they did, to answer 'why' questions. Finally, matrices and networks are useful to capture the sequence of events and activities over time, when analyzing process in response to 'how' questions.
- It is essential to verify your findings to ensure the trustworthiness of your study. Verification techniques include triangulation, participant validation, and looking for negative evidence.

Presenting qualitative data involves careful attention to respecting commitments to anonymity and confidentiality. Data extracts and visual displays should be presented one at a time using the 'hamburger' technique of introducing, presenting and commenting on the material.

NEXT STEPS

14.1 Getting ready. Organize your data into files and give them descriptive names. Transcribe your audio and video recordings, if relevant. Type and save your field notes, using the same filing and naming system used for your data files. Decide whether you are going to use software to analyze your data and, if relevant, find out what training and support are available.

14.2 Familiarizing yourself with your data. Read and reread your data carefully. Use memos to capture your ideas and emerging themes. Ensure that your memos are cross-referenced with your data so that you can easily locate and retrieve that piece of data later, if needed.

14.3 Coding your data. Ensure that you keep an index of your codes and their definitions, including any hierarchical relationships between them. If you rename or change your codes, remember to revisit the coded material to assess whether the chosen label is still relevant.

14.4 Staying organized. Ensure that you save all relevant output. Make a note of preliminary findings in your memos and their implications for your research questions. As you work, keep a detailed log of what you do, to help you write up the final report.

14.5 Reviewing your analysis plan. Review your analysis plan to ensure that it is still appropriate in the light of your data exploration. Decide what changes, if any, need to be made (for example, collect more data). If appropriate, you should discuss these with your supervisor.

14.6 Answering your research questions. Develop visual displays for your data, depending on whether you are pursuing a what, why, or how type of project.

    a. Experiment with alternative matrices and networks.

    b. Develop displays for various level of analysis.

    c. Revisit previous displays as the analysis progresses and your understanding of the data improves.

    d. Draw out and review the trustworthiness of your conclusions.

    e. Keep a log of what you do and save relevant output for your report.

FURTHER READING

For further reading, please see the companion website.

REFERENCES

Attride-Stirling, J. (2001). Thematic networks: An analytic tool for qualitative research. *Qualitative Research*, 1(3): 385–405.

Blumer, H. (1954). What is wrong with social theory? *American Sociological Review*, 19(1): 3–10.

Braun, V. and Clarke, V. (2006). Using thematic analysis in psychology. *Qualitative Research in Psychology*, 3(2): 77–101.

Braun, V. and Clarke, V. (2022). *Thematic Analysis: A Practical Guide*. London: SAGE Publications.

Canhoto, A. I. (2007). *Profiling Behaviour: The Social Construction of Categories in the Detection of Financial Crime*. PhD thesis, London School of Economics, London.

Castillo, D., Canhoto, A. I. and Said, E. (2021). The dark side of AI-powered service interactions: Exploring the process of co-destruction from the customer perspective. *The Service Industries Journal*, 41(13–14): 900–925.

Corbin, J. and Strauss, A. (2015). *Basics of Qualitative Research*. 4th ed. Thousand Oaks, CA: SAGE Publications.

Dey, I. (1993). *Qualitative Data Analysis*. London: Routledge.

Hahn, C. (2008). *Doing Qualitative Research Using Your Computer: A Practical Guide*. London: SAGE Publications.

King, N. (2004). Using templates in the thematic analysis of text. In: Cassell, C. and Symon, G. (eds) *Essential Guide to Qualitative Methods in Organizational Research*. London: SAGE Publications.

Lewins, A. and Silver, C. (2009). *Choosing a CAQDAS Package: NCRM Working Paper*. Available at: http://eprints.ncrm.ac.uk/791/1/2009ChoosingaCAQDASPackage.pdf (Accessed 7 November 2009).

McNaught, C. and Lam, P. (2010). Using wordle as a supplementary research tool. *Qualitative Report*, 15(3): 630–643.

Miles, M. B., Huberman, M. A. and Saldaña, J. (2020). *Qualitative Data Analysis*. 4th ed. Thousand Oaks, CA: SAGE Publications.

Poole, M. S., Van de Ven, A. H., Dooley, K. and Holmes, M. E. (2000). *Organizational Change and Innovation Processes*. Oxford: Oxford University Press.

Saldaña, J. (2021). *The Coding Manual for Qualitative Researchers*. 4th ed. London: SAGE Publications.

Silverman, D. (2022). *Doing Qualitative Research: A Practical Handbook*. 6th ed. London: SAGE Publications.

PART V

Communicate

Part V addresses how to communicate the output of your research to interested audiences. As these audiences may vary, we look at three specific types of research reporting: an academic report being submitted for assessment as part of an academic qualification, writing an academic paper for a journal, and a report for a practitioner audience. We provide guidance on the structure and content for each and identify the typical differences between them. This is supported by advice and tips on the process of writing and editing. We conclude the chapter with a look at alternative ways of communicating your results including via digital channels.

Chapter in Part 5:
15: Reporting your research

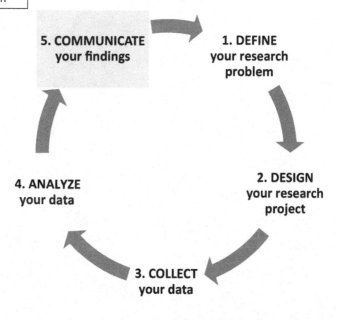

5. COMMUNICATE
your findings

1. DEFINE
your research
problem

2. DESIGN
your research
project

3. COLLECT
your data

4. ANALYZE
your data

DOI: 10.4324/9781003381006-19

Reporting your research

15.1 INTRODUCTION

You are now reaching the final stage of your research project. You have collected and analyzed your data, and the task before you now is to communicate your findings. If you cannot do so successfully, then it does not matter how well you have done or how hard you have worked up to this point: people either will never hear of your research or will ignore it if they do. Reporting your research is therefore a key stage in your project. It is also one that can be very demanding, especially if you are new to research and/or new to report writing. In essence, reporting will involve answering four questions about your research.

1. What? The topic of your research.
2. Why? The problem that your research addresses.
3. How? The research methods you used to carry out your research.
4. So what? The conclusions and recommendations from your findings.

How you communicate the answers to those questions and to what level of detail will depend on the purpose of your project and the audience you are trying to reach. In this

DOI: 10.4324/9781003381006-20

chapter we therefore look at different ways of reporting your research and for different audiences. We begin by looking at written reports, starting with writing for an academic qualification such as a dissertation or thesis. We then discuss what to consider when writing for an academic journal or for a practitioner audience should you wish to publish your research internally or externally. We then take a more detailed look at the writing process itself. We end the chapter by introducing other ways of communicating your research results particularly using the opportunities offered by digital channels.

15.2 WRITING FOR AN ACADEMIC QUALIFICATION

If you are doing your research project as a student researcher you will almost certainly be expected to produce a written report which will form all or part of the assessment for your academic or professional qualification. Depending on the qualification, its level, and where you are studying, the report may be referred to as a research project, dissertation, or thesis. In the UK, the word dissertation is typically used at master's-level and thesis at doctoral level; in the USA it is usually the other way around.

Regardless of the terminology, reports written for an academic qualification share a number of characteristics. Firstly, the primary audience for your report will be your supervisor and other academic tutors who will read it in order to assess and examine whether it meets the required standard for your course of study. Make sure therefore that you understand the assessment process and the criteria against which your project will be marked. Secondly, particularly at master's level and above, you will typically be expected to demonstrate an understanding of existing theory and prior research in your topic area and where your own research fits within that. This is usually assessed by requiring a critical review of the literature in the report. Thirdly, you will have to explain and justify the way you carried out your investigation, usually by way of a section of the report focused on the research design. Finally, you will be required to conform to the structure and format laid down by your academic institution for your particular degree, as we discuss next.

15.2.1 Structure and content of a report for an academic qualification

Although academic institutions and different qualifications vary in terms of their detailed requirements, there is a generic structure that is followed for many academic reports, which we outline in Table 15.1 before discussing key elements in more detail.

Title page

The detailed content of the title page will probably be specified by your academic institution. The one item that you will have freedom over, however, is the title of your report. In your research proposal, you will have given your project a working title (Chapter 8) that captured the intention of the research at that point. Now is the time to review that provisional title. Does it still reflect the actual nature of the research undertaken and/or the

TABLE 15.1 Typical structure and components of a report for an academic qualification

Part	Component	Description
Front matter	Title page	Indicates the title, author, and the qualification for which submission of the report forms all or part.
	Abstract	A concise summary of the report for the reader.
	Acknowledgements	Thanks or other acknowledgements for support or help during the research.
	Table of contents	Section and subsection headings and page numbers.
	Lists of tables and figures	If required, lists of tables, figures, or other numbered items, with page numbers.
	List of abbreviations or technical glossary	If required (may be needed in some research projects, depending on the subject matter).
Body of report	Introduction	Background to the research problem, why it is significant, the overall purpose of your research, and the structure of the report.
	Literature review	A critical review of the literature in the topic, locating your own research within it, and leading into your research questions.
	Research questions/ hypotheses	Statement of the specific research questions and, if included, any research hypotheses (often supported by a conceptual model).
	Research design	An overview and justification of the research design used in the project.
	Results	Presentation of the results of the analysis, supported by appropriate extracts from the data or output from the analysis. Sometimes combined with discussion into a single section.
	Discussion	Discussion of the results of the analysis in the context, for example, of the literature. This section may include a discussion of research limitations.
	Conclusions and recommendations	Conclusions of the research in relation to the research questions and recommendations for theory/practice as a result. This section often includes a discussion of research limitations, if not discussed earlier. Suggestions for further research are often made at this point.
End matter	Reference list	List of all works cited in the report in the required format.
	Appendices	Additional information that may be relevant to readers of the report but does not form part of the main body.

outcomes? Does the wording convey the essence of what the research is about, including the key concepts or variables involved? If it needs to, does it communicate the context of the research or the method used so as to help the reader judge its relevance? If the answer to any of those is 'no', you should review and edit your title.

In Research in Practice 15.1 we list the titles of a selection of articles to show different ways in which the writers have presented their work. Note the use of two-part titles, with the parts separated by a colon (:). This can be used to separate a more general statement of the topic area from details about the specific subject, the research method, or the context of the research. It is sometimes employed to separate an attention-grabbing or humorous headline from a more serious statement of the subject matter. As we noted in Chapter 8, however, humour or catchy phrasing should be used only if it is likely to be acceptable to the target audience. If you do use the colon method, you should still keep your title concise and to the point.

Research in practice 15.1 Research titles

Here is a selection of titles from research articles that illustrate different approaches. Consider how effectively the titles communicate to you the nature of the project and how it influences your expectations about the research.

- 'Women and the labyrinth of leadership' (Eagly and Carli, 2007)
- 'Does VRIO help managers evaluate a firm's resources?' (Knott Paul, 2015)
- 'Snakes and ladders: Unpacking the personalisation-privacy paradox in the context of AI-enabled personalisation in the physical retail environment' (Canhoto et al., 2023)
- 'Shaken and stirred: A content analysis of women's portrayals in James Bond films' (Neuendorf et al., 2010)
- 'Coaching the "ideal worker": female leaders and the gendered self in a global corporation' (Gray et al., 2019)
- 'Does Agile work? A quantitative analysis of agile project success' (Serrador and Pinto, 2015)
- 'The influence of the Five Factor Model of personality on the perceived effectiveness of executive coaching. International Journal of Evidence Based Coaching and Mentoring' (Jones et al., 2014)
- 'Factors for success in customer relationship management (CRM) systems' (Wilson et al., 2002)
- 'Chocs away: Weight watching in the contemporary airline industry' (Tyler and Abbott, 1998)
- 'MNCs and religious influences in global markets: drivers of consumer-based halal brand equity' (Butt et al., 2017)

Abstract or executive summary

Research reports may vary as to whether they begin with an executive summary or an abstract, so be aware of the requirements for your qualification. An executive summary often appears at the beginning of business documents or reports and is no more than a page or two at the most. It is intended to be a concise and easy way for a busy executive to understand the objective(s) and key outputs of the report without reading it in full. It should provide the reader with a clear understanding of the topic, the key conclusions, and any recommendations being drawn. It may also include concise details of the data used or basis for the report's findings. Similarly, executive summaries may be used at the start of a research report to provide the reader with a concise understanding of the research and similarly inform the reader of the research problem, how it was conducted, and the key conclusions and recommendations.

An abstract appears at the start of an academic report or academic journal article. It provides a short, concise, and accurate summary of the content of the report. It should allow the potential reader the opportunity to familiarize themselves with the content of your report and decide whether or not to read the full document. Typical content includes the following:

- the research topic
- the purpose of the research
- outline of the research design
- key findings and conclusions

The length of the abstract varies. For a short report, a single page is sufficient, although your institution may give specific guidelines or word count. Students often fail to provide sufficient information about the findings of the research in the abstract. Craswell (2005) suggests that about two-thirds of the abstract should be devoted to the findings and conclusions, but again, you may be given more specific guidance. Abstracts do not normally include figures or references. Along with your title, the abstract is the first thing the reader will encounter, so it is important to get it right. Our suggestion is that you write it last, but not at the last minute: give yourself time to refine and edit it before submission.

Table of contents

This is an essential component of your report and should accurately show all chapters and subsections of chapters, along with their page numbers. If appropriate, include lists of tables and figures as well, and a list of abbreviations and technical glossary (as in Table 15.1).

Introduction

The introduction should review the background to the research problem, establish its significance, explain the overall purpose of your research, and lead the reader into the report itself by setting out the structure of the document. At the end of the introduction you and your reader will have a shared understanding of what is to follow. Building on ideas by Booth et al. (2008) and Minto (2009), we suggest the following general structure for your introduction:

- *Background.* Introduce the background to the research problem. In applied research this will relate primarily to the organizational/business context; in pure research, relevant context is likely to be the area of theory to which the research will contribute.

This part of the introduction should be self-sufficient and noncontroversial and establish 'common ground' with the reader (Booth et al., 2008: 235).

- *The problem.* Introduce the 'complication' (Minto, 2009: 27) that disrupts the situation you have described in the background and that gives rise to the problem that motivates your research.
- *The research aim.* You should explain the aim of the research, which is most often framed as a research question(s) and/or a series of research objective(s) that the study aims to answer. Research objectives and/or research questions are crucial as they provide the guidance for the subsequent research process. Depending on the requirements of your institution, these may appear in the introduction or in a separate section later.
- *The solution.* This is where you indicate how your research will contribute to resolving the problem. At doctoral level it is most often the convention to provide a brief summary of your findings as well as the key contributions given the extensive nature of the research. At master's level and below, this may be a discussion of how your research objectives/research questions will enable you to explore the research problem.
- *Report structure.* Finally, your introduction should provide the reader with the structure of the report, giving indications of the content and running order of chapters or sections.

The length of the introduction depends on the length of the overall report and any word count restrictions or guidance. We illustrate these elements in use in Research in Practice 15.2; for a longer introduction, each element should be expanded as required to provide adequate coverage. Your introduction should also be appropriately referenced and make use of supporting data, such as industry statistics, particularly in the background section.

Research in practice 15.2 Writing your introduction

Here we show you the way in which we can use the framework to write a short introduction. Note that your own introduction is likely to be much longer and contain more detail under each of the four areas shown in bold type, including citations as appropriate.

With the development of e-retailing, more consumers are shopping online, including for high-involvement, high-priced products such as furniture or cars. Sensory information such as sight, touch, or sound can be important when purchasing but are constrained or not available online. [Background].

Sensory-enabling technologies are now increasingly available. E-retailers want to understand the value of investing in them and the impact that lack of sensory input has on online purchase intentions. [Problem].

The objective of the study was to test a model of the effects of sensory stimulation during purchase of online high-involvement products. [Research aim].

This research investigates the effects of varying levels of sensory experience upon other factors that influence purchase intention such as buyer concerns about risk, trust, and the role of the store versus the website. [Solution].

The report is organized. . . . [Structure].

Literature review

Chapter 3 gave advice on the role of the literature review in research and how to carry one out. We will not repeat all of that advice here but instead stress the need to ensure that your review is successfully integrated into your research report. Remember that if you have adopted a deductive, theory-testing approach, your literature review forms the basis for the development of your conceptual model and any hypotheses you are planning to test. In an inductive approach, your literature review will frame the problem and may provide sensitizing concepts that will have informed your data collection and analysis.

Research questions/hypotheses

This may be a relatively short section but is very important to the reader's understanding of the research. Here you should state your research questions if you have not already done so, numbering them, if you have more than one, so that they are clear to the reader. If you have adopted a deductive approach, you may also choose this point, rather than the end of the literature review, to present the full version of your conceptual model, along with any hypotheses.

Research design

As we noted earlier, one of the characteristics of academic research reports is that they contain details of the research methods used. This section may go under different labels, such as 'research methodology', 'research methods', or 'investigation design', but whatever the terminology, it should provide a comprehensive account of the research design, which will allow the reader to evaluate the approach taken and whether or not it was suitable. Key elements in this section include

- overall approach to the research, including the philosophical orientation taken (Chapters 1 and 4 provide additional guidance on describing your overall approach);
- research design adopted;
- sampling method used and details of the sample obtained;
- data collection techniques used (such as questionnaire, in-depth interviews), including the following:

  - data collection instrument, for example, how you developed your questionnaire and the measures used
  - pretesting and piloting of your data collection techniques
  - field procedures used in interviews or observation, or details of questionnaire administration

- data analysis techniques used to analyze your data (although results are not presented until later);
- quality control measures used in the research (see Chapter 4 for guidance on quality criteria);
- ethical issues faced and how they were dealt with (see Chapter 5).

The detailed structure of this section and the language that you use should reflect the research design that you have adopted, but the headings provide an outline structure. Throughout this section you should aim to describe what you did and how you did it and to justify why that was appropriate. This includes the strategic-level decisions about why a particular research design was chosen and the more tactical-level choices of particular techniques, such as online rather than face-to-face interviews.

Results

In this section of your report you provide the reader with the results of your data analysis. You will therefore need to decide what to include. Go back to your research questions and consider how each can best be answered by the data analysis you have carried out. Be selective in what you use, and do not overwhelm your reader with too much raw data or pages of graphs, tables, or visual displays. Instead include the material that most clearly illuminates the points you wish to convey. Remember that in a research report, the data that you present in your results section provide the evidence for your conclusions and subsequent recommendations.

When presenting your results, whether in the form of tables, charts, quotations, or visual displays of qualitative data, make sure that you provide supporting commentary. Use the hamburger or sandwich technique as we have recommended in earlier chapters to top and tail each piece of data or analysis output:

- Introduce the data
- Present the data in a suitable format
- Bring out the 'so whats?' by commenting on its relevance

In addition, if you are using charts, tables, or figures, ensure that each is clearly numbered, captioned, and referred to in the text.

Think about how you will structure your results section. A common mistake in student projects is simply to organize and report the results one question at a time, with each question forming, in effect, a separate section. Aside from taking up a lot of space, it is difficult to convey a coherent message to the reader. Instead, try to group your results into logical subsections. When reporting quantitative research, this may involve presenting related questions, such as classification variables, together. In qualitative research you can use your higher-level codes (Chapter 14) to help you structure your results in a thematic way. Remember that qualitative results are not normally reported using quantitative display techniques such as graphs or bar charts. This is because the sample size will be too small but more importantly because the purpose of qualitative data is not to measure but rather to explore and gain rich data on the phenomenon. If you have conducted a mixed methods project, you should also think about how to organize your results. For sequential designs, a simple technique is to report each as a separate stage of the project. For parallel mixed method designs, a thematic presentation of the results, in which findings from both the quantitative and qualitative components of the research are discussed together for each theme, may be more suitable.

Discussion

Having presented the output from the analysis of your data, the next section moves to a discussion of the significance of the findings that you have made. Here you are discussing what you have found (via your own research) in relation to existing knowledge and theoretical understanding (identified in your literature review), as well as how it informs your research problem. If your research adopted a deductive approach, you should discuss the results of your hypothesis tests and other analysis in terms of the statistical and practical significance in relation to your original conceptual model. If your research adopted an inductive approach, you should discuss the extent to which your findings provided a fresh understanding of the research problem. Revisit your literature review and ask yourself, 'are my findings consistent with the existing work on the topic?' If they are, then you can write about the consistency found in your work; if not, then discuss how your findings diverge or are different from existing theory. In your discussion section, try to be aware of the difference between description of your findings and your interpretation of them. Description merely retells what is in the data; interpretation brings out what is significant about them.

Conclusions and recommendations

The focus of the conclusions section is on the contribution of your research to answering the research questions. It can therefore be helpful to start your conclusions section with a brief reminder of the research problem and research questions that you set at the start of the project and to structure the presentation of your conclusions so that they clearly answer the research questions. A mistake sometimes made at this point is to confuse conclusions with findings. Your findings are the outputs from your data analysis. The conclusions are statements that are based on these findings. For example, the findings of a survey may be that '85 per cent of Millenials compared to 60 per cent of Generation X' prefer to shop online. Further analysis suggests that this difference is both statistically and practically significant for the target population. From these findings we conclude that there are generational differences in the usage of online retail websites amongst the target population.

Your conclusions should form the basis on which you make any recommendations regarding your research problem. In pure research, this may involve drawing out the implications for the existing theory in your topic area and how it may need to change to accommodate the results of your project. In applied research, on the other-hand, the focus of the recommendations will be in the area of management practice. Ensure that your recommendations are grounded in your research findings and avoid speculation that is not justified by your own research.

The conclusions section should include a discussion of any limitations of your research (although this may also be done in the discussion section) by reflecting on your research in the light of the quality criteria for research discussed in Chapter 4. No research is perfect, and it is important to be reflective about limitations in your own research, for example, in relation to your sampling strategy or data collection procedures. Finally, you can end your report by discussing how further research may be undertaken in order to progress the investigation of the research problem or to further understand some of the new insights thrown up by your research findings.

Reference list

Referencing is a key part of academic writing. Ensure that you follow the guidelines in Chapter 3 and include a full reference list (or bibliography if required) in the format expected by your institution.

Appendices

Your appendices should contain information that the reader may need to access but that is not part of your main report. Typical material includes the following:

- Copies of your data collection instrument (questionnaire, interview guide etc.)
- Additional output from your analysis (such as more detailed SPSS tables) to support the analysis in the main body
- Examples of briefing letters sent to participants and informed consent forms to document procedures that were followed

The decision about what to include in your appendices is yours, and you need to be selective in what you include in order that the appendices do not grow too large. In most institutions the appendices and reference lists do not form part of the final word count, but this should not be a reason to pack them too full. Make sure that you title and number all appendices, cross-reference them in the main text, and include them in your table of contents.

15.2.2 Telling the story

Table 15.1 has provided a formal structure for your report, but you will also need to think about the storyline for your research report. This storyline should take the reader along a journey from the research problem, via the literature and your research design, to your results and conclusions. This means not developing each section of the report in isolation but seeing instead how they link together to provide a coherent account of your research. You also need to communicate that to the reader. A good introduction will help, but especially in a long report, you should also provide regular signposts or pointers in the report that enable the reader to keep on track. You should also think about the 'shape' of your report. Bem (2003) uses the analogy of an hourglass to describe this idea. The report begins with the broader background to the problem and increasingly narrows its focus through the literature review to the research questions. The research design and results sections are the 'neck' of the hourglass, which starts to broaden out again as you discuss your findings, move on to conclusions and recommendations, and finally, recommendations for further research. By thinking of the hourglass shape of your research report, you can avoid losing focus at the critical point where you present your own research design and your results whilst ensuring that the research is placed in context.

15.3 WRITING FOR AN ACADEMIC JOURNAL

Whilst the initial outlet for your research may well be the dissertation or thesis required by an academic programme, it does not have to stop there. In this section we take a look at writing for an academic journal.

15.3.1 Why write for an academic journal?

There are many motivations that novice researchers may have for deciding to write up their research and submit it to an academic journal for publication. First, publishing in subject-specific academic journals ensures that your work becomes known and recognized to a wider audience in the same discipline. This is how knowledge is captured and shared with others, and if your research findings are new or different, then an academic journal may publish your work. Second, if you are aiming to develop an academic career, it will be essential that you become recognized for the expertise you have in a particular area as you progress in your career. Getting published provides evidence of your work and often connects you with others researching in the same topic.

As a novice researcher, particularly at masters or PhD level, your research may be the first opportunity to become a published author and start your future career. Having publications listed on your CV will be important to becoming visible within your discipline. Achieving first publication of your work can be very exciting and can motivate you and also others to want to work with you. A third reason to publish academically is that in most academic institutions, it is a performance requirement to conduct research and achieve publications. Such academic outputs are an important source of reputational value both for the individual academic and the institution. Finally, academic publication can be a satisfying and rewarding return for your research work. If you are thinking of going for publication, do discuss this with your supervisor, who may be interested to support you.

15.3.2 Selecting a journal

An important first step in getting published academically is to select an appropriate journal for your work. It is more time efficient to write your paper to meet the requirements of a specific journal from the start. From your own knowledge of the topic and your literature review, you will be familiar with the leading journals in the field. It is also possible to find complete listings of academic journals from sources such as the *Academic Journal Guide* issued annually by the Chartered Association of Business Schools (CABS) in the UK or similar.

You should aim to publish in a recognized peer-reviewed academic journal. All academic journals are ranked in terms of the standard and quality of the research as well as having an impact factor. The higher the ranking of the journal, the greater the expectation in terms of the contribution being made by the research (how much it adds something new and different) as well as the robustness of the methodology and data analysis. It can be difficult to publish in a high quality journal so this may be aspirational for you as your career develops.

In addition to looking at the ranking of a journal, it is important to identify a journal that is relevant to your topic and will be sympathetic to the contribution that your research is making, as well as aligned to your methodology. You should spend time looking online at the information that journals provide about their scope and areas of interest in order to identify one that is relevant. Often journals may have a forthcoming 'Special Edition' focusing on a particular topic that may align to your research, and this is often an opportunity to fit with the journal requirements. You are advised to discuss the selection of a targeted journal with your supervisor, who is likely to be also involved in the writing process. When selecting a potential journal, take all of these issues into consideration in order to maximize your likelihood of getting published.

15.3.3 The structure of your paper

All journals provide detailed information for prospective authors including 'Authors Guidelines', which tell you the specific requirements for any paper being submitted (e.g. word count, formatting, referencing style, etc). You should also look at recent example articles provided on their website or via your library. Journals will vary slightly, particularly in terms of how they wish the abstract to be written. In Table 15.1 we offered a general outline structure for an academic qualification. Journal articles can be very similar, but do check with the journal you are targeting. However, while the structure may be similar, the style of writing is different. The word count for an academic paper is likely to be lower, so the style of writing needs to be more concise and direct. Keep in mind that the audience has changed and will now be knowledgeable academics in the field rather than academics, marking your work using assessment criteria. It is not possible merely to cut and paste from your dissertation or thesis but rather the content needs to be written with a different audience in mind. You will need to ensure you quickly communicate the aim and contribution(s) of the research in the introduction and demonstrate in the remainder of the paper how your research achieves this.

15.3.4 The review process

When writing for an academic journal there is no guarantee that your paper will be published. After submission it will pass through a review process that begins with a 'desk review' where an editor will give initial consideration of the submission before deciding whether to pass it on for peer review. 'Blind' peer review involves your paper being reviewed by other expert academics in the field without the authors' names attached. This review process often takes time and may result in a request for some revisions to be made. Most publishers use online submission platforms that allow you to track the progress of your paper. Revisions may take place a number of times, and whilst these may be frustrating, they do most often result in a better finished paper. Alternatively, the review may result in rejection of the paper. Whether rejection occurs at the initial 'desk review' stage or after peer review, this can be demoralizing to receive. Feedback is provided, however, and this can help you to make improvements to the paper. At this stage you will need to begin again the process of looking for a suitable home for your academic paper.

15.4 WRITING FOR A PRACTITIONER AUDIENCE

Communicating the results of your research to practitioners is an important part of many research projects. For some projects, particularly in commercial or policy-making environments, practitioners rather than academics will be the primary audience. Even if your project is for an academic qualification, you may still be expected to communicate your results to other stakeholders, such as members of the organization that requested the research or supported it in other ways. In other situations you may have offered to share your findings with research participants. An academic research report is unlikely to be suitable for a broader audience because of its size, style, and focus. Instead you will need to produce a report (or more than one) tailored to the needs of a different audience.

15.4.1 Understand your audience

You should start, therefore, by understanding what your audience expects. If you have carried out the research for a client organization, you should have agreed the reporting format in the planning stage, so you should revisit that agreement and confirm that it is still applicable. If not, you should discuss the format with the intended recipient, if possible, or if not, seek guidance from experienced colleagues, other researchers, your supervisor, or others who have produced similar reports in the past. You should also consider whether a single format will suit everyone. You may, for example, need to tailor your report to meet the needs of particular groups; for example, a very short nontechnical summary for a broad audience and a more detailed report containing recommendations for managers wanting to use your research to support their decision-making or as a basis for setting future policy.

15.4.2 Structure and content of a practitioner report

Given the diversity of potential audiences, a practitioner report can take many different formats. It will still need to address the four key questions of what you did, why you did it, how you did it, and what your conclusions were, but the emphasis will be different compared to an academic report. Table 15.2 shows what a typical practitioner research report might include.

You will notice three key differences in structure and content, as compared to an academic report (Table 15.1). Firstly, an executive summary will replace the academic abstract. This is not just a change in name. As previously discussed, an executive summary is intended to be read by a busy reader, such as the CEO or head of policy, who wishes to understand the project in an efficient and quick way. It should provide a nontechnical summary of the report that can be understood by a competent lay reader without specialist expertise. The executive summary should typically cover the following:

1. What the research was about.
2. Why the research was done.
3. How it was done.
4. Main conclusions drawn from the research.
5. Recommendations made as a result.

TABLE 15.2 Structure and content of a typical practitioner report

Part	Component	Description
Front matter	Title page	Indicates the title and author
	Executive summary	A concise, nontechnical summary of the report for the reader (replaces the academic abstract)
	Table of contents	Section headings and page numbers; keep this simple
	Lists of tables and figures	If required, lists of tables, figures, or other numbered items, with page numbers; only include in longer reports
	List of abbreviations or technical glossary	If required (may be needed in some research projects, depending on the subject matter)
Body of report	Introduction	Background to the research problem, why it is significant, the overall purpose of your research, and the structure of the report, emphasizing the practice-related dimensions of the research rather than the literature-related ones
	Method	A brief, nontechnical overview of how the research was done (further details may be contained in an appendix or separate document)
	Findings	Nontechnical presentation of the research findings; more detailed analysis
	Conclusions and recommendations	Conclusions of the research in relation to the practical dimensions of the research problem; presentation of recommendations
End matter	Reference list	List of any works cited in the report; number-format referencing may be more suitable for a practitioner report
	Appendices	Additional information that may be relevant to readers of the report but does not form part of the main body (if required)

Keep the executive summary short and focus on those aspects of the project that are relevant to your audience. Note that for very large research reports, such as a major policy review, the executive summary may be somewhat longer and issued as a separate document.

The second area of difference is the absence of a literature review. This does not mean that the research project did not include one, but a formal literature review does not usually form part of a report intended for a practitioner audience (unless one is requested). In some research projects, a literature review is included as an appendix or issued as a separate document for those who are interested. If, however, you are writing a practitioner-style report to be included as part of an assessment for an academic or professional qualification, you may still be expected to include some discussion of literature in the main body. Ensure that you understand what is required if that is the case.

The third area of difference is the method section. This is usually much briefer and less technical than the academic equivalent. It should give the reader an outline of the key features of how the research was conducted, but not attempt to provide an in-depth, critical discussion of design issues. More details can be given in an appendix, if required.

In general, reports for a practitioner audience should focus on what is relevant to that audience. That will usually mean addressing the implications of your research for practice rather than engaging in 'academic argument' (Craswell, 2005: 142). As a result, writing a practitioner report can be very demanding because it involves hard decisions about what is included and what has to be left out. Always start by understanding your audience's perspective when writing your report.

15.5 THE PROCESS OF WRITING

If you are new to research, you may find the idea of writing a lengthy report quite daunting. Even if you are used to writing big documents, preparing a research report may be new to you. In this section we will therefore offer some guidance on the process of writing and share some techniques that may be useful.

15.5.1 Understanding what is expected

Begin the planning process by reviewing any guidelines that you have been given regarding your report. For an academic qualification these will normally include recommended section headings and a maximum word count. Indicative content and word count within each section may also be provided. Alternatively, a percentage split for the marking may suggest the approximate length of each section. Knowledge of the allocation of words per section enables you to set a target for your writing. Exceeding (or falling short) of that target will alert you to the likelihood that your final report is going to be unbalanced in terms of the contribution of the main sections. If no written guidance is available, discuss expectations with your supervisor or other intended recipient of the report. Tables 15.1 and 15.2 can also be used to help you decide on an overall structure. At this point you should also remind yourself of the criteria by which your report will be assessed, if it is for a qualification, or revisit any commitments you have made regarding deliverables in your research proposal.

15.5.2 Planning what you are going to write

The guidelines may provide an outline structure for your report, but you still have to decide what to write, to create your storyline linking the different parts together, and establishing a logical flow between them. You will also need to plan what you are going to say in each section. To help you do this, we recommend that you start by developing an outline plan for your report using one or more of the following techniques.

Develop a linear outline for your report

Developing a sequential, linear outline is the most obvious way of developing your overall report content. Start by listing all of the major section headings for your report; usually this will be based on guidelines you have been given. Next, identify what each section should contain and list these as subheadings. Note what each subsection will cover, adding sub-sub-headings if necessary. Note the planned word count for each section. Now review the structure to check that the flow is logical and that you have covered all of the key points that need to be made. Check also that the balance between the sections is appropriate, for instance, in terms of the word count. The main advantage of linear outlines is that they provide an immediate structure for you to write against. They are also easy to create in a word processing package. The disadvantage is that it can be difficult to visualize the connections between the parts of the report. In addition, creating a linear structure very early can lock you into a way of organizing your report that later may turn out to be unsuitable.

Use visual mapping techniques

Visual mapping techniques are an alternative planning device that can help you to make connections and visualize the relationships between the different components of your report. Mind mapping (Buzan, 2010) is a very useful technique for doing this. Start with a blank sheet of paper. In the centre of the paper, write the title of your report (or the relevant section heading if you are mapping only a part of it). Draw some lines coming out of the central title and label each one with your proposed section headings. Add branches to each line to represent subheadings or the key content that will be included. Continue this until you have mapped out the report or the section in sufficient detail. You can use colour, arrows, pictures, and so on to help you develop your thinking. A mind map can capture a whole report on a single piece of paper, making it easier to see how the different components fit together and to gain sense of the coverage. Mind maps can be drawn by hand or using one of the specialist software packages available. Figure 15.1 shows an example of a mind map developed for this chapter by one of the authors.

Developing a storyboard

In this technique you start working on the structure of your report by viewing it as a story which you are creating on a series of 'boards'. This is very similar to how film-makers or

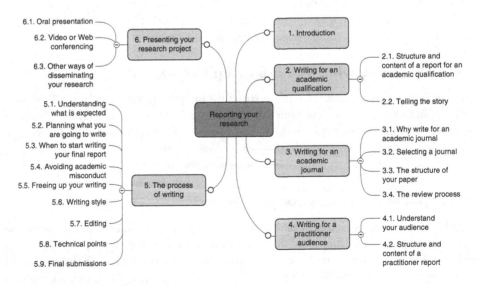

FIGURE 15.1 Example mind map

advertisers develop a storyline for a film or advert. It involves the following steps (Hunter, 2009).

On a large, blank piece of paper, draw a series of boxes. Alternatively, you can use sticky notes or PowerPoint slides.

- Each box represents a section or subsection of your report.
- In each box, write down the main point it will cover, for example, 'impact of changes in information technology'.
- Next, rewrite the points as active phrases to indicate what you plan to cover in that section, for example, 'describe how changes in information technology are impacting on the decision to outsource'.
- Add notes on key content, including data, key references, and so on that you will include in the section.
- Check the structure and the flow. Reorder or regroup sections and subsections as necessary.

Using sticky notes or PowerPoint slides gives more flexibility to rearrange the structure and to add or remove sections as required. The completed storyboard then becomes the structure for your report. Storyboarding provides some of the flexibility of visual display techniques, whilst offering the sequential structure of a linear outline.

15.5.3 When to start writing your final report

Even a small research project report can take lot of time and effort to write, so do not leave it until the end of your project, and definitely not until just before the submission deadline. Instead, start writing your research report as your project progresses or, as a colleague told one of the authors, don't write up, write down. In other words, write as you go. As well as using your research diary to record what you have been doing and your emerging thinking about your research questions, start drafting the major report sections as you carry out the work. Composing the final report then becomes more a matter of structuring, crafting, and editing than just brute writing. Not only can this make it easier for you to hit your delivery deadline, it can also help you to create a better-quality report.

Writing can also help you to develop your ideas, and once they are on paper, it is easier to share them with others and get feedback, so start early in the project. Once you have started, try to write regularly, every day if possible, to form what Creswell and Creswell (2023: 85) call the 'habit of writing'. Not only does this give you practice in writing, it can help you not to lose contact with your project and so find it hard to get started again.

15.5.4 Avoiding academic misconduct

When writing a research report for any audience, it is essential that you write the report yourself using your own words. For academic submissions all institutions have regulations relating to academic misconduct which relate to plagiarism and cheating in the preparation of work that you subsequently submit for assessment. Plagiarism 'involves presenting someone else's work or ideas as your own without proper attribution'

(Khalil and Er, 2023: 4). Plagiarism can take place intentionally when an individual includes words or text taken from elsewhere for example by copy and pasting from another source without acknowledgement by using quotation marks and citation. However, with the increased ease with which information can be sourced and downloaded from the Internet, it is important that you are alert to the words and phrases of others unintentionally appearing in your work. This can happen for example by copying text directly from an article into your own notes without care to identify them as quoted words. You may subsequently use your notes in your own report and thereby copy direct text. Be scrupulous in your process for note-taking and subsequent use of Internet-derived text. Other practices may be viewed as plagiarism, such as unattributed paraphrasing, which involves the writer rewording the original text. Whilst paraphrasing as a writing style is not prohibited, note that the definition of plagiarism includes 'ideas', so even paraphrasing of a concept, idea, or thought must be acknowledged by citation of the original source.

Other forms of plagiarism that will lead to a charge of academic misconduct by your institution include asking someone else to write your work, or use of 'contract cheating', or what are commonly referred to as 'essay mills', which Medway et al. (2018: 393) define as 'a colloquial term for websites that provide pre-written assignments to students'. With effect from April 2022 the Skills and Post-16 Education Bill made it illegal in the UK for an organization to provide paid cheating services, and therefore you should not engage with such organizations. Similarly new advances in artificial intelligence (AI) technology can potentially be used for the generation of written text such as academic essays or assignments. The use of AI technology such as ChatGPT for the preparation of assessment where not permitted in the assessment guidance may be considered academic misconduct by your institution. Plagiarism detection software is used by academic institutions (e.g. Turnitin® or ithenticate®), and academic institutions are now aware of the need to ensure that detection now extends to AI-generated work (Khalil and Er, 2023). We strongly advise you to make yourself aware of how to correctly reference your work, the academic misconduct regulations of your institution (including the use of AI), and attend training provided to students regarding prevention of plagiarism.

15.5.5 Freeing up your writing

It can be hard sometimes to find time to write, so it is incredibly frustrating to find that the words will not come when you do sit down at the computer. 'Freewriting' is one technique that can be helpful in such situations (Wolcott, 2009: 22). As its name suggests, it involves writing freely without stopping to check for spelling or grammar. It means silencing what is sometimes called the 'internal editor', that voice inside us that keeps telling us to stop, go back, and edit something. Write freely for a short period, such as 10 or 15 minutes. It is better to begin writing by getting your ideas onto the page and then editing them later. As Creswell and Creswell suggest (2023), if you have an hour to write something, it is better to write four drafts, one every quarter of an hour, than just one which is usually written in the final 15 minutes. As the old saying goes: don't get it right, get it written. Once it is written, you can improve and refine it.

15.5.6 Writing style

Whether writing for practitioner or for academic purposes, you should always write as clearly and concisely as possible. Here we offer some tips on writing style for your report:

- *Professional tone.* Research reports should not normally contain slang, colloquialisms, or jargon. Where technical, industry, or other specialist terms, including acronyms, need to be used, they should be defined clearly, and a glossary should be added if necessary.
- *Write in the third person.* It is still standard to write reports in the third person in business situations. This gives greater objectivity to your writing. Although there is more latitude in this respect than previously, you should use the third person unless advised or invited to do otherwise.
- *Use the active voice.* Where possible, use the active rather than the passive voice when writing.
- *Spelling, grammar, and punctuation.* Check your report thoroughly for errors. Your report should be free from spelling mistakes and basic grammatical errors. Watch for punctuation, in particular the correct use of apostrophes, commas, colons, and semi-colons. If you are concerned about the accuracy of your written English, you should ask someone to check your work at the draft stage. Use of the grammar and spelling checker within Word can be useful here, but be careful of using other web-based software packages which can interfere with plagiarism software that may be subsequently used by your institution and result in a false match.
- *Non-discriminatory language.* When writing your report, you should ensure that you avoid language bias or language that is discriminatory towards groups or individuals. For example, your language should be gender neutral, using terms such as 'flight attendant' rather than 'air hostess' or 'staff' rather than 'manpower'.

15.5.7 Editing

Editing should take place at both macro- and micro-levels. At the macro level, changes involve looking at the overall structure and the sequence of the report. Here you should focus on the logic of the storyline, the flow between sections and the appropriateness of the weight given to each section. Check your report against any marking criteria or other guidelines. Micro-level editing involves looking at the structure of sections and paragraphs, the logic of the arguments presented, and issues of style such as grammar, punctuation, and language use.

We strongly recommend that you prepare a draft of your work, either in sections/chapters or as a whole, and have this read by someone else. This can be particularly helpful in identifying areas where your writing is not clear or where you fail to explain a key concept adequately. If you are a student researcher, you may be entitled to have drafts of your work read by your supervisor. Do take advantage of this, but make sure that you allow sufficient time for your supervisor to review and return work and for you to make any changes as a result. When preparing and circulating drafts, make sure that you keep track of the different versions and always work on the latest one.

15.5.8 Technical points

As well as the structure and content of your report, you will have to ensure that it is correctly formatted. Review any specific guidance that you have been given. Important points to note include the following:

- *Headings*. Use text formatting such as bold and italics to emphasize your headings and any hierarchy. Consider numbering your headings. For most reports, up to three numbered levels (as in this book) will be adequate.
- *Captions*. Ensure that you number and caption all figures and tables and use the figure and table numbers when referring to them in the text.
- *Page numbers*. Include page numbers; if not specified by a required format, place the page number in the header or footer on the right (or outside if printing double-sided).
- *Page layout*. Confirm what is expected regarding page layout. Points to consider include the following:
    - Margins. If your report is to be bound, you may need to have a larger left (or inside) margin.
    - Line spacing. For drafts and reports for academic qualifications, 1.5 or double line spacing may be expected.
    - Font. If font type and size are not specified, use a clear, easy-to-read font such as Calibri or Times New Roman in 11 or 12 point.

15.5.9 Final submission

Lastly, make sure that you are aware of and follow any special instructions for final submission of your report, including supporting documentation such as informed consent evidence if required. Allow sufficient time for binding and delivery if a bound copy has to be provided. If the document is to be submitted online, ensure you understand the upload process and can access the system in sufficient time in advance of the submission deadline.

15.6 PRESENTING YOUR RESEARCH PROJECT

Whilst the conventional form of research reporting is to provide a written document, alternative forms of reporting can also be used to share your research with others. We consider three here: oral presentation, video or web conferencing, and other online distribution channels.

15.6.1 Oral presentation

Most often an oral presentation is prepared in conjunction with a more detailed written report. Do not be tempted merely to repeat or read the written report. The value of a face-to-face presentation is to provide richness and clarity, along with the opportunity to respond to questions or discuss particular points in depth. Presentations may range from informal discussions with a key stakeholder in the research, through to very formal presentations to a large group. The audience may be made up of practitioners, such as the members of a client organization, or it may be composed of academics, for example, at a research colloquium or academic conference. Here we provide you with some points to consider when preparing to give an oral presentation.

Preparing the presentation

Ensure that you are clear about the purpose of the presentation. Consider the audience for your research and what their expectations are. Who is in the audience? How big will the audience be? What aspect of the research will be most relevant to them? Will a formal or informal style be appropriate? If you are presenting a piece of research undertaken by you as a student researcher in an organization, you may need to agree in advance with the organization what particular topics it is appropriate for you to cover.

- Establish how much time you have available for your presentation and any expectations regarding format, time allowance for questions, and what aspects of your research are of particular interest.
- Plan the structure of your presentation carefully. Think about the storyline you will use to convey your message. Make sure that you prepare a clear introduction that leads the audience into the presentation and an effective conclusion that leaves the audience with a clear understanding of your key points.
- Use visual aids thoughtfully (e.g. diagrams or graphs), to elaborate and clarify what you are saying. Do not make slides overly complicated or too 'busy' with too much text or elaborate graphics.
- If using slides, do not have too many. A useful rule of thumb when planning is to allow at least two minutes per slide.
- Practise your presentation in advance, for example, by doing a rehearsal in front of colleagues.

Delivering the presentation

When presenting, do not merely read out the slides in the presentation. Instead, use the slides as prompts to ensure your key messages are received and understood. During your presentation ensure that you maintain good eye contact with your audience, looking at them rather than at any slides or other visual aids you are using. Speak confidently and at a pace that allows your audience to follow what is being said. Ensure that you allow sufficient time for questions and discussion after your presentation.

If you are not an experienced presenter, seek advice from colleagues, tutors, or others who can help you to prepare and deliver an effective presentation. Whatever else, it is worth heeding consultant Peter Block's advice about presenting research:

> The mistake with most presentations is that they are too long and too intricate. When we have spent all that time analysing data, we fall in love with it. . . . Go

ahead and fall in love with your data – but don't tell everyone about it. Keep your presentation short and simple.

Block (2011: 230)

15.6.2 Video or web conferencing

It may be that the audience for your research includes people who are widely distributed geographically, for example, management of the organization in overseas locations for whom you have conducted the research. With the capability of communication technology today, it is possible to provide presentations efficiently to a wide audience. Cloud-based video conferencing systems such as Zoom or MS Teams enable the presenter to load and deliver a slide presentation using audio and visual channels (including webcam). All participants are able to access and view the slides, although the order and pace of presentation is controlled by the presenter. The presenter provides an oral presentation to all participants and questions, and answers can be enabled via either voice or text via chat. There are a number of advantages and disadvantages to such web-based reporting of research, as summarized in Table 15.3.

15.7 OTHER WAYS OF DISSEMINATING YOUR RESEARCH

The capability of the Internet today enables us all to upload and share content of all types. This opens up new ways of sharing our research findings, for example, by self-publishing our research report via a personal website, sharing it via social media sites, via a dedicated YouTube channel, or through the websites of commercial or other organizations. This can allow the dissemination of findings to a much wider audience, if required. Neither are we limited to written formats; videos, podcasts, slide shows, and other formats can also be

TABLE 15.3 Advantages and disadvantages of web conference research presentations

Advantages	Disadvantages
Able to reach a geographically dispersed audience	May be less engaging for participants than a face-to-face presentation
Cost-efficiency in terms of time and money	Lack of visual cues from the audience can make it difficult for the presenter to judge pace and audience reaction
Useful for short, immediate feedback of research findings or update on an on-going research project	Control of the flow of questions and discussion can be difficult for the presenter, so interactions in a large group may be limited
Can allow for two-way discussion between participants and for the capture of feedback (either audio or text, depending on the technology being used)	Can be difficult to convey the depth of engagement and passion that the researcher has for the topic

used to share our research with others. Before doing so, however, you must always consider the confidentiality of the report and any agreements that you have made regarding who has access to it. Equally important, you must respect the confidentiality and privacy of research participants. If you intend to place the results of your research on the Internet, this information should be included in the briefing documents to participants at the time of informed consent, and in your report you must ensure that it is not possible to identify the research participants or their organization from the material you publish online. We discuss the growth of Internet-based open access dissemination of research in Critical Commentary 15.1.

CRITICAL COMMENTARY 15.1

Disseminating research via open access

In Chapter 1 we introduced you to the distinction between pure and applied research. Today in the UK and other countries there is a discernible move towards trying to achieve impact from pure research beyond the academic domain, where impact can be understood as 'the demonstrable contribution that excellent research makes to society and the economy' (ESRC, 2022).

One way in which impact may be increased is by using more immediate and accessible forms of communication to reach wider audiences. An example of where this is occurring is via 'open access' forms of publication. In this context, open access is a term used to refer to the process of making scholarly articles freely available to everyone via the Internet. This may be via open-access journals or via e-documents made available via authors' websites or other repositories (Antelman, 2004). This act of freeing up the channel of publication is fraught with many concerns on the part of academics, institutions, and publishers. Concerns include the effect that this approach may have on the traditional and recognized high standard of peer-reviewed articles, issues of copyright, the costs associated with publication, fees to authors, and revenue to publishers. Under the 'gold' open access model, authors are charged fees upon publication. In some instances this has led to what Beall (2013: 11) describes as 'unscrupulous publishers . . . exploiting the model for their own profit'. A predatory journal may actively approach researchers and may have no peer review or editorial process in place but exists more for financial purposes. This clearly undermines the standards of academic publishing and can lead to exploitation of researchers. A list of predatory journals is now listed regularly (see openaccessjournal.com).

Despite this, scholars and researchers are turning to open access to disseminate their work more freely. However, we can ask if opening up the channel of access will in itself increase the flow of knowledge from the pure to the applied domain. Some issues still remain, such as, will a wider audience necessarily understand the language of pure research? Should such research be made available in different formats? Who will make the assessment of the quality and standard of the research? Whilst these are concerns to be addressed as the practice of open access develops, it is obvious that practitioners can benefit from wider access to knowledge derived from outside their own organization or sphere of interest. Watch this (web) space.

CHAPTER SUMMARY

- At the end of a research project we need to communicate the outcomes to as wide an audience as possible, which may be academic or practitioner.
- A report for an academic qualification (often referred to as a thesis or dissertation) will have a specific structure, often dictated by the academic institution to which it will be submitted. It will be relatively detailed and will provide the reader with a review of the theoretical support for the research undertaken and full technical information regarding the research method applied and data analysis. A discussion of the relevance of the findings to both existing theoretical knowledge and current practice, with conclusions drawn, will be included.
- You may decide to publish your research in an academic journal. This is a more rigorous form of reporting and will require you to adhere to the structure stipulated by the journal.
- A practitioner report is likely to be shorter and more succinct. It will focus more on the practitioner's problem or opportunity that is the focus of the research and how the findings provide useful input to solutions rather than the academic aspects of the research.
- A number of techniques are available to help the researcher to prepare a written report. These include linear outline, storyboarding, and mind maps.
- Whilst most research continues to be disseminated via written report and/or oral presentation, technology now enables us to use alternative channels through which to reach our audience(s). These include video recordings (potentially distributed online), online platforms, webinars, and teleconferences or podcasts. In the field of pure research, open access publication is now enabling a wider dissemination of research outputs.

NEXT STEPS

15.1 **Understanding what is required**. Locate any guidance document that you have been given by your institution for your qualification or other requirements for your research report. Read it thoroughly and find out the following points.

- Is there a required/suggested structure for the document? If so, look at it and consider how the proposed chapters/sectors relate to your own research.

- If there is no template structure provided to you, look back at Table 15.1 and Table 15.2 and create an outline structure for your report.

15.2 **Planning your report**. Use one or more of the planning techniques discussed in this chapter to develop the overall structure for your report. Make notes of the content that will occupy each section.

15.3 **Get writing**. Choose one of the sections of your report and try free writing on the topic for 10–15 minutes. After your session, reflect on the process and recognize the degree to which your 'internal editor' is influencing your flow of writing.

15.4 **Developing a timetable for writing**. Set out a time schedule for your writing and aim to generate some form of written output on a regular schedule (daily, every two days or weekly).

15.5 **Presenting your research**. If you are not already required to do so, find an opportunity to present your research to interested parties, for example, at a research colloquium or seminar. Use the opportunity to get feedback on your research to date.

FURTHER READING

For further reading, please see the companion website.

REFERENCES

Antelman, K. (2004). Do open-access articles have a greater research impact? *College and Research Libraries*, 65(5): 372–382.

Beall, J. (2013). Unethical practices in scholarly, open-access publishing. *Journal of Information Ethics*, 22(1): 11.

Bem, D. (2003). Writing the empirical journal article. In: Darley, J., Yanna, M. and Roediger III, H. (eds) *The Compleat Academic: A Practical Guide for the Beginning Social Scientist*. Washington, DC: American Psychological Association.

Block, P. (2011). *Flawless Consulting*. 3rd ed. San Francisco, CA: Jossey-Bass.

Booth, W. C., Colomb, G. G. and Williams, J. M. (2008). *The Craft of Research*. Chicago, IL: University of Chicago Press.

Butt, M. M., Rose, S., Wilkins, S. and Ul Haq, J. (2017). MNCs and religious influences in global markets. *International Marketing Review*, 34(6): 885–908.

Buzan, T. (2010). *The Mind Map Book: Unlock Your Creativity, Boost Your Memory, Change Your Life*. Harlow: BBC Active.

Canhoto, A. I., Keegan, B. J. and Ryzhikh, M. (2023). Snakes and ladders: Unpacking the personalisation-privacy paradox in the context of AI-enabled personalisation in the physical retail environment. *Information Systems Frontiers.* https://doi.org/10.1007/s10796-023-10369-7.

Craswell, G. (2005). *Writing for Academic Success.* London: SAGE Publications.

Creswell, J. W. and Creswell, J. D. (2023). *Research Design: Qualitative, Quantitative and Mixed Methods Approaches.* 6th ed. Thousand Oaks, CA: SAGE Publications.

Eagly, A. and Carli, L. (2007). Women and the labyrinth of leadership. *Harvard Business Review,* 85(9): 62–71.

ESRC (2022). *Defining Impact.* Economic and Social Research Council. Available at: www.ukri.org/councils/esrc/impact-toolkit-for-economic-and-social-sciences/defining-impact/ (Accessed 18 March 2023).

Gray, D., De Haan, E. and Bonneywell, S. (2019). Coaching the "ideal worker": Female leaders and the gendered self in a global corporation. *European Journal of Training and Development,* 43(7/8): 661–681.

Hunter, I. (2009). *Write that Essay.* North Ryde: McGraw-Hill.

Jones, R. J., Woods, S. A. and Hutchinson, E. (2014). The influence of the five factor model of personality on the perceived effectiveness of executive coaching. *International Journal of Evidence Based Coaching and Mentoring,* 12(2): 109–118.

Khalil, M. and Er, E. (2023). Will ChatGPT get you caught? Rethinking of plagiarism detection. *arXiv preprint arXiv:2302.04335.* https://arxiv.org/abs/2302.04335

Knott Paul, J. (2015). Does VRIO help managers evaluate a firm's resources? *Management Decision,* 53(8): 1806–1822.

Medway, D., Roper, S. and Gillooly, L. (2018). Contract cheating in UK higher education: A covert investigation of essay mills. *British Educational Research Journal,* 44(3): 393–418.

Minto, B. (2009). *The Pyramid Principle.* 3rd ed. Harlow: Pearson Education.

Neuendorf, K. A., Gore, T. D., Dalessandro, A., Janstova, P. and Snyder-Suhy, S. (2010). Shaken and stirred: A content analysis of women's portrayals in James Bond films. *Sex Roles,* 62(11–12): 747–761.

Serrador, P. and Pinto, J. K. (2015). Does Agile work? A quantitative analysis of agile project success. *International Journal of Project Management,* 33(5): 1040–1051.

Tyler, M. and Abbott, P. (1998). Chocs away: Weight watching in the contemporary airline industry. *Sociology,* 32(3): 433–450.

Wilson, H., Daniel, E. and McDonald, M. (2002). Factors for success in customer relationship management (CRM) systems. *Journal of Marketing Management,* 18(1–2): 193–219.

Wolcott, H. (2009). *Writing Up Qualitative Research.* 3rd ed. Thousand Oaks, CA: SAGE Publications.

Glossary

a priori codes In qualitative data analysis, codes that have been developed prior to analysis (e.g. from the literature).

Abductive approach An approach to research involving inference to the best explanation response to an observed anomaly and characterized by the interplay of theory and observation. The terms retroduction and retroductive approach are sometimes used as a alternatives to abduction and abductive approach.

Action research A research design involving collaborative partnership between researcher and a group in a cyclical process of joint planning, action, observation, and reflection that contributes to actionable knowledge for both the practitioner and academic communities.

Alternative (alternate) hypothesis Another term for the research hypothesis.

Analytic survey A survey study that tests theories by investigating the associations between variables of interest.

Axiology The study of values.

Bar chart A chart showing data in the form of a vertical or horizontal bar used for displaying frequency counts or other data.

Bias A systematic error in a particular direction.

Bibliography A list of all the works consulted during the preparation of the report whether cited in the text or not.

Big data An evolving term used to refer to data sets characterized by very large volume, from a wide variety of sources, and generated at very high speed.

Bimodal A frequency distribution with two modes (peaks).

Bivariate analysis The analysis of two variables simultaneously.

Box plot A chart showing summary measures of an ordinal or metric variable's distribution. Also known as box-and-whisker plots.

Common-method bias A form of bias that can arise in survey research when data are collected using the same method from the same person, leading to (e.g.) inflated or deflated measures of relationships between variables.

CAQDAS Computer-aided qualitative data analysis software.

Case In sampling, an element within a sample. Also referred to as an observation. In case study research, the case which is the object of the study.

Case study A research design involving the study of a relatively small number of naturally occurring cases, in depth and in context, often using multiple sources of evidence.

Causal description Identifying that a causal relationship exists between X and Y.

Causal explanation An explanation of how X causes Y, for example in terms of causal mechanisms.

Causal mechanism Causal mechanisms explain how and why a hypothesised cause contributes to an effect.

Census Research that collects data from all members of the target population.

Citation chaining The process of following up on literature sources cited by a particular reference (backward chaining) or citing that reference (forward chaining).

Chi-square (χ^2) test of independence Significance test of association between two categorical variables (nonparametric).

Closed questions Questions with a set of predefined response from which to answer.

Cluster analysis A multivariate statistical analysis technique used to sort cases (e.g. respondents to a questionnaire) into groups whose members have similar properties.

Cluster sampling A form of probability sampling in which the target population is grouped into clusters from which a sample is drawn, before further sampling from each cluster.

Clustered bar chart A bar chart in which observations for each category are clustered side-by-side.

Code A numerical or textual label applied to segments of raw data to facilitate subsequent analysis.

Coding In quantitative analysis, the process of assigning meaningful numerical values to nonquantitative data (such as responses to open-ended questions) to facilitate analysis. In qualitative analysis the process of applying thematic codes to data segments.

Coding Schedule A document that specifies which actions or behaviours are to be recorded during an observation and how they will be categorized.

Coefficient of determination (R^2) In regression analysis, a measure of what per cent of the variability in the dependent variable is explained by the regression model.

Coefficient of variation   A measure of dispersion for metric data: usually calculated as the standard deviation divided by the mean; it can be used to compare the degree of dispersion between variables measured on different scales.

Computer simulation   The use of computer software to model the behaviour of a real-world process or system.

Concept   A mental category that groups observations or ideas together on the basis of shared attributes.

Conceptual model   Diagrammatic representation of a theory or real-world phenomenon, usually identifying concepts (variables) and their relationships.

Confidence interval   An interval estimate, giving a range of plausible values for a population parameter to a given confidence level (typically 95%).

Confirmability   A dimension of trustworthiness. Showing that the findings of the study are shaped by the respondents and not by researcher bias, motivation, or interest.

Confirmation bias   The tendency for the collection or analysis of data to be biased in a way that confirms the researcher's preconceived opinion.

Constant comparison   In grounded theory, the process of constantly comparing emerging theory with data.

Construct validity   The extent to which a measure actually measures the underlying concept it is intended to measure.

Content analysis   A research design for the systematic analysis of text through the application of a structured coding scheme for purposes of description or prediction. Used here to refer to quantitative content analysis; a variant form is qualitative content analysis.

Content validity   The extent to which a measure captures all of the dimensions of the concept it is intended to measure.

Contingency table   A cross-tabulation showing the relationship between two or more variables in tabular and displaying the frequency counts and/or per cents for each combination of categories. Described in terms of the number of rows × number of columns (r × c), so a 3 × 4 contingency table has three rows and four columns.

Control group   In an experiment, a group that does not receive treatment.

Convenience sampling   A non-probability sampling method in which participants are chosen on the basis of their accessibility or availability.

Convergent validity   The extent to which a measure for one concept is correlated with another measure that measures the same underlying concept. Contrast with discriminant validity.

Conversation analysis   The detailed study of talk in interaction.

Correlation A relation between two entities (e.g. two variables) such that they vary together. A positive correlation means that as the value of one increases, so does the other; a negative correlation means that as the value of one decreases, the other increases.

Correlational study A nonexperimental quantitative research design in which the researcher measures two or more variables as they exist naturally for a set of individual cases (e.g. people) and then tests the association between them. (Note that the analysis procedures used in these studies are not limited to correlation but include regression analysis and related techniques.)

Cramer's V Measure of the strength of association between two categorical variables (nonparametric).

Credibility A dimension of trustworthiness. Giving confidence in the 'truth' of the findings, in terms of the alignment between the researcher's findings and the lives and experiences of respondents.

Criterion validity The extent to which a measure of a chosen variable predicts the value of another variable known to be related, for example, how well a score on a course entry test predicts performance on that course.

Critical discourse analysis A form of discourse analysis that investigates the relationships between text and talk and wider social relations, practices, and structures.

Critical incident technique (CIT) A technique that can be used to investigate significant happenings identified by the interviewee and how they were managed, why they happened, what the consequences were, and so forth.

Cronbach's (coefficient) alpha A measure of reliability of multi-item scales.

Cross-sectional study A study in which data is gathered at a single, specific point in time. Also known as a one-shot study. Contrast with a longitudinal study.

Data cleansing The process of detecting and correcting data entry errors, corrupt data, and missing data prior to quantitative data analysis.

Data collection instrument A means by which we collect research data, such as a questionnaire.

Data-driven research Exploratory (quantitative) research that analyzes data inductively to extract insights such as patterns and correlations within the data.

Data matrix Visual display in which the data are presented as a cross-tabulation.

Data reduction Techniques to make large data sets more manageable by identifying the aspects of the raw data that are relevant for the project at hand.

Data transformation In quantitative data analysis, the process of changing the format of the original data to a new format to facilitate analysis or reporting.

Deductive approach A research approach that seeks to test theory against data.

Degrees of freedom (df)   The number of values that are free to vary when calculating some common test statistics (such as the t-test).

Dependability   A dimension of trustworthiness. Demonstrating that the findings are consistent and could be repeated.

Dependent variable   The variable that is identified as the effect; it is dependent on changes in other variables. Also referred to as the outcome variable. Conventionally labelled Y in diagrams, graphs, and mathematical models.

Descriptive statistics   Statistical techniques used to analyze, summarize, and report sample data.

Descriptive survey   A survey study that generates a description of phenomena in terms of the distribution of variables of interest.

Digital Object Identifier (DOI)   A unique digital identifier for an electronic document such as a book or journal.

Directional hypothesis   A hypothesis in which the expected direction of the association is specified (e.g. A is greater than B, or X is positively associated with Y).

Directionality problem   The problem of deciding, if two variables co-vary, which one is the cause and which is the effect.

Discourse   A term with a wide variety of meanings. Used here to refer to the linguistic and other social practices that constitute the objects and subjects to which they refer.

Discourse analysis   The study of discourse. See also critical discourse analysis.

Discriminant validity   The extent to which a measure for one concept is not correlated with another measure that measures a different underlying concept. Contrast with convergent validity.

Dummy variable   In regression analysis, an independent variable with two levels coded 0 and 1 used to incorporate the effect of different levels of a nominal variable (such as gender).

Ecological validity   The extent to which findings from a research in an artificial environment, such as a laboratory, hold in natural settings, such as the home or workplace.

Effect size   The magnitude of the effect being measured, such as the difference between pre- and posttreatment in an experiment.

Emic perspective   Adopting the perspective of those involved in the situation being investigated. Often associated with qualitative research.

Empiricism   The view that valid knowledge must be based on observation and experience.

Epistemology   Epistemology refers to questions of how we know what we claim to know.

Ethical risk   Any uncertain event or condition that, if it occurs, causes physical or psychological harm or loss of dignity, anonymity, or confidentiality for stakeholders.

Ethnography Used here to refer to a research approach involving in-depth investigation of a culture-sharing group in which participant-observation and/or informal interviews play a significant role.

Ethnomethodology The study of how people produce and reproduce social structure through their everyday actions.

Etic perspective An approach in which concepts are specified by the researcher, based for example on the theory being tested. Often associated with quantitative research.

Experiment A research design involving manipulation of a variable to observe its effects.

Experimental control The management of extraneous variables that could threaten internal validity of a study by direct intervention by the experimenter, for example, by ensuring standardization of treatment.

Experimental design Research designs that involve the manipulation of an independent or treatment variable by the researcher to observe the effect.

Experimenter-expectancy effects Influence on the conduct of a study as a result of the researchers expectations about the findings, for example, by behaving differently towards the treatment group compared to the control group in an experiment.

External validity See generalizability.

Extraneous variable A variable that produces a correlation between two variables that are not causally related.

Face validity A subjective judgement of the extent to which a measure appears 'on the face of things' to measure what it is supposed to measure.

Factor analysis A multivariate quantitative data analysis technique used to reduce a larger set of variables to a smaller set of factors.

Field experiment An experiment conducted under conditions that are not created by the researcher.

Field notes The notes produced by the researcher during fieldwork, for example as a participant-observer.

Fisher's exact test Significance test of association between two categorical variables (nonparametric).

Focus group A form of interview where research participants are interviewed in a group setting because the research wants to study not only the participants' views or experiences of the topic under discussion but also the interactions between members of the group.

Frequency distribution The number of observations or cases that fall within each category of a variable.

Frequency table A table showing the number and per cent of observations or cases that fall within each category of a variable.

Gantt chart   A form of bar chart used to depict a time schedule.

Gatekeeper   A member of the group being studied who has insider status and can facilitate access to potential participants.

Generalizability   The extent to which your research findings are applicable to people, time, or settings other than those in which the research was conducted. Also known as external validity.

Grand theory   A theoretical system applicable to large-scale social phenomena.

Grounded theory   A research design in which the aim is to build theory systematically from data through an iterative process of constant comparison.

Hierarchical coding   An arrangement of codes in a way that reflects increasing levels of abstraction.

Histogram   A form of bar chart used to display the frequency distribution of a metric variable.

Hypothesis   A testable proposition about the expected association between two or more concepts or variables.

Hypothetico-deductive approach   A deductive research approach involving the formulation and testing of hypotheses derived from the theory under investigation.

Idealism   The ontological position that only minds and their ideas exist.

in vivo codes   In qualitative data analysis, naming codes based on a word or phrase used in the data being coded.

Independent two-sample t-test   Significance test of the difference between the means of two independent (not related) samples (parametric)

Independent variable   The variable that is identified as the cause of changes in the dependent variable. Also referred to as a predictor or treatment variable. Conventionally labelled X in diagrams, graphs, and mathematical models.

In-depth interview   A format of interview where the researcher asks open-ended questions and where the choice of words and order of the questions is flexible.

Indicator   Something used as a measure of a more abstract concept, for example, answers to questions in a questionnaire to measure attitude.

Inductive approach   A research approach that seeks to build theory from data.

Inferential statistics   Statistical techniques used to make inferences about a population on the basis of sample data.

Insider researcher   A researcher undertaking research within and about their own organization.

Internal consistency reliability   The extent to which items in a multi-item scale are related. Often measured using Cronbach's Alpha.

Internal validity The extent to which causal inferences about the relationship between two or more variables can be supported by the research design.

Interpretivism A philosophical orientation that stresses the difference between the objects of natural science and the subjects of social science and emphasizes the importance of understanding and meaning in social research.

Interquartile range A measure of dispersion: the difference between the top 25 per cent and the bottom 25 per cent of the distribution.

Inter-rater reliability The degree of consistency between two or more coders when coding the same set of data. Also known as inter-coder reliability.

Interval data Data measured at the interval level can be placed in rank order, but it is also possible to measure the size of the difference between the values. Interval data do not have a naturally occurring zero point.

Interval estimate An interval calculated from sample data to give a range of plausible values for a population parameter.

Interview guide The topics or questions to be used in a qualitative interview. Also referred to as an interview schedule or interview protocol.

Interview study A research design in which qualitative interviews are the means of data collection.

Investigative question Questions asked in interviews or questionnaires that generate the data needed to answer your research questions.

Kendall's tau (τ) Measure of the strength and direction of association between two ordinal variables (nonparametric).

Kolmogorov-Smirnov test Significance test of whether or not the sample is drawn from a normally distributed population.

Kurtosis A measure of the extent to which a distribution is flat (platykurtic) or peaked (leptokurtic) compared to a normal distribution.

Laboratory experiment An experiment conducted in a laboratory or other artificial condition created by the researcher.

Level of precision The maximum difference the researcher is prepared to tolerate between the estimated sample value obtained and the actual value that would be obtained in the population.

Linear regression A statistical technique for predicting the value of a metric dependent variable from knowledge of the value of one or more independent variables.

Literature The body of written material on a particular topic, whether published or unpublished.

Longitudinal study A study which gathers data on subjects or events over time. Contrast with a cross-sectional study.

Mann-Whitney test   Significance test for difference between two groups (nonparametric).

Maturation effects   A threat to internal validity that arises from changes in a participant over the course of a study and that can influence the results irrespective of any treatment, for example, the effects of growing older or gaining experience.

Mean   A measure of central tendency: usually refers, as here, to the arithmetic mean, which is the arithmetic average of the data.

Measures of central tendency   Statistics such as the mode, median, and mean that measure the average or typical value for a variable.

Measures of dispersion   Statistics such as range, interquartile range, and standard deviation that measure degree of spread or dispersion among the observations in a sample.

Median   A measure of central tendency: the value that is in the middle of the distribution.

Mediating variable   A variable that represents a mechanism through which an independent variable influences a dependent variable. Also known as an intervening variable.

Member checking   See respondent validation.

Memo   A term originating in grounded theory to refer to notes written by the researcher for their own use to track progress, record emerging ideas, serve as a basis for writing up, and so on.

Memoing   The act of creating memos.

Meta-analysis   The use of statistical techniques to synthesize the findings from multiple studies to provide a single quantitative estimate (for example as part of a systematic review).

Metric data   Used in this book to refer to data measured on an interval or ratio scale.

Middle-range theory   A theory providing an explanation of a particular phenomenon.

Missing value   In quantitative data analysis, a value for a particular observation that is missing due to nonresponse, data entry error, or other reason

Mixed methods study   A study combining quantitative and qualitative methods.

Mode   A measure of central tendency: the most frequently occurring value in the data.

Model   The term 'model' may be used to convey a number of meanings, including:

- A synonym for theory.
- A mathematical representation of a theory or real-world phenomenon.
- A diagrammatic representation of a theory or real-world phenomenon.

Moderating variable   A variable that influences the nature of the relationship between an independent variable and a dependent variable.

Mono method study   A study using either quantitative or qualitative methods but not both.

Multicolinearity   In regression analysis, the correlation between independent variables.

Multi-item scale   A scale which consists of several questions (items) that are combined (summated) to produce a single measure for the chosen variable. Also known as a summated scale.

Multimodal   A frequency distribution with more than two modes (peaks).

Multiple regression   Linear regression featuring more than one independent variable.

Multistage sampling   Sampling involving two or more stages in sample selection; may involve both probability and non-probability sampling strategies.

Multivariate analysis   The analysis of more than two variables simultaneously.

N n   Uppercase N is usually used to refer to the population size and lowercase n to the sample size, e.g. $n = 25$ would indicate a sample size of 25.

Natural experiment   A study investigating a naturally occurring comparison between a treatment and a control condition that is as close as possible to those that would have been created in an experiment.

Netnography   A form of ethnography that studies behaviour in online environments. Also referred to as webethnography, online ethnography, and virtual ethnography.

Network   Visual display in which the data are presented as a network of nodes and links.

Nominal data   The lowest level of measurement used when numbers are applied to distinguish different categories such as gender (male/female); the categories have no natural rank order.

Nondirectional hypothesis   A hypothesis in which the direction of the association is not specified; nondirectional hypotheses are the most commonly encountered type in business and management research.

Nonexperimental design   Research design that does not involve manipulation of a treatment variable.

Nonparametric tests   Statistical tests that do not make the assumptions regarding the type of probability distribution of the population from which the sample were drawn.

Non-probability sampling   Any non-randomized procedure for generating a sample from a target population.

Nonresponse bias   Bias introduced when nonrespondents are systematically different from respondents.

Normal distribution   A probability distribution sometimes called the bell curve because of its shape. It is an important distribution in statistical analysis. Also known as the Gaussian distribution.

Null hypothesis   The reverse of the research hypothesis indicating that what you expect to find is not present (for example, that there is no difference or no association).

Objectivism An epistemological position that assumes the possibility of gathering data through theory-neutral and value-free observation.

Observation A data collection technique involving the purposeful observation, recording, and analysis of activities, events, or behaviours. Also used in sampling and quantitative analysis to refer to individual elements, such as respondents.

Observer effect Potential bias arising from participants' knowing they are being observed during an observational study.

One-sample t-test Significance test of whether the sample comes from a population with a specified mean (parametric).

One-tailed test A significance test of a directional hypothesis.

One-way, independent analysis of variance (ANOVA) Significance test of the difference between the means of three or more groups (parametric).

Online Survey Survey method that uses questionnaire delivery via an Internet browser.

Ontology Ontology is concerned with the nature of what is out there to know in the natural and social world.

Open Questions Questions that do not have a definitive set of option answers but rather the respondents answer freely in their own words.

Operationalization The process of turning concepts into measurable variables.

Ordinal data Data measured at the ordinal level can be placed in rank order from highest to lowest but do not allow measurement of the difference between categories.

Outcome variable See dependent variable.

Outlier An observation or combination of observations with characteristics that are distinctly different from other observations in the data set.

Paired (or dependent) two-sample t-test Significance test of the difference between the means of two paired samples (parametric).

Panel study A longitudinal study that follows a specific group of subjects (the panel) by repeated observations over time.

Parametric tests Statistical tests that make assumptions regarding the type of probability distribution of the population from which the sample were drawn. If using a parametric test, you must ensure that any required assumptions are met by your data.

Participant-observation A form data collection in which the researcher is an active participant as well as an observer.

Participatory research Research involving the collaboration between researcher and respondents with respect to the goals, process, and outcomes of the research.

Pearson's correlation coefficient (r) Measure of the strength and direction of linear association between two metric variables.

Peer review The process of expert review of work prior to its being accepted for publication (also known as refereeing).

Phi Measure of the strength of association between two categorical variables (nonparametric).

Pie chart A chart that represents the relative proportion of each category of a variable by representing it as a slice of a pie.

Pilot study A small-scale study carried out to test aspects of a research project such as a questionnaire, ideally with a group from the intended sample and using the same administration methods, prior to beginning full data collection.

Plagiarism The representation of someone else's work as your own.

Point estimate A single-number statistic estimate of a population parameter.

Population The universe of people, entities, or events in which the researcher is interested and from which a sample is drawn.

Population parameter A statistic that characterizes a population.

Positivism A philosophical orientation that seeks to apply the methods of the natural sciences to the social sciences.

Post-positivism A philosophical orientation that shares some features of positivism but accepting the conjectural and fallible nature of knowledge (Note: the term is used also by other writers to refer to a range of philosophical orientations that came 'after' positivism).

Predictor variable See independent variable.

Pretest A test of a data collection instrument, such as a questionnaire, to check clarity, time to complete, and so on prior to a pilot test.

Primary data Data that are collected specifically for the purposes of the research project being undertaken.

Probability sampling A procedure for generating a sample from a target population that involves randomization.

Process model Conceptual model showing stages or event sequences over time.

Projective technique A technique for eliciting responses in an interview whereby the researcher taps into the respondents' underlying feelings and attitudes that may remain dormant, by use of ambiguous objects or stimuli.

Proportionately stratified sampling A form of stratified random sampling in which the sample size for each subgroup in the population is proportionate to its size within the total population.

Prospective study A longitudinal study that follows events as they happen.

Pure research Research associated with an academic agenda that focuses upon adding to the existing body of theoretical knowledge in relation to a particular topic.

Purposive sampling A form of non-probability sampling which involves the selection by the researcher on the basis of theoretical relevance to the study.

p-value The probability of observing a test statistic at least as extreme (positive or negative) as the one observed, assuming the null hypothesis is true.

Qualitative content analysis A qualitative variant of content analysis.

Qualitative interview Refers to in-depth, semi-structured, or unstructured interviews used to generate qualitative data.

Quasi-experiment An experiment in which individuals are not assigned randomly to groups.

Questionnaire A data collection instrument that uses a standardized, structured set of questions to measure variables that are of interest to the researcher.

Quota sampling A form of non-probability sampling in which the researcher determines quotas for specific subgroups within the population.

R^2 See coefficient of determination.

Randomized control trial A term referring to a true experiment; often used in evaluation research, including pharmaceutical trials.

Range A measure of dispersion: the difference between the maximum and the minimum value for a variable.

Ratio data Data measured at the ratio level can be placed in rank order, have equal distance between measurement intervals, and a meaningful zero point.

Realism The ontological position that there exists a reality independent of the mind of the observer.
A philosophical orientation that combines ontological realism with epistemological subjectivism.

Reference list A list of all the works cited in a text.

Reflexivity The practice as a researcher of reflecting on one's own position and role in research.

Regression coefficient (*b*) In regression analysis, a measure of the strength of the relationship between an independent variable and the dependent variable; it shows the change in the dependent variable associated with a one-unit change in the independent variable.

Reliability The degree of stability and consistency of the measures used in a study.

Research A purposeful, systematic process of investigation in order to find solutions to a problem.

Research design The plan adopted for the research in order to answer the research question(s).

Research diary or log A record of relevant information and activities that take place which you document as you proceed through your project.

Research ethics committee (REC) A group of individuals charged with ensuring adherence to appropriate ethical standards in an institution such as a university.

Research hypothesis A statement about what you expect to find in your data in terms of, for example, an association between two variables or differences between two or more groups. Typically written as H_1, H_2 ... H_n, etc. Also referred to as the alternative or alternate hypothesis.

Research methods The general form of data collection and analysis procedures (e.g. quantitative or qualitative).

Research problem The specific problem, issue, or opportunity that is the subject of your research.

Research proposal A document that provides an overview of the intended research. It sets out the purpose of the research and a plan for how it will be carried out and is often the basis for research approval.

Research question The specific question(s) that your research needs to answer in order to resolve your research problem.

Research risk Any uncertain event or condition that, if it occurs, has an effect upon the project.

Research techniques The specific tools and techniques used to collect and analyze data.

Respondent validation A process used in some research in which respondents are asked for feedback on emerging and/or final findings of the research. Feedback may be seen as part of a validation process or as a means of gathering additional insight into the research findings. Also referred to as member checking.

Response rate The proportion, expressed as a percentage, of those contacted who actually participate in the research as respondents and whose data is included for analysis.

Retrospective study A form of longitudinal study that takes place after the events of interest has happened.

Reverse coding The process of reversing the direction of an ordinal or interval scale, usually carried out to ensure that all scales run in the same direction prior to analysis.

Sample A smaller set of cases or observations drawn from a larger target population.

Sample statistic Statistics that characterize a sample.

Sampling The process of selecting a sample from the target population.

Sampling bias Bias arising as a result of systematic error in sampling leading to a non-representative sample.

Sampling error The naturally occurring difference between a sample statistic and the true population parameter.

Sampling frame A listing of all the elements that make up the population from which the sample will be drawn.

Scatter plot A chart plotting one variable against another; used with metric or ordinal data.

Secondary data Data that were collected, usually but not necessarily by someone else, for purposes other than your own investigation.

Secondary data analysis The reanalysis of secondary data to answer a research question that is distinct from that for which the data were originally collected. Also known as secondary analysis.

Self-selection sampling A form of non-probability sampling in which participants self-select to take part in a study.

Sensitizing concept Concepts that are tentative and subject to change and which can guide data collection by suggesting initial lines of inquiry and can help structure data analysis. Sensitizing concepts can be drawn from existing literature.

Shapiro-Wilk test Significance test of whether or not the sample is drawn from a normally distributed population (nonparametric).

Significance level In statistical significance testing, the level at which the null hypothesis will be rejected. Also referred to as α. For business and management, commonly set at 0.05. It represents the risk of committing a Type I error.

Simple random sampling A form of probability sampling in which each individual is drawn at random from the target population.

Skewness A measure of the extent to which a distribution departs from symmetry. Positive (right) skewness indicates that the observations are clustered around the lower values of the distribution with a tail of higher values. Negative (left) skewness indicates the opposite.

Snowballing A form of non-probability sampling in which the researcher starts with a few known members of the population who meet the sample characteristics, and these are approached to participate and also identify others they know who also meet the sample characteristics.

Social constructionism A philosophical orientation that emphasizes the 'constructed' nature of phenomena which are seen as constructed through our social processes and, in particular, through interaction and language.

Social desirability bias The tendency for respondents to choose answers that conform to what is seen to be socially desirable or responsible.

Spearman's rho (ρ) Measure of the strength and direction of association between two ordinal variables or between one ordinal and one metric variable (nonparametric).

Spurious correlation A statistical correlation between two variables that is not directly related causally.

Stacked bar chart   A bar chart in which the observations for each category are stacked in a single bar rather than clustered side-by-side.

Standard deviation   A measure of dispersion: for metric data, measured in the same units as the mean, it indicates how far the distribution is spread out from the mean (the standard deviation is the square root of the variance).

Statistical control   The use of statistical techniques to identify and control for the influence of extraneous variables.

Statistical inference   The process of using inferential statistics to draw conclusions based on data; in research it commonly refers to drawing conclusions about a population on the basis of data drawn from a sample of that population.

Statistical representativeness   The extent to which a sample is representative of the population from which it was drawn.

Simple random sampling   A form of probability sampling in which the population is divided into smaller groups or strata from which the sample is drawn.

Structured interview   A format of interview where the researcher asks close-ended questions, in the same order, the same way, and only the predefined answer choices can be given – e.g. surveys.

Structured observation   A form of observation that involves the coding of observed behaviour or activities against a defined coding schedule for subsequent numerical analysis.

Subject-expectancy effects   Influences on research findings as a result of participants reacting to being part of the research, irrespective of any actual treatment administered.

Subjectivism   An epistemological position that assumes all observation is at the very least value-laden.

Substantive theory   A theory providing an explanation of a specific phenomenon in a specific setting.

Summated scale   A scale which consists of several questions (items) that are combined (summated) to produce a single measure for the chosen variable. Also known as a multi-item scale.

Survey study   A nonexperimental research design that collects and analyzses quantitative or quantifiable data on variables of interest for the population being studied.

Systematic random sampling   A probability sampling method involving the systematic selection of sample elements from a list at a predetermined sampling interval.

Systematic review   A type of literature review that seeks to provide a systematic, transparent, and reproducible method for locating, appraising, and synthesizing all of the relevant studies in the chosen topic area.

Systems model   Conceptual model showing system components and their interrelationships.

Target population   The totality of all elements (individuals, organizations, documents, and so on) of interest to our research problem.

Taxonomy   A classification scheme derived from data.

Test statistic   A value that is calculated as part of statistical test and used to determine the degree to which the sample data are consistent with the null hypothesis.

Test-retest reliability   The extent to which a measure will give the same result if it is repeated.

Thematic map/network   A form of visual display showing the relationships between themes in thematic analysis.

Theoretical sampling   Another term for purposive sampling.

Theoretical saturation   A term originating in grounded theory to refer to the point at which the cycle of data collection and analysis generates no new categories or new dimensions of existing categories. Can be used as a guide in qualitative research that sample size is adequate.

Theory-driven research   A term used to refer to hypothetico-deductive approaches to research.

Thick description   A form of description associated with ethnography allowing an interpretation of the understanding of those involved in a particular situation or action.

Time series   A form of longitudinal data that consists of a sequence of observations, usually the observations are of a single entity at regular intervals over a fairly long period.

Transferability   A dimension of trustworthiness. Providing sufficient information to allow the reader to assess the relevance of the findings to other contexts; analogous to generalizability (external validity) in traditional quality criteria.

Treatment group   In an experiment, a group that receives a treatment.

Treatment variable   A term used in experimental designs. See independent variable.

Trend   The long-term direction of a time series (e.g. up, down, or stationary).

Triangulation   The process of using multiple sources of data or multiple methods to cross-check the validity of your findings.

True experiment   An experiment which uses random assignment of participants to groups.

Trustworthiness   A set of quality criteria proposed for qualitative research consisting of credibility, transferability, dependability, and conformability.

Two-tailed test   A significance test of a nondirectional hypothesis.

Type I error   Rejection of the null hypothesis when it is, in fact, true.

Type II error   Acceptance of the null hypothesis when it is, in fact, false.

Typology   A classification scheme derived in advance and then applied to the data.

Unimodal   A frequency distribution with a single mode (peaks).

Unit of analysis   The level of aggregation of the data that are used during analysis and for which you report your results.

Univariate analysis   The analysis of single variables individually.

Validity   The extent to which research findings are really about what they claim to be about.

Variable   A concept, characteristic, or attribute that can take on different values (e.g. satisfaction, income, or gender).

Variance   A measure of dispersion: for metric data, it indicates how far the distribution is spread out from the mean.

Variance model   Conceptual model specifying cause-and-effect relationships between concepts, identifying dependent and independent variables.

Within-subjects design   Another term for repeated-measures design.

Name index

Subject index

Note: Page numbers in *italics* indicate a figure and page numbers in **bold** indicate a table on the corresponding page

Printed in the United States
by Baker & Taylor Publisher Services

Printed in the United States
ʾv Baker & Taylor Publisher Services